CONTEMPORARY DIRECT MARKETING

Lisa D. Spiller, Ph.d
Christopher Newport University

Martin Baier

PEARSON
Prentice
Hall

UPPER SADDLE RIVER, NEW JERSEY 07458

Library of Congress Cataloging-in-Publication Data

Spiller, Lisa.
  Contemporary direct marketing / Lisa Spiller, Martin Baier.
    p. cm.
  Includes bibliographical references and index.
  ISBN 0-13-101770-5 (pbk.)
    1. Direct marketing. I. Baier, Martin. II. Title.

  HF5415.126.S65 2004
  658.8'72—dc22

                                        2004041525

Acquisitions Editor: Katie Stevens
Editor-in-Chief: Jeff Shelstad
Assistant Editor: Melissa Pellerano
Editorial Assistant: Rebecca Cummings
Developmental Editor: Elisa Adams
Media Project Manager: Jessica Sabloff
Marketing Manager: Michelle O'Brien
Marketing Assistant: Amanda Fisher
Managing Editor (Production): John Roberts
Production Editor: Maureen Wilson
Manufacturing Buyer: Michelle Klein
Cover Design: Kiwi Design
Cover Illustration/Photo: Photodisc
Composition/Full-Service Project Management: Carlisle Communications, Ltd.
Printer/Binder: Phoenix

Credits and acknowledgments borrowed from other sources and reproduced, with
permission, in this textbook appear on appropriate page within text.

Pearson Education LTD.   Pearson Education Australia PTY, Limited
Pearson Education Singapore, Pte. Ltd   Pearson Education North Asia Ltd
Pearson Education, Canada, Ltd   Pearson Educación de Mexico, S.A. de C.V.
Pearson Education–Japan   Pearson Education Malaysia, Pte. Ltd

10 9 8 7 6 5 4 3 2 1
ISBN 0-13-101770-5

Contents

Foreword

It has been apparent, especially since the advent of the interactive medium called the World Wide Web, that those engaged in *direct* marketing require expanded knowledge in certain aspects of marketing as these have been traditionally taught. It is these elements of direct marketing with which this new textbook, *Contemporary Direct Marketing,* is concerned.

The elements of special interest to students aspiring to careers in direct marketing, as well as professional direct marketers already there, include: customer relationship management and recognition of the lifetime value of a customer, market segmentation and customer profiling, database development and utilization, research and testing, measurement and accountability which emphasizes response, offer creation, benefit-oriented promotion, interactive multimedia planning as well as fulfillment strategies.

All of these concepts are expanded herein . . . as an *extension of*–not as an *alternative to*–basic marketing instruction.

The utilization of direct marketing methods has shown spectacular growth . . . to the point that its tools and techniques are now employed by virtually every organization, for-profit as well as not-for-profit. A major deterrent to continued explosive growth, though, is a dearth of trained talent.

That is why the positioning of this textbook and expanded curriculum dealing with direct marketing, already happening at some universities, is so vital. I am in accord with that.

Philip Kotler
*Professor at the Kellogg School of Management,
Northwestern University*

Preface

Contemporary Direct Marketing, conceived as a college textbook for a core course in direct marketing, was developed to have practical relevance for those interested in, about to enter, or already involved in direct marketing. It is designed to encourage interactivity and creative discussion both in and out of the classroom.

We two authors have endeavored to combine theory and practice for college students as well as for experienced professionals. Our objective has been to identify and organize the proven principles and correct concepts of direct marketing. Mind-boggling technologies have appeared only recently ... yet what appears in this text has been evolving long before that among mail-order merchants and users of direct mail.

There was significant innovation in direct marketing tools and techniques during the last half of the twentieth century. Unfortunately, an abundance of overzealous "dot-coms," coupled with what they felt to be unlimited potential of an "e-commerce economy," did not know these proven principles and correct concepts of direct marketing. A host of failures inevitably resulted.

From our combined learning (spanning many decades), from our extensive classroom work, and from our on-the-job practical experiences, we have watched direct marketing evolve to what it has become today. Our backgrounds are extensive, yet diverse.

It must be remembered that instruction in direct marketing is an *extension of*–not an *alternative to*–basic marketing. The roots of direct marketing, as it emerged as a discipline in its own right, lie in the basic philosophy of the total marketing concept. It interacts with the two other major functions of organizations—finance and production—as well as many related academic disciplines including computer science, quantitative analysis, economics, and the behavioral sciences. These related disciplines are often viewed and sometimes even repeated in this text, but always in the context of direct marketing.

Key attributes of direct marketing, distinguishing it from traditional marketing, are these: measurement and accountability along with reliance on lists and databases. As costs have soared, business firms as well as nonprofit organizations of every size have recognized that the efficient use of the elements of direct marketing can be one of the best ways to produce positive results. Most direct marketers are practical, pragmatic people. They do enough things right, but they can improve by measuring what they do against proven theory. Theory guides practice. Understanding "why" is as important as knowing "what" or "how." Virtually everyone uses direct marketing in today's environment.

Today, mounting numbers of both commercial firms and nonprofit organizations are initiating or expanding direct marketing in their operations. These actions can be observed in a broad range that includes big corporations and entrepreneurial companies as well as organizations and associations like educational and health institutions, theater and arts groups, services, financial firms, in fact, all types of enterprises. The effective use of the elements of direct marketing has become one sure means of increasing profits, fundraising contributions, attendance, memberships, or political actions.

The explosive growth of direct marketing has made it difficult to find enough people with the skills demanded in the discipline. By gaining the knowledge needed to guide firms and organizations to direct marketing success, trained professionals also boost the chances for their own career advancement. Inevitably, college education in direct marketing has been advancing rapidly.

ORGANIZATION AND PEDAGOGY

The total marketing concept serves as a basic philosophy in understanding the elements—concepts and theories—of direct marketing. Tools and techniques relative to these elements are presented in this text as appropriate. Many principles derived from other course work (statistics, for example) are covered, but all are positioned in the context of direct marketing so as to provide completeness and continuity.

Four major sections of the book deal with (1) Basics: an overview of direct marketing; (2) Media: print, broadcast, telecommunications, Internet; (3) Strategies and tactics: fulfillment, research, and regulation; (4) Applications: business-to-business, not-for-profit, and international. Individual chapters within these four major sections deal with such subjects as customer relationship management and the lifetime value of a customer, market segmentation and customer profiling, database development and utilization, research and testing, measurement and accountability, offer creation, benefit-oriented promotion, interactive multimedia planning, and fulfillment strategies.

As pedagogical aids to learning, all chapters are summarized. Additionally, key terms, review questions, and challenging exercises appear at the end of each chapter. And, for each chapter there is a case specifically structured to the content of that chapter. These are real-world cases, with real names, facts, and figures. They were developed with the cooperation of the organizations themselves.

All of the material in this book has been classroom tested; most has been field tested. Much of the theory espoused herein has been put into practice by the authors themselves. Although the individual instructor using this text may see fit to rearrange his or her own teaching order, the real-world fact is that decision making in direct marketing must be at the beginning, not the end of the process. Unlike a language or mathematics text, *Contemporary Direct Marketing* does not progress from the "easy" to the "difficult."

ACKNOWLEDGMENTS

We are the authors and personally responsible for this comprehensive textbook in direct marketing, but we hasten to acknowledge lots of input and lots of help from lots of others. Much has been derived from our direct marketing career experiences: from the firms that provided us with the opportunities and field laboratories, from our work colleagues at these firms as well as from literally hundreds of other direct marketers who have shared their own successes and failures with us. In college classrooms, many seeds were planted by those who taught us. And, our own presentations of concept and theory have been considerably enriched by challenging and perceptive interaction with students.

We are grateful to three CNU professors who contributed information to select chapters of our textbook. Thanks to Dr. Walter Wymer for his contributions to the Internet and Nonprofit chapters; Dr. Carol Scovotti for her contributions to the Telemarketing and International chapters; and Dr. Stephanie Hunneycutt for her contributions to the Telemarketing and Legal chapters. Special praise goes to Iris Price for going beyond the call of duty in providing secretarial services and administrative support with the many aspects of manuscript completion. Thanks to CNU Librarians Doris Archer and Andrea Kross for their timely research assistance. We appreciate the efforts of the following former CNU students who assisted with data collection, case research, and development of chapter review questions: Noel Vermeire, Jason McKinley, Sharon Brown, Terri White, Pam Todd, Mara Hudgins, Christy Hill, Meredith Kalmbach, Katie Baker, and Keri Vierra.

Thanks to Dr. Donna Mottilla, Dean of the School of Business at CNU and to the University Administration (President and Provost) and CNU Board of Visitors for their support in the form of a semester sabbatical to enable the lead author to dedicate time to conduct research and write many of the chapters of this text.

We are indebted to the many business professionals who kindly assisted in providing case information and textbook examples. These business executives include

David Hochberg, Lillian Vernon Corporation
John Gerke & Van Rhodes, Newport News, Inc.
Allison Scherer, The Spiegel Group
Pat Overton, McDonald Garden Center
Meredith Hines, TreadMoves
Jim Schloss, Smithfield Packing, Inc.
Lindsay Poteat, Peninsula Rescue Mission
Martina White, National Trust for Historic Preservation
Shannon Johnson, The Martin Agency
Annie Hurlbut, The Peruvian Connection
Paula Schumacher, P. S. Graphics
Earl Hogan, Hogan & Associates
Roland Kuniholm, Fundraising Consultant

The authors owe a debt of gratitude to the Direct Marketing Association and the Direct Marketing Educational Foundation for the wealth of information and assistance provided over the years in keeping up with the dynamic field of direct marketing. Special thanks go to Laurie Spar, Pat Faley, and Ann Zeller for their personal assistance.

We also sincerely thank the many reviewers and colleagues at various institutions and organizations who read and provided comments on early chapter drafts. Their comments and suggestions have been invaluable. These reviewers include

Dennis B. Arnett, *Texas Tech University*
Bruce C. Bailey, *Otterbein College*
John J. Cronin, *Western Connecticut State University*

Wenyu Dou, *University of Nevada, Las Vegas*
Richard A. Hamilton, *University of Missouri, Kansas City*
Susan K. Harmon, *Middle Tennessee State University*
Barry E. Langford, *Florida Gulf Coast University*
Marilyn Lavin, *University of Wisconsin, Whitewater*
Carmen Sunda, *University of New Orleans*
William Trombetta, *St. Joseph's University*

The authors also wish to thank the many people at Prentice Hall who helped develop this book. Our sincere thanks to Katie Stevens, Acquisitions Editor, Bruce Kaplan, Managing Editor, Maureen Wilson, Production Editor, John Roberts, Production Manager, Michelle O'Brien, Executive Marketing Manager, Rebecca Cummings, Editorial Assistant, and Bill Beville, Prentice Hall Sales Representative for their assistance during the various stages of manuscript development, manuscript revision and completion, edit, publication, and marketing. The authors also thank Elisa Adams for her developmental editing and Ann Imhof for her copyediting services.

To all of these, we express our thanks.

Finally, we owe many thanks to our families—James "Dooley," Suzanne, Chad and Jack Spiller, and Dorothy Baier, and Donna Baier Stein—for their constant support and encouragement. To them, we dedicate this book.

Lisa Spiller
Martin Baier

About the Authors

As a team, Lisa Spiller and Martin Baier provide a blend of experience uniquely suited to writing a direct marketing text. Professor Spiller is an award-winning teacher with twenty years of experience teaching direct marketing to undergraduate business students. Martin Baier, a legendary member of the Direct Marketing Association's Hall of Fame and author of the very first direct marketing textbook, was a highly successful direct marketing professional who has dedicated more than thirty-five years to academia in an attempt to bridge the gap between what is learned in the classroom and what is practiced in the business world. In 1984, the two met at the University of Missouri–Kansas City, where Baier taught the graduate direct marketing classes and Spiller taught the undergraduate direct marketing classes. The rest is history . . . and their years of teaching experience and knowledge of direct marketing is captured in this text.

LISA D. SPILLER

Lisa Spiller is a professor of marketing in the School of Business of Christopher Newport University in Newport News, Virginia. She has been teaching direct marketing courses to undergraduate business students for 20 years and has recently helped her university pioneer a concentration in direct marketing. Dr. Spiller's marketing students have won the coveted Collegiate Gold ECHO Award from the Direct Marketing Association in 2003 and the Collegiate Silver ECHO Award in 2002. Professor Spiller has received awards for her teaching, including 2003 and 2002 Faculty Advisor Leader Awards from the Direct Marketing Association, a Distinguished Teaching Award in 1997 from the Direct Marketing Educational Foundation, and an Outstanding Teaching Award in 1986 from the University of Missouri–Kansas City. Her research studies, the majority of which have been related to some aspect of direct and database marketing, have been published in numerous journals. She is an active member of several editorial boards, including the Abstract Editorial Board of the *Journal of Interactive Marketing,* where she has served for the past 10 years. Professor Spiller received her B.S.B.A., and M.B.A. degrees from Gannon University and her Ph.D. from the University of Missouri–Kansas City. Prior to joining academia, Spiller held positions as a marketing director with an international company and account executive with an advertising agency. Through the years, she has served as a marketing consultant to many organizations. Professor Spiller possesses a true passion for teaching and has been a strong advocate of direct marketing education throughout her entire academic career.

MARTIN BAIER

Martin Baier has been a direct marketing consultant and educator since retiring in 1987 as executive vice president of the marketing group at Old American Insurance Company. He is founder of the Center for Direct Marketing Education and Research in the Henry Bloch School of Business and Public Administration of the University of Missouri–Kansas City (UMKC), where he served for 25 years as adjunct professor. He has consulted with a variety of organizations now involved in or adopting the discipline of direct marketing.

His education includes an M.A. in Economics (1970), a B.A. in Business Administration (1943), and a B.S. in Economics (1943)—all from UMKC. His *Elements of Direct Marketing,* the first college textbook on the subject, was published by McGraw-Hill in 1983. A Japanese edition was published by Nikkei in Tokyo in 1985; an international student edition was published in Singapore in 1986. His *How to Find and Cultivate Customers Through Direct Marketing* was published by NTC Business Books in 1996. *Contemporary Database Marketing: Concepts and Applications,* co-authored with Kurtis Ruf and Goutam Chakraborty, is an interactive college textbook/CD, published by Racom Books in 2001.

Martin Baier has been affiliated with many professional organizations and listed in *Who's Who in Finance and Industry* and in *Who's Who in Advertising.* He has taught direct marketing at many universities and has conducted numerous seminars throughout the United States and in Europe, Australia, New Zealand, and Asia. His presentation of "ZIP Code—New Tool for Marketers" in the January–February/1967 *Harvard Business Review,* created substantial interest and caused the *Kansas City Star* to name him the "Father of ZIP Code Marketing."

He was inducted into the Direct Marketing Association Hall of Fame in 1989, number 34 to be so honored. The Direct Marketing Educational Foundation presented him its Ed Mayer Award and the Direct Marketing Insurance Council named him Direct Marketing Insurance Executive of the Year, both in 1983. The Mail Advertising Service Association honored him with its Miles Kimball Award in 1990. The Ed Sisk Award for Direct Marketing Vision was presented to him by the Direct Marketing Association of Washington Educational Foundation in 1994. The Andi Emerson 1995 Award, for contribution of outstanding service to the direct marketing creative community, was awarded by the Direct Marketing Creative Guild and the John Caples Awards Board. In 1995, he was elected International Fellow of The Institute of Direct Marketing (U.K.) in recognition of exceptional services to the profession. The New England Direct Marketing Association honored him with its 1996 Lifetime Achievement Award.

CHAPTER

1

ELEMENTS OF DIRECT MARKETING

Like most college students, Catesby Jones needed some extra cash, so in 1985 he decided to create beach volleyball shorts to sell around campus at the University of Virginia. He wanted an unusual design that would appeal to his target market, so he arranged an eye-catching assortment of national flags all over the boxer shorts. To put flare into his design, Catesby added a frog holding two digits in the air, forming a peace sign, and after receiving numerous orders he began manufacturing and selling the unique boxer shorts from his dorm room.

Catesby saw the potential in his creation, so he and a few buddies decided to place a $15,000 direct marketing advertisement in *Rolling Stone* magazine. The advertisement generated a total of 1,000 orders. By the time Catesby finished his degree in international relations, he was already four years into what would become his passion and a very successful business.

Peace Frogs began to dispense products through multi-channel distribution using a mail-order catalog, retail stores—company-owned and licensed—from wholesale to department stores and specialty retailers, and the Internet at www.peacefrogs.com. These channels allowed the company to distribute its products to a vast number of consumers and save resources through cross marketing. They also helped to create brand recognition

Original Advertisement in *Rolling Stone* Magazine 1987

and loyalty because the consumer could see the merchandise at many different outlets.

Now a million-dollar company, Peace Frogs operates a 37,000-square-foot distribution center at its home office in Gloucester, Virginia. This multipurpose facility houses Peace Frogs' merchandise, ordering systems, and a retail store. The 25 employees who work in the distribution center try to ensure that customers are completely satisfied.

The company not only has unique clothing; it has also found a distinctive way to distribute merchandise—psychedelic painted VW vans driving the roads and highways of the United States. Peace Frogs chose this vehicle both as a means of transportation and as a marketing statement, a representation of "reliability and freedom." As it did with its products, the company has taken something ordinary and transformed it into a unique message that leaves a distinct impression and has a positive impact on its customers. And the peace frog and its related "positively peaceful thinking" message have become a significant symbol that many can relate to.

The company's line now includes t-shirts, sweatshirts, hats, boxer shorts, lounge pants, jewelry, accessories, and school supplies. In the process of building a business through direct marketing, Catesby Jones showed that with dedication, hard work, and daring to be a little different, people can make an impact.

W hat is direct marketing? What are its objectives, and how is it carried out? What makes it different from traditional marketing? In this chapter we'll find the answers to these (and many other) questions commonly raised about the exciting and dynamic field of direct marketing. Welcome to "Elements of Direct Marketing 101!"

ELEMENTS OF DIRECT MARKETING

Direct marketing is an interactive system of marketing that uses one or more advertising media to effect a measurable customer response or transaction at any location and stores information about that event in a database. Direct marketing is often referred to as **interactive marketing** because it is expected to be two-way communication with the customer or prospect. It is both a channel of distribution with no middlemen and a selling method where the advertising copywriter is the salesperson. Of course traditional retailers who want to generate store traffic or provide alternative shopping channels for their customers via catalog, telephone, or Web site purchase opportunities can also use direct marketing.

The single most notable differentiating feature of direct marketing is that it always seeks to generate a *measurable response.* This response can take the form of an order, an inquiry about the product or service, or traffic brought into a store. The activities of direct marketing are *measurable* and the direct marketer must be *accountable,* always relating results to costs. Unlike most of the activities of traditional marketing—creating awareness for a product, service, or organization or enhancing the image of a product, brand, or a company—direct marketing activities can always be measured by the response of targeted customers and/or prospects.

One of the most important tasks of direct marketing is capturing these customer responses and storing them in a **database.** It is the creation of a database that enables direct marketers to target their best prospects and best customers, to build customer relationships, and to maintain long-term customer loyalty—the hallmarks of customer relationship management. Thus, the goal of direct marketers is not just to make a sale . . . but also to *create a CUSTOMER!* Although traditional marketers have a long history of building relationships with customers, their activities and interactions with customers are not normally measurable, accountable or captured and recorded in a database.

Traditional marketers also have seemed to focus more on acquiring new customers than on retaining current ones. However, direct marketers have long known the long-term value of customers and have exercised customer relationship management strategies to retain them. The goal of direct marketers is to interact with customers on a one-to-one basis, with reference to the information obtained and stored about each customer in the customer database. Direct marketers then provide the customer with information and product/service offers that are relevant to each customer's needs and wants. This too is different from the activities of traditional marketers who normally attempt to communicate with customers on a mass or segmented basis but not normally on a personal individual basis.

Figure 1-1 shows the traditional marketing cycle of both an indirect channel (with the marketing activities carried down through the channel from the manufacturer to the wholesaler to the retailer to the targeted customer) and a direct channel (where there

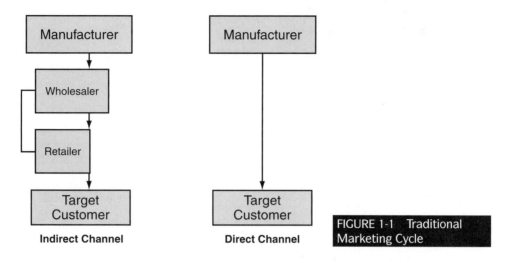

FIGURE 1-1 Traditional Marketing Cycle

are no middlemen involved). There is no emphasis on interactivity, on achieving a measurable response, or retaining customers via database marketing activities. The marketing process often ends with the product or service being purchased by the target customer. This is vastly different from the direct marketing cycle shown in Figure 1-2.

You can see that in the direct marketing cycle, the marketer (who could be a manufacturer, wholesaler, retailer, non-profit organization, governmental agency, or politician) sends a *direct response communication,* an advertising message often personalized and intended to generate a measurable action (such as order, inquiry, store visit, or vote for a candidate), directly to the target customer or prospect. The response generates information that is stored in the organization's database and is used by the direct marketer in future marketing activities. The direct marketer processes the response, whether an inquiry or an order that needs to be filled. Customer service and fulfillment activities,

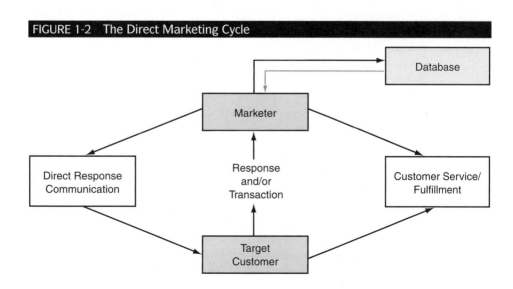

FIGURE 1-2 The Direct Marketing Cycle

Direct Marketing	Traditional Marketing
Direct selling to individuals with customers identifiable by name, address, and purchase behavior	Mass selling with buyers identified as broad groups sharing common demographic and psychographic characteristics
Products have the added value of distribution direct to the customer, an important benefit	Product benefits do not typically include distribution to the customer's door
The medium is the marketplace	The retail outlet is the marketplace
Marketing controls the product all the way through delivery	The marketer typically loses control as the product enters the distribution channel
Advertising is used to generate an immediate transaction, an inquiry or an order	Advertising is used for cumulative effect over time for building image, awareness, loyalty, and benefit recall; purchase action is deferred
Repetition of offers, promotional messages, toll-free numbers, and Web addresses are used within the advertisement	Repetition of offers and promotional messages are used over a period of time
Customer feels a high perceived risk—product bought unseen and recourse is distant	Customer feels less risk—has direct contact with the product and direct recourse

FIGURE 1-3   Comparison between Direct and Traditional Marketing

often called "back-end" marketing, include delivery of information and/or order shipment directly to the target customer.

How does the marketing manager carry out the direct marketing cycle for each individual customer on a one-to-one basis? The manager follows each direct marketing campaign with a response analysis that examines the results for effectiveness. He or she can then initiate future communication designed specifically for each target customer by using the customer information stored in the database. And the process begins again: Each direct response communication builds on the relationship the direct marketer has with each individual customer and reinforces that customer's loyalty to the company or organization. We'll expand on these characteristics of direct marketing later in this chapter and in subsequent chapters in this textbook.

In summary, traditional marketing and direct marketing are similar in being guided by the marketing concept, but the tools and techniques, the elements described in this textbook, are often quite different. Figure 1-3 provides a summary and comparison of direct marketing and traditional marketing.

THE MARKETING CONCEPT AND CUSTOMER RELATIONSHIP MANAGEMENT

With its historical roots in direct-mail advertising and mail-order selling, direct marketing has evolved as an aspect and an extension of the marketing concept. For-profit businesses and not-for-profit organizations, as well as political entities, seek out target market segments, whether the desired response is a sales transaction, a fundraising contribution, or a political action. They interact with these market segments through a variety of media—*direct mail, printed newspapers and magazines, broadcast radio and television,* and/or *electronic channels (telephone, Internet)*—to offer tangible products and intangible services. Their objectives are the creation and cultivation of ongoing customer relationships.

The **marketing concept,** which emerged out of the post-World War II production-oriented economy, was seen to be customer-oriented. Peter F. Drucker, an architect of the marketing concept, observed, "There is only one valid definition of business purpose—to create a customer. Companies are not in business to make things . . . but to make customers."[1]

The marketing concept is a philosophy, an attitude which says that all planning, policies, and operations should put the needs and wants of the customer above the desire to sell a particular product or to use a particular promotional strategy, a particular distribution system, or a particular medium for communicating its messages. Today's customer relationship management (CRM) requires every function of a marketing system to be operating smoothly. In such a marketing system, products/services are distributed to customers in defined markets, segmented in a variety of ways, with consumer markets distinguished from industrial markets.[2] Distribution channels are negotiated and logistics (shipping, warehousing, etc.) are determined.

Both message and media are especially important in direct marketing promotions. Feedback is essential for the marketer, as are positioning, product differentiation, and market segmentation, and the process must start with customers. *Who* are they? *What* do they need and want? *Where* are they located? *When* are they ready to buy? *How much* will they buy? *Why* do they buy? The product or service that results from such planning is a combination of tangible and intangible attributes directed toward satisfying customer needs and wants. These attributes are frequently psychological as well as functional. All of this is carried out on a personal basis.

Creating and then cultivating customers doesn't end with developing the right product/service to meet their needs. That's just the beginning. Promotion is vital in direct marketing. Promotion consists of personal selling, advertising, publicity, and an array of techniques commonly called sales promotion. Direct marketing embraces the professional coordination of these elements. Remember, direct marketing is especially concerned with communicating relevant, benefit-oriented messages that motivate *response* (not just awareness) through appropriate media such as direct mail, print, broadcast or electronic via the telephone, and/or the Internet. It also is concerned with finding the most efficient channels for distribution of products/services to appropriate market segments.

The overall management of direct marketing embraces a variety of related academic disciplines including production, finance, operations, control, and organizational development, as well as accounting, computer science, and quantitative analysis. In-depth knowledge of all these areas is a prerequisite to the management of customer relationships. An advertising copywriter, for example, must possess writing skills but must also possess some knowledge of the science of consumer behavior so as to understand what motivates people to respond.

To understand your customers, and write copy that will motivate them to action, you will need to understand the concepts of the behavioral sciences. Psychology, sociology, cultural anthropology, and human ecology are all relevant. At direct marketing's core are the disciplines of economics and statistics. The jobs and functions of direct marketing are widespread and diverse. All of the jobs in a marketing system come into play. The scientific mind is a prerequisite, and the objective thinker is a necessity. Job tasks in direct marketing range from the creativity of the arts to the discipline of the sciences. You will find yourself, as a direct marketer, using many techniques from other courses you've studied, such as the scientific method and critical thinking skills.

DIRECT MARKETING IS AN EXTENSION OF TRADITIONAL MARKETING

As we have stated, direct marketing is multidisciplinary, as is traditional marketing. A traditional marketing system is sometimes presented in terms of the four "Ps": *product, price, place,* and *promotion.* Direct marketing can be viewed in these terms, too. The *product* can be a book, a record, a magazine, a computer, a job offering, an insurance policy, an item of clothing, a box of grapefruit, a worthy cause, or a political agenda.

We can think of *place* in terms of databases, or **market segments** to which we distribute direct response advertisements. Segments include mailing lists (if the advertising medium is direct mail) or lists of readers, listeners, viewers, or Internet browsers. Market segmentation can be thought of as lists. Thus, the various media of direct marketing become targeted, selective like an aimed rifle shot as opposed to a shotgun scatter. Market segments can describe "senior citizens" or "collectors" or "outdoorsmen" or specific industrial classifications.

In terms of *promotion,* we can utilize direct mail or a printed magazine/newspaper advertisement or a broadcast television/radio commercial or a well linked and executed Web site. We can present our offerings in a virtually endless variety of formats. Figure 1-4 shows the various direct marketing promotion formats and activities.

When all of its elements are put together, we view direct marketing as an aspect and an extension of traditional marketing. Direct marketing is differentiated in that it is always measurable and the direct marketer is accountable. Its goal is to achieve a response. It relies on lists and databases describing these lists. Marketing research gathers information and applies the scientific approach to objective decision making.

CHARACTERISTICS OF DIRECT MARKETING

Direct marketing is *database-driven* marketing. It is a process, a discipline, a strategy, a philosophy, an attitude, a collection of tools and techniques. It is a way to run a for-profit business, a not-for-profit organization, or a political entity so as to *create* and *cultivate* customers, whether these customers are themselves consumers, buyers for industrial organizations, or voters. Direct marketing is characterized by

- Customer/prospect databases that make targeting possible
- A view of customers as assets with lifetime value
- Ongoing relationships and affinity with customers
- Data-based market segmentation
- Research and experimentation (testing)
- Benefit-oriented direct response advertising
- Measurement of results and accountability for costs

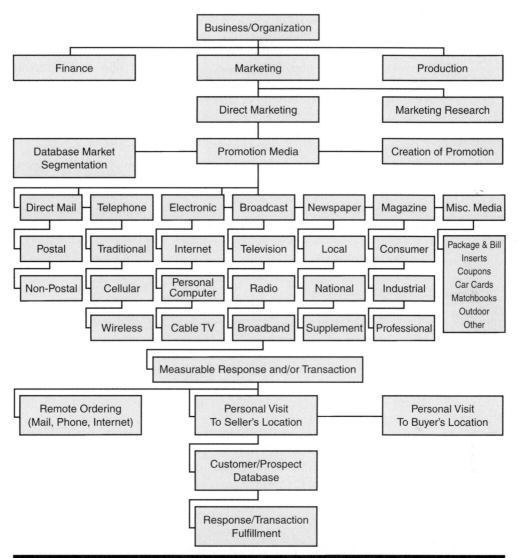

FIGURE 1-4 Various Direct Marketing Formats and Activities

- Interactivity
- Multimedia promotion
- Multichannel distribution

In today's business world, many traditional marketers are beginning to realize the benefits of these attributes of direct marketing.

Measurability and Accountability

Direct marketing is measurable, with results always being related to costs. The direct marketer is accountable for her actions. Marketing managers must usually justify their promotion expenditures. A retail department store may not always be able to measure the specific results from a newspaper or television advertising expenditure except, possibly, by measuring total sales of a particular offering as advertised. On the other hand, the marketing manager might issue a periodic or seasonal catalog inviting orders by mail, telephone, or the World Wide Web. Through the proper "keying" of the response device, such as a preprinted code on a mailed order form or a request for a specific department or individual in an electronic response, the sales transactions resulting from a particular promotional effort can be measured and the total expenditure can be accounted for. It is not so easy to measure or account for, however, the store traffic that this same catalog generates, with buyers coming to the seller's location. (The tools and techniques of measurement and analysis are presented in Chapter 11.)

A political candidate or charitable organization that mails a letter to you or circulates a handbill to your front door is using the elements of direct marketing. It's possible to measure your response only by tallying the votes or contributions received, but even then it is impossible to ascertain how many of the total votes were stimulated by the direct promotion efforts.

Lists and Databases

Direct marketing makes extensive use of lists and databases. Lists can be looked at as market segments to which promotion efforts are directed and from which databases are generated. **Lists** have been commonly thought of as mailing lists. They also might be thought of as readers of a particular publication, as viewers of a particular television program, or as visitors to a Web site. The readers of *Fortune,* for example, represent a different market segment from the readers of the *National Enquirer.* These segments of readers may have different purchase preferences and will probably respond to different promotional strategies. Likewise, browsers of a Web site who do not purchase on-line likely have different purchase preferences from on-line buyers at that site.

Lists are even more useful when selective data accompany them. Such data records the nature of the response, whether an inquiry for follow-up or an actual transaction, as well as such vital information as the product/service ordered, the recency and the frequency of purchase, and the monetary value of the transaction. You might also record characteristics of the respondent, such as age or gender. Geographic location of the respondent, such as residence within an identifying ZIP code area, can further enhance the customer's data record.

HISTORY AND GROWTH OF DIRECT MARKETING

The first mail-order catalogs are said to have appeared in Europe in the mid-fifteenth century, soon after Gutenberg's invention of movable type.[3] There is record of a gardening catalog, the predecessor of today's colorful seed and nursery catalogs, issued by William Lucas, an English gardener, as early as 1667. By the end of the eighteenth century, there was a proliferation of such catalogs in England and William Prince published a catalog in 1771 in colonial America. It is reported that George Washington visited Prince's Gardens in 1791 and that Thomas Jefferson was a mail-order buyer, in both America and England.

Benjamin Franklin, America's first important printer, published a catalog of "near 600 volumes in most faculties and sciences" in 1744. That catalog is especially notable, in a direct marketing sense, in that it contained a guarantee of customer satisfaction along with this statement on its cover:

> Those persons who live remote, by sending their orders and money to said B. Franklin, may depend on the same justice as if present.

A Connecticut custom clockmaker, Eli Terry (whose neighbor and sometimes adviser was the inventor Eli Whitney), deserves mention in the evolution of direct marketing in that he is credited as being the creator of the free trial offer. A Yankee peddler (a direct seller), Terry would pack his custom-made clocks in his saddlebags and would leave them, on trial, with the farmers on his route, collecting for them, in installments, during ensuing trips along the route.

The Birth of Mail-Order Catalogs

From these beginnings there followed a proliferation of catalogs during the post-Civil War period when agrarian unrest, through the National Grange, fueled the popular slogan "eliminate the middleman." Then, as now, mail-order catalogs reflected social and economic change. Beginning as books featuring seed and nursery products, mail-order catalogs of the late nineteenth century included sewing machines, dry goods, medicines, and musical instruments. Most sellers were product specialists and mail order was an alternative mode of distribution. It was during this period in 1872 that Aaron Montgomery Ward produced, on a single unillustrated sheet of paper, a mere price list offering the rural farmer savings of 40 percent. Just 12 years later in 1884 Ward's single sheet of prices had been expanded to a 240-page catalog containing 10,000 items. He, too, featured a "guarantee of satisfaction or your money back."

Two years later came the forerunner of what was to become by 1893 Sears Roebuck & Company. Young Richard Warren Sears, a telegraph operator in the remote location of North Redwood, Minnesota, acquired a shipment of undeliverable gold-filled watches. He reasoned that the best prospects for the purchase of these watches would be other railroad agents, like him, and he had a mailing list of 20,000 railroad agents. By 1897 his original offer of a fine watch to a specific market segment had expanded to a catalog of more than 750 pages with 6,000 items (see Figure 1-5).

By 1902 the sales of Sears Roebuck & Company exceeded $50 million annually. Ward and Sears were followed in 1905 by Joseph Spiegel, who introduced credit terms with catalog copy reading: "We are willing to trust you indefinitely . . . and to receive our pay by the month, so that no purchase is a burden."

Mail Order Diversifies

While mail-order merchandise catalogs were becoming more accepted, new cultural, social, and economic phenomena were breeding another form of mail order. Magazines reflecting these changes, such as *Time,* the *New Yorker,* and the *Saturday Review of Literature,* appeared during the early 1920s, with subscriber-prospects solicited by direct mail. In 1926 Harry Sherman and Maxwell Sackheim, direct marketers who had earlier noted how few bookstores there were relative to the number of post offices capable of delivering direct mail ads as well as books, created the Book-of-the-Month Club.

FIGURE 1-5   1897 Sears Roebuck & Company Catalog

Sherman and Sackheim innovated the "negative option" offer, where books were sent to subscribers on a regular basis, unless the publisher was advised against it. Today, the majority of books is sold by mail order, aided and abetted via the Internet.

Direct marketing has played a major role in the evolution of business-to-business distribution, too. John H. Patterson, founder of the National Cash Register Company, was first to use direct mail to get qualified leads for follow-up by salespeople. Today, his basic method of sales prospect qualification, augmented by direct response advertising media other than mail, plays a role in the total scheme of industrial direct marketing.

Print Media

The versatility of laser printing, personalization possibilities of inkjet printing, advances in press technology, and computerized typesetting are important examples of how the printing process is becoming more and more conducive to the "demassification" of the printed word. Further enhancing the growth of direct marketing, during the 1960s and to this day, has been the increasing availability of advertising media, other than direct mail, suitable for direct response advertising, especially those geared to highly defined market segments. The readers of selective publications, such as the magazines *Sports Illustrated* and *Organic Gardening* as well as *The Wall Street Journal* newspaper, are not only mailing lists in and of themselves but also provide an audience for direct response print advertising geared to specialized market segments.

Broadcast Media

The same evolution has been occurring in the broadcast media, television and radio, through special programming geared to market segments. Cable and satellite transmissions, now appearing with interactive capabilities, offer an array of channels appealing to special interests like news, sports, food, and home shopping.

Electronic Media

AT&T introduced Wide Area Telephone Service (WATS) in 1961, providing direct response promotions the convenience of toll-free telephone calling. This has been a tremendous stimulus to response. And, the telephone itself has become another major medium for direct marketers, enhanced by cellular and wireless technologies.

The proliferation of telephone usage (wired and wireless) has been augmented by access via computers to the Internet and its World Wide Web.

There have been advances as well in other electronic communication involving cable, satellite, and interactive television. Certainly a major media breakthrough has been the technology of the Internet and its commerce affiliate, the World Wide Web. Especially in tandem with print and broadcast media, direct response advertising entices buyers to well-structured Web sites.

The E-Commerce Economy

A watchword for today's direct marketers is *interactivity*.[4] Customers now respond via personal computer, telephone, and television. The Internet's *e-commerce economy* puts a new perspective on how organizations transact as well as on how businesses are valued. A new mathematics of business looks to future productivity, whatever the medium used for response. Mass-market advertising, having survived for years in a largely unaccountable manner, now faces a future of measurement.

Information has become a key economic resource. The ability to access, understand, and communicate that information is a necessity in today's economy. Yet, as futurist John Naisbitt has said, "we are drowning in information but starved for knowledge."

Database-driven direct marketers utilizing the Internet are obtaining that knowledge, enabling them to profile their customers and determine their prospects. At the same time, they are predicting future behavior and using promotional strategies that will not only drive prospects to their Web sites but also engage them in meaningful and ongoing transactions once there.

Interactivity in creating and cultivating customer relationships has its roots in mail order as well as the combined use of direct mail and telephones as media. Today's Internet-based electronic media have tremendously extended these opportunities.

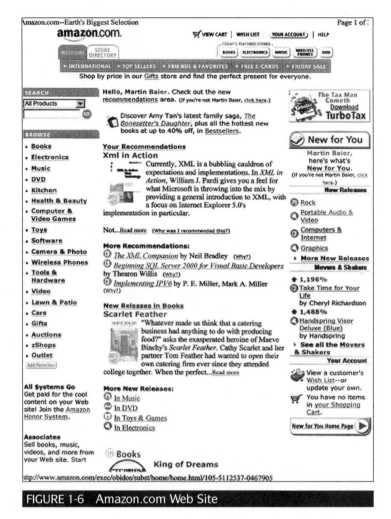

FIGURE 1-6　Amazon.com Web Site

Benefit-oriented and relevant promotion remains a key, as does development of relationships with customers.

The e-commerce case of Amazon.com is a notable one. At its core is a database of customers and their transactions for continuity selling (which encourages customers to make a repeat purchase at a regular interval of time—monthly, quarterly, etc.) while diversifying product lines, to music and video and more, provides cross-selling opportunities (where related and unrelated products/services are sold to an existing customer base). Their Web-site home page greets a visitor as shown in Figure 1-6.

Continuity selling and cross-selling to Amazon.com visitors enhance customer relationships in a variety of ways. Pointing out

- "Customers who bought this book also bought:..."
- "Our auction sellers recommend:..."
- "Look for similar books by these subjects:..."

FIGURE 1-7   Peruvian Connection Home Page

- "This book is especially popular in these places: . . ."
- "We've included the top five titles for your browsing pleasure below. (At least these were the top five as of when we sent this message.)"

Multichannel Marketing

Most direct marketers now view the Internet not just as a technological marvel, but also as an alternative advertising medium as well as a distribution channel. Many direct marketers are tapping the synergy among the various media through **multichannel marketing,** which allows customers to select the media or channels they prefer when shopping for products and services. In fact, many traditional marketers have recently become direct marketers by offering consumers a catalog, toll-free number, and/or a Web site from which they may shop.

Many shoppers want convenience while others still want to see, touch, and feel the items they buy and then take immediate delivery. The bottom line: consumers want choices! And multichannel marketing is giving them just that.

The Peruvian Connection is one example of the many direct marketers using multichannel marketing. It obtains inquiries for its catalog from direct mail and magazine ads. It has retail stores in selected locations, where it sells surplus stock. And, a good many new sales now originate at its Web site, the home page of which appears in Figure 1-7.

Direct marketers actively seek out and identify those target customers to whom they will send a catalog. A Web site, however, does not permit the direct marketer to make this selection; the customer makes it. Thus, a Web site is actually more of a reactive tool that relies on other media to generate traffic.

The Growth of Direct Marketing

According to the Direct Marketing Association, direct and interactive marketing contributes $2 trillion in the U.S. economy. The industry employs 16.1 million individuals.

FIGURE 1-8   Peruvian Connection Catalog Cover

And this sector of the economy is growing faster than all other sectors.[5] The social and economic changes that have given impetus to the burgeoning rise of direct marketing since the mid-twentieth century have been coupled with equally impressive advances in the technology used in various elements of direct marketing. A few of these technological and social advances are worth mentioning.

Printing Technology: The versatility of laser printing, personalization of inkjet printing, advances in press technology, and computerized typesetting are important examples of how the printing process is becoming more and more conducive to the "demassification" of the printed word. Desktop publishing enables businesses to create newsletters, brochures and other print material that can have a highly professional look at a fraction of former cost. Graphic capabilities have also taken major strides. Compare, for example, the cover page from the mailed 2001 catalog of The Peruvian Connection, shown in Figure 1-8, with that of the introductory page from the mailed 1897 catalog of Sears Roebuck & Company, shown in Figure 1-5. Indeed . . . much has changed!

Credit Cards: Since the advent of credit cards during the 1950s, there has been enormous growth of mail order as a selling method. Credit cards greatly enhanced and expedited transactions, which up to that time had been mainly cash with order. The ready availability of worldwide credit systems, together with rapid electronic funds transfer, has contributed to the feasibility and viability of direct marketing by simultaneously offering convenience and security.

Personal computers: These have revolutionized direct marketing, making possible the record keeping, work operation, and model building that are so much a part of the art and science of direct marketing. The complex maintenance of lists and the retrieval of data associated with them are but two examples of the computer's contribution. The processing of orders and the maintenance of inventories are others. And, of course, the use of highly sophisticated analysis can mean the difference between direct marketing success and failure. The computer's contributions of great speed, lower-than-human error, and low cost have made it indispensable to users of direct marketing.

Changing Consumer Lifestyles: As travel becomes more expensive and communication becomes less expensive, there is further impetus to the use of mail, telephone and the Internet. Mailed catalogs, Web sites and toll-free telephone numbers provide the convenience of shopping at home. Further, as more women have entered the work force, families are placing a greater emphasis on time utilization. Once a leisurely pastime, shopping has become more of a chore, especially for the majority of households in which both spouses work. The advent of mail order and the World Wide Web have made anytime day-or-night shopping even more convenient for these working spouses.

Negative Aspects of Retailing: Many consumers enjoy shopping in traditional retail stores. However, there is a strong belief that traditional retail shopping has a number of negative aspects associated with it. Some of these include inadequate parking facilities, concerns about safety, long walking distances, uninformed sales clerks, difficulties in locating retail sales personnel, long waiting lines at check-out, in-store congestion, difficulty in locating certain sizes, styles or colors of products, and the hassle of juggling packages out of the retail stores. For these consumers, direct marketing, with all of its modern methods and conveniences, has been a welcome alternative.

THE CREATION AND CULTIVATION OF CUSTOMERS

Customers are the life-blood of an organization.[6] Enterprise thrives on customers. They are the reason for its existence. The creation and cultivation of customers is what direct marketing is all about. Much has been written in recent times about **customer relationship management (CRM).** We will look in this section at *interactive customer relationships* as well as the related subjects of customer affinity and loyalty, pointing to the need for determining the lifetime value of a customer, to be presented in more detail in Chapter 3.

Interactive Customer Relationships

Customers are not a homogeneous lot. Their one common characteristic is a relationship or affinity they form with those they favor with their purchases and their ongoing loyalty. In return they expect quality, value, and service. Businesses, in turn, seek customer loyalty, in the hope of creating an affinity that keeps customers coming back.

It is well known that loyal customers generate greater profitability for a company than do new customers. When compared with new customers, loyal customers (a) spend more money over time—that is the amount of their purchase transactions increase along with the length of their relationship with the organization; (b) cost less to serve—since they are more familiar with the products/services and policies of the company; (c) are less price sensitive than are new customers—since they pay less attention to competitor offerings; and (d) generate referrals for the company by spreading positive word-of-mouth communication. Therefore, direct marketers actively plan to keep their customers happy and loyal to their business by attempting to exceed customer expectations instead of merely meeting them.

Often products/services outside a firm's usual offerings, when offered to the firm's loyal customer base under the company's brand, may garner response greater than if that same offer came directly from the unknown, unrelated manufacturer. Products as diverse as insurance and automobiles have been sold successfully to **affinity** groups such as credit union members. Oil companies, department stores, and credit card companies all sell a great variety of unrelated merchandise to customers with whom they enjoy a relationship. These are examples of **continuity selling** and **cross-selling** to loyal customers.

Airlines are active relationship marketers. Frequent flyer programs offer mileage points for many purchases charged to a selected credit card. Other affinity partnerships have offered an insurance plan from Allstate to Sears' customers and a Seiko watch "exclusively" to Daughters of the American Revolution. Some companies use the power of affinity marketing to sell other merchandise under their brand (another example of cross-selling). Eastman Kodak, claiming its cameras were the world's largest consumers of batteries, sells batteries under its valuable brand name. John Deere's catalog offers an array of home and garden products far different from the farm machinery with which the Deere brand had long been associated. Many brand names, trading on their affinity relationships with customers, also have been licensed to unrelated organizations.

Customer Affinity and Customer Lifetime Value

Customers have intrinsic value; the first sale to a new customer is but a forerunner of possible future sales to that customer. However, customers are also the most elusive of intangible assets an organization has. Their *goodwill*—the ability of the organization to keep them—is the source of future revenues and future profits, which can go well beyond recovering the initial cost of attracting or acquiring them. In fact, over the years direct marketers have been able to calculate that a current customer will generate five times the amount of profitability as a newly acquired customer.

The creation of customers is only a first step in building a successful business. The next, and equally important, step is to *keep and cultivate them.* Though businesses in the past may have known that the number of customers increased or decreased, that advertising attracted some new customers, or that competitors took away others, there were few ways of knowing *which* customers came or went or *why.*

A company's investment in keeping its customers can be just as real as its investment in plant and equipment, inventory, and working capital, and perhaps even more valuable. Mail-order firms, faced with high front-end promotion costs, long ago adopted the concept of the lifetime value of a customer to guide marketing decision making. **Lifetime value of a customer (LTV)** is the discounted stream of revenue a customer will generate over the lifetime of his or her relationship with a company. The LTV concept is presented in detail in Chapter 3.

So, now that you know what direct marketing is and how it differs from traditional marketing, let's examine who uses direct marketing and for what purposes.

WHO USES DIRECT MARKETING AND HOW

You can immediately recognize a direct response advertisement, regardless of the medium used, by noting whether the reader, listener, or viewer is requested to take an immediate action: mail an order form, call a telephone number, log on to the World Wide Web, come to a store or event, fill in a coupon, ask for a salesperson to call, send a contribution, vote for a particular candidate, or attend a meeting. If so, it is an example of direct marketing.

Users of Direct Marketing

At some time or another, virtually every business and every organization—charitable, political, educational, cultural, and civic—and even every individual uses direct response advertising and, indeed, has a database for so doing. As individuals, we use direct mail whenever we send greeting cards, wedding invitations, and birth or graduation announcements. Job hunters find the mail is an excellent way to get their résumés to prospective employers. Businesses, especially small businesses, use a variety of media for direct response advertising and also employ many of the other elements of direct marketing. This is true of giant corporations as well as small retailers and industrial service organizations. The leading enterprises using many of the elements of direct marketing include, among others

- Periodical publishers
- Food stores and distributors
- Mail-order houses
- Department stores
- Book and record publishers
- Automotive manufacturers
- Pharmaceutical manufacturers
- Book and stationery stores
- Newspaper publishers
- Home furnishing stores
- Insurance companies
- Credit card companies
- Financial institutions

Among non-profit organizations—civic, charitable, political, educational, and cultural—the list of users of the elements of direct marketing is virtually endless. Religious organizations, PTAs, colleges, and universities, as well as charities, use direct marketing techniques to keep members informed, to solicit funds, and to promote understanding. Political organizations use direct response advertising to change public opinion, to inform constituents, and to raise campaign funds.

The range of businesses/organizations that have embraced direct marketing is diverse. The exploits of Aaron Montgomery Ward and Richard Warren Sears now range from the sophisticated and expensive products of Neiman-Marcus, Gump's, and Saks Fifth Avenue to the fine sporting goods of L. L. Bean and Eddie Bauer to the art products of the Metropolitan Museum of Art and Lincoln Center to the specialty products of Omaha Steaks and Vidalia Onions.

Applications of Direct Marketing

Let's look at a sampling of the many applications of the tools and techniques of database-driven direct marketing in use:[7]

- *Traffic-building at the seller's location:*   Retailers like Bloomingdale's, Neiman-Marcus, Macy's, and Saks use direct mail, Web sites, and telemarketing—in addition to traditional print and broadcast media—to drive store traffic. They build databases in the process, as do very many specialty stores like Radio Shack. Countless manufacturers, Hewlett-Packard among them, do the same for their resellers.
- *Lead-generation at the buyer's location:*   Business-to-business (industrial) direct marketers like IBM and Pepsi-Cola Bottlers use direct mail, Web sites, and telemarketing to generate leads so as to enhance their personal sales forces.
- *Mail order (remote location):*   The term "mail order" is really a misnomer as consumer and industrial organizations go beyond traditional direct mail and catalogs. They now utilize telephones, Web sites, broadcast, and print media. They solicit responses via the World Wide Web. Then the United Parcel Service and FedEx, as well as the U.S. Postal Service, fulfill the responses. "Mail" often never enters the picture!
- *Multi-channel distribution:*   Williams-Sonoma, Abercrombie & Fitch, Sharper Image, Talbot's, and Laura Ashley are but a few examples of enterprises whose roots are in mail-order catalogs but who now populate shopping malls and the World Wide Web. From catalog shopping to buying via the Internet and from personal selling to mail order and telecommunication, the channels have become blurred. What is the common denominator of all of these? A *database* . . . and *customer relationship!*

The list of organizations that can benefit from a database and direct marketing is virtually all-inclusive:

- *Product and service enterprises:*

    American Express builds customer relationships with financial services, travel services, and related products.

    IBM offers hardware and software products through its Web site. It generates leads for its sales staff. Gateway and Dell sell direct in a variety of media. Apple and Compaq sell direct and support resellers, too.

    Bland Farms uses the tools and techniques of direct marketing . . . as a purveyor of its Vidalia onion products.

    So do travel agents, stockbrokers, and banks.

- *Consumer and industrial enterprises:*

    Packaged goods companies harness the power of coupons, whether mailed, in newspapers, in-store, or on the Internet. One packaged goods company built a database from coupons redeemed for fitness foods and used this to develop ongoing customer relationships with other of their products appealing to fitness lifestyles.

    Manufacturers of heavy cranes or earth-moving equipment find prospective customers through various construction and building permit databases.

- *For-profit and not-for-profit organizations:*

    The United States Treasury encloses order forms for U.S. Mint Liberty Coins with income tax refunds.

    The University of Missouri's Repertory Theater utilizes databases to get prospects to a single performance and then upgrades those to season ticket buyers.

- *Fundraising organizations:*

    Jerry Lewis raised upwards of $60 million to fight Muscular Dystrophy during his 2003 Labor Day Telethon.

    City Union Mission puts together a list of 4,000 prior contributors from which it gets contributions of $350,000 from a single letter. Sisters of Mercy do likewise.

- *Political action groups:*

    Do you want to be elected president, governor, or mayor? Do you want to be elected to a School Board?

    Do you want to build support or raise funds for the National Women's Political Caucus or Planned Parenthood?

    Do you want to overcome objections of legislatures to conversion of railroad right-of-ways to Rails-to-Trails?

    Do you want to garner political and financial support for environmental causes like The Nature Conservancy, World Wildlife Fund, American Rivers, and starving elk?

    If you answered "yes" to any of the above, you will rely on direct marketing activities to obtain votes and financial support!

TRENDS IN DIRECT MARKETING

There has been a major increase in diversity of *non-store retailing*. Direct marketing has become a way of life, especially since the advent of on-line shopping. Not only has there been a proliferation of mail-order catalogs, but now more than ever catalogs are generating transactions at both store locations, called "bricks," and other non-store, on-line retailers, called "clicks" retailers. Catalogs have been responsible for generating a great deal of Internet traffic and telephone orders, too. It is clear that the advent of the Internet, together with its World Wide Web, has ushered in a whole new type of "store."

Many of the traditional store retailers capitalized on their recognizable brands and images and expanded their distribution with mail order. Early catalog entrants were Neiman-Marcus, Bloomingdales, and Saks Fifth Avenue, although L. L. Bean had been selling clothing from a catalog since 1912!

Several years ago a futurist had predicted that by the year 2000 as much as 80 percent of consumer purchases would be made from "electronic cottages." While the advent of the World Wide Web made "electronic cottages" a reality, a look at the stores populating today's malls indicates that the reverse process has also happened. Mall tenants like Eddie Bauer, Sharper Image, Anne Taylor, Laura Ashley, Abercrombie & Fitch, Talbot's, and Williams-Sonoma all had their beginnings as successful mail-order catalogs. A key consideration of these merchants in opening mall stores has been the recognition and loyalty they built with their catalogs to create store traffic and not just remote sales via catalog, telephone, or Internet.

A multimedia synergy also has developed embracing all forms of advertising: broadcast television and radio, printed publications, direct mail, and telephones. Most recently, personal computers have provided electronic access to what may become the most powerful medium of all: the Internet. The Internet has driven several recent trends in direct marketing, such as the interaction of *bricks* and *clicks*. Rapid advances in technology have encouraged this as have changing lifestyles. More and more, direct marketing has become characterized as multimedia and multichannel.

Creating In-Store Traffic

Direct marketing plays a major role in boosting store traffic and not just remote ordering. Many retailers, however, have tended to view catalogs (and Web sites) as an *alternative*, rather than as an *adjunct* that can create store traffic at the same time as it generates added direct sales.

Customers, especially those at some distance from stores, are offered the convenience of shopping by mail, telephone, or Web sites for items featured in promotions in a variety of media. Many also like to "shop" from catalogs or on the Internet, but prefer to make their purchase in the store, where they can see and feel the merchandise, check colors, get a proper fit, and then take immediate delivery.

Oil companies have justified inclusion of circulars with their monthly billing that offer merchandise in order to promote traffic to their service station retail locations. Knowing that they are already receiving a monthly billing for their gasoline purchases, customers will be inclined to favor the company from which they purchase gas with extended-payment merchandise purchases, such as power tools or luggage, to be added to their monthly gasoline bill and thus avoid a second bill from another company. The oil companies have found that such regular monthly billing also encourages your future loyalty for gasoline purchases.

An interesting example of retail traffic building comes from the motion picture industry. Warner Brothers capitalized on its affiliation with publisher Time, Inc., in the formation of a new organization, Time Warner. To promote its World War II movie, *Memphis Belle,* Warner Brothers called on the direct marketing experts at its affiliate, Time-Life, Inc. It then mailed 700,000 postcards offering a special $1.00 discount to each recipient and a guest at evening performances of the new movie. The recipients of this discount offer were purchasers of books or videos from Time-Life on such subjects as World War II, Nazi Germany, and aviation—all likely to be interested in the movie.

Manufacturers, too, have utilized the tools and techniques of direct marketing to create retail traffic for their products. Many have built databases from warranty cards returned by recent purchasers of their products.

Coupons, mass-distributed through direct mail, newspapers, magazines, and the Internet have been used to promote retail store traffic. One major packaged goods manufacturer compiled the names of those who had redeemed coupons for fat-free and sugar-free foods. It used this to develop a database to send a quarterly nutrition newsletter to these calorie-conscious users in order to identify and build brand relationships. Coupons sent with the newsletter to a segmented market were redeemed at a rate five times that of coupons sent at random.

Directing On-Line Traffic

A major consideration for Internet retailers is creating traffic to their Web sites. A good many techniques have been developed to accomplish this for traditional "brick-and-mortar" retailers who have opted to also sell on-line. These typically involve initiative on the part of the retailer who usually directs promotions offering exclusive benefits, such as price discounts, to store customers, utilizing a variety of media to get their attention and to describe the benefits they offer. The same can be done to direct traffic to Web sites of those without stores, of course, but it appears that many of the failed dot-coms did not understand the nuances of such direct marketing. Neither did most of the now-defunct dot-coms recognize the importance of building a customer database so that future continuity and cross-selling promotions could be directed to them. The Internet retail merchant success stories seem to be about those who have direct marketing and database expertise—Sharper Image and Lillian Vernon, to name just two.

Web sites make available an endless array of information for those who want it and for those who prefer to shop at their leisure and convenience, just as they have been doing for some time with mail-order catalogs and direct-mail offers. A notable example of this is Internet pioneer Amazon.com, which who has mastered the art and science of direct marketing in a way that has demonstrated the lifetime value of a customer. Amazon.com has built great market valuation in the form of a database with millions of active customer records. Its major asset seems to be its database of customers, coupled with its ability to continuity-sell and cross-sell new product lines in a manner that provides added benefits to its customers.

Certain products are best purchased on a visit to a retail store. As we write this, Amazon.com is recognizing that fact in the marketing of home theater components: highly technical and multi-choice digital monitors, sound systems, receivers, and disk/tape players. The firm has entered into a partnership with Circuit City retail stores, so prospects can deliberate over specifications on-line and then take delivery and receive service off-line at a retail store.

Membership (Affinity) Clubs

France Loisirs, a French mail-order book club unit of the German publishing group, Bertelsmann, strategically located its retail bookstores by studying the geographical distribution of its book club members. A single retail location serves about 10,000 members, and admission to a store is by membership card only. Typical direct-mail catalogs announce current selections, which members (if they so choose) can purchase at their local limited-access store. To provide meaningful service on each customer visit, store clerks can access a database of the individual customer's reading preferences and prior purchases.

Following the success of airline frequent flyer programs, scores of retailers have created frequent buyer programs. Usually, like Hallmark Cards' Gold Crown Card program, these programs encourage store traffic and continuity of customer relationships with reward points that can be redeemed for future purchases. While a television presentation like the *Hallmark Hall of Fame* does much to promote its brand among those "who care enough to send the very best," dealers laud the Gold Crown Card, which generates store traffic that results in measurable sales.

FIGURE 1-9   Example of Loyalty Program Card

Such membership programs are very much in evidence now. They register customers in a database and thus provide promotion opportunities together with an identification card entitling the customer to substantial discounts. Retailers scan purchases at checkout and record them in a database so they can recognize buying patterns as well as develop customer profiles. These buyer continuity programs, like those for frequent flyers, provide an air of exclusivity and affinity with the store. Some, like those of large-volume, high-discount retailers Sam's Club and Costco, even charge annual membership fees for the privilege of spending money with them. Membership programs also have proliferated among food stores; examples are the Kroger Plus Card, the Giant BonusCard, the Food Lion MVP Card, and the Harris Teeter VIC Card (as shown in Figure 1-9).

Going hand in hand with these membership or loyalty club marketing activities is the issue of information privacy. Although privacy issues will be discussed in greater detail later in this book, its importance merits a brief overview here.

Issues of Privacy and Security

The important issues of privacy and security will be discussed in greater detail in Chapters 8, 9, and 12, however a brief overview is provided here to help you put into perspective the uncontrollable and ever-changing legal developments affecting direct marketers. With regard to the issues of privacy and security, one thing is certain—the privacy policies are changing, and they will have a great impact on direct marketing. With that in mind, let's look at a few of the key issues surrounding privacy and security.

The use of data culled from interactive customers and their transactions alarms privacy advocates. Will these concerns about information privacy affect the future of database-driven direct marketing? Databases provide opportunities to fulfill customer preferences through targeting of relevant messages and media. This minimizes intrusive or "junk" advertising—that which is not relevant to the interests of the recipient. As a reality, though, people do not always react favorably when what they buy triggers further solicitations.

Privacy advocates also point to potential harm or injury to individuals as a result of data disclosure. It thus behooves the direct marketer to be responsible in both the acquisition and the use of data. Certainly not the least of the reasons for this is that it is inefficient, as well as costly, to send irrelevant direct mail advertising to those not interested. Some customers, of course, continue to view any promotion as an intrusion or a nuisance and feel it is an invasion of their privacy. Others, seeking to minimize the time they spend reviewing advertising for things they will never buy, welcome the database-driven offers they receive because of their relevance.

A few facts about information privacy are clear. Opinions about information privacy vary depending on the type of consumer. Governmental regulations and privacy legislation are on the rise. Information privacy is an area upon which direct marketers must keep close watch. It is a nebulous area and one that is changing rapidly.

Also changing are the laws governing Internet security. Both current legislation and new technology are being developed to block telemarketers and e-mail marketers. These are areas that are changing almost daily! Direct marketers must constantly monitor the legal policies affecting interactive media—especially on-line marketing activities. It's impossible to understate the impact of these important issues of privacy and security on their work.

Summary

Direct marketing is a measurable, accountable, response-driven system of marketing that interacts with customers on a one-to-one basis with all customer interaction information stored in a database and used to drive future marketing activities. Thus, direct marketing is database-driven marketing.

Almost all types of business can and do conduct direct marketing activities, including organizations and individuals whose goal is to establish long-term relationships with their customers. Direct marketing uses many different types of media and formats including, direct mail, catalogs, newspaper, magazine, radio, television, telephone, and the Internet. The industry has a long history and has experienced rapid growth primarily due to credit cards, computers, advances in the printing industry, changing lifestyles of consumers, and the negative aspects of in-store retailing.

Customers are at the heart of the direct marketing process. The main goal of the direct marketing process is to develop and strengthen long-term relationships with customers. Many direct marketers are finding great success in using membership clubs to enhance customer loyalty. These are becoming very popular among direct marketers and among consumers. However, as with any area of marketing, there are many uncontrollable variables affecting the way direct marketing activities can be carried out. The issues of privacy and security are the most pertinent at the moment and will require direct marketers to constantly seek ways to satisfy consumer needs and wants while adhering to the regulations governing their industry.

Key Terms

- direct marketing, 4
- interactive marketing, 4
- database, 4
- marketing concept, 7
- market segments, 8

- lists, 10
- multichannel marketing, 15
- customer relationship management (CRM), 17
- affinity, 18

- continuity selling, 18
- cross-selling, 18
- lifetime value of a customer (LTV), 18

Review Questions

1. Name and elaborate on the characteristics that distinguish *direct* from *traditional* marketing.
2. What is meant by measurability of and accountability for marketing decisions?
3. What is the difference between a list and a database?
4. What are the "Ps" of marketing and how do they relate to direct marketing?
5. "Direct marketing is an aspect of marketing characterized by *measurability* and *accountability* with reliance on *databases*." Explain this statement.
6. Discuss the historical roots and the emergence of direct marketing; how has it been influenced by technological, economic, and social change?
7. Compare and elaborate on the evolution of direct response advertising from Figure 1-5 (1897 Sears catalog) to Figure 1-8 (2001 Peruvian Connection catalog).
8. Just where do the Internet and its commerce subsidiary, the World Wide Web, fit into the total marketing scheme of things and the distinguishing characteristics of direct marketing?
9. What is direct response advertising and how does it relate to direct mail as well as print, broadcast, and Web sites?
10. Describe the use of direct marketing by a business. Describe its use by a non-business organization. Describe how it fits into the political scheme of things.

Exercise

Think of your favorite cuisine. Pretend you have just opened a restaurant featuring all of your favorite foods.

a. How will your marketing plan use direct marketing techniques to build your business?

b. Pretend a year has gone by and you have been successfully operating your restaurant. How will your direct marketing activities change over the next few years?

CASE: TREADMOVES™—AN INTERNET SUCCESS

OVERVIEW

This case is an example of how direct marketing methods provide a cost-effective alternative and improvement over traditional marketing methods. It demonstrates how a new entrepreneurial venture was successfully launched on a very small budget by concentrating on direct-response communication channels, customer relationship management, and measurement. The case specifically details how the Internet can be used as both a promotional medium and a selling method. It is proof that direct marketing can work for any company, organization, or entrepreneur—regardless of size.

As a learning experience, the student should focus on the basic elements of direct marketing, including marketing research, database development, customer relationship management, measurability and accountability, and multi-channel distribution. Show how this case demonstrates the application of the newest direct marketing medium—the Internet. Then, examine how direct marketing strategies and techniques play an integral role in the development and execution of a twenty-first-century business.

CASE

In response to the fitness craze of today's consumers, a new product has been born—TreadMoves™. TreadMoves is a series of four exercise videos for treadmill users. It is providing a much-needed rejuvenation for treadmills. Research has shown that there are approximately 14 million treadmills in U.S. consumers' homes today, however approximately half are NOT being used for exercise—but as a place to hang clothes! And why?? It has been suggested that the consumer got bored with his/her walking or running routine on the treadmill. Well ... TreadMoves deals with that!

Gone are the days of jumping on a treadmill only to stare at the timer and wait for the treadmill workout to end. Now, TreadMoves provides so many new moves and combinations from which to choose—treadmill exercisers never have to do the same workout twice. The TreadMoves video series, as shown in Figure 1-10, consists of many different workouts to meet the needs of different target market segments. For example,

FIGURE 1-10   TreadMoves™ Video Covers

some videos include moves and combinations such as shuffling, boxing, knee lifts, and kicks to appeal to exercisers who enjoy choreographed classes like step aerobics. Conversely, other videos consist of strictly walking, running, hill climbing, sprinting, and weight training to appeal to sports enthusiasts. Additionally, each video also includes moves that can be performed while the treadmill is turned off, such as push-ups, abdominal exercises, and stretching; however, all components of the workouts are performed *on a treadmill.*

Founded in 2001, TreadMoves was created by Meredith Hines, a 24-year-old graduate student with an intense passion for health and fitness. Meredith lacked the financial backing needed to mass market her exercise videos through traditional retail channels and or advertise via traditional mass media—fitness magazines, newspapers, and television. Her challenge was to create the look of a professional and credible business on a very limited budget. Given this considerable financial constraint, certain decisions were critical to the viability of the business. Some of these key decisions included determining how to conduct marketing research, how to promote the videos to target consumer segments, how to select marketing channels through which to distribute the products, and how to measure the effectiveness of the marketing techniques she utilized. Direct marketing techniques provided the solution to each of her needs. We'll look at how she used direct marketing methods for each of the following five phases in marketing TreadMoves:

- Phase I: Marketing Research
- Phase II: Promotion
- Phase III: Database Development and Customer Relationship Management
- Phase IV: Channel Selection
- Phase V: Measurement

Phase I: Marketing Research
The Internet provides a wealth of general market data such as industry trends. However, gathering very specific information about customer segments and demographics is very expensive to purchase and was not an option for TreadMoves. So, the TreadMoves team utilized chat rooms to gather this specific type of information. In order to find these types of chat rooms, the TreadMoves team searched the Internet for sites that hosted chat rooms related to fitness, weight loss, and exercise videos. One of the Web sites that the TreadMoves team discovered was VideoFitness.com—a Web site that is dedicated to people who work out at home with exercise videos.

This site has a very robust chat room with thousands of members who participate in discussions on a wide range of topics. The TreadMoves team read through many discussion threads (which are groups of posted comments that are responding to one original question or posted comment) to gather information about demographics and consumer behavior. This information heavily influenced the exercise content of the initial set of videos.

Once the first two TreadMoves videos were available for sale, the TreadMoves team visited the VideoFitness.com Web site and was actually able to read discussion threads about their own videos. The information gathered from these threads allowed the TreadMoves team to tailor new videos and products to the needs of their targeted customer segments and ultimately, create even better products.

Phase II: Promotion
Promotion objectives for TreadMoves were twofold—first, to generate awareness of the videos and second, to stimulate product purchase. To generate awareness for the new product the TreadMoves team created a direct response brochure. Since these brochures were quite expensive and the entrepreneur was operating on a small budget, their use was somewhat limited. Thus, the brochures were primarily used in an attempt to gain publicity for TreadMoves.

Figure 1-11 demonstrates other promotional activities included the development of

FIGURE 1-11 Home Page of TreadMoves™ Web Site

a Web site to be used for both promotion and selling. The TreadMoves team mailed complimentary copies of the new videos to the Webmasters of the chat rooms (discussed above) for them to review. Once the Webmasters posted their review of the workouts, the Webmasters' reviews intrigued the members of the chat rooms enough for them to visit the TreadMoves Web site and buy their own copies. Once the members of the chat rooms tried and loved the workouts, they posted their own discussion threads about TreadMoves and generated additional traffic to the TreadMoves Web site, which further sold the videos to other chat room members.

Once the team had introduced the product the initial market introduction was made via the Internet, the team researched several other promotional methods were researched, such as acquiring lists of e-mail addresses, placing banners on related Web pages, buying magazine advertising space, etc.; however, the costs of each of these methods was prohibitive. Therefore, the TreadMoves team decided to focus their promotional efforts on database marketing activities.

Phase III: Database Development and Customer Relationship Management

Once the initial two videos were successfully introduced to the market, the TreadMoves team took advantage of its most valuable resource: its customer database. Information about each customer who purchased products from the Web site or inquired about information was captured in the database. When the second set of videos was ready for market introduction, all current customers and inquirers were sent an introductory e-mail offer to be the first to try out the new TreadMoves workouts. The response to this offer was very good—it garnered a 20 percent return within two days!

The company developed, in addition, customer profiles and used these to enable the identification of prospective buyers who possessed characteristics similar to those of the TreadMoves customers. The TreadMoves team then surfed the Internet in an attempt to compile lists of prospective buyers. For example, Gold's Gym posts e-mail addresses for the managers of each of its gyms. It took quite some time, but the TreadMoves team was able to gather their e-mail addresses and add them in to their database. They then sent information about product offerings to all of the new e-mail addresses in the database.

Each customer and prospect also received information or news related to TreadMoves. For example, when TreadMoves™ was ranked in the top 10 videos for 2002 by *Fitness* magazine, the following e-mail message in Figure 1-12 was sent to each customer and prospect in the TreadMoves database.

The TreadMoves team constantly used their database to interact with their customers and prospects. In addition to promoting new products or sharing newsworthy information, the TreadMoves Web site encourages feedback from their customers and provides answers to customer questions about fitness. Such interaction is strengthening customer relationships and enhancing the value of the TreadMoves™ brand.

Phase IV: Channel Selection
Through the TreadMoves Web site, customers could obtain information and purchase products. Minus the initial cost of designing the site,

this channel enabled TreadMoves to conduct business for just the cost of Web site hosting, credit card processing, and domain name registration, which totaled about $100 per month. Additionally, the Internet store was also easy to update with new products and information, so the content of the site could be quickly and inexpensively changed to grow with the business.

As a result of being able to demonstrate significant Web site traffic as well as a 30 percent repeat purchase rate, the TreadMoves team investigated other channels of distribution. Today, TreadMoves is sold via multi-channel direct marketing. In addition to the TreadMoves Web site, customers can purchase the videos from multiple catalogs (such as Collage Video), through on-line retailers (such as Amazon.com), and via bricks-and-mortar retailers (such as Barnes & Noble retail stores). This enables TreadMoves to reach even more customers. With the exception of consumers who purchase the videos from retail stores, all video orders are fulfilled by mail.

FIGURE 1-12   TreadMoves™ E-Mail Advertisement

Phase V: Measurement

The company that hosts the TreadMoves Web site on its server provides Web site statistics, such as number of visitors per day and click-through patterns. These data provide infinite amounts of information and allows small companies, like TreadMoves, to have an inexpensive way to test and measure the effectiveness of their creative appeals. For example, each customer who visits the TreadMoves Web site has a unique "fingerprint" that can be tracked and monitored. So, the TreadMoves team has experimented with two different copy appeals and has compared the percentage of people who make an immediate purchase with each.

They also cross-tested this data with another variable—the buying season—to provide additional information. The test results showed that more people made an immediate purchase on their first visit to the TreadMoves Web site during the holiday season than during the New Year's resolution month of January, when shoppers seemed to take longer to make their purchase decision. Based on this information, the TreadMoves team was able to tailor their marketing efforts towards these different types of buying patterns.

The measurability and accountability aspects of direct marketing provide a great advantage over traditional marketing methods. For example, the TreadMoves team sends animated e-mail advertisements to each customer in its database. Since the actions of each customer can be tracked, TreadMoves is able to measure the effectiveness of each advertisement. TreadMoves can also measure how the advertisement was effective, whether it simply built traffic or actually increased sales. Finally, the TreadMoves team also was able to use the Web site statistics, specifically site traffic statistics, to influence other distributors to carry their products. By demonstrating that thousands of unique visitors explored the TreadMoves site monthly, the TreadMoves team was able to prove that there is significant demand and interest for TreadMoves' products that would in turn build traffic to the distributors' Web sites, too. Thus, direct marketing measurement, by itself, has proven to be a very profitable marketing tool for TreadMoves.

SUMMARY AND CONCLUSION

As of January 2003, TreadMoves has sold over 10,000 videotapes worldwide and continues to get recognition from top fitness publications, such as *Fitness* magazine. Given the success of the TreadMoves video series in the residential market, the TreadMoves team has since expanded its product offerings to include an audio series for treadmill users who want to take their workouts to the gym, on vacation, or any other location without TV/VCR accommodations. Additionally, TreadMoves has ventured into the commercial markets, offering instructor certifications and license packages so that TreadMoves exercise techniques can be taught in commercial gyms and fitness centers. This means that TreadMoves will be utilizing additional methods to communicate to its business customers, such as trade shows and conventions. However, regardless of the media, the TreadMoves team will apply the same basic tenants of direct marketing wherever they go. At each trade show, there will be a clipboard that collects e-mail addresses of customers who want more information. And then the direct marketing process of creating and cultivating a customer one at a time will begin again.

So if you're tired of your same old exercise routine, go and check out your school fitness center or local gym, you might be able to enjoy a taste of twenty-first-century fitness called TreadMoves. Or you can find out more information about TreadMoves videos by giving your fingers a little exercise and visiting www.TreadMoves.com today. ■

Case Discussion Questions

1. What was the single most important direct marketing technique that the TreadMoves team employed early on?
2. What other ways could the TreadMoves team use the Web site statistics to make their e-mail marketing even more effective?
3. Given TreadMoves recent entry into the commercial market, in what other ways could the TreadMoves team use their customer database to promote to the commercial market?
4. Taking into consideration the limited budget of the entrepreneur, what else could be done to increase the size of the TreadMoves database?
5. Overview the various direct marketing methods that have lead to the success of this new business venture. Could traditional marketing methods have achieved the same level of success? Why or why not?

Notes

1. Peter F. Drucker, *The Practice of Management* (New York: Harper, 1959), 37.
2. Refer to Chapter 2 for extended discussion of market segmentation.
3. Many of the early historical references contained in this section are based on documentation prepared by Nat Ross for the Direct Marketing Association.
4. Adapted from Martin Baier, Goutam Chakraborty, and Kurt Ruf, *Contemporary Databased Marketing* (Evanston, IL: Racom, 2001).
5. DMA 2003 Statistical Fact Book, *The Direct Marketing Association,* October 2002, pp. 256, 264.
6. Martin Baier, *How to Find and Cultivate Customers Through Direct Marketing* (Lincolnwood, IL: NTC Business Books, 1996), 3ff.
7. Adapted from Martin Baier, Goutam Chakraborty, and Kurt Ruf, *Contemporary Databased Marketing* (Evanston, IL: Racom, 2001).

CHAPTER

2

DIRECT MARKETING LISTS AND SEGMENTATION

The Nature of Market Segmentation
Product Differentiation
Product Positioning
Industrial Market Segmentation

The Bases for Market Segmentation
Geographic Segmentation
Demographic Segmentation
Social Factor Segmentation
Psychographic Segmentation
Behavioral Market Segmentation

ZIP Code Areas as Market Segments
Geographic Structure
ZIP Plus Four
Clustering Areas to Segments
Availability of Statistical Data

Lists as Market Segments
A Perishable Commodity
Types of Lists
Development of House Lists

The List Industry
List Users
List Owners
List Brokers
List Managers
List Compilers
Service Bureaus

Evaluation of Lists
Measurement of Results
Response Differences Attributable to Timing

Customers can be served best by organizations that know their characteristics. Since all buyers are not alike, marketing managers have developed ways to place them into groups or market segments, according to geographic, demographic, social, psychological, or behavioral factors. These market segments are the focal points of product differentiation and positioning.

Direct marketers have been using market segmentation strategies in their efforts to effectively promote and distribute products and services to consumers for many years. Think of a sports magazine. Its readers probably are interested in many different sports. It could easily identify its golf-enthusiast consumers and offer them golf products and services. Likewise, it could offer its tennis-playing readers tennis equipment and clothing. The concept and theory of market segmentation and its special relevance in both consumer and industrial direct marketing are the subjects of this chapter. We will also be concerned with ZIP codes as a segmenting tool and mailing lists as market segments.

THE NATURE OF MARKET SEGMENTATION

Market segmentation is a marketing strategy devised to attract and meet the needs of a specific submarket. These subgroups are referred to as **market segments**. A company may target marketing strategies to several market segments. Each segment should be homogeneous—that is, its members should be similar to one another; heterogeneous—meaning its members should all be different from the members of other segments; and substantial in size—so as to be profitable.

Product Differentiation

Marketers target products and services to select market segments, rather than the total market, unless the product or service is unique and appeals equally to everyone. Many times it is necessary to *differentiate* products for particular market segments and to *position* these products so that they will have special appeal to the intended market. **Product differentiation** is a strategy that uses innovative design, packaging, and positioning to make a clear distinction between products and services serving the same market segment. Product differentiation, like market segmentation, is an alternative to price competition. The difference might be real or simply an advertised difference. For example, a brand of toothpaste that contains fluoride is intrinsically different from one that does not. An airline may call its Boeing 727 aircraft a "Star-Stream Jet" without making it any different from the planes of its competitors. Product differentiation can distinguish a product from that of its competitors.

Product Positioning

Product positioning is the way the product is defined by consumers on important attributes. It enables consumers to rank products or services according to perceived differences between competing products or brands within a single product category.

Marketers can position products based on quality, size, color, distribution method, time of day that the product is used, time of year, and price. Examples include: "7-UP: the Uncola"; "Avis . . . We Try Harder"; "Think Small—the Volkswagen Beetle." When all other soft drinks manufacturers were competing in the cola market, 7-UP took a different direction. The same thing occurred in the automobile industry when most automotive manufacturers were producing big cars, Volkswagen introduced a small car. Most big-ticket marketers, such as the manufacturers of Rolex watches and Mercedes-Benz automobiles, thrive by positioning their products as exclusive, high-quality items. So do the well-known direct marketers of specialty products like Harry and David, The Sharper Image, and Victoria's Secret.

Industrial Market Segmentation

Like consumer markets, industrial markets break down into smaller, more homogeneous segments of the heterogeneous total industrial market.

Standard Industrial Classification

The Standard Industrial Classification (SIC) coding system developed by the federal government serves as a basis for classifying statistical data and has been widely used by government, trade associations, and business enterprises. SIC codes classify business customers by the main economic activity in which they engage. All major activities are assigned a two-digit code number. Some of the major industry divisions include, but are not limited to, agriculture, mining, construction, manufacturing, transportation, wholesale trade, retail trade, financial services, and public administration.

As a company's business activity becomes more specialized, up to six digits can be added to the two-digit SIC code to identify subgroups. SIC codes can also designate the primary and secondary lines of a business as well as additional segmentation information based on the following statistical data: sales volume, credit rating, age of business, number of employees, net financial worth, and subsidiary and geographic location. Most direct marketers have used SIC codes in conjunction with proprietary information as the primary tool for segmenting business and industrial consumers. However, SIC codes posses certain limitations and are no longer in such wide use.

North American Classification System (NAICS)

The North American Industry Classification System (NAICS, pronounced as "nakes") has largely replaced the SIC coding system. Many business people felt that the SIC system failed to recognize the growth of information technology, the service industry, high technology, and international trade. The new NAICS system offers several improvements over the former SIC system. Figure 2-1 overviews the main differences between them.

SIC Codes	NAICS Codes
SIC codes classify establishments by the type of activity in which the business is primarily engaged.	NAICS is based on a production-oriented, or a supply-based, conceptual framework.
SIC is a 4-digit code.	NAICS is a 6-digit code.
SIC system lacked current information.	NAICS will be reviewed every five years so classifications will change with the economy.
SIC have 10 classifying sectors: • Agriculture, Forestry, and Fishing • Mining • Construction • Manufacturing • Transportation, Communications, and Public Utilities • Wholesale Trade • Retail Trade • Finance, Insurance, and Real Estate • Services • Public Administration	NAICS have 20 classifying divisions: • Agriculture, Forestry, Fishing, and Hunting • Mining • Construction • Manufacturing • Utilities • Transportation and Warehousing • Wholesale Trade • Retail Trade • Accommodation and Food Services • Finance and Insurance • Real Estate and Rental and Leasing • Information • Professional, Scientific, and Technical Services • Administrative Support; Waste Management and Remediation Services • Educational Services • Health Care and Social Assistance • Arts, Entertainment, and Recreation • Other Services (except Public Administration) • Public Administration • Management of Companies and Enterprises

FIGURE 2-1   Comparison of SIC Codes and NAICS Codes

Source: From the NAICS Association Web site, accessed online at http://www.naics.com/info.htm, February, 2003.

The first improvement is relevance. NAICS identifies over 350 new industries, including high-tech areas, and 9 new service industry sectors that now contribute to the economy. The second improvement is comparability. NAICS was developed by the United States, Canada, and Mexico to produce comparable data for all three nations. Industries are identified by a 6-digit code, in contrast to the 4-digit SIC code, to accommodate a larger number of sectors and allow greater flexibility in designating subsectors. The first five digits denote the NAICS levels common to all three NAFTA countries, while the sixth digit accommodates user needs in individual countries. Figure 2-2 shows the new hierarchical structure of NAICS.

The third improvement is consistency. NAICS uses a consistent principle: businesses that use similar production processes are grouped together. This is entirely different from the SIC system which focused on the industries served. The fourth improvement is adaptability. NAICS will be reviewed every five years, so classifications and information keep up with our changing economy. Finally, quality has been

xx	Industry Sector
xxx	Industry Subsector
xxxx	Industry Group
xxxxx	Industry
xxxxxx	U.S., Canadian, or Mexican national Specific

FIGURE 2-2   NAICS Hierarchical Structure

improved with key measures of U.S. economic activity such as retail services, manufacturers' shipments, and service industry receipts.[1]

THE BASES FOR MARKET SEGMENTATION

The needs, wants, or interests of the consumers belonging to various segments are different. However, it would be almost impossible to conduct marketing research for every product and service that could determine which market segment each consumer would best fit into; therefore marketers use other, more general, indicators for segmenting markets. These indicators include: geographic, demographic, social, psychological, and behavioral factors. A brief overview is provided here.

Geographic Segmentation

Potential geographic subdivisions range in size from the country as a whole down through census divisions and Federal Reserve districts to states, counties, trading areas, cities, towns, census tracts, neighborhoods, and even individual city blocks. In addition, there are numerical codes such as ZIP codes, geocodes, telephone area codes, computer "match" codes, and territory and route numbers. Once upon a time, census tract numbers were the best means of geographical segmentation. Do you know which census tract you live in? Most people probably do not. However, our ZIP code number *is* meaningful to us and everyone knows that number.

An important form of geographic market segmentation is that which recognizes inherent differences among those buyers who reside in central cities, suburban, urban fringe, and rural areas. The last may be further divided between farm and non-farm households. Geographic location can also affect the future purchase activity of consumers. For example, the level of consumer interest in purchasing nursery plants or snow blowers is often related to the climate of the geographic area in which the consumer lives.

Population changes within geographic areas, such as the decreasing population of a specific geographic area or the high mobility of the population in another, have significance to the marketer. Census data is invaluable for research regarding the changing geographic and demographic profile of the American population. The recent CensusCD Neighborhood Change Database (NCDB) is a very powerful product that presents four decades (1970, 1980, 1990, and 2000) of census tract series data. Additional information about this new product is available at www.uscensus.net.

Another geographic segmentation tool, the **Global Positioning System (GPS),** associates latitude and longitude coordinates with street addresses. Direct marketers use this system to identify geographic locations, establish business sites, locate competition, measure distance, and generate data about the demographics of a business location. Given this information, combined with the technological mapping capabilities of most businesses, the direct marketer can better determine the business penetration and market potential in certain geographical areas.

Demographic Segmentation

Demographics are identifiable and measurable statistics that describe the consumer population. The primary unit of observation in demography is the individual; the family unit and household are secondary concerns. Common demographic variables include age, gender, education level, income level, occupation, and type of housing.

There are three main sources for such data: (1) population enumeration as in a census; (2) registration on the occurrence of some event, such as birth, marriage, or death; and (3) sample surveys or tabulation of special groups. The data obtained in these ways are generally available for marketing and other uses from governmental sources, especially the Census Bureau.

To indicate the wealth of demographic data available, we offer some data from the 2000 Census of Population and Housing in Figure 2-3. It is often wise to tabulate the effect of the interaction of many demographic variables at the same time. For example, it is highly valuable for a direct marketer to know the marital status of a certain 25-year-old male consumer. Just think, of two male consumers, both age 25, one might be married with two children and the other single with no children. These two consumers probably belong in totally different market segments—based on their

Demographic Characteristics:
- Sex and Age
- Race
- Hispanic Origin and Race
- Relationship
- Household by Type

Social Characteristics:
- School Enrollment
- Educational Attainment
- Marital Status
- Fertility
- Grandparents

Economic Characteristics:
- Employment Status
- Commuting to Work
- Occupation
- Industry
- Class of Worker

Housing Characteristics:
- Units in Structure
- Year Structure Built
- Rooms
- Year Householder Moved into Unit
- Vehicles Available

FIGURE 2-3   Data Available from the U.S. Census Bureau

Source: From U.S. Census Bureau, American Community Survey Change 2000–2001, www.uscensus.net, February, 2003.

market needs. In this case, the more demographic data you can collect, the better. Oftentimes, a single demographic statistic can be misleading.

Marketers know that currency is the key to accuracy and validity of demographic data. *Changes* in demography, such as when someone marries or has a baby, therefore have marketing significance.

Social Factor Segmentation

Social factors include a person's culture, subculture, social class rank, peer group references, and reference individual(s). Social factors demonstrate the impact that other people in our society have on our decision-making process and consumption activities.

Society may well have an impact on our behavior beyond our control. For example, **reference groups** (also called "peer groups") are the people a consumer turns to for reinforcement. This reinforcement normally comes *after* the consumer makes a purchase decision. Reference groups may have a direct and powerful influence on the consumption behavior of adolescents and teenagers. A **reference individual** is a person a consumer turns to for advice. This person or persons will influence the consumer *before* he or she makes a purchase decision. Therefore, reference individuals normally have a stronger impact on consumer decision making than do reference groups.

Psychographic Segmentation

Psychographics is the study of lifestyles, habits, attitudes, beliefs, and value systems of individuals. Even though buyers may have common geographic, demographic, and social characteristics, they often have different buying characteristics. Psychographic segmentation divides consumers into different groups based on lifestyle and personality variables. Individual buyer behavior is influenced not only by geographic, demographic, and social factors, but also by variables that are more difficult to define such as environment, self-perception, and lifestyles. When marketers can identify and measure these influences, they can use them effectively in segmenting mailing lists.

Direct marketers have the ability to identify psychographic market segments and thus predict potential consumer response by recognizing and evaluating the simultaneous appearance of a prospect's name on a variety of lists. For example, a registered owner of a particular type of automobile might also appear on the subscriber lists of *The Wall Street Journal* and *Better Homes and Gardens* as well as the customer lists of up-scale catalogs such as Neiman-Marcus and Gump's. This same prospect might even be a contributor to Planned Parenthood and a member of the National Geographic Society. When merged, such multiple list identifiers can describe the psychographics of consumers (activities, interests, and opinions) more specifically than consumer surveys. Another means of psychographic identification of specific prospects is a comprehensive data file developed by Equifax, under the trade name The Lifestyle Selector. The Lifestyle Selector is the direct marketing industry's largest and most comprehensive database of self-reported consumer information. More than 500 response segments cover all aspects of how consumers live, what they spend their money on, and what interests they possess. This file is primarily derived from two sources: responses to consumer surveys and product registration cards filled out voluntarily by consumer after they have completed a product purchase. Included for each of the 47 million consumer names and addresses are a variety of demographic characteristics and activities or hobbies. It is possible for a consumer direct marketer to develop a psychographic and demographic profile of his or her company's house lists by matching the lists with The Lifestyle Selector, and to extend his or her prospect base by adding other names from the data file.

Thus, measurement of environmental influences within geographic units combined with demographic and psychographic indicators derived from list cross-referencing and other expressions of activities, interests, and opinions all interact to enable the direct marketer to reach individual consumers within market segments. Such list selection is obviously more efficient and can be more effective than directing pinpointed messages to the total marketplace.

Behavioral Market Segmentation

The actions taken by consumers are certainly a viable base for market segmentation. The specific types of products and services consumers have purchased, the time the transactions took place, the method or location of their purchases, and the method of payment they choose can all reveal similarities among consumers. Each behavioral factor can indicate a consumer preference that may be shared by other consumers, consequently identifying a market segment.

"Cookies" provide marketers with the ability to segment consumers according to their on-line activity. A **cookie** is an electronic tag or identifier that is placed on a personal computer. Cookies (which we will discuss in greater detail in Chapter 9) are presently the best tool for recognizing Web users again after they have interacted with a marketer's Web site in some capacity. The process is quite simple: whenever a Web site visitor makes a request to a Web server, that server has the opportunity to set a cookie on the personal computer that made the request. The Web-site host can then use the cookie for tracking beyond the initial click to determine how often that visitor returns to the Web site, the length of time of each visit, and the particular Web pages visited, which can often detail the specific products or services in which the visitor is interested. Cookies provide valuable insight into consumer behavior.

ZIP CODE AREAS AS MARKET SEGMENTS

ZIP code areas, although originally conceived and developed by the U.S. Postal Service for the purpose of sorting and distributing mail, have become a convenient and logical method of geographic segmentation, especially in direct marketing. ZIP code areas have become a key basis for market segmentation in direct marketing, combining the characteristics of geographic, demographic, social, psychological, and behavioral factors. The value of ZIP codes for marketers is based on the simple fact that the codes tend to enclose homogeneous neighborhoods and geographical boundaries.

The old saying, "birds of a feather flock together," explains why ZIP code areas constitute market segments. Because people with like interests tend to cluster and because their purchase decisions are frequently influenced by their desire to emulate their friends, neighbors, and community innovators, ZIP code areas provide the means to *identify* clusters of households that have a high degree of *homogeneity*. This homogeneity is inherent in the manner in which ZIP code areas have been constructed and

- Establish and define market segments, including sales potentials based on environmental data about the unit.
- Evaluate direct marketing results performance, based on a measurement of actual penetration against the projected potential, and realign market segments as such analysis warrants.
- Process inquiries and orders more efficiently and effectively without need for reference to a map, since the address immediately identifies the sales territory.
- Forecast more accurately based on objective analysis of the marketplace rather than on a collection of individual opinions about it.
- Pinpoint market segments in relation to profits.
- Increase regional and national advertising effectiveness when direct mail, magazines, or newspapers are used.
- Determine optimum distribution centers.
- Set up a territorial rating system for credit evaluation and perform continuing analysis of accounts receivable.
- Conduct market research, especially if demographic cross sections or probability sampling is called for.
- Develop differentiated products that have special interest to specific market segments that can be defined by ZIP code areas, certain educational levels, or target occupation groups, for example.
- Analyze penetration of present customers according to specific ZIP code area characteristics to more effectively direct and control marketing efforts.
- Identify growth areas, with updated demographics.
- Direct new product sampling more effectively.
- Control inventories according to historical territorial patterns.
- Coordinate data processing and information systems through use of the ZIP code as part of the computerized "match code."
- Distribute seasonal and climate-oriented products and information on a chronological schedule by ZIP code area.

FIGURE 2-4   Uses of ZIP Code Area Data

relies on accepted principles of reference group theory as well as the concept of environmental influences on buyer behavior.

Marketers can use ZIP code areas in many specific ways; we outline some of them in Figure 2-4.

Geographic Structure

The socioeconomic usefulness of these units, especially from a direct marketing perspective, results from the three criteria the U.S. Postal Service used in establishing each ZIP code:

1. A hub city is at the center of each cluster of ZIP code areas (termed a sectional center) that is the natural center of local transportation.
2. An average of 40 to 75 individual post offices lie within each sectional center, resulting in units with fairly consistent population density.
3. Each natural transportation hub is about 2 to 3 hours driving time away from the farthest post office in the sectional center.

An obvious convenience of these geographic units, which sets them apart from commonly used divisions such as counties, is that each household and business within the unit is readily identifiable by a five-digit number assigned to it as a part

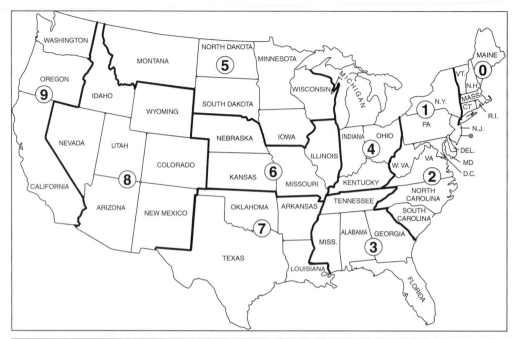

FIGURE 2-5   ZIP Code National Area Designations

Source: Courtesy of the United States Postal Service.

of its street address. In dissecting the ZIP code, you will find that the first digit of the five-digit codes identifies one of 10 (0 through 9) geographic areas of the nation, with the digit ascending from east to west. These regions are identified in Figure 2-5.

The next two digits of the five-digit number identify a major city or major distribution point (sectional center) within a state. The last two digits of the five-digit ZIP code fall into two geographic categories: (1) key post offices in each area, which normally have stations and branches in the city's neighborhoods; and (2) a series of associated small town or rural post offices served by the sectional center transportation hub or a specific neighborhood or delivery unity within a city.

ZIP Plus Four

Figure 2-6 summarizes what the five-digit ZIP code designations represent. The U.S. Postal Service has added a four-digit extension to the original five-digit code. The sixth and seventh digits denote a *sector* and the last two denote a *segment* within a sector. These additional four digits permit mail to be sorted to carrier delivery routes. An example of the meaning of the additional four-digits is as follows:

> Digits 6 and 7—could denote the location of a specific organization, like a university.
> Digits 8 and 9—could represent a specific segment or department within the university, perhaps the office of admissions.

ZIP CODE DIGIT DESIGNATIONS

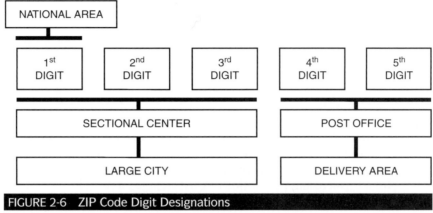

FIGURE 2-6   ZIP Code Digit Designations

Source: Courtesy of the United States Postal Service.

Clustering Areas to Segments

A key advantage of ZIP code areas is that they can be combined like building blocks to suit the individual need of the direct marketer relative to product differentiation or promotional strategy. A ZIP code–based marketing information system enables direct marketers to know more about their markets and to organize them according to local transportation patterns. Many major coupon distributors segment their markets on the basis of ZIP code areas. These companies also know which ZIP code areas possess a heavy concentration of residential households and coupon users.

Availability of Statistical Data

During the past few decades increasing amounts of data for ZIP code areas have become available. Some of these include organizations' own records along with consumer survey data compiled by the Census Bureau, Market Research Institute (MRI), and Simmons Market Research Bureau.

ZIP Code Business Patterns is a service published by Economic Information Systems. It identifies the top 10,000 five-digit ZIP code areas in terms of business activity measured by number of employees. This service identifies the number of business establishments within 10 major economic sectors (based on the first digit of the SIC code) for each ZIP code area. The following information is provided for each ZIP code area and for each SIC category:

- Number of employees
- Number of business establishments (by employment class)
- Identification of the city and state in which located
- Total payroll levels in the ZIP code

ZIP Code Business Patterns provides segmentation information that is invaluable for direct marketers.

LISTS AS MARKET SEGMENTS

Lists and data are at the very core of direct marketing. Lists identify prospects as well as customers who have something in common. Perhaps these individuals made a response and/or transaction with the direct marketer. Perhaps the prospects on a list are all females who enjoy surfing as a hobby. Or a different list could identify all of the customers who purchased a surfboard from a certain sporting goods store within a given year. Yet another list could possess the names and addresses of males, between the ages of 20 and 25, who are independently wealthy and own a horse! Therefore, lists cannot be thought of as mere mailing lists, since customers and potential customers on marketing lists are often reachable through media other than direct mail such as: telephone, the Internet, magazines, newspaper, television, and radio. Lists are the marketplace, the "place" of the 4 Ps of marketing (product, place, price, and promotion). A list denotes a market segment. Therefore, it follows that the direct marketer needs to accumulate data about the customers and prospects on them. Marketers must identify relevant geographic, demographic, social, psychological, and behavioral information using information they discover about their customers to identify prospects with similar characteristics. In the case of customer lists, the direct marketer needs to record activity in terms of responses and/or transactions. What direct response medium triggered the activity? Did the person buy, inquire, or take some other action? What product was involved? Did the customer pay by credit card? Direct marketers also want to know how frequently the activity occurs, how recently it last occurred, and the dollar amount of the transaction.

A Perishable Commodity

A list is a perishable commodity. Not only does the degree of activity (or inactivity) fluctuate, which means a list could be less valuable tomorrow than it is today, but also the people and organizations on lists are far from static. They move. They marry. They die. Their attitudes change. In 12 months, for example, as many as 25 percent of the addresses on an average customer list could change.

The direct marketer must not only be aware of the condition of lists acquired from others, but also be assured that the maintenance of the house list is current and adequate. Otherwise, part of the communication with an out-of-date list will be undeliverable and result in cost without potential benefit. List maintenance involves not only name and address correction, but also continual updating of the data within the customer's record. Figure 2-7 shows an example of a layout for a mailing list record. It shows the customer name and mailing address as well as the initial and latest order dates. Figure 2-7 also shows order and payment characteristics. The mailing list record could also show demographics of the customer.

Data about a list are also perishable. No direct marketer wants to distribute messages indiscriminately. He wants to make sure not only that the message is delivered, but also that it is delivered to the right prospect. Direct marketers are particularly sensitive to the downside of indiscriminate mass communication, not only in terms of the waste of resources but also in terms of the possible antagonism sparked among non-prospects.

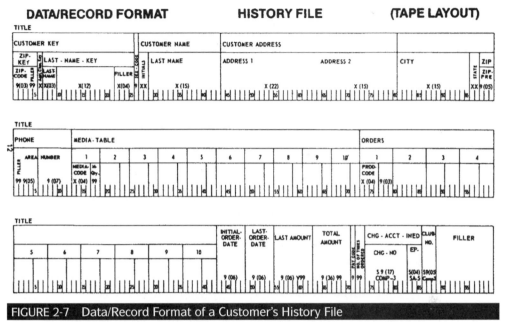

FIGURE 2-7 Data/Record Format of a Customer's History File

Source: From the Direct Marketing Association, *Direct Marketing Manual.* Courtesy of the DMA, 1120 Avenue of the Americas, New York, NY 10036–6700.

Types of Lists

There are three basic types of lists. In descending order of importance to the direct marketer, these are:

1. House lists
2. Response lists
3. Compiled lists

House Lists

House lists are lists of an organization's own customers, active as well as inactive. Because of the very special relationship that an organization enjoys with its own customers, sometimes called "goodwill," house lists are the most productive mailing lists available in terms of future response. Of lower potential (in terms of future response), but probably still more productive than lists from sources outside the organization, are the names of customers who have become inactive, who have inquired but not purchased, and who have been referred or recommended by present customers of the firm.

These four segments of a house list may be among an organization's most valuable assets, inasmuch as they generate future business at a cost much less than that of acquiring responses from outside lists. It is not uncommon for a house list to be four times, or even ten times, as productive as an outside list with which there is no existing customer relationship.

The kind and degree of customer activity is also relevant in terms of products purchased as well as the recency, frequency, and dollar value of such purchases. The source of the customer as well as the promotional strategy the marketer used to acquire that customer is information that can also help determine future response. The original list source and whether this source was direct mail, space advertising, broadcast media, the Internet, or even a salesperson have bearing on future productivity. With inquiries, there is only an expression of interest rather than an actual purchase. Although this information is important, inquiries do not have equal value compared with customer purchase information. With referrals, the recommendation by a customer of the organization could offer an advantage, especially when the name of the present customer can be used in the promotional effort sent to the referred prospect.

Response Lists

Response lists are lists of those who have responded to another direct marketer's offer by mail, e-mail, telephone, or even by personal visit. In terms of future productivity, these lists rate right behind house lists. Obviously, the lists of those direct marketers offering similar products and services will yield the greater potential for response to a similar, or even directly competitive offer. A customer who has subscribed to a news magazine by mail, *USA Today,* for example, could be an ideal prospect for a competitive news magazine such as *Newsweek*. Similarly, a consumer who has purchased fitness equipment by mail could be an ideal prospect for a sporting goods store such as The Sports Authority. The first important qualification is that the name on a list from an outside source has a history of response to direct marketed offers. The second and possibly equally as important characteristic would be an indication of response to a similar direct marketed offer. Beyond this could be a history of purchase of related items. Those who have purchased gourmet meat products, for example, might be good prospects for gourmet fruit products. They might even be good prospects for classical records or a book on interior decorating.

Lists of directly competitive firms, if available, are obvious choices. On the other hand, one of the real challenges to direct marketers is to determine *why* the purchaser of a home study course by mail, for example, might be a particularly good prospect for a book club.

Like an organization's house lists, other response lists should be looked at in terms of geographics, demographics, and social and psychological factors. They should also be segmented by type of response and/or ultimate transaction or purchase. Direct marketers should consider response lists in terms of source as well as the promotional strategy that caused them to be responsive in the first place.

Compiled Lists

Falling behind both house lists and response lists in expectations, usually, are compiled lists. **Compiled lists** are lists generated by a third party or market research firm. Individuals on compiled lists do *not* have a response history. Examples of such lists include: telephone directory listings; automobile and driver's license registrations; the newly married and the newly born; high school and college student rosters; public records such as property tax rolls and voter lists; rating services such as Dun & Bradstreet; and a multitude of rosters such as those for service and civic organizations. Other potential sources of compiled lists include manufacturer warranty cards and coupon redemptions.

Although compiled lists typically do not have a response qualification built into them, market segmentation techniques coupled with sophisticated computer systems for duplication identification make possible selection of the best prospects (those most likely to effect a response and/or transaction) from very large compiled lists. Modern technology can also cross-identify characteristics of compiled lists, such as telephone or automobile registration lists, with known response and thus even further improve response potential. Combining a response list with an automobile registration list and further identifying those on the response lists who own a mini-van, for example, is a way of identifying responsive households with children. Direct marketers use compiled lists in market segmentation and in further qualifying response and house lists.

Development of House Lists

The discussion of house lists earlier anticipates that direct marketers must compile and develop the list along with relevant data through some appropriate mechanical means. Computerized systems hold a great deal of flexibility as well as long-range economy.

The marketer must first determine just what useful data, other than accurate names and addresses, she needs to qualify individual members of the list, how to collect and record it, and in what form. Consider, too, just what purpose the data will serve in the future. Keep in mind that collection of information costs money and must therefore produce benefits commensurate with its cost. How will the data be used and can they be analyzed and evaluated properly?

THE LIST INDUSTRY

List owners and list users often come together through the efforts of list brokers, list managers, list compilers, and even service bureaus. Typically, marketers rent response lists under an arrangement allowing them to make a specific use of the data. Sometimes they buy compiled lists outright; then there is no limit on the number of times these names can be mailed. List owners usually maintain rented response lists, so these lists often have better deliverability than do compiled lists that have not been updated regularly. Service bureaus interact with all members of the list industry, providing expertise in the areas of data processing and analysis. Check out these Web sites for more information on list building: www.fastlist.com and www.alistnow.com.

List Users

Virtually every direct marketer uses lists. For example, Victoria's Secret, L. L. Bean, Lands' End, Eddie Bauer, American Eagle, and Abercrombie & Fitch all use lists. There are literally thousands of response and compiled lists available from which to choose, but the starting point is usually the direct marketer's own list.

A direct marketer using lists must obviously know its own customer profile in order to match it against available lists. Sometimes the marketer will use only segments of these lists, selecting them according to geographic, demographic, social, psychological, or behavioral characteristics. Matching one's house list against potential response and compiled lists is in itself a stimulating exercise. It often provides the direct marketer with basic knowledge of the marketplace the marketer can use to develop new products and determine successful promotional strategies.

List Owners

List owners are those who describe and acquire prospects who show potential of becoming customers of the list user. A key attribute of direct marketing, aside from its measurability and accountability, is the acquisition of lists and data about the individuals or organizations on these lists. Every direct marketer is a list owner. The lists that he compiles during new business acquisition activities are described as house lists.

Although the primary reason for acquiring house lists is to build and perpetuate an organization through contact with its customers, many direct marketers view their house lists as profit centers in their own right. Firms rent their house lists to other direct marketers, under specified conditions, and this activity becomes an important source of added revenue. Nearly all credit card companies participate in list rental activities. Also, if you subscribe to any major magazines, your name appears on the magazine's house list.

All respondents to a renter's offer become additions to the renter's own house list. Under the usual rental arrangement, the rented list may be mailed only one time, and the list owner must approve the offer in advance. Directly competitive offers may not be approved except in an "exchange" that occurs when two competitive list owners provide each other with comparable numbers of their respective house lists, or lists of active or inactive buyers.

An obvious advantage of renting a list rather than purchasing it outright (as is sometimes done with compiled lists) is that the list owner maintains the list, keeping it current and accurate. Another obvious advantage is that the names on such lists have a history of responding to direct marketing activity; thus they are termed "response" lists. A history of prior response, whether by mail, telephone, or the Internet, is another important advantage to direct marketers.

Owners of response lists or compiled lists provide descriptions of them in a standard format such as the example shown in Figure 2-8. The information normally includes list quantities, pricing, and general descriptions of the lists, including available selections (such as gender or marital status), as well as mechanical considerations such as the type of labels desired, the label format, or the output medium in which the file is to be delivered. The type of label is normally pressure sensitive, which is peel and stick, or Cheshire, which is cut and paste. Label format decisions address the number of labels to be placed horizontally across a page—normally referred to as "1, 4, or 5 up."

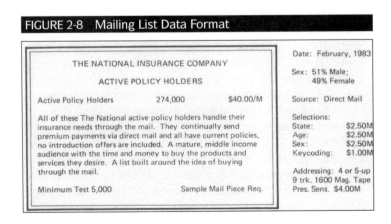

FIGURE 2-8   Mailing List Data Format

THE NATIONAL INSURANCE COMPANY

ACTIVE POLICY HOLDERS

Active Policy Holders   274,000 $40.00/M

All of these The National active policy holders handle their insurance needs through the mail. They continually send premium payments via direct mail and all have current policies, no introduction offers are included. A mature, middle income audience with the time and money to buy the products and services they desire. A list built around the idea of buying through the mail.

Minimum Test 5,000   Sample Mail Piece Req.

Date: February, 1983

Sex: 51% Male;
     49% Female

Source: Direct Mail

Selections:
State: $2.50M
Age: $2.50M
Sex: $2.50M
Keycoding: $1.00M

Addressing: 4 or 5-up
9 trk. 1600 Mag. Tape
Pres. Sens. $4.00M

List files are normally delivered via magnetic tape/cartridge, file transfer protocol (FTP), CD-ROM, or ZIP disk. Other output mediums exist but are not commonly used given today's technology.

The costs of lists can range from less than $10 per thousand names for large quantities of broad-based compiled lists to more than $100 per thousand for highly selected up-scale response lists. The average list rental charge of approximately $40 to $50 per thousand for one-time use usually includes provision of these names on either labels or disks for computer processing.

Not all direct marketers make their house lists available for use by others. Perhaps the list contains proprietary information, or the list owner wishes to safeguard a very valuable asset from improper use. For example, some non-profit organizations never rent their donor lists to ensure donor privacy. Most colleges and universities do not allow their student lists to be used by other businesses. Can you think of some businesses that would like to rent the list of students enrolled at your school? Some list owners also feel that there is a tendency for a list to wear itself out. Even offers that do not directly compete can vie with each other for discretionary spending, these list owners contend.

The counterargument is that it is virtually impossible for individuals and organizations to be left off response and/or compiled lists. Thus, although a list owner has a proprietary interest in a house list, individuals and organizations on the list will inevitably appear on lists owned by others. Another counterargument contends that the more opportunities individuals and organizations are provided, the more likely they are to respond.

List Brokers

Like real estate brokers or stock brokers, **list brokers** serve as intermediaries who bring list users and list owners together. They do not actually own lists but rather serve as middlemen in the list industry. In so doing, they perform the following functions:

- Find new lists
- Verify information
- Report on performance
- Check instructions
- Clear offer
- Check mechanics
- Clear mailing date
- Work out timing
- Ensure delivery date

List brokers are specialists in the process of bringing list owners and list users together. They should have a very clear picture of the products of the list owner as well as the needs of the list user. List brokers usually work on a commission basis, which is paid by the list owner.

List Managers

Although list rental can be an attractive profit center, direct marketers usually run it as a by-product of their basic business. Thus they often try to maximize returns from this activity through list managers. **List managers** represent the interests of list owners and assume the responsibility, on behalf of list owners, of keeping in contact with list brokers and lists users. They perform the advertising and sales functions and often maintain the lists they manage in their own facility. Like list brokers, list managers receive a commission from the list owner.

List Compilers

Organizations that develop lists and data about them, often serving as their own list managers and list brokers, are called **list compilers.** The form of list compilation they do is different from that which direct marketers do in developing their own house lists through generation of responses and/or transactions.

List compilers usually develop their lists from public records (such as driver's licenses or motor vehicle registrations), newspaper clippings, directories, warranty cards, and trade show registrations. In fact, the compiler owns such lists and then resells them, rather than renting them for one-time use. Instead of regularly maintaining such lists, compilers usually recompile periodically. Names and addresses in telephone directories, for example, are compiled regularly, at least annually, on issuance of newly published volumes.

Service Bureaus

Service bureaus provide data processing, data mining, outsourcing, on-line analytical processing (OLAP), and other services to support the interchange of lists and database information within the direct marketing industry. (These items will be discussed in the next chapter.) Some of the larger direct marketing companies have its own service departments that perform this function on a regular basis.

EVALUATION OF LISTS

Record keeping is essential to properly evaluate the profitability of response lists as well as compiled lists. Marketers also rely on record keeping to predict future response from lists or segments of lists. Record keeping includes accurate measurement of results and evaluation of response differences attributable to timing. A sample form for ongoing recording of lists/segments is shown in Figure 2-9.

Measurement of Results

Evaluating a list begins with selecting a **key code,** a unique identifier placed on the response device or order form prior to mailing a promotional piece. Key codes can be simple preprinted numbers identifying the source of the mailing list, or they can be so complex as to incorporate not just the source, but the category of list, type of product offered by the list owner, or even the degree of prior direct marketing activity.

Direct marketers structure key codes so that they can accumulate information across several individual lists by different categories. Thus, the direct marketer can tabulate response not only by individual lists, but also by sources of list, product lines, geographic location (ZIP code), and a variety of other broad qualifiers. The marketer then groups individual lists into such categories and makes assumptions about the overall efficiency of certain list sources, particular ZIP codes, or specific product lines.

CLASS NUMBER--- LIST OWNER--- PRODUCT---

QUANTITY AVAILABLE | YEAR | COST | USED
.........M ☐Buy. ☐F. Buy. ☐Inq. | ...... | $............/M
.........M ☐Buy. ☐F. Buy. ☐Inq. | | $............/M

B.N. | ADDRESS ☐Form ☐Label | SOURCE ☐D.M. ☐Pub. ☐Comp. ☐Misc. | ARRANGED ☐Geo. ☐Chron. ☐None | LABELS EXTRA $............/M | SELECT EXTRA $............/M

SALES

Date Mailed	Key	No. Mailed	1 Week		2 Weeks		3 Weeks		4 Weeks		5 Weeks		6 Weeks		7 Weeks		8 Weeks		9 Weeks		10 Weeks		11 Weeks		12 Weeks		13 Weeks		COST PER SALE
			No.	P/M	No.	P/M	No.	P/M	No.	P/M	No.	P/M	No.	P/M	No.	P/M	No.	P/M	No.	P/M	No.	P/M	No.	P/M	No.	P/M	No.	P/M	

CONVERSIONS

At End of →		1st Mo.		2nd Mo.		3rd Mo.		4th Mo.		5th Mo.		6th Mo.		Final			PAR RATIO
Date Mailed	No. Mailed	No.	%	No.	%	No.	%	No.	%	No.	%	No.	%	No.	%	Comments	

FIGURE 2-9 Mailing List Evaluation Form

Marketers should keep ongoing records of lists and monitor them even if they frequently contact the names on the list. The character and nature of lists change over time, just as the character and nature of the list owner's business may change. Many direct marketers have achieved the highest response rate when they have used so-called "hotline" names. **Hotline names** are those most recently acquired, but there is no consensus in the industry about what chronological period "recent" describes.

Response Differences Attributable to Timing

Response differences can occur as a result of timing alone. Certain exogenous factors over which the direct marketer can exert no control (beyond the quality of the list itself), such as economic conditions or climate variations, can have a profound effect on results when lists are developed over a period of time. Other uncontrollable factors include major events or even catastrophes that divert public attention from the everyday.

Certain offers, such as a catalog of Christmas gifts, are timely and are targeting seasonal differences in consumer buying habits. Some offers can be affected by the income tax season or by the vacation season. Some direct marketers try to time their promotional efforts so as to avoid arrival during any type of holiday event, especially those that take people outdoors. For example, if Lands' End were to send consumers a catalog offering winter sweaters in the early portion of summer when most consumers are enjoying wearing light summer clothing, the response to their offer may be affected by the season. In addition, offers with expiration dates may need to be lengthened during the summer months due to the fact that many consumers take summer vacations are not at home to receive their mail.

Even for non-seasonal offers, however, an apparent month-to-month cycle affects direct response advertising. All other factors being equal, many direct marketers have noted these ebbs and flows. For example, Bally's and other fitness centers probably receive a greater response to their direct marketing efforts during the months of January and February, although they are open for business 12 months a year. Each direct marketer should develop an index of monthly responses and determine which month generates the highest relative response. Noting monthly variances is useful to the direct marketer who is testing lists on an ongoing basis. It makes it possible to consider the variable of timing in comparing one list with another when these are released during different months of the year. When direct marketers add customer response information to their house list, they will be creating a customer database. Let's take a closer look at the differences.

LISTS VERSUS CUSTOMER DATABASES

What is the difference between a list and a customer database? A customer database may begin as a simple name and address listing, but it incorporates additional customer information beyond what would normally appear on a list. It includes geographic, demographic, social, psychological, and behavioral information about each customer and serves as a record of the interactions between the organization and the customer, which details the depth of the relationship between the two parties. In sum, the information contained on a list is only a fraction of that which is normally contained in a customer database. The next chapter will provide more details on how this customer database information is organized, stored, and used to maximize customer relationships.

However, an organization's customer database is also likely to be segmented, since all customers do not have the same needs, wants, or interests. Thus, direct marketers apply the principles of market segmentation prior to interacting with customers on a personalized basis. We'll demonstrate this strategy in this chapter's case on Lillian Vernon Corporation.

Summary

Most direct marketers conduct market segmentation to better serve consumer needs and wants. Direct marketers segment final consumers according to geographic, demographic, social, psychological, and behavioral characteristics. Direct marketers also segment businesses or industrial consumers according to Standard Industrial Classification (SIC) codes or the North American Industrial Classification System (NAICS). Direct marketers consider ZIP code areas to be geographic market segments that provide important customer information.

Lists are also important market segmentation tools. There are three basic types of lists: house, response, and compiled. Each list is of value for direct marketers, although house lists are considered to be the most valuable. The list industry is comprised of list owners, list users, list brokers, list managers, list compilers, and service bureaus. Each member plays an important role in the list rental activities of direct marketers. Direct marketers strive to keep lists current and accurate. House lists normally hold a customer's name, address, and pertinent contact information on them. These lists often serve as the foundation of a customer database. When additional customer information is appended to each customer record, the list is no longer considered a *list*, but is considered to be a *customer database*—which is the topic of the next chapter.

Key Terms

- market segmentation, 34
- market segments, 34
- product differentiation, 34
- product positioning, 35
- Global Positioning System (GPS), 37
- demographics, 38

- reference groups, 39
- reference individual, 39
- psychographics, 39
- cookie, 40
- house lists, 45
- response lists, 46
- compiled lists, 46

- list owners, 48
- list brokers, 49
- list managers, 49
- list compilers, 50
- service bureaus, 50
- key code, 50
- hotline names, 51

Review Questions

1. What is *market segmentation* and how do direct marketers use it?
2. How is segmenting industrial markets different from segmenting final consumer markets?
3. Overview the differences between SIC Codes and NAICS. Name some companies who might use industrial classifications in segmenting their industrial or business consumer market.
4. What are *psychographics?* In what way are they useful to direct marketers?
5. In the four-digit extension of an original five-digit ZIP code, what does each of the numbers stand for?
6. How can ZIP codes help achieve product differentiation or promotional strategy?
7. What type of list is most important to an organization? Why?
8. Identify a few products or services that probably incur response differences attributable to timing.
9. Explain the difference between a *list user* and a *list owner.*
10. What are list brokers, list managers, and list compilers each responsible for?

Exercise

The company you work for sells snow skiing equipment on-line. Not only do they sell snow skis, but they also sell snowboards, skiing apparel, and packages to ski resorts all over the United States. To better target its customers, the company has decided to segment its markets and "get the word out" about its products. It has asked you to segment the company's customers and potential customers in terms of geographic location, demographics, social factors, and psychographic information. How will you go about obtaining this information? What resources would aid you in determining the different segments? How might this information about the company's customer segments be helpful to the direct marketing efforts of the firm?

CASE: LILLIAN VERNON CORPORATION

OVERVIEW

This case study demonstrates the importance of a company's house list. It examines the processes used in prospecting to acquire new customers, as well as the segmentation strategies used in retaining current ones.

Technology has dramatically improved the manner by which direct marketers create, store, and use lists. Today, the lists of almost all direct marketers are computerized and sophisticated. However, most direct marketing lists originated long before the computer age—and were housed on simple 3x5-inch index cards. With computerization came the ability to rent lists and conduct precise market segmentation of lists. Your objective in completing this case is to better understand the application of list and segmentation strategies of one of America's leading direct marketing companies—Lillian Vernon Corporation.

CASE

On a little yellow kitchen table one of America's largest specialty catalog companies, Lillian Vernon Corporation, was founded in 1951. Lillian Vernon started the firm when she placed a $495 advertisement for a personalized pocket book and belt in *Seventeen* magazine (a copy of this ad is presented and discussed in Chapter 4). With her initial investment of $2,000 in wedding gift money and the success of that first ad, which resulted in $32,000 in orders, Vernon's business was off and running.

The response to this initial ad also marked the start of a valuable house list for Lillian Vernon Corporation. From the very beginning, entrepreneur Vernon knew that her customer list was the most valuable asset of her business (even though her bankers mistakenly thought the company's physical plant and computer systems were its main assets). Vernon exerted great care in maintaining her customer list. She would

sit at her yellow kitchen table laboriously noting customer names and orders on 3x5 index cards. Every two months she would pore over her cards—adding, deleting, and revising the information on each. Why? Because people relocate, stop ordering, get married, and die, and the customer list must be constantly updated.

Lillian's efforts have really paid off. When the Lillian Vernon catalog was first published in 1960, the customer list had 125,000 names on it. By the early 1980s it had more than ten million names, and by 1995, more than eighteen million.[2] Today, Lillian Vernon Corporation's mailing list identifies more than 26 million households throughout the United States.[3] According to David Hochberg, Vice-President of Public Affairs at Lillian Vernon Corporation, the number of *recent buyers* (defined as those customers who have made a purchase from the company within the past 12 months) totaled 2.7 million in 2003. Today, the 52-year-old firm has become a leading national catalog and online retailer that markets gifts, housewares, and gardening, seasonal, and children's products.

How Does Lillian Vernon Corporation Get Names?
Back in the 1950s Lillian Vernon simply added customer names to her list as new customers placed orders. This process continued for about a decade and the firm built its house list slowly. In fact, some of Lillian's very first customers—who were teenagers when they bought her bags and belts—are now grandmothers who still buy from the company. Thus, retaining satisfied customers is the foundation upon which the customer list is built. However, every direct marketer must prospect for *new* customers as well. Lillian Vernon Corporation loses about 20 percent of its customers annually, which means that expanding the list requires prospecting to secure new customers on an ongoing basis.[4]

At first, most of the prospect names were found via ads in select magazines that target the same customer type (*House Beautiful, Better Homes and Gardens, Women's Day*) or through word-of-mouth referrals. Ever since the first Lillian Vernon catalog was mailed, each catalog has included space on the order form that asks customers for the names of other people who might also like to receive a catalog.

In the 1970s, Lillian Vernon Corporation began participating in the list rental industry. The firm rented out its customer names and also rented names from other direct marketers. Frequently the company would also trade names with different direct marketers—essentially a non-cash swapping of lists. Lillian Vernon Corporation focused primarily on renting *response lists,* since consumers who possessed some history of purchasing via direct marketing proved to be better prospects than someone who had no such history. The primary criteria used by Lillian Vernon Corporation when renting lists include[5]

- *Merchandise compatibility*—select companies that have similar products (never rent a list from a company whose merchandise is incompatible, has inferior quality, or is in poor taste).
- *Customer compatibility*—select companies that target similar customers (never rent a list from a men's clothing company or a catalog specializing in power tools when the target customer is women).
- *Price compatibility*—select companies with similar price ranges (never rent a list that markets to the upper class when your catalog specializes in moderately-priced merchandise for middle-income consumers).

In 2002 Lillian Vernon Corporation hired the list managing services of ALC New York to be responsible for all list rental activities. It continues to actively rent response lists (Newport News, Inc.) but no longer rents compiled lists (financial services lists using income as the primary selection variable) with which it has had little success. ALC New York will also screen all list rental requests the company receives. The

types of companies that have recently requested to rent Lillian Vernon's customer list include book and magazine publishers and retailers of collectibles. Lillian Vernon Corporation does not rent its list for offers the company knows would be inappropriate for its customers.

The list managing service will also conduct tests of potential lists prior to making a major commitment to rent the entire list. Most direct marketers permit other direct marketers to test a cross-section sample of 10,000 or 15,000 names. Once the response to the test has arrived, the renter may require additional tests (of larger sample sizes) before deciding whether to rent the entire response list. Through testing, Lillian Vernon Corporation can project the profitability a particular response list.

Who Are Lillian Vernon's Customer Segments?
Over 90 percent of Lillian Vernon Corporation customers are women, with an average age of 44 and an average household income of $65,000—57 percent above the national average. Over 64 percent are employed outside the home, and more than half have children living at home.[6] However, all these customers are not alike. They have different lifestyles and different needs, wants, and interests, so the corporation segments its customer list accordingly. Each customer segment must be substantial in size and responsive to the product category. There must also be a large and compelling product assortment in a given category to warrant a separate catalog title.

The corporation publishes seven catalog titles, Lillian Vernon, Favorites, Christmas Memories, Rue de France, Lilly's Kids, Personalized Gifts, and a sale catalog. Each catalog averages 96 pages with over 700 products in each edition. Target markets are kept in mind when selecting the products to be presented in each catalog. The Lillian Vernon catalog, the Favorites catalog, and the Christmas Memories catalog all target the core Lillian Vernon customer. The Lilly's Kids catalog specifically targets those Lillian Vernon customers who are mothers and grandmothers. (See Figure 2-10 for these catalogs.)

FIGURE 2-10   Lillian Vernon Catalogs

Over the years, Lillian Vernon Corporation has tested other catalog titles, such as Lillian Vernon Gardening, and found that the market segment did not meet its segmentation standards of size and/or responsiveness. In such cases the firm has dropped the catalog.

The Rue de France catalog is the only one that does not bear the well-known Lillian Vernon brand name. (See Figure 2-11 for the Rue de France catalog.) The company acquired the Rue de France product line along with the catalog in 2000; it targets a more up-scale consumer. The price-range for the products offered in the Rue de France catalog is significantly higher than in the other Lillian

Vernon Corporation catalogs. Thus, a multi-brand strategy is being employed to target this customer segment.

Lillian Vernon Corporation also serves the business-to-business (B2B) or organizational consumer market segment. The B2B segment of Lillian Vernon Corporation originated back in the 1960s but has recently gained increased market share. Pursuing the business segment was a logical move for the company—given the fact that Lillian Vernon was a pioneer in offering personalized products. The B2B division of the company sells corporate gifts, premiums and incentives (personalized with corporate names or logos) and gift certificates to more

FIGURE 2-11   Rue de France Catalogs

than 1,000 firms, including many Fortune 500 companies.[7]

SUMMARY AND CONCLUSION

According to an Opinion Research poll, more than 39 million Americans are familiar with the Lillian Vernon name. Since 1951, the Lillian Vernon logo has appeared on three billion catalogs, 172 million shipping boxes, and 485 million products.[8] The corporation is an incredibly successful direct marketer. Why? Because Lillian Vernon meticulously created, updated, refined, and segmented her house list, always believing that it was the corporation's greatest asset. She built her business by segmenting her customers and satisfying the individual needs and wants of each market segment. Customer satisfaction is also a company tradition at Lillian Vernon Corporation. Through precise market segmentation, the company has tailored each of its catalogs to different customer segments. Through direct marketing, each customer has been marketed to on a personal basis. ∎

Case Discussion Questions

1. Discuss the various methods used by Lillian Vernon Corporation to acquire names of prospective customers. Which methods have been most productive?
2. Given the three criteria used by Lillian Vernon Corporation when renting a response list, name some response lists that Lillian Vernon Corporation should pursue.
3. Identify some direct marketing companies that might have an interest in renting Lillian Vernon Corporation's customer list. Explain why each company would possess such an interest and whether or not Lillian Vernon Corporation should permit such a list rental transaction.

Notes

1. From the "North American Industry Classification System (NAICS)" Web site, accessed online at http://www.census.gov/naics, February, 2003.
2. Lillian Vernon, *An Eye For Winners: How I Built One of America's Greatest Direct-Mail Businesses* (CITY: HarperCollins Publishers, Inc., 1996), 131–132.
3. 2003 Overview of Lillian Vernon Corporation.
4. Lillian Vernon, *An Eye For Winners: How I Built One of America's Greatest Direct-Mail Businesses* (New York, NY: HarperCollins Publishers, Inc., 1996), 131.
5. Lillian Vernon, *An Eye For Winners: How I Built One of America's Greatest Direct-Mail Businesses* (New York, NY: HarperCollins Publishers, Inc., 1996), 135–136.
6. 2003 Overview of Lillian Vernon Corporation.
7. Ibid.
8. Ibid.

CHAPTER

3

DATABASE-DRIVEN DIRECT MARKETING

All direct marketers seek to maximize the profits of their business. Two ways to achieve this are attracting new customers and encouraging your current customers to buy more from you. We saw in Chapter 2 that often a direct marketer seeks to obtain new customers by renting a response and/or a compiled list of prospects and directing promotional efforts toward list members.

However, it is very well established that a new customer acquisition program may *not* be as profitable as a customer retention program. Did you know that it costs (on average) about 5 times as much money to acquire a new customer than it does to keep a current customer?[1] Thus, direct marketers may be better served by directing their marketing efforts towards retaining the customers they already have. This is the concept behind database-driven direct marketing, which will be the focus of this chapter.

We will also discuss what a customer database is, its importance in developing customer loyalty, and how to build, maintain, and secure a customer database. In addition, this chapter will detail how to utilize a customer database for the purposes of calculating the lifetime value of a customer, conducting continuity and cross-selling activities, and creating a customer communication program.

CUSTOMER DATABASE

A **customer database** is a list of customer names to which the marketer has added additional information in a systematic fashion. Just as a house list contains active as well as inactive customers, inquirers, and referrals, so does an organization's customer database. Thus we can think of a customer database as a computerized house list that contains more than merely a listing of customer names.

A customer database is the key to developing strong customer relationships and retaining current customers. The customer database is the vehicle through which a company documents comprehensive information about each customer. This information could include the consumer's past purchases (buying patterns), demographics (age, birthday, income, marital status, etc.), psychographics (activities, interests, and opinions), and much more. Marketers use this information to direct all future marketing activities with each customer on an individual basis. For example, the customer database is used for purposes such as lead generation, lead qualification, sale of a product or service, and promotional activities. Armed with this information, marketers are able to develop a closer relationship with each customer on a personalized basis. The stronger the relationship with each customer, the more likely that customer will continue purchasing from the company. That is why current customers, with whom the direct marketer already has an established relationship, are more likely to be retained as future customers.

How does a company retain its customers? By keeping the customer satisfied and happy. Highly satisfied customers tend to be loyal customers and loyal customers generate greater profits for an organization over their lifetime of patronage. This is due to the following reasons:

1. Loyal customers tend to increase their spending over time. Thus, retained customers normally spend more with an organization than do newly acquired ones.[2]

2. Loyal customers cost less to serve than new customers. Repeat customers have greater familiarity with an organization's processes and procedures and, therefore, are more quickly and easily served.
3. Loyal customers are normally happy customers who tell others about the organization, which in turn, generates additional business.
4. Loyal customers are less price sensitive than are new customers. They see value in their relationship with the organization and may spend more freely because of their high level of satisfaction with the firm.

In addition, according to Frederick Reichheld, author of *The Loyalty Effect,* a five-percentage-point increase in customer retention in a typical company will increase profits by more than 25 percent — and growth by more than 100 percent.[3]

The task of creating and maintaining loyal customers is what customer relationship management (CRM) is all about. (Chapter 10 will provide an expanded discussion of CRM along with customer service issues.) In an attempt to retain current customers, marketers are investing in programs and activities to create and enhance customer loyalty. The development of a customer database is the first step in this process.

DATABASE DEVELOPMENT

In building a customer database, management must first determine the company's primary goals. For example, an organization might want to get to know its customers better in order to develop more effective future promotional activities. Other objectives may include selling them different products/services; thanking them for their patronage; encouraging referral business; introducing a new product or service; distributing information about an upcoming event or sale; or introducing a new staff member or employee . . . the list goes on! Customer loyalty programs are commonly used in the process of creating a customer database.

Customer Loyalty Programs

Customer loyalty programs are programs sponsored by an organization or firm to encourage customer repeat purchases through program enrollment processes and the distribution of awards and/or benefits. Airlines, hotels, cruise lines, retail stores, and many other organizations have rewarded customer loyalty through structured programs for years.

Organizations primarily offer customer loyalty programs to strengthen customer relationships. Customer loyalty programs are also used to develop and/or provide additional information to a company's customer database. The beauty of customer loyalty programs is that you can obtain information about customers on a direct basis and use this information to more effectively target customers' future needs and wants.

Examples of Loyalty Programs

An example of a successful customer loyalty program is the revamped Marriott Honored Guest Program. Marriott launched the Marriott Rewards program in 1997 to

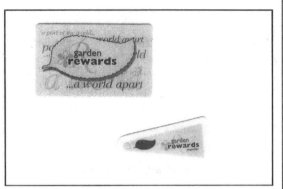

FIGURE 3-1   McDonald Garden Center Garden Rewards Program

increase usage across all brands and to be a strong incentive for frequent travelers to switch from competitive offers. Members of this program can redeem points for more than 85 award options such as hotel stays, travel packages, room upgrades, frequent-flyer miles, airline awards, cruises, and golf and skiing packages. In one year, the program has resulted in 10 million members, with members spending approximately 2.5 times more than non-members.[4]

Figure 3-1 provides an example of how McDonald Garden Center, with three retail locations in Virginia, rewards customer loyalty via its Garden Rewards Program. The Garden Rewards Program was established to allow McDonald Garden Center to know its customers and communicate with them based on the value of the relationship. It enabled the company to improve customer loyalty while reducing long-term marketing expenses through more precise market segmentation and tailored communication. The program has quickly become a success. In less than six weeks from the launch date, the number of customers enrolled in the Garden Rewards Program totaled 15,375—which was almost 60 percent of the customers on the company's house list. Of the reward program cards issued, 70 percent were used at least one time during that same six-week period; 42 percent were used two or more times.[5]

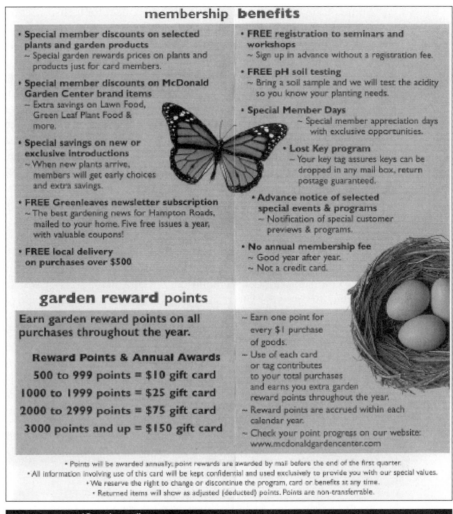

membership **benefits**

- **Special member discounts on selected plants and garden products**
  ~ Special garden rewards prices on plants and products just for card members.
- **Special member discounts on McDonald Garden Center brand items**
  ~ Extra savings on Lawn Food, Green Leaf Plant Food & more.
- **Special savings on new or exclusive introductions**
  ~ When new plants arrive, members will get early choices and extra savings.
- **FREE Greenleaves newsletter subscription**
  ~ The best gardening news for Hampton Roads, mailed to your home. Five free issues a year, with valuable coupons!
- **FREE local delivery on purchases over $500**

- **FREE registration to seminars and workshops**
  ~ Sign up in advance without a registration fee.
- **FREE pH soil testing**
  ~ Bring a soil sample and we will test the acidity so you know your planting needs.
- **Special Member Days**
  ~ Special member appreciation days with exclusive opportunities.
- **Lost Key program**
  ~ Your key tag assures keys can be dropped in any mail box, return postage guaranteed.
- **Advance notice of selected special events & programs**
  ~ Notification of special customer previews & programs.
- **No annual membership fee**
  ~ Good year after year.
  ~ Not a credit card.

garden reward points

Earn garden reward points on all purchases throughout the year.

Reward Points & Annual Awards

500 to 999 points = $10 gift card

1000 to 1999 points = $25 gift card

2000 to 2999 points = $75 gift card

3000 points and up = $150 gift card

~ Earn one point for every $1 purchase of goods.
~ Use of each card or tag contributes to your total purchases and earns you extra garden reward points throughout the year.
~ Reward points are accrued within each calendar year.
~ Check your point progress on our website: www.mcdonaldgardencenter.com

• Points will be awarded annually; point rewards are awarded by mail before the end of the first quarter.
• All information involving use of this card will be kept confidential and used exclusively to provide you with our special values.
• We reserve the right to change or discontinue the program, card or benefits at any time.
• Returned items will show as adjusted (deducted) points. Points are non-transferrable.

FIGURE 3-1   (Continued)

Once managers have determined the objectives of the database and the method by which they will gather customer information, they can identify the data they need to collect from their customers.

Source Data

The information contained in a customer database is called **source data.** Each direct marketer must determine the particular source data needed for their customer database—which often varies vary based on the specific products or services or the competitive situation of the direct marketer. Collecting data that will not be used simply drives up the organization's marketing costs. Within their house records, direct marketers usually capture certain key data such as product preferences or credit experience, if relevant.

Some of the basic data marketers should collect for a customer database are the customer's name and address including ZIP code, telephone number, and e-mail address. Many direct marketers document how the customer first learned about the product or service. Additional data called **"transactional data"** includes what products each customer has purchased; how recently (recency) and how often (frequency); and how much the customer spends (monetary). This information provides an avenue to analyze each customer through some variation of the **recency/frequency/monetary (R/F/M)** assessment. By carrying the date and volume of purchases, in the master list record over a period of time marketers can determine the transaction record of each customer in a given period, which helps determine the future potential of that customer. Many direct marketers, such as Lillian Vernon Corporation and Newport News, Inc., use this approach in determining who will receive catalogs and how often. It relates the cost of promotion to the potential benefits to be derived from each customer.

The Recency/Frequency/Monetary Assessment

The exact R/F/M formulation for each direct marketer will, naturally, vary according to the importance given to each of the variables in relation to each other. For some promotions, marketers might need to manipulate their calculations by weighting one of the factors, so that, for example, the results will show those customers who had purchased most recently. More sophisticated direct marketers use multivariate statistical techniques to mathematically determine the R/F/M weights and use them with greater reliability.

Figure 3-2 shows how to evaluate customers on a mailing list according to the combined R/F/M values of their transactions over time. For purposes of this textbook example, the following weights are assigned to the variables: recency (x 5), frequency (x 3), and monetary (x 2).

FIGURE 3-2   Evaluation of Customer Mailing List Record by Recency, Frequency, and Monetary Values of Transactions (R/F/M)

ASSUMPTIONS:

Recency of Transaction:
20 Points If within Past 3 Months
10 Points If within Past 6 Months
 5 Points If within Past 9 Months
 3 Points If within Past 12 Months
 1 Point If within Past 24 Months

Frequency of Transaction: Number of Purchases within 24 Months Times 4 Points Each (Maximum: 20 Points)

Monetary Value of Transaction: Gross Dollar Volume of Purchases within 24 Months Times 10% (Maximum: 20 Points)

Weighting Assumption:
Recency = 5
Frequency = 3
Monetary = 2

EXAMPLE:

Cust.	Purchase #	Recency	Assigned Points	(x5) Wght. Points	Frequency	Assigned Points	(x3) Wght. Points	Monetary	Assigned Points	(x2) Wght. Points	Total Wght. Points	Cum. Points
A	#1	3 Mths.	20	100	1	4	12	$ 30	3	6	118	118
A	#2	9 Mths.	5	25	1	4	12	$100	10	20	57	175
A	#3	24 Mths.	1	5	1	4	12	$ 50	5	10	27	202
B	#1	12 Mths.	3	15	2	8	24	$500	20	40	79	79
C	#1	3 Mths.	20	100	1	4	12	$100	10	20	132	132
C	#2	6 Mths.	10	50	1	4	12	$ 60	6	12	74	206
C	#3	12 Mths.	3	15	2	8	24	$ 70	7	14	53	259
C	#4	24 Mths.	1	5	1	4	12	$ 20	2	4	21	280

In the example in Figure 3-2 three customers (identified as A, B, and C) have a purchase history calculated over a 24-month period. We assigned numerical points to each transaction, according to the derived R/F/M formula and further weighted these points. The resulting cumulative point calculations, 202 for A, 79 for B, and 280 for C, indicate a potential preference for customer C. C's R/F/M history, and perhaps A's, justifies a greater amount of promotion dollars. Customer B might be an unlikely promotion dollar risk. In order to apply R/F/M assessments, marketers must keep the customer database—especially the transaction data—current by means of continuous database maintenance.

DATABASE MAINTENANCE

As noted in Chapter 2, a list is a perishable commodity that needs constant oversight and maintenance. Direct marketers must establish maintenance schedules and adhere to them rigorously. An initial requirement for proper list maintenance is that the list be compiled and developed in a uniform manner. Only when such uniformity exists within a computerized list is it possible to use match codes with any assurance of control.

Database maintenance activities include identifying and eliminating any duplicate records, identifying consumer names that appear on a number of different direct marketing response lists, and keeping the customer records current. Let's look more closely at each of these activities.

Match Codes and Merge-Purge

A serious and often cumbersome problem in compiling and maintaining lists is the potential for duplicating the same individual or organization, not only within house lists but also within and between response and compiled lists and even between these lists and house lists. If lists are computerized, marketers can extract from a name/address record abbreviated information about this record. This abbreviation is called a **match code** and it is constructed so that each individual record can be matched with each other record. Since such matching requires a tremendous amount of computer memory, the match code is abbreviated to minimize the need for such storage. The match code abbreviation should be designed so that it addresses each area where errors are likely to occur within key parts of a record, such as transposition within a street address number as shown in the two examples below:

Ann Stafford   Ann Stafford
9330 West Arlington Road   3930 West Arlington Road
Alexandria, VA 22301   Alexandria, VA 22301

An example of a simple 18-digit match code derived from the name/address above is shown in Figure 3-3. Quite often, direct marketers will add other data to the match code such as a unique identification number or an expiration date for a magazine subscription. Mailing labels for catalogs or periodicals often demonstrate match codes of this type. An example is the ten-digit customer number used by the Newport News catalog of the Spiegel Group. This unique customer number reveals information about the particular market segment to which each customer belongs, their credit card status, whether or not they are a member of the Newport News Discount Club, and more.

Position	Item	Description
1	State	A unique alpha-numeric code assigned to each state
2-5	ZIP code	Last 4 numbers of 5-digit ZIP code
6-8	Surname	1st, 3rd, and 4th alpha characters of surname or business name
9-12	Address	House or business number
3-15	Address	1st, 3rd, and 4th alpha characters of street name
16	Surname	Alpha-numeric count of characters in surname
17	Given name	Alpha initial of first name
18	Given name	Alpha-numeric count of characters in first name

EXAMPLE ADDRESS

Ann Stafford
9330 West Arlington Rd
Alexandria, VA 22301

DERIVED MATCH CODE

82301SAF9330AEX8A3

FIGURE 3-3   Match Codes

An alternative to match codes is a unique identification number, such as a Social Security number, which identifies only one individual, but the customer or prospect has to provide this number for the marketer to be able to use it.

Using the abbreviated match codes, the computerized **merge-purge process** identifies and deletes duplicate names/addresses *within* house lists. It can also eliminate names on house lists from outside response and/or compiled lists that the marketer is using for new customer solicitation. Thus, the organization's own house list will not be duplicated within that promotion effort to prospects. The merge-purge process can eliminate duplication between these outside response and compiled lists as well.

Merge-purge is a highly sophisticated and complex process, but essentially it generates a match code for each name/address on each list and these match codes, potentially many million of them at a time, are matched, with every other name on the list in sequence. Duplications are identified for special handling (which we will discuss later).

It is doubtful that a "perfect" match code could be developed, one that would compensate for *all* the idiosyncrasies and potential errors inherent in a name/address record. However, the one shown in Figure 3-3 has a pretty good track record. As demonstrated in the direct mail example shown in Figure 3-4, even a 5 percent "hit" rate, eliminating the need to mail 5 percent duplications, can result in substantial savings. This is especially true when several million name/address records are merged and purged. With reference to Figure 3-4, identifying a duplication of 15 percent of the names, when one million names on various lists are merged and purged, would eliminate 150,000 pieces of unnecessary mail. At an assumed cost of $200 per thousand names mailed, this results in a savings of $30,000. Against this savings, of course, would be the cost of the merge-purge itself, possibly as much as $10 per thousand names examined or $10,000 for a one million name/address input.

% DUPLICATION (OR MULTI-BUYERS)	TOTAL NUMBER OF NAMES/ADDRESSES MERGED					
	100,000	500,000	1,000,000	2,500,000	5,000,000	10,000,000
5%	$1,000	$ 5,000	$10,000	$ 25,000	$ 50,000	$100,000
10%	$2,000	$10,000	$20,000	$ 50,000	$100,000	$200,000
15%	$3,000	$15,000	$30,000	$ 75,000	$150,000	$300,000
20%	$4,000	$20,000	$40,000	$100,000	$200,000	$400,000
25%	$5,000	$25,000	$50,000	$125,000	$250,000	$500,000
30%	$6,000	$30,000	$60,000	$150,000	$300,000	$600,000

Assumption: Mailing cost is $200 per thousand names mailed (or not mailed).

FIGURE 3-4   Economic Value of Merge/Purge of Mailing Lists Utilizing Match Codes to Identify Duplication as Well as Multi-buyers

The merge-purge process can also effectively remove names of individuals who have expressed a desire not to receive solicitation as well as those who are poor credit risks or otherwise undesirable customers. Figure 3-5, adapted from an actual merge-purge procedure, displays the manner of showing duplicate names/addresses on two or more lists. Shown are both name and address variations.

Multi-Buyers

Eliminating duplicate names/addresses, saving costs, and minimizing irritation to those receiving duplicate mailings all are obvious advantages of the merge-purge process. But there is another possibly even greater advantage. If the same name/address is found on

FIGURE 3-5   The Various Ways Duplicate Records May Exist in a Database

Name	Address	City	State	Zip
Samantha Fox	12353 N. Oak Drive	Arlington	VA	22301
Samantha Fox	12353 N. Oak Drive	Arlington	VA	22301
Christina Smith	250 Elders Drive	Arlington	VA	22301
C Smith	250 Elders Drive	Arlington	VA	22301
Jerry Matthis	9372 Nasaw St	Arlington	VA	22301
Jerry Matthis	9372 Nasaw St	Arlington	VA	22301
Dale Armstrong	700 Mosac Ln	Arlington	VA	22301
Nancy Armstrong	700 Mosac Ln	Arlington	VA	22301
Steven Samson	3662 S 11th St	Arlington	VA	22301
Steve Samson	3662 S 11th St	Arlington	VA	22301
Regina Jones	251 12th Ave	Arlington	VA	22301
Regina Jones	252 12th Ave	Arlington	VA	22301
Elaine Lowell	261 N Second St	Arlington	VA	22301
Claire Lowell	261 N 2nd St	Arlington	VA	22301
Carson Snyder	690 42nd St	Arlington	VA	22301
Carson Snyder	690 42nd St	Arlington	VA	22301
Catherine Marlin	Apt 963 561 N 5th St	Arlington	VA	22301
Catherine Marlin	561 N 5th St	Arlington	VA	22301
Elizabeth Parks	68 Waverly Lane	Arlington	VA	22301
Elizabeth Parks	68 Waverly Ln	Arlington	VA	22301
Elizabeth Parks	68 Waverly Ln N	Arlington	VA	22301
Elizabeth Parks	68 Waverly Ln N	Arlington	VA	22301

two or more response lists simultaneously, that individual may be a better prospect for a direct marketing offer since he or she is a **multi-buyer**. Experimentation has shown, in fact, those whose names appear on three lists have a higher response rate than those appearing on two lists. Likewise, names appearing on four lists are even more responsive.

In addition to identifying multi-buyers, direct marketers perform database maintenance activities to keep their customer records current and accurate. These activities will be discussed in the next section.

Keeping Records Current

If incorrect addresses or telephone numbers result in misdirected advertising promotions, the cost is twofold: (1) the wasted contact and (2) the sacrifice of potential response. That is what is at stake if the direct marketer does not keep his or her records current. In an effort to keep customer records current and accurate, direct marketers regularly perform change of address investigations, nixie removal, and record status updates. Let's examine each of these activities in greater detail.

Whenever possible, direct marketers request address corrections through the Postal Service. The United States Postal Service assures that mail prepaid with first class postage is automatically returned if undeliverable or else forwarded without charge, if the new address is known. In the latter instance, for a fee, the change of address notification can be sent back to the direct marketer. In the case of advertising mail, the use of the "address correction requested" legend on the mailing envelope guarantees prepayment of any return postage and service fees. There are many variations of this particular list correction service relative to either individual mail or catalog mail, concerning forwarding and/or return postage guarantees.

Additionally, direct marketers encourage the recipient of mail to inform them of any change of address or telephone number. If available, customers are encouraged to reference a unique account code when requesting changes. If the account number is unavailable, customers are asked to provide both the old and new address; the former for entering into the system and removing the old record, and the latter for future addressing.

Using the "address correction requested" service on each and every customer mailing is not necessary; once or twice a year should suffice to clean the database. Using the legend more frequently, because of lags in handling times, could result in duplication of returned mail and unnecessary duplication of costs. The term **nixie** refers to mail that has been returned by the United States Postal Service because it is undeliverable as addressed, often due to a simple error in the street address or the ZIP code. Or the person to whom the piece is addressed is deceased or has moved and left no forwarding address. The marketer will remove such names from the mailing list; unless the list owner can obtain updated information, they cannot be reinstated. Approximately 20 percent of U.S. households change addresses each year. Perhaps this is why e-mail addresses are quickly becoming the preferred address—since they do not necessarily change each time the person moves to a new geographical location. However, some Internet service providers are local and if you move to a new location, you have to change your e-mail address. Also, keep in mind that a lot of consumers switch Internet providers due to personal preferences and many more consumers prefer to change their screen names.

Changes in telephone numbers should be made periodically to house lists that are accessed by telephone. Customers who have changed to unlisted numbers should be contacted by mail or an effort should be made to obtain these numbers.

The U.S. Postal Service, for a nominal handling fee, will provide direct marketers with correct address information, if available. Often, however, mail addressed to a deceased person will go to the surviving spouse. Or, business mail to an individual who has changed positions or even left an organization will go to the replacement in that position. Although the U.S. Postal Service will not send notifications in such instances, some direct marketers correct their lists in other ways. Special notices might periodically be sent with mailings requesting list correction. Additionally, sales representatives can request consumer information changes each time he or she calls on a customer. In some cases the mail recipient sends such notice directly. Other ways in which list owners can update their lists include news items, periodic updates from telephone and other directories, and public records such as birth and death notices and marriage and divorce proceedings.

It is important to perform database maintenance not only from the perspective of nixie and otherwise undeliverable mail, but also to keep the record status of customers up-to-date. List owners should enter new orders from customers into the database promptly as they have major impact on the R/F/M formulation described earlier. Such prompt record keeping also avoids unnecessary mailings, telephone calls, or e-mails to customers who already have what the direct marketer is offering.

DATABASE SECURITY

Customer databases are assets, much the same as buildings, equipment, and inventories. Because their value is intangible, however, databases are not easily insurable (except for replacement or duplication costs) even if we can determine their future value. And, unlike other assets, they're portable, especially when several hundred thousand names can be packed on a single computer disk or CD-ROM.

For these reasons, marketers must take special precautions to prevent theft, loss, or unauthorized use of the database and to guarantee the information privacy rights of all consumers.

Information Privacy
As we will address in greater detail later in Chapter 12, organizations that maintain a customer database also have a responsibility to safeguard the personal information contained in it. Direct marketers must use the information only in a highly ethical manner and honor any consumer requests to have their personal information kept confidential—which means not sharing it with other direct marketers. For example, numerous organizations have been asked to allow the authors of this textbook to reprint their marketing materials. Many have agreed. Some have refused. One organization, the Christian Foundation For Children and Aging (CFCA), was not able to grant our request to reprint a letter written from one of their volunteers to one of the authors, a sponsor of the CFCA. What was their reason? It was due to the fact that the organization wanted to protect the privacy of the volunteer, the sponsored child, and the donor. So, although you won't be viewing the CFCA volunteer letter when you read the non-profit chapter later in this text, you may be able to better appreciate the actions of many organizations to safeguard information privacy. Therefore, regular database maintenance should include activities to protect the information privacy rights of consumers, as well as to ensure that the information in each database record is accurate and kept up to date.

Proper Database Storage

A logical first step in database security is the provision of adequate storage. Usually, such storage protects against natural hazards of fire and water damage, as well as theft or unauthorized use. To discourage theft, marketers should limit and control access to database files at all times. This often involves certain passwords used to protect the database and permit only select individuals access to the information stored in the database. Should records become lost, adequate backup should be available in the form of duplicate records at a remote location.

List Seeding

Direct marketers have developed a variety of marking techniques to ensure that their customer lists are not misappropriated or misused especially when rented to outside parties. One commonly used technique is called salting or seeding a list. **Seeding** (also called **salting**) a list is when the direct marketer places decoys, which are either incorrect spellings or fictitious names that appear nowhere else, on the customer list so as to track and identify any misuse. While a seeded list may reveal such misuse, it may not lead to the guilty person. Marketers should construct identification programs like seeding so that the decoy names will not be removed through match coding. And of course the decoy names should be confidential and access to them limited.

Direct marketers discourage list theft by placing seeds on lists. Direct marketers must communicate their use of list seeds to all parties involved in the list industry. By fully disclosing the actions to protect their lists, direct marketers may discourage list theft.

DATABASE USES AND APPLICATIONS

Once we have captured and stored data, we can convert it into real information to better serve customers and maximize profitability. The uses of a database are virtually endless; we'll discuss seven of them in this chapter. Keep in mind the real beauty of a customer database is that it enables direct marketers to communicate with small market segments or individual customers without other customers knowing. This kind of secrecy enables direct marketers to extend different types of offers to individual customers on the basis of their customer information. For example, Harris Teeter, a local grocery store, sends elaborate gifts on a regular basis to its *very best* customers. These customers also receive a $10 Harris Teeter gift card at Thanksgiving along with a personally signed thank-you letter from the store manager. Gifts of lesser value and thank-you letters not containing the $10 Harris Teeter gift card may be sent to those regular customers who are not as *valuable* to Harris Teeter based on the amount spent at Harris Teeter. Further, Harris Teeter may send other direct-mail letters containing coupons encouraging other customers (those even less valuable) to shop more often at Harris Teeter. This kind of one-on-one communication is made possible by the source data contained in a customer database. This is critical to successful direct marketing since building customer relationships is most effectively carried out on a one-to-one basis. The ability to know their customers and communicate with them individually is the basic premise of a customer database for direct marketers.

Seven Ways a Direct Marketer Can Use a Customer Database

1. **Profile customers.** By developing a geographic, demographic, social, psychological, and behavioral profile of their customers, direct marketers can better understand the various consumer market segments they are serving. For example, Carnival Cruise Lines passenger database of more than 2 million households includes information on prior travel habits.[6] Carnival collects information regarding passenger anniversaries and birthdays, what cruises passengers took, what they paid, their sailing date, how many people traveled in their party, and whether they traveled with children. This information enables the company to better understand the needs of their typical customer.

2. **Retain the best customers.** According to the well-known 80/20 principal, approximately 80 percent of an organization's business is generated by 20 percent of its customers. Thus, it is critical that direct marketers analyze their customer database to determine who their best customers are and to spend more effort (and promotional dollars) in keeping these customers satisfied and coming back for more! Just think of the Harris Teeter example discussed earlier. Harris Teeter can afford to spend more money in terms of promotional dollars to keep those customers who spend more money in groceries satisfied and coming back on a regular basis. Harris Teeter cannot justify sending its occasional shoppers gifts and personally signed thank you notes from the store manager.

3. **Thank customers for their patronage.** All customers deserve to be recognized and thanked for their decision to purchase from a given organization. This is especially true when the direct marketer has a number of competitors from which the customer could have purchased. Customers expect to be satisfied with their purchase decisions; however, follow-up activities can often provide an avenue for future dialogue with each customer to ensure that satisfaction. Thanking customers is also an effective way to both reinforce purchase decisions and promote future purchases. An example is the thank-you letters containing bumper stickers that are mailed to individuals who make donations to the various state and local police associations. Donors take pride in displaying those bumper stickers, which state: "I Am A Proud Supporter of the Virginia State Police."

4. **Capitalize on cross-selling and continuity selling opportunities. Cross-selling** refers to selling your current customers products and services that are related (and even unrelated) to the products/services they currently purchase from your organization. By analyzing the products and services your customers have purchased from your organization, you can identify and capitalize on numerous cross-selling opportunities. **Continuity selling** has also been referred to as "club offers"; here consumers purchase on a regular basis—either, weekly, monthly, quarterly, or annually. *Time* magazine, for example, cross-sells other of its publications—*People, Sports Illustrated, Fortune*—to certain current subscribers.

5. **Develop a customer communication program.** As mentioned earlier, the real beauty and power of a database is that it enables the direct marketer to communicate on a one-to-one basis with each customer. Thus, the marketer can segment the promotional strategies based on the customer group and individual with whom the

direct marketer is communicating. For example, newer customers could receive "welcome to . . . " letters, while established customers might receive "thank you for your loyalty . . . " letters. Of course, each customer does not know what is being communicated to other customers. Unlike general advertising, a database also enables marketing communications to occur between the direct marketer and their customers without the competition knowing. This is another powerful use of the customer database.

In addition, a direct marketer can afford to spend more promotional dollars to communicate with regular customers who generate a substantial amount of business for the organization, spending less on new customers who may or may not purchase from the organization a second time. Therefore, a firm may distribute an annual newsletter to some customers, while communicating on a quarterly or monthly basis with others with whom it has a stronger relationship.

Finally, a customer communication program implies two-way communication. Direct marketers use customer feedback to revise and improve their marketing activities to better serve the customer and maximize profitability. Examples of customer communication programs are numerous. Hotels, airlines, grocery stores, non-profit organizations, magazines, and just about every direct marketer has one. If you purchase a new car, chances are likely that you will receive a variety of follow-up communications from the automobile manufacturer. Say you purchased a Honda Prelude. The first message you receive should be a "thank you" for your purchase of the Prelude. Next might be a mini-survey to assess the quality of your Honda shopping experience. After that, you might receive a number of "updates" about what is new at Honda and regular reminder notices about when you should bring your Prelude back to the Honda dealer for servicing. Of course, at some point in time, Honda will suggest that it is time to trade your Prelude in for a new one!

6. Perform marketing research. The database is a natural arena for direct marketers to conduct marketing research to better understand the current and future needs and wants of their customers. Marketing research gathers, classifies, and analyzes information about customers. This information is normally "problem specific" or "purpose specific." For example, if the direct marketer is thinking of bringing a new product or service to the market, investigating the potential response from current customers is a natural application of marketing research. Marketing research activities can include customer satisfaction surveys, new product research, customer needs assessments, brand preference studies, media preference research, and much more.

An example is Carnival Cruise Lines periodically sending surveys to its past-guest database. The company uses the surveys to update information about passengers' current cruise interests, what they'd like to see in new itineraries and new products, their cruise planning lead times, and general travel and vacationing patterns. The marketing research results are used to update their services and send special offers and targeted mailings to prospective passengers.[7]

Another form of marketing research is to analyze customer information housed within the customer database to draw inferences about each individual customer's needs. This is referred to as **data mining**. Data mining uses statistical and mathematical techniques to extract knowledge from data contained within a database. For example, Teredata, a division of NCR Corporation, analyzed the sales data of a well-known retailer and found some interesting correlations. Based on the analysis, Teredata found a direct relationship between the purchases of beer and diapers in the evening hours.[8] Thus, retailers and merchandisers wanting to predict and model future consumer behavior, use information like the beer and diapers relationship in their attempts to maximize the effectiveness of their marketing efforts.

7. Generate new customers. We've seen that analyzing the customer database enables the direct marketer to develop a profile of average customers and best customers. Armed with this information, direct marketers can seek out new customers who may have needs and wants similar to those of their current customers. This also enables direct marketers to rent response and/or compiled lists of prospects who match the profile of their best customers and target them with promotional offers to attract new customers. This is a much more effective and efficient way to generate new customers than merely blanketing the mass audience with advertisements in hope that someone with a need or want for the product/service will respond.

DATABASE ENHANCEMENT

Database enhancement is adding and overlaying information to customer records to better describe and understand the customer. Direct marketers also call it "appending" the database. It is a means to an end, not an end in and of itself. There are at least three specific reasons to enhance a customer database:

1. To learn more about the customer;
2. To increase the effectiveness of future promotional activities targeted to current customers; and
3. To better prospect for new customers who are similar to current customers.

The kinds of information that enhance a database in this way include geographic, demographic, social, and psychological data. We can obtain the data either *internally* or *externally*.

Internal Data Enhancement

Direct marketers can obtain information *internally* when they conduct marketing research activities with their existing customers. Of course, each customer must be willing to furnish the given data. Examples of information that direct marketers, such as Carnival Cruise Lines, Gateway Computers, or Hallmark Cards, can collect internally from their customers include

- Age
- Gender
- Income
- Marital status
- Family composition
- Street address
- E-mail address
- Length at current residence
- Size of household

- Type of housing
- Telephone number
- Do not mail (preference)
- Lifestyle data

Direct marketers cannot gather all enhancement data internally, therefore they must rely on some external sources as well. For example, when applying for a JC Penney credit card, the company must obtain some historical information about your credit rating prior to approving your application and establishing the limit of your line of credit.

External Data Enhancement

Direct marketers purchase external data from many different sources. They purchase data compiled by companies like Experian, Equifax, and R. L. Polk, and electronically overlay this information to their customer database. It is usually demographic, although some companies compile consumer lifestyle and leisure activity data. Examples of the data that direct marketers such as L. L. Bean or Lands' End may obtain to enhance their customer database externally include

- Geographic address
- Telephone number
- Gender of head of household
- Length of residence
- Number of adults at residence
- Number of children at residence
- Income
- Occupation
- Marital status
- Make of automobiles owned

Companies like Equifax, Experian, and R. L. Polk purchase census data from the government, sometimes for small geographic areas known as census tracts; direct marketers can purchase the data from these intermediary firms for a fee. Census data can help identify

- Specific age segments (i.e., adults ages 18 to 24)
- One-person households
- Households with children
- Households with specified income levels
- Households with homes greater than specified amounts
- Adults with some college
- Adults in college
- Adults with specified occupations

Finally, firms can purchase external data about businesses, rather than final consumers. Companies such as Dun & Bradstreet and Experian collect data on businesses and make it available to direct marketers for a fee. Such data can include

- Company name/address/telephone number
- Industrial classification code
- Number of employees

- Gross sales
- Primary products produced
- Branch locations
- Name/title of key employees

In summary, direct marketers enhance their customer database in an effort to better serve the future needs and wants of their customers. This should result in a stronger relationship with each customer. While each customer is valuable to the direct marketer, all customers are not of equal value. Let's examine how direct marketers determine the value of each customer.

THE LIFETIME VALUE OF A CUSTOMER

The **lifetime value of a customer (LTV)** can be calculated as the discounted stream of net revenues that a customer will generate over the period of its lifetime of patronage with a company.[9] The information for calculating LTV is derived from transactions recorded in an organization's database. The term *LTV* is interchangeably called PAR . . . meaning it is an objective, as in the game of golf.

Whenever we gain or retain a customer as a result of good customer relations, we earn not only the revenue generated in one month or one year but we also earn the *present value* of the *future profits* generated for as long as the customer remains active as a customer.[10] Just think . . . if a business were to be totally consumed in a fire, its tangible assets such a buildings, equipment, and inventory could be rebuilt in time and each of these tangible assets is likely to be covered by insurance. The business would continue. However, if an organization lost its database of customers, an intangible but very valuable asset, the business likely could not continue. Without customers, there is no business! You might argue, well, the business would simply have to go out and get new customers. That may be true, but it would require much greater effort and cost than most companies could sustain.

Direct marketers spend a major portion of their time, effort, and money developing lists of customers and qualified prospects. In fact, many in direct marketing believe that such lists, along with descriptive databases, are, in fact, the key ingredients that differentiate *direct* marketing from general marketing. Therefore, direct marketers especially should view their customers as assets, as investments. They are the lifeblood of a direct marketing organization from which future sales accrue at a cost that is generally significantly lower than that attributed to the first sale.

It follows that, if a marketing expenditure can result in the acquisition of *new* customers who will generate value over future time, then that action is desirable even though the initial cost to obtain those customers might be greater than the short-term return on that investment. Some might call this long-term return on investment, LTV, the cost of goodwill. Savvy direct marketers call it "the value of a customer."

Naturally, when a new customer is acquired, the direct marketer does not know whether that customer will make only a single purchase or become an ongoing customer. The direct marketer cannot determine if that customer will purchase only low-margin products that have limited profitability or purchase without paying attention to price at all. However, direct marketers know that in most cases the cost of acquiring customers will yield a positive return on the investment. Let us look at how we can quantify it.

The Concept of "PAR"

PAR is the continuity value of a customer over future time . . . an amortized return of the investment firms make in acquiring new customers. It can be thought of as an alternative term for customer lifetime value (LTV). Calculation of PAR/LTV typically is associated with the continuity of the initial product sold to a customer. As additional products are cross-sold to this customer, each of these products needs to have its own long-term value calculated. Determining the value of a continuity customer over time can be an extensive, involved, and sometimes complex calculation. In its simplest form, however, the procedure is this

1. Develop a stream of total revenues over a period of future time or, possibly, over the life of a catalog customer, taking into account ordering frequency as well as average order size. Provide, too, for **attrition,** the assumed (historic) drop off in active customers from one time period to the next.

2. From this total revenue stream, deduct for each time period the cost of goods sold and general/administration expenses. The residuals derived from total revenues, in each period, represent a series of contributions available for two purposes: to defray promotion costs associated with acquiring new customers and to produce a profit.

3. Discount this stream of contributions to new customer acquisition cost at some rate appropriate to the risk of investing in new customers. This rate may be determined by the interest rate or the bank rate paid for alternative uses of the money. Therefore, the rate is the relevant interest rate or opportunity costs of money. The sum of these discounted values represents the *present value of a customer,* or PAR, and provides a measure of how much we could or should spend to acquire this customer at the yield rate assumed when discounting.

It's best to calculate PAR by product and, if feasible, even by source of new business for that product if we know that certain fulfillment costs (such as credit loss) will vary by source. In certain cases, an organization might willingly spend more than a customer appears to be worth, or it might spend less as a result of its own marketing effectiveness.

An Example of Continuity Break Even

An example of calculating the lifetime continuity value of a customer (also called PAR) over time is shown in Figure 3-6. This calculation assumes an initial base of 100 new customers amortized over a 5-year period with assumed attrition of 35 percent during the first year; 20 percent of the remainder during the second year; 15 percent of the remainder during the third year; and 10 percent of the remainder during the fourth year. We further expect cost of goods sold plus general/administration expenses to average 65 percent of revenue during the first year, increasing to 75 percent of revenue during the fifth year. We discount the contribution to acquisition by an assumed interest factor of 10 percent to arrive at present value. Assuming a promotion mailing cost of $250/M and an initial fulfillment (order entry and order processing) cost of $5/customer, we calculate, as shown in Figure 3-6, a break-even point of 18.08 sales/M at a separately calculated LTV of $18.83.

So far, we have considered the value of a customer, as an investment, in terms of the initial sale and renewal sales of a single product (such as an insurance policy or a magazine subscription), and beyond that, we have calculated the value of such a continuity

Time Period	Customers Active	% Retention	Total Revenue (@ $25/Customer)	Cost/ Revenue	Total Cost	Contribution To Acquisition	Discounted Contribution
1	100		$2,500	65%	$1,625	$875	$ 795
2	65	(65%)	$1,625	68%	$1,105	$520	$ 430
3	52	(80%)	$1,300	70%	$ 910	$390	$ 293
4	44	(85%)	$1,100	72%	$ 792	$308	$ 210
5	40	(90%)	$1,000	75%	$ 750	$250	$ 155

Total Present Value of 100 Initial Customers $1,883

Total Present Value of One Customer $18.83

Assume:

Mailing Cost: $250/M

Fulfillment Cost: $ 5 per customer

Customer Value: $18.83 (present value @ 10% discount)

B/E Sales/M =   A (to be determined)

Continuity Break-Even Calculation:

(Mailing Cost) + [(Fulfillment Cost) x A] = (Customer Value) x A

$250 + [$5.00 (A)] = $18.83 (A)

or . . . $250 = $18.83 (A) - $5.00 (A) = $13.83 (A)

A = $250/$13.83 = 18.08

thus . . . B/E Sales/M = 18.08/M

FIGURE 3-6   Continuity Value of a Customer Calculated Over Time

sale over time, arriving at a break-even level for the long run. Now let's look at a situation in which the true lifetime value of a customer would be *greater* even than that required to simply break even with an initial product sale followed by continuity renewals of that sale, as we calculated in Figure 3-6. This might occur, as an example, when direct marketers create and cross-sell new products (each with its own PAR value) to a specific segment of an existing customer base. These incremental sales to present customers likely will cost less to produce than their PAR value because, typically, less promotional cost is required to resell to an existing customer than to acquire a new one.

Here's an example: The Stafford Company wishes to acquire 70 new customers. In an effort to do so, the company mails out 3500 direct-mail packages to prospective customers. If the company receives a 2 percent order response rate on that mailing, the company will succeed in gaining 70 new customers. However, *retaining* those 70 customers will not require mailing as many direct-mail packages, perhaps as few as 100 if the direct marketer targets its house list as opposed to prospect lists. The reasoning behind this is simple. Those 100 customers are already familiar with the company and have a relationship with the company; therefore, Stafford is not selling itself, as it was in the initial mailing. In addition, 70 of the 100 customers are also more receptive to other products the company has to offer because of their proven response history and relationship with the company. Previous purchase history, as reflected in a database, is often a precursor of future business; consequently, fewer mailing pieces will be needed to reach a narrower, more targeted segment of customers. When marketing is particularly effective, PAR value of an *additional* product sale might exceed the cost of making *that* sale. Comparing PAR to cost provides us with a useful measure called PAR ratio, which we discuss next. Keep in mind, direct marketers calculate PAR and PAR ratio to establish the cumulative value of each customer in their database, resulting from both continuity and cross-selling . . . and to determine the amount of money that can be spent on acquiring new customers to grow their business.

Calculating PAR Ratio: The Ultimate Value of a Customer

PAR ratio, as derived from customer transaction data recorded in a database, is the relationship of marketing cost to PAR value, thus:

$$\text{PAR ratio} = \frac{\text{cost}}{\text{PAR value}}$$

If the PAR ratio is 1.00, new customers are being acquired at exactly what they are worth over future time, yielding an assumed rate of return on investment, and discounted to a present value. If the PAR ratio is less than 1.00 (0.85, for example), we are acquiring new customers at a cost somewhat less than their ultimate value over time. Discounted to a present value, this yields *more* than the assumed rate of return. If the PAR ratio exceeds 1.00 (1.40, for example), we are paying more for the acquisition of a customer than that customer is seemingly worth unless there is another source of revenue, such as related or increased sales to that customer base.

If the direct marketer is, in fact, to view the cost of acquiring new customers as a value received, to be amortized over time in terms of present and future profits from the initial as well as subsequent and related sales, it behooves him to itemize and display every marketing effort, calculating for each a ratio of total cost to total value. From such an itemization, shown in Figure 3-7, individual marketing efforts can be ranked from best to worst, in ascending PAR ratio order, until one of three criteria stops the ranking

FIGURE 3-7	Using PAR Ratio in Accumulative Selection of Direct Marketing Efforts			
Effort	$ Cost (000)	Par Ratio	Accum. $ Cost (000)	Accum. Par Ratio
A	75	.40	75	.4000
B	125	.71	200	.5500
C	235	.98	435	.7196
D	120	1.00	555	.7658
E	115	1.12	670	.8097
F	145	1.19	815	.8589
G	125	1.20	940	.8928
H	75	1.23	1015	.9112
I	245	1.24	1260	.9611
J	240	1.30	1500	1.0027
K	185	1.40	1685	1.0349
L	145	1.70	1830	1.0681
M	220	2.00	2050	1.1243

Product	Source	Promotion Cost	Inquiry Fulfillment Cost	Product and Fulfillment Cost	Total Cost	Mailing Volume (or Circulation)	Inquiries #	Inquiries Per M	Sales #	Sales Per M	Sales Volume	Value (Par) Per Cust	Total Value	PAR Ratio	Cum. PAR. Ratio
A	1 Customers	$ 17,500		$ 20,000	$ 37,500	100,000			4000	40	$100,000	$12.19	$ 48,750	.77	
	2 Direct Mail	$ 40,000		$ 12,500	$ 52,500	250,000			2500	10	$ 62,500	$12.19	$ 30,475	1.72	
	3 Space	$ 15,000	$ 10,000	$ 10,000	$ 35,000	(500,000)	5000	10	2000	4	$ 50,000	$12.19	$ 24,380	1.44	
	Subtotal	$ 72,500	$ 10,000	$ 42,500	$125,500	—			8500		$212,500	$12.19	$103,605	1.21	1.21
B	1 Customers	$ 17,500		$ 7,200	$ 24,700	100,000			3600	36	$ 54,000	$ 7.55	$ 27,183	.91	
	2 Direct Mail	$ 39,000		$ 12,600	$ 51,600	300,000			6300	21	$ 94,500	$ 7.55	$ 47,565	1.08	
	3 Space	$ 2,700	$ 5,480	$ 8,100	$ 17,280	(270,000)	3240	12	1620	5	$ 24,300	$ 7.55	$ 12,231	1.41	
	Subtotal	$ 59,200	$ 6,480	$ 27,900	$ 93,580	—			11520		$172,800	$ 7.55	$ 86,979	1.03	1.15
C	1 Customers	$ 50,000		$ 8,000	$ 58,000	200,000			2000	10	$120,000	$28.55	$ 56,700	1.02	1.12
D	1 Customers	$ 35,000		$ 8,400	$ 43,400	200,000			4200	21	$147,000	$14.94	$ 62,748	.69	1.03
E	1 Customers	$ 2,000	(Stuffer)	$ 1,200	$ 3,200	200,000			1200	6	$216,000	$11.12	$ 13,344	.24	1.00
	TOTAL	$218,700	$ 18,480	$88,000	$323,180	—			27420		$673,900	$11.79	$323,376		1.00

FIGURE 3-8 Product and Source Mix Forecast, Viewing Customer Acquisition as an Investment

process. First, all available alternatives for promotion have been exhausted, a possible but unlikely occurrence. Second, all available new customer acquisition funds have been committed, certainly possible and also likely at times. Third, all the present alternatives, when relative (cost) weights are given to each PAR ratio, represent a strategy that yields a *cumulative* PAR ratio of 1.00. That is, the ranking process continues, beginning with the best alternative, until the weighted average PAR ratio of all chosen alternatives equals 1.00. In Figure 3-7, that would be at the conclusion of marketing effort "I."

A rank-ordering such as is presented in Figure 3-7, represents the ultimate value of a customer, a procedure by which direct marketers can systematically select the best from among a rank ordering of alternative marketing efforts with some calculable measure of yield resulting from progressive investment in each new customer acquisition opportunity. If budget constraint is a consideration and, for example, there is a desired limited expenditure of $1 million, the direct marketer would conceivably stop after having processed marketing effort "G" according to the costs shown in Figure 3-8.

An Example of the Use of PAR Ratio

Figure 3-8 summarizes what we've accomplished so far. This figure is a product and source mix forecast wherein customer acquisition is viewed as an investment. Product alternatives are designated A, B, C, D, and E. Three sources of business are shown: present customers, prospective customers reached through direct-mail promotion, and prospective customers reached through space advertising promotion. PAR ratio is demonstrated to vary by product as well as by source. The bottom line objective, all product lines and all sources of business combined should not exceed a cumulative PAR ratio of 1.00, when cost exactly equals PAR value.

The direct marketer should always relate results to costs, rewards to risks. Further, she should view customer acquisition as an investment, just as is the acquisition of buildings, equipment, and inventory, and she recaptures this investment over future time through continuity sales as well as corollary sales.

Ultimately, a favorable PAR ratio (less than 1.00) enables her to invest in still more new customers at an accelerating rate. Ultimate profit becomes an objective. Customer orientation remains a cornerstone.

Summary

A customer is the company's most important asset. Customer retention is more beneficial to most companies than is new customer acquisition. A customer database is a tool used to retain customers. It enables a company to establish and strengthen relationships with customers by allowing the company to interact with each customer on a personalized basis. The information captured and stored in a database provides the company with knowledge about the particular needs, wants, and interests of each customer. Armed with this knowledge, marketers are better able to develop products and services that will satisfy each customer's needs and wants. In addition, the information housed in the customer database may assist the marketer in more effectively communicating with each customer. The end result is this—a highly satisfied customer—a loyal customer!

Database marketing employs a number of activities designed to acquire, store, and use customer information. Database marketing activities commonly include customer loyalty programs, such as the many airline, hotel, and grocery programs. In addition, direct marketers regularly assess the value of their customers. This may include applying the recency/frequency/monetary assessment and calculating PAR, the lifetime value of a customer over a period of time. Of course, direct marketers must keep their customer database current and accurate in order for it to be of value. Direct marketers perform common database maintenance activities such as applying match codes and a merge-purge process to identify and delete duplicate customer records, identifying multi-buyers, and performing record status updates to keep each customer record current. Direct marketers also carry out a variety of activities designed to safeguard their database against improper use or theft. Some of these activities include salting or seeding their customer lists, applying access passwords, and ensuring information privacy protection for their customers. Each of these database marketing activities is critical in maintaining strong customer relationships that in turn lead to the retention of customers.

Key Terms

- customer database, 60
- customer loyalty programs, 61
- source data, 63
- "transactional data", 64
- recency/frequency/monetary (R/F/M), 64
- match code, 65
- merge-purge process, 66
- multi-buyer, 68
- nixie, 68
- seeding, 70
- salting, 70
- cross-selling, 71
- continuity selling, 71
- data mining, 72
- database enhancement, 73
- lifetime value of a customer (LTV), 75
- PAR, 76
- attrition, 76
- PAR ratio, 78

Review Questions

1. What is a *customer loyalty program?* Identify three customer loyalty programs with which you are familiar. What are the benefits to each of the organization's sponsoring these loyalty programs?

2. When building a customer database, what must an organization first determine? What must they first identify?

3. What is a *match code?* Explain its importance for database development and maintenance.

4. Describe the activities required to maintain a customer database? How often do you think database maintenance should be performed?

5. What is the purpose of the merge-purge process? How does it work?

6. If incorrect addresses or telephone numbers result in misdirected advertising promotions, what is the cost to the organization? How can this be avoided?

7. Explain the value of applying the recency/ frequency/monetary assessment to an organization's customer database. Is it possible to determine when an organization should place more weight on one of the three variables over the other? If so, explain why. If not, explain why not.

8. Describe the value of each of the seven ways a direct marketer can use a customer database. Provide examples of each use.

9. Explain what is meant by the term *lifetime value of a customer.* How is this calculated?

10. Imagine that you have recently started a new business venture and that you already have a database of 10,000 customers. You are going to a financial institution to obtain a loan to expand your business. The financial officer asks you "What is the biggest asset of your business?" How will you respond? Provide support for your answer using the information presented in this chapter.

Exercise

Select any catalog of your choice. Pretend you are the list manager of the house list for this catalog. Write a description of the catalog's customer list for use in generating list rental income. Identify a minimum of 10 companies that you believe would have an interest in renting your list. Identify five companies that would NOT be permitted to rent your list and explain why.

CASE: SMITHFIELD FOODS, INC.

OVERVIEW

As lifestyles change, so do consumer needs and wants. Marketers must be keenly aware of consumer's changing needs and wants and must constantly strive to produce products and services that meet their desires. All consumers are not alike—which is why database marketing is so effective. Armed with detailed customer information, marketers are able to profile their customer base, segment their customers and provide more customer-specific information, products, services, and promotional appeals. Database marketing is highly effective in generating transactions, building customer relationships, and enhancing customer satisfaction. This case examines the uses of database marketing in building customer relationships, with diverse market segments. It demonstrates how various types of information can be collected to profile customers, select the media, and create more effective promotional offers.

CASE

Smithfield Foods, Inc., headquartered in Smithfield, Virginia, is the largest hog producer and pork processor in the world. This $8 billion plus corporation supplies foodservice customers and retailers, and owns some of the most popular retail and foodservice protein brands in the world. Publicly owned and traded on the New York Stock Exchange under the symbol of SFD, it specializes in the vertical integration, processing, and marketing of pork products. Smithfield Foods, Inc., is known through the activities of its operating subsidiaries.

The company operates through subsidiaries in the United States Poland, France, Canada, and Mexico, which produce value-added fresh pork and processed meats under scores of strong regional brands including Smithfield Lean Generation Pork™, Smithfield Premium, John Morrell, Patrick Cudahy, Schneiders, Krakus, and Ember Farms. Each meat processing company is responsible for aggressively pursuing marketing opportunities for its own products and brands.

Prospective customers of Smithfield Packing (a subsidiary of Smithfield Foods, Inc.) include supermarket food service operators or organizational consumers, grocery stores, and final consumers. The typical final consumer is a woman between 18 and 54, with children and an income level of $50,000 and below. When considering these final consumers Smithfield Packing pays particular attention to lifestyle changes and the effect those changes have on purchasing behavior. Contrary to past purchasing behavior, today's U.S. families are always on the go and their cooking habits reflect that. The typical consumer now spends less than 30 minutes preparing and cooking meals. He or she has less time to shop and cook and families typically have at least two incomes that result in more disposable income to spend on prepared foods. The busy household needs food products that meet consumers' needs. What do these lifestyle changes mean to Smithfield Packing Company? They mean new business opportunities if the company can continue to bring products to market that meet these needs.

In order to take advantage of this new business opportunity, the company must know its customer. Smithfield must be aware of purchasing behavior, such as recency, frequency, and the monetary value of customer purchases. This type of data must be gathered, measured, and stored in a database that is capable of qualifying and quantifying the data into useful information. Smithfield Foods is aware of the significance of an effective database and the powerful results of going one-on-one with the consumer. This type of direct marketing can only be achieved through database management.

As Jim Schloss, Vice President of Marketing for Smithfield Packing Company explains it, "Why do we use database marketing? Because it works." It is that simple—database management is an effective tool in keeping the company focused and directly targeted at the prospective consumer. Database marketing clearly identifies known targeted users and prospective users of Smithfield products. It is a tool that is used in conjunction with the overall marketing mix. Recognizing the significance of database marketing, Smithfield Packing Company incorporated database marketing into their company's marketing mix by obtaining customer purchasing data from various supermarket chains.

Database marketing enables Smithfield, working in cooperation with its retail partners, to gather and organize data based on customer purchases. Prospect information is obtained through grocers' incorporation of customer loyalty card programs. Smithfield currently works with many major grocers such as Kroger, Harris Teeter, Food Lion, Giant Landover, Acme, Pathmark, selected Albertson's divisions, and Safeway. These grocery chains organize their customer data according to customer transactions—the product category and the amount and frequency of purchases. Smithfield evaluates the customer purchase data and searches for buying patterns and behaviors, such as whether or not they ever purchase, how often they purchase, and what other products besides Smithfield products do they purchase. For example, Smithfield Packing closely examines consumer purchases of other competing protein products, such as chicken breasts, as well as related items such as marinades, breads, and salads.

The objectives of the customer loyalty card program include increasing product usage with average-to-frequent Smithfield customers, encouraging repeat purchases by low frequency buyers, and developing users among non-users who buy related items. The 1–800–LINE Loyalty Program supports the card program with data gathering. Customers may call the line and receive information, callbacks, coupons, recipes, and/or special offers, which correspond directly to their needs. This program increases the potential for long-term relationship building, while enabling Smithfield to gather

customer-specific information about that customer's preferences.

When marketing to the final consumer segment, Smithfield uses broadcast television and radio, print (free-standing inserts and run-of-press ads), and sales promotions (sweepstakes, in-store demonstrations, coupons via News America, Catalina Marketing, and ADVO). For example, one supermarket chain segments its customers based on who bought pork valued at more than $7 in the past three months. The trade segment approaches marketing with ad allowances, ad payments, slotting fees for placement, contents— store level display, same store sales contests, and store promotions, grill-outs, and special events. The public relations segment at Smithfield focuses on opinion leaders in food, nutrition, trade publications, newspapers, television, and radio. Unfortunately, this segment offers no instrument for measurement, no means to track.

Smithfield Packing Company's database contains more than 20,000 non-duplicating and growing customer records that are obtained in a variety of ways. The company obtains customer information using several tactics. For example, the company maintains a 1–800–LINE, manned by Telerex on all sale packages. The recent implementation of the Web site has proven highly effective for database improvement purposes. The Web site (www.smithfield.com) is extensively linked to provide an increase in customer benefits and potential to capture customer data. The Web site provides the ability to capture customer data without an intermediary—thus, it is crucial to the continued success of Smithfield. It allows the company to rise above the competition. During the second week of operation, the Web site had over 100 counter hits. Customer service handles 25 to 30 percent of these Internet hits. Figure 3-9 shows Smithfield's Web site.

Smithfield Packing Company has successfully integrated database marketing into the pork and beef products industry and maintaining the database is in essence protecting the company's assets. The company also relies on Telerex for database maintenance.

FIGURE 3-9   Smithfield Packing Company's Web Site (http://www.smithfield.com)

The objectives of the database are to identify prospects, decide which consumer receives which offer, deepen customer loyalty, and reactivate consumer purchases. Smithfield Packing has had and will continue to have tremendous success with their database marketing programs. For example, the company has recently incorporated Spectra demographic profile software. With a ZIP code map of every grocery store within 10 miles that has the ability to categorize pork product usage and types, Smithfield will be able to market more effectively. This new software gives Smithfield a clearer picture of the demographics of a particular store or cluster of stores and the consumers' propensity to buy certain items.

The following response rates are a result of a typical mass-market consumer incentive program: 1 to 2 percent for Sunday consumer coupons and 1.5 percent for Wednesday through Saturday. Compare these figures with the almost 40 percent redemption rate that Smithfield has experienced via database marketing. The figures speak for themselves. In fact, database marketing has worked so well that Smithfield Packing is increasing its marketing focus on database marketing activities. Currently, the company's promotional marketing mix targets include final consumer, trade, public relations, and database categories. In 1998, the company allocated its promotional budgets with 50 percent directed at final consumer promotion, 30 percent trade, 10 percent public relations, and only 5 percent for database marketing. Currently, the company has increased the database marketing allocation to 15 percent with a projected increase to 25 percent in 2005.

Database marketing allows Smithfield access to information about how many offers are being accepted, the value of those offers, and which promotion produced the best value for the investment. No form of marketing is as effective at measuring results as database marketing. ■

Case Discussion Questions

1. Think about the three objectives of Smithfield's customer loyalty card program. What other objectives could they try to achieve with their database marketing program?
2. How does Smithfield currently obtain customer information?
3. Identify some additional mechanisms by which they could gather customer data. How are the promotional budget alloca-

tions of Smithfield changing? Why? If you were the president of Smithfield Packing, how might you allocate your promotional budget?
4. What kinds of data does Smithfield Packing Company normally obtain about its customers? Why does it collect this information? What additional data would be useful for the company to collect about its customers?

Notes

1. Tom Peters, *Thriving on Chaos* (New York: Harper and Row, 1988).
2. Jon Anton and Natalie L. Petouhoff *Customer Relationship Management: The Bottom Line to Optimizing Your ROI* (Upper Saddle River, NJ: Prentice Hall, 2002).
3. Frederick F. Reichheld, *The Loyalty Effect: The Hidden Force Behind Growth, Profits and Lasting Value,* (Cambridge, MA: Harvard Business School Press, 1996).
4. Adapted from "Program Snapshot: Marriott® Marriott Rewards," *Colloquy* 6, no. 3, (1998): 9.
5. Pat Overton, Marketing Director, McDonald Garden Center, 2002.
6. *Colloquy* 5, no. 3 (1996).
7. *Colloquy* 5, no. 3 (1996).
8. "Taking data mining beyond beer and diapers," *iStart: New Zealand's e-Business Portal* <http://www.istart.co.nz/index/HM20/PCO/PV21906/EX224/CS22580> (August, 2002).
9. Martin Baier, Kurtis M. Ruf & Goutam Chakraborty, *Contemporary Database Marketing: Concepts & Applications* (Evanston, IL: Racom Communications, 2002), 151.
10. Adapted from Jon Anton & Natalie L. Petouhoff, *Customer Relationship Management: The Bottom Line to Optimizing Your ROI* (Upper Saddle River, NJ: Prentice Hall, 2002), 138.

CHAPTER

4

PLANNING THE OFFER

I t's August. The summer is winding down. Your school mails you a letter welcoming you back to the new academic year. The letter is encouraging you to stop by campus and purchase your textbooks early to beat the rush. In fact, the letter states if you buy your textbooks before August 15th you will receive a $15 rebate on your purchase providing your bill totals $200 or more. What you have just received is called an *offer* and that is the topic of this chapter. We will define the offer, discuss the elements of an effective offer, the steps in planning the offer, the components of an offer, and how to create, target, and test the offer. In addition, this chapter will examine a variety of different types of offers that have been successfully used by direct marketers through the years. Since creating the offer is both a science and an art, we can learn much from examining offers that have "worked" *as well as* those that have not worked.

WHAT IS THE OFFER?

The **offer** is the proposition to the prospect or customer stating what you will give the customer in return for taking the action your marketing communication asks him to take. In essence, it is the terms under which a direct marketer promotes her product or service. The offer encompasses both the manner of presentation by a direct marketer and the all-important request for a response.

Creating need-satisfying offers is a part of ongoing customer relationship management (CRM) that drives the direct marketing process. Without an attractive offer, consumers would not initially respond to an organization and, thus, the customer relationship would never originate. And without continuous monitoring of customer needs and wants, direct marketers could not create appropriate offers to keep their customers satisfied and encourage them to return and purchase again and again. The offer is the all-important "front-end" activity in the CRM process.

The Offer as a Component of Direct Marketing Strategy

According to Edward Nash, author of *Direct Marketing: Strategy, Planning, Execution,* there are five essential elements of direct marketing strategy: product, offer, medium, distribution method, and creative.[1] The offer must be created with these other five elements in mind. However, Nash claims that the offer is the element most quickly and easily revised for an improved result in the direct marketing effort. Nash claims, "even the slightest change in the price, though buried in body copy or coupon, can have dramatic effects on front-end performance."[2] Just think about all of the products that are priced at odd numbers, such as $19.99 or $199.97. These figures are pennies away from the even dollar amounts, however, consumers often perceive them to be far less. Research has proven that odd prices are very effective in generating consumer response and, therefore, many direct marketers use odd prices in their offers.

Other direct marketers believe in the "40-40-20 rule," which states that the success of any direct marketing effort is 40 percent reliant upon using the right lists, 40 percent reliant upon having an effective offer, and 20 percent reliant upon creating the right creative mix (copywriting, photographs, illustrations, etc.) in your direct marketing effort. However we may try to quantify its importance, the offer is clearly a major contributor to the success or failure of any direct marketing campaign.

Elements of an Effective Offer

In order to create an effective offer, the direct marketer must research and really know the target audience and the customers' likes, dislikes, "hot buttons," and, most of all, needs and wants. Without this information, it is difficult, at best, to create an effective offer. In addition, marketers must research how consumer needs and wants change. Direct marketers must constantly revise their offers, including the creative materials used to convey each offer. This normally requires printing a number of different catalogs or changing a company's Web site throughout the year to provide timely offers that appeal to consumers during a particular season or holiday. Figure 4-1 features a few of

FIGURE 4-1   Examples of Seasonal Offers from Harry and David

the various catalog covers used by the well-known specialty food and gift direct marketer, Harry and David, when marketing to their customers. Note that the creative appeal used and the products offered are appropriate for each season or holiday.

According to Lois Geller, author of *Response: The Complete Guide to Profitable Direct Marketing,* effective offers have three characteristics: believability, involvement, and creativity.[3]

1. *Believability.* Using common sense when creating the offer can go a long way toward making it believable. An offer has to make sense to the consumer. It cannot give so much in the form of gifts or "freebies" that it makes the consumer wonder "what's wrong with the product or service?" For example, a sale offering 80 percent off at the end of a season makes sense to the consumer, since we all know that marketers need to make room for new inventory, but 80 percent off at any other time makes the consumer wonder "what's wrong with this product that it didn't sell?" Therefore, the offer should be believable.

2. *Involvement.* Geller believes that most shoppers suffer from what she calls the "glaze-over effect." She claims that some offers are so common that consumers' eyes simply glaze over when we see one.[4] For example, an offer of 10 percent or 15 percent discount is very common. It usually gets passed over. However, the offer that promises "buy one, get one at half price" is more exciting and appealing and may motivate the consumer to calculate his or her potential savings. The offer must attempt to get the consumer involved.

3. *Creativity.* The most creative offers usually get the highest response. Creativity can set your offer apart from all the other offers bombarding consumers. Geller believes that "exclusive offers" are very appealing and should be featured prominently if the product or service is really exclusive to the market. "Exclusive" means that the product is in limited supply or not available in stores and is special to your company.[5] An example of an exclusive offer is

> The recipe for these peanut butter balls has been in the Stafford family for fifty years. For decades, friends and neighbors have been savoring these tasty sweet treats. Buy one box of these peanut butter balls, and we'll throw in Grandma Stafford's special recipe for oatmeal cookies with a cinnamon swirl. You can't find this recipe in any cookbook or baker's magazine. We keep it so we can give it to our special customers. Enjoy!

PLANNING THE OFFER

The right offer can sell almost anything, but it must be carefully planned. Let's walk through a four-step process to heeding the details that can make or break an offer.

Step 1: Establish Objectives of the Offer

What is the offer designed to do? Get orders? Generate sales leads? Sell subscriptions? Encourage repeat purchases or renewals? Introduce and sell new products? Increase the amount that the customer is presently purchasing? Raise funds? Without clearly established objectives, you won't be able to measure the success or failure of the offer—and remember that measurement is imperative in direct marketing.

The underlying objective of any offer is to maximize profitability for a company or organization. Two of the most common methods of achieving increased profitability include (a) encouraging repeat purchases from existing customers, and (b) encouraging a company's current customers to purchase additional related or unrelated products beyond what they normally buy. The three direct marketing strategies that achieve this profit-maximization objective are continuity-selling, cross-selling, and up-selling. Let's take a look at each of these strategies.

Continuity selling describes offers that are continued on a regular basis, whether weekly, monthly, quarterly, or annual. These offers are also called "club offers" and are a hallmark of direct marketers, who want to acquire customers who will remain active for an extended period of time. In continuity selling, customers buy related products or services as a series of small purchases, rather than all at a single time. Books, magazine subscriptions, insurance policies, and many other products are sold by means of club offers, as are periodic shipments of fruit, cheese, or other food items. An example of continuity selling is provided in Figure 4-2. Harry and David's Fruit-of-the-Month Club ® offers consumers an opportunity to receive select fruit throughout the year. The customer can choose to give or receive or giving as a gift the 3-Box Club, 5-Box Club, 8-Box Club, or the 12-Box Club.

The continuity selling offer includes a **positive option** where the customer must specifically request shipment for each offer in a series, or a **negative option** where the shipment is sent automatically unless the customer specifically requests that it not be. The "negative option" is a controversial marketing technique because some consumers don't realize that they must request the shipments be stopped or else they are responsible for paying for the products delivered. Most consumers normally expect to pay for what they order, but with negative option, they pay unless they request the shipment to be stopped. It is different from the norm. An example of a negative option club offer is a continuity mail-order marketer called "Around-the-World-Shoppers Club." They shipped a variety of unusual gift items monthly to subscribers, each month from a different foreign country. Of course, if the consumer received an undesired shipment, it could be returned at anytime for credit.

Another example of a negative option offer is a "till-forbid." A **till-forbid (TF)** is an offer that prearranges continuing shipments on a specified basis and is renewed automatically until the customer instructs otherwise. Till-forbid offers are commonly used with insurance policies or magazine subscriptions. Other examples include some clubs, such as senior citizen groups or automobile clubs, which may include specific services with an annual membership fee.

Cross-selling offers new products to existing customers. The products may be related or unrelated to those the customers are already buying. For example, a purchaser of books and software might be offered other books and software or possibly an insurance policy, a home power tool, or a vacation package to a tropical resort. The most important element of successful cross-selling is the manner in which the customer views the direct marketer's reputation, reliability, and overall image.

Up-selling is the promotion of more expensive products or services over the product or service originally discussed or purchased. You might think of up-selling as suggestive selling, since the marketer is suggesting the more expensive product or service as opposed to the consumer requesting it.

FIGURE 4-2   Example of Continuity Selling

In summary, continuity selling, cross-selling, and up-selling are important direct marketing strategies used to achieve different objectives when planning the offer. Each strategy has been used by direct marketers and has been met with great success. It is important that the direct marketer decides which strategy he or she will employ when planning an offer.

Step 2: Decide on the Attractiveness of the Offer

Generally, the more attractive you can afford to make the offer, the better the response will be. How do you make an offer attractive? You dress it up with lots of freebies. However, direct marketers must be careful that the cost of the incentives like free gifts does not outweigh the added profit of the additional orders. This step entails close examination of the budget constraints within which the direct marketer must operate. An example of an attractive free gift offer by Busch

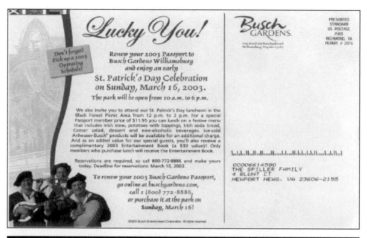

FIGURE 4-3   Example of an Attractive Free Gift Offer

Gardens® appears in Figure 4-3. Note that the complimentary 2003 Entertainment Book is a $30 value.

Step 3: Reduce Risk of the Offer

The direct marketing consumer bears risk, usually greater than in traditional retail buying, whenever he or she purchases a product without the added benefit of actually seeing, touching, feeling, and personally examining the product. Therefore, the goal of the direct marketer is to reduce the perceived risk associated with purchasing the product unseen and unfelt.

Two basic components of the offer are designed to reduce the risk, a *free trial* or *examination period,* and a *money-back guarantee.* We'll talk about these in greater detail later in this chapter. For now, understand that their importance is magnified by their role in reducing the risk associated with any offer.

Step 4: Select a Creative Appeal

The appeal of an offer can be either rational or emotional. The rational appeal targets a consumer's logical buying motives. It presents facts in a logical, rational manner and targets basic needs such as the need for food, shelter, clothing, and safety. An example of a rational appeal is the National Association of Letter Carriers' Food Drive. This organization distributes a direct-mail postcard to residents asking them to help "stamp out hunger" by placing a food donation at their mailbox on a certain day before their letter carrier arrives. The carrier will pick up the food donation and deliver it to a local food bank or pantry. The offer is clear, logical, and doesn't attempt to invoke great emotion on the part of the local resident that is being asked for a food donation.

The emotional appeal focuses on a consumer's desires and feelings. It targets the consumer's wants, such as social status, prestige, power, recognition, and acceptance, as opposed to physical needs. An example of an emotional appeal is the offer extended by Emode, the World's Leading Self-Assessment Company. Their offer is for a free IQ test to see how smart you are. This assessment test can determine how your IQ score affects your ability to compete and provide a comparison to other people. Although the offer may pique the consumer's curiosity and may provide some nice-to-know information, it is appealing to a person's wants. Nobody *needs* to have this information. The type of appeal selected must be appropriate to the media used to distribute the offer. For example, if a direct marketer is making an on-line offer to regular or prospective customers, the offer must be direct and to the point since most people only spend a few seconds on Web sites. In addition, the offer must enable the consumer to respond via a quick click of the mouse or keyboard. The offer must include messages that encourage the consumer to "*click here*" or "*view online now!*" as in the on-line offer shown in Figure 4-4.

FIGURE 4-4   An On-line Offer

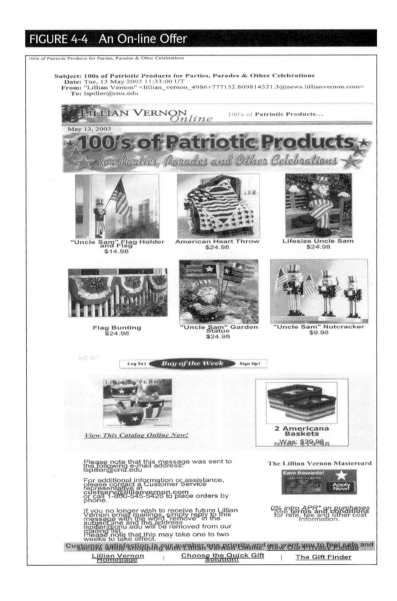

Regardless of the creative appeal used, each offer must have the same basic parts or components. Let's investigate the components that encompass the offer.

COMPONENTS OF THE OFFER

The components of the direct marketing offer fall into two categories: those that are required and must be present in all offers, and those that are optional and may be included depending on strategy and costs.[6] The *required* elements are product, price, payment terms, length of commitment, and risk-reduction mechanisms. The *optional* elements are: incentives, multiple offers, and customer obligations.

Product or Service

The actual tangible product or intangible service is critical to the success of any offer of course. It must satisfy the needs or wants of the target consumer to whom it is being presented. Physical features such as weight, dimensions, color, model, accessories, and any extended properties such as gift-wrapping, alterations, delivery, and service are very important, as is the basic benefit the product will provide. Services have unique properties such as type of service, length of time or duration of the service, location, and frequency or schedule of the service. Appropriate timing of the offer can also affect the consumer's response, particularly if the product or service is seasonal, as we've discussed.

Marketers must understand these product or service features well in order to create an effective offer that garners a response from the target consumer. If the product/service itself does not satisfy the needs or wants of the consumer, then no matter how attractive you make the rest of the offer, it will be to no avail. Simply stated, consumers are not interested in purchasing products and services for which they have no need or want.

Pricing and Payment Terms

Direct marketers must decide whether their price objective is to maximize profit or maximize sales. If the price is meant to generate the largest possible return on investment (ROI), that is, the objective is to maximize profit, then the direct marketer must use a **price skimming** strategy. This strategy establishes the price at the highest possible level in order to "skim-the-cream" off the top of the market and target only a select number of consumers who can *afford* to buy the product/service. Of course, a high price will result in fewer sales transactions, but greater profitability per sale.

A **price penetration** strategy will help the direct marketer maximize sales volume. This strategy sets the price at a very low level so that almost any consumer who wants to buy the product can afford to do so.

The price elasticity of a product is another factor to take into account when establishing the price of the product. **Price elasticity** is the relative change in demand for a product given a change in its price. It measures the consumer's responsiveness or sensitivity to price changes. For example, let's pretend the Gap Inc. decreased the price of its jeans from $35 to $25. Would consumers buy two pairs of jeans instead of one? Let's also pretend Starbucks Coffee increased the price of their coffee by two dollars.

Basic price statement:	"Receive one year subscription for only $10.99"
Basic price statement (expressed as units):	"Only 99 cents per copy"
Price expressed in fractions:	"Only half-price"
Savings dramatized by units:	"Five issues free"
Savings expressed numerically:	"Save $6"
Savings expressed in percentages:	"Save 30 percent"

FIGURE 4-5   Examples of Ways to Express Price in an Offer

Source: Edward L. Nash, *Direct Marketing: Strategy, Planning, Execution*, 2nd ed. (New York: McGraw-Hill, 1986).

Would consumers continue purchasing Starbucks or would they switch to either a different brand of coffee or substitute product, such as hot cocoa or tea, instead of coffee? The direct marketer, in initially estimating the demand for products, first determines whether there is a price the market expects and then develops an estimate of the sales volume he or she expects at different price levels. If the consumer's demand for a product doesn't change substantially regardless of price increases, then the product has an inelastic market demand. If, however, the consumer is very sensitive to price changes and market demand for the product decreases greatly as price increases, then the product has an elastic market demand. A product with an *elastic* market demand should usually be priced lower than an item with an *inelastic* market demand.

It is not just price level that is important. Equally important is the manner in which we state the price. Is it a buy-one-get-one-free offering? Is it a sale? Figure 4-5 shows various ways to present price in an offer.

Finally, payment method is a vital part of the offer. The payment methods direct marketers have offered in the past, cash with the order (CWO) and collect on delivery (COD), lacked convenience and often were a deterrent to ordering. On the other hand, an offer to absorb shipping costs if cash payment is sent with the order can be a distinct incentive.

A bill me later (BML) payment offer that includes credit card options, either the direct marketer's own, a bank card, or a travel and entertainment card, not only provides convenience but also spurs the customer not to procrastinate when placing an order. In certain cases, such as a free trial offer with full return privileges, the BML offer isn't just nice to have, it's a necessity.

Delayed payment is sometimes extended to provide installment terms. This option is usually confined to higher priced products and can be with or without an interest charge. Payment in installments is an attractive incentive to many consumers and such an offer can be a strong one. However, marketers must weigh the advantages of this incentive against the cost of financing the resulting accounts receivable, the potential for bad debts, and the ultimate return on the direct marketer's investment.

Trial or Examination Period

Typically, the buyer does not have the opportunity to see or feel the product before ordering. The free trial or free examination offer helps overcome this distinct disadvantage of ordering by mail or telephone.

The trial offer might be an introductory one requiring payment of a nominal amount, such as 25 cents for the first 30 days of coverage under an insurance policy or $1.97 for the first 3 months of subscription to a magazine. If the buyer's examination reveals that the insurance policy or magazine does not meet expectations, even the small introductory payment might be refunded.

Full return privileges are, of course, a vital part of any offer.

Guarantees

Direct marketers have been using guarantees for many years. In fact, the 1744 catalog of colonial America's first important printer, Benjamin Franklin, guaranteed customer satisfaction with the following statement on its front cover:

> *Those persons who live remote, by sending their orders and money to said B. Franklin, may depend on the same justice as if present.*

A guarantee of "complete satisfaction or your money back" is an inherent necessity of direct marketing. This assurance, and the manner in which it is presented, is a vital part of the offer. L.L. Bean, Inc., offered this "100 percent guarantee" in one of their recent catalogs:

> *Our products are guaranteed to give 100% satisfaction in every way. Return anything purchased from us at any time if it proves otherwise. We will replace it, refund your purchase price or credit your credit card. We do not want you to have anything from L.L. Bean that is not completely satisfactory.*

Certain direct marketers of collectible items even guarantee to buy back some products at a later time and certain direct marketers of insurance guarantee to accept all applicants for some types of policies. Guarantees have been developed for extended time periods. Some even offer "double your money back" if the buyer is less than completely satisfied.

Sweepstakes or Contests

Direct marketers have used many sweepstakes and contests as an ordering stimulus. To avoid being considered a lottery, which requires a purchase as a condition for entry and is illegal in most states, a contest or sweepstakes must guarantee a winner, and making a purchase must not be a requirement though it can be an option for entering. In addition, the law requires that the odds of winning the sweepstakes or contest be published on promotional materials. You should readily see that attractive prize offerings, such as trips to lavish resorts or big-ticket electronic devices such as flat-screen televisions, yield a large response in terms of contest or sweepstakes participation.

Winners selected by random drawing sometimes are made in advance of the mailing, so that the contest will not be construed as a lottery. How can a direct marketer choose a winner before people enter the contest? That may seem odd, however, based on the mailing list that will be used to distribute the contest or sweepstakes offer, the direct marketer can actually select a name or multiple names and then if that person does not enter the contest, they will not be awarded the prize. Remember, lotteries require a prior purchase while contests and sweepstakes only require an entry form to be submitted. A key to the success of sweepstakes and other forms of contests is getting the respondents involved in some way, such as by returning perforated tear-offs, die-cuts, tokens, and stamps, as well as by giving answers to questions, problems, or puzzles. Direct marketers should be creative when designing contest or sweepstakes entry forms.

Gifts and Premiums

An effective device for stimulating response to a direct marketing promotion is the offer of a free gift or premium, either for purchasing or for simply examining or trying the product. Although such incentives increase response, as do sweepstakes and contests, they may also attract less qualified respondents in terms of credit worthiness and/or final product acceptance.

Some gifts are termed "keepers," meaning that the customer can keep the premium whether or not they keep the product. To be most effective, the premium should be related to the product or the specific audience. Sometimes, direct marketers offer customers a choice between multiple gifts. In other situations, direct marketers keep the gift "a mystery" and consumers do not know what particular gift they will receive until it is delivered. It can have tangible and apparent value or the value can be intrinsic, such as a booklet containing advice. Sometimes the free gift offer can be as nominal as information or a price estimate.

Time Limits

A limited time offer typically specifies a deadline, an enrollment period, a charter membership, a limited edition, or a pre-publication offer. An example of a limited time offer can be seen in Figure 4-6. Lillian Vernon Corporation sent this on-line offer to its regular customer base. Note that the offer uses words such as "pre-order now!" and "hurry!" to encourage consumers to act quickly since it is an initial limited shipment of the product. The offer can even quote "while supplies last."

Do all offers possess all the components we've discussed? Probably not. However, these are the essential parts of most basic offers. Now you know the pieces of the puzzle, what do you do with them? You begin creating an offer for your consumers.

CREATING AN OFFER

The offer is not independent of the entire direct marketing strategy. While creating it marketers must keep the other strategic elements of direct marketing in mind, especially the needs and wants of the customer. Let's discuss the five steps direct marketers should follow when creating an offer.

Step 1: Perform Market Research

When direct marketers attempt to predict and determine consumer needs and wants they often rely on certain indicators, such as geographic, demographic, social, psychological and behavioral characteristics of the consumer. (These were overviewed in Chapter 2.) Direct marketers strive to understand consumer needs and wants, not merely predict them. Thus, they often conduct consumer research to determine what *motivates* the consumer to purchase a given product/service. After all, consumer motivations drive the purchase process. **Motivations** are needs that compel a person to take

FIGURE 4-6   A Limited Time On-line Offer

action or behave in a certain way, such as purchase a product/service. Consumers have both internal and external motivations for their behavior. Internal motivators can stem from basic physiological needs, such as hunger or thirst, or other needs, such as the need for acceptance. However, external motivators can take the form of advertisements, free samples, a sales pitch, or even a persuasive offer.

In any event, direct marketers must understand what needs the consumer is attempting to satisfy in order to effectively create offers that will meet these needs and wants. Direct marketers are concerned with creating, caring for, and keeping customers. They want to create a customer . . . not just make a sale! The difference between the two is that a sale means a one-time purchase, whereas, a customer is someone who will come back and make repeat purchases from an organization throughout his/her lifetime. Thus, long-term customer relationship management (CRM) is a constant focus of direct marketers.

Therefore, the underlying theme in creating any offer is the consumer. The development of an offer cannot occur without an understanding of the consumer's needs and wants. Think of it in this way: Creating an offer without careful analysis of consumer needs and wants is like driving off in a car without making sure there is gasoline in the tank! Not a good idea, right? It is only by carefully researching the consumer and the competitive situation, that the direct marketer will have the needed information upon which to create an offer. The market research data collected by the direct marketer will also provide specific details pertaining to the terms of the offer.

Step 2: Determine the Terms of the Offer

Although brand names, packages, and labels along with advertising and other promotional strategies create product and supplier preferences, it is the quality of the product itself that must ultimately lead to repurchases. The quality (and this includes any warranty and service) must be consistent with customer expectations, and it is the terms of the offer that creates those expectations. Therefore, it is critical to meet (and even exceed) what is set forth by the terms of the offer.

Direct marketers must consider five specific product details when determining the terms of the offer. These product details include:

1. *A Choice of Sizes.*   Whether the direct marketer will make the product available in a wide array of sizes, including extra-small, extra-large, and half-sizes are specific details that must be determined. Another term of the offer pertaining to product sizes is whether or not the direct marketer will allow consumers to place a special order for an unusual size if desired. Direct marketers must spell out these specific product terms.

2. *A Choice of Colors.*   Whether the direct marketer will make the product available in a wide variety of popular colors is an important product detail. In addition, can the consumer select certain colors to be mixed and matched with other colors when ordering products with more than one component or piece? For example, when placing an order with Victoria's Secret, can a consumer select a bathing suit top in one color or design and a bathing suit bottom in a different, yet coordinating, color or design? Will the direct marketer allow consumers to place special orders for a unique color if desired? Direct marketers make these and similar determinations when creating the terms of an offer.

3. *Product Specifications.*   Direct marketers must disclose the dimensions of the product including such elements as the weight, height, length, texture, and scent of the product in the offer. Direct marketers often utilize photographs or illustrations to depict the product, however, they must also be careful to spell out the exact specifications in words as well as photographs.

4. *Product Accessories.*   Direct marketers must specifically state what product accessories are available. It is also important to specify which accessories are included with the purchase of the product and which can be purchased separately if so desired. Once again, the more specific the product details are identified in the offer, the smaller the chance of unmet consumer expectations.

5. *Personalization.*   Personalization enhances the sale of a direct-marketed product, and thus should, if possible, be made available to the customer. The cornerstone of some very successful direct marketing companies has been offering personalized products. Lillian Vernon founded a mail-order business by offering a leather bag and belt that could be personalized. See Figure 4-7 for a copy of the ad that

FIGURE 4-7   Example of the Use of Personalization in the Offer

launched Lillian Vernon Corporation, which appeared in the September, 1951, issue of *Seventeen* magazine. The response to that personalized offer was beyond her wildest dreams! She sold $33,000 worth of merchandise.

Step 3: Target the Offer

In creating an offer and developing the copy or jargon that will position the offer, Donna Baier Stein and Floyd Kemske in their book, *Write On Target,* insist that every direct marketer or copywriter must ask themselves four essential questions:[7]

1. What am I selling?
2. Who am I selling to?
3. Why am I selling this now?
4. What do I want my prospect to do?

They believe the key to effective direct marketing is unlocking the selling power that comes from knowing who you are targeting your offer to. Knowing the target consumer requires market research on that target profile of consumers. It is only by knowing and understanding the target consumer that the offer can be "right on target" to generate the maximum response rate. Of course, not all consumers are the same. There are differences (and similarities) between them. That is the basis of market segmentation and is also the starting point of effectively targeting an offer.

The process of targeting the offer is directly related to the important concepts of market segmentation and product positioning we reviewed in Chapter 2. Market segmentation enables a marketer to view consumers as belonging to certain select groups based on shared characteristics and/or needs and wants. Thus, instead of trying to target a product or service to the total market, most marketers will select certain groups of customers called market segments to whom they will target their promotional efforts.

Positioning is a marketing strategy that enables marketers to understand how each consumer perceives a company's product or service. This perception is based in part on the strengths and weaknesses of the product or service compared to other competing products or services. Knowing what that perception is, we can more effectively create an offer and target it toward a particular consumer segment. Of course, offers may or may not generate a positive reaction or consumer response. This is why direct marketers normally test different offers to determine which one is most effective with which particular consumer market segment.

Step 4: Test the Offer

We'll discuss research and testing in greater detail in a later chapter in this textbook, but let's look at it briefly here because it is of such great importance to the success of the offer.

We might consider testing to be the ultimate consumer opinion poll. The research question we are asking each consumer is, of course, "does the offer make you want to buy the product or service?" If the offer is not attempting to sell something, but rather trying to obtain a specific outcome, such as a vote for a politician or attendance at an upcoming meeting, then does it make the target individual want to take the action for which the offer is requesting? The test determines the effectiveness of the offer and provides an answer to the critical question—does the offer *work?*

How do direct marketers conduct the tests? The answer is simple. They first determine what they want to test or investigate. For example, direct marketers may want to determine the free gift or premium they will offer consumers who make a purchase during some specified time period. Let's say a local restaurant wants to distribute direct mail offers to local residents in a particular ZIP code area to encourage consumers to patronize the restaurant. Prior to creating the offer, the restaurant wants to determine if consumers will respond more readily to an offer for a free appetizer or a free dessert. Next, the direct marketer creates two-direct mail cards, one containing the offer for the free appetizer and the other containing the offer for a free dessert, and mails these cards to a sample of consumers in the ZIP code area of interest. When consumers present their direct-mail cards to the restaurant waiter or waitress, the cards are kept. At the end of the time period specified for the test, the direct marketer counts how many responses each free gift offer generated. The offer that generates the largest response wins the test. Direct marketers then use the test results to determine which free gift to include when creating the offer. Of course, direct marketers may perform multiple tests if they want to investigate other terms or components of the offer.

Lois Geller has offered a simple, four-step approach to testing the offer:[8]

1. *Test only one feature at a time.*   When you are testing an offer, be sure to only change one variable at a time. If you change more than one variable, whether it is creative, product or service, or price, you will not know what variable change caused the change in consumer response.
2. *Code your tests so you can measure results.*   Each version of a promotion must have its own specific/individual code so that you will know which offer has generated the best response. For example, if you are testing the same offer in two different magazines, then the only difference between the two offers should be the code printed on the response device so that when consumers respond to the offer, you will know which magazine was responsible for generating that consumer's order.
3. *Keep accurate records.*   Record all coded tests so that you can measure and analyze the test results. Recording test results can be as simple as writing them

in a ledger book, or as sophisticated as computing an ongoing summation in a computerized database.

4. *Analyze test results and take action.*   Whenever a test for an offer is complete, you will want to know which offer polled best, in other words generated the largest consumer response rate, so that you repeat the most effective offer.

Marketers should test their offers on an ongoing basis. In fact, early testing of an offer on a small market segment, rather than waiting until the offer is complete and ready to be rolled out to the entire consumer market, saves time and money. Remember that given time and preparation, *all* components of an offer can be tested— one at a time. Keep in mind, the ultimate goal of testing is to determine what will work the best in generating a response from the consumer.

Step 5: Execute the Offer

Once the direct marketer performs marketing research, decides on the terms of the offer, appropriately targets the offer to the right consumer market segment, and employs tests on various components of the offer, it is then time to execute the offer. The first part of offer implementation is where the direct marketer uses the results of each test to revise the offer and make it more attractive to consumers. Once the direct marketer makes the necessary revisions, he ro she is now prepared to put the offer into action.

What does executing the offer mean? It means that the direct marketer must now be ready to implement the decisions that he or she has made thus far. The direct marketer must be poised and prepared to fulfill the terms of the offer at the time of implementation. This means that if the direct marketer offers a consumer a free gift with a purchase, then the direct marketer must now have an adequate supply of the free gifts to distribute to those consumers making a purchase. If the direct marketer is offering a new innovative color of a given product, then that new color of product is ready to be packaged and shipped as soon as an order is received from a consumer.

In summary, creating the offer is a step-by-step process that culminates when a consumer accepts the offer and carries out the action that the direct marketer has asked him to take. Direct marketers who follow the steps described in this section should find greater success in both the execution of the offer and consumer acceptance of that offer. Creating the offer is a bit of science and art. The science is the logical sequence of steps that direct marketers should follow when creating the offer and the art is the many different kinds of offers that direct marketers can create. Let's take a look at some popular offers that are used in direct marketing.

POPULAR OFFERS

Although some offers may be unique and no offer is "right" for all situations, most are extensions of common offers that have stood the test of time. With that said, the following is an overview of nine popular offers:

1. *Free gift offers.*   Providing a gift for inquiring, trying the product, purchasing the product, or for spending a certain dollar amount can be very effective given the right situation.
2. *Other free offers.*   Offering a free catalog, information booklet, estimate, demonstration, tour, delivery, and more is generally effective.

3. ***Discount offers.*** Everybody loves a bargain! Discounts can come in many different forms: cash discounts, quantity discounts, seasonal discounts, "early-bird" discounts, and trade discounts to name a few. Discounts are most effective when the product or service has a well-established value. However, discounting the price can also generate a negative image. If a watch is priced at $15, consumers may perceive that it is either a bargain, or it is simply "cheap." Therefore, direct marketers must use discount offers in conjunction with the promotional message that the offer is trying to convey.

4. ***Sale offers.*** Sale offers are similar to discount offers; there has to be a reason for the sale such as pre-season sales, post-season sales, and holiday sales. Direct marketers often repeat seasonal sale offers on an annual basis if they are successful. Examples of sale offers include the Mother's Day sale or Presidents' Day sale. There are other reasons why sale offers, such as inventory reduction or clearance sales, provide an explanation for the sale and thus make it more believable to the prospect. Unlike discount offers, sale offers tend to be held at certain times of the year and usually provide explanatory terms for their existence.

5. ***Sample offers.*** Sample offers are designed to get the product into the hands of a prospective buyer. Usually, they are offered in conjunction with continuity selling. An example is a free sample issue of a magazine offered along with a trial year subscription.

6. ***Time-limit offers.*** Time-limit offers work because they *force* the consumer to make a decision by a certain time. It is normally more effective to use an exact date, opposed to a time period (10 days), when implementing a time-limit offer. Examples of time-limit offers include magazine publishers who offer consumers a special price on a subscription if the consumer places their order by a specified date and amusement parks that offer consumers a free gift for purchasing a season pass by a specified date. In addition, book publishers commonly extend pre-publication offers to consumers who place an order for a new book prior to the official publication date of the book. In this case, the publisher uses the pre-publication orders to help in determining the printing quantity.

7. ***Guarantee offers.*** We've seen that guarantees are very common in direct marketing. Direct marketers commonly use money-back or extended guarantees. However, it is important to use common sense when offering time limits with the guarantee. For example, when selling fishing lures, be sure to allow enough time for the consumer to use the lures for a fishing season, prior to returning them if not satisfied.

8. ***Build-up-the-sale offer.*** The objective of a build-up-the-sale offer is to increase the dollar amount of the average order. An example is offering a volume of books for $19.95, and then offering the same volume of books, leather bound, for $24.95.

9. ***Sweepstakes offers.*** Contests or sweepstake offers add the element of excitement to an ordinary direct marketing appeal. There are, however, certain rules that must be followed in executing a sweepstakes offer. In addition, they may not be used in some states due to local restrictions.

These nine sample offers are only a few of the many creative types of offers that direct marketers have effectively used throughout the years. Jim Kobs, a leading authority in direct marketing, developed an extensive listing of tested, successful propositions. See Figure 4-8 for "Kobs' 99 Proven Direct Response Offers."

FIGURE 4-8   Kobs' 99 Proven Direct Response Offers

99 PROVEN DIRECT RESPONSE OFFERS

Basic Offers
1. Right Price
2. Free Trial
3. Money-Back Guarantee
4. Cash with Order
5. Bill Me Later
6. Installment Terms
7. Charge Card Privileges
8. C.O.D.

Free Gift Offers
9. Free Gift for an Inquiry
10. Free Gift for a Trial Order
11. Free Gift for Buying
12. Multiple Free Gifts with a Single Order
13. Your Choice of Free Gifts
14. Free Gifts Based on Size of Order
15. Two-Step Gift Offer
16. Continuing Incentive Gifts
17. Mystery Gift Offer

Other Free Offers
18. Free Information
19. Free Catalog
20. Free Booklet
21. Free Fact Kit
22. Send Me a Salesman
23. Free Demonstration
24. Free "Survey of Your Needs"
25. Free Cost Estimate
26. Free Dinner
27. Free Film Offer
28. Free House Organ Subscription
29. Free Talent Test
30. Gift Shipment Service

Discount Offers
31. Cash Discount
32. Short-Term Introductory Offer
33. Refund Certificate
34. Introductory Order Discount
35. Trade Discount
36. Early Bird Discount
37. Quantity Discount
38. Sliding Scale Discount
39. Selected Discounts

Sale Offers
40. Seasonal Sales
41. Reason-Why Sales
42. Price Increase Notice
43. Auction-By-Mail

Sample Orders
44. Free Sample
45. Nominal Charge Samples
46. Sample Offer with Tentative Commitment
47. Quantity Sample Offer
48. Free Sample Lesson

Time Limit Offers
49. Limited Time Offers
50. Enrollment Periods

51. Pre-Publication Offer
52. Charter Membership (or Subscription) Offer
53. Limited Edition Offer

Guarantee Offers
54. Extended Guarantee
55. Double-Your-Money-Back Guarantee
56. Guaranteed Buy-Back Agreement
57. Guaranteed Acceptance Offer

Build-Up-The-Sale Offers
58. Multi-Product Offers
59. Piggyback Offers
60. The Deluxe Offer
61. Good-Better-Best Offer
62. Add-On Offer
63. Write-Your-Own-Ticket Offer
64. Bounce-Back Offer
65. Increase and Extension Offers

Sweepstakes Offers
66. Drawing Type Sweepstakes
67. Lucky Number Sweepstakes
68. "Everybody Wins" Sweepstakes
69. Involvement Sweepstakes
70. Talent Contests

Club & Continuity Offers
71. Positive Option
72. Negative Option
73. Automatic Shipments
74. Continuity Load-Up Offer
75. Front-End Load-Ups
76. Open-Ended Commitment
77. "No Strings Attached" Commitment
78. Lifetime Membership Fee
79. Annual Membership Fee

Specialized Offers
80. The Philanthropic Privilege
81. Blank Check Offer
82. Executive Preview Charge
83. Yes/No Offers
84. Self-Qualification Offer
85. Exclusive Rights for Your Trading Area
86. The Super Dramatic Offer
87. Trade-In Offer
88. Third party Referral Offer
89. Member-Get-A-Member Offer
90. Name-Getter Offers
91. Purchase-With-Purchase
92. Delayed Billing Offer
93. Reduced Down Payment
94. Stripped-Down Products
95. Secret Bonus Gift
96. Rush Shipping Service
97. The Competitive Offer
98. The Nominal Reimbursement Offer
99. Establish-the-Value Offer

Source: Jim Kobs, Kobs & Brady, Inc., *Profitable Direct Marketing*, NTC Business Books, Lincolnwood, IL 1993.

Summary

In summary, planning the offer is a critical part of the success of any direct marketing campaign. It is reliant upon a solid understanding of consumer needs and wants. All direct marketing offers are response-driven. Direct marketers must plan each offer. This planning includes establishing objectives, deciding on offer attractiveness, reducing offer risk, and selecting a creative appeal. Every offer consists of basic components and decisions that must be made by the direct marketer. These components include the product or service, pricing or payment terms, trial or examination period, guarantees, sweepstakes or contests, gifts or premiums, and time limits. Direct marketers must carefully create the offer in order to ensure success. The step-by-step process to follow when creating the offer involves performing marketing research, determining the terms of the offer, targeting the offer, testing the offer, and, finally, revising and executing the offer. Direct marketers can create many different types of offers. Many direct marketers vary the offer based on the season. Some popular offers include free gift offers, discount offers, sale offers, sample offers, time-limit offers, guarantee offers, build-up-the-sale offers, and sweepstakes offers. These different types of offers have been presented in this chapter. In the next chapter you will learn how the creative strategy is used to position the offer to the target market.

Key Terms

- offer, 87
- continuity selling, 90
- positive option, 90
- negative option, 90
- till-forbid (TF), 90
- cross-selling, 90
- up-selling, 90
- price skimming, 94
- price penetration, 94
- price elasticity, 94
- motivations, 97
- positioning, 100

Review Questions

1. Why is it important for direct marketers to understand consumer motivations when creating an offer? What can drive these motivations?
2. What is an *offer?* What are the elements of an effective offer?
3. What are the main differences between continuity selling, cross-selling, and up-selling?
4. What are the basic components to include in planning an offer?
5. Describe the four-step process to planning an offer. Is the order of this process important? Why or why not?
6. There are several popular offers. Name a few of the popular offers described in this chapter. How can you determine which offer will work best given a specific situation?
7. What are the four questions Donna Baier Stein and Floyd Kemske, in their book *Write on Target*, suggest every direct marketer or copywriter ask? What do they believe to be the key to effective direct marketing?
8. How do market segmentation and positioning strategies play a role in planning an offer?
9. Review Lois Geller's four-step approach to testing the offer. Apply these steps in the creation of a test to determine the best price for a new set of golf clubs.
10. Name the five specific product details direct marketers must consider when planning the offer. Select any direct marketing catalog and determine whether it provides each of these important product details.

Exercise

You are a part of the marketing team of a new brand of cola just introduced to the market. Your job is to plan the offer to promote the new product to the 21 to 35 age group via an on-line and direct-mail campaign. As you already know, you have several variables to consider. To start with, examine the basic components to planning the offer. Next, follow the four steps to planning the offer. Of all the common popular offers presented in the chapter, which type of offer would you choose or what combination would you use? Why do you think they would be effective?

CASE: OLD AMERICAN INSURANCE COMPANY

OVERVIEW

There is nothing new about offers—in fact, direct marketers have been creating and using them for centuries. What you are about to read is a success story from long ago. It is a great example of how a direct marketer can use different offers to target different markets and achieve different objectives. This case focuses on planning and creating effective offers. It demonstrates how a direct marketer can utilize a variety of different offers to achieve numerous marketing objectives. It provides examples of how creatively the offer must be worded in order to maximize the rate of customer response. Finally, it illustrates how planning the offer is critical when attempting to maximize customer value by creating, cultivating, and retaining customers.

CASE

In 1939, when Old American Insurance Company began to offer personal insurance to older Americans who were largely bypassed by traditional insurance agents, "senior citizens" were a widely dispersed minority group and difficult to reach. The best strategy for reaching this market segment seemed to be mail order—then a completely new, untried strategy for selling insurance.

At that time, no one had compiled a list of senior citizens—no one, that is, except the Departments of Motor Vehicles of the various states issuing driver's licenses. These early public records contained a wealth of customer identity factors, including color of eyes and hair, weight, and date of birth. Now, here was more than a "list." Here was a *database*. It was now up to Old American Insurance Company to compile this market segment from driver's licenses records. And it did.

Let's look at how Old American Insurance Company used a series of offers emphasizing continuity selling and cross-selling strategies to pioneer its Building-a-Customer program. Initially, Old American engaged in mail-order direct sales, without involving an agent. Later, it applied its expertise in direct marketing to lead-generation programs for agent sales.

An older-age prospect, identified from a databased mailing list, might first become a policyholder of Old American Insurance Company through purchase of an introductory term of a low-cost Senior Accident Policy, from an initial short-term introductory offer such as this:

> You are invited to spend 25 cents and receive 30 days of coverage under Old American Insurance Company's $25,000 Senior Accident Policy.

(A Short-Term Introductory Offer.)

Upon conversion from the 30 days' introductory term, that is, when the prospect became a buyer or made a subsequent renewal, he or she might receive a thank-you letter like this one, along with another offer—an application form to pass along to another member of the family:

Dear Policyholder:

Thank you for renewing your Senior Accident Policy. Your payment has been received and we have extended your coverage for the full period you requested.

You made the right decision to continue your Senior Accident protection. Now you can face the future more confidently, knowing that in case you have a covered accident, you'll be able to claim important cash benefits right when you need the money most.

Since you're a satisfied policyholder, I'm asking you to share this protection with others. That's why I've enclosed a Senior Accident Policy application for you to give to another member of your family. You'll see it makes the same offer that you took advantage of.

There is also enclosed with this letter a reply card on which can be listed names and addresses of friends and other relatives to whom you would like us to mail information on the insurance policies we offer . . . "

(A Member-Get-A-Member Offer)

The Senior Accident policyholder may also need supplemental life insurance. So, a cross-selling strategy follows, inviting the customer to buy *another product*—Guaranteed Acceptance Life Insurance—with the offer stating

". . . the plain facts about our revolutionary plan of life insurance that guarantees to accept you if you are between the ages of 50 and 80."

To express appreciation and strive for continuity, a month or so in advance of the life insurance policy's renewal date, the company sent each customer a reproduction of a Norman Rockwell illustration suitable for framing. Of course, the objective of this incentive is to boost the response rate to the above offer.

From its increasingly sophisticated database, Old American observed that its customer is approaching the age of eligibility for Medicare and quite likely will need private coverage to *supplement* Medicare benefits in order to reimburse the deductible and co-pay amounts.

So, Old American used another cross-selling strategy and provided the following "bill-me-later" offer:

HOW CAN YOU SAY "NO"
TO OUR INVITATION

TO TAKE A FREE LOOK AT
OUR MEDICARE-PLUS POLICY?

Dear Customer:

You can't possibly say "no"—it would be imprudent to pass up this offer to apply for this Medicare supplemental plan . . . for people 65 and over . . . for a full 30 days.

I believe you can only say "yes" once you see all the benefits this plan provides. And you do not have to send any money to apply.

(Bill-Me-Later Offer)

Still another product cross-selling opportunity was used to present a related product—a Cancer Indemnity Protection Policy. This new product was offered to specific customers about whom Old American has information in its database. That offer used a free gift for inquiring and it read

Here's some of the best news you'll ever hear about coping with cancer!

Get this book free—*CANCER . . . There's Hope*—

just for reviewing our CANCER INDEMNITY PROTECTION POLICY

(Free Gift for Inquiring Offer)

The gift book by H&R Block co-founder, Richard Bloch, tells how Bloch used his positive mental attitude, prayer, and a will to fight, to beat his malignancy, diagnosed as terminal.

Here's a final cross-selling offer that Old American used to create, care for, retain, and cultivate customers, whose lifetime value turned out to be it's the company's greatest asset. Old American wanted its customers to examine and be protected temporarily by a new product: coverage for surgical procedures. It sent each customer another bill-me-later offer with an actual policy labeled

OFFICIAL POLICYHOLDER NOTIFI-
CATION
Valuable Insurance Policy
Enclosed for Old American Policyholder:

(The Customer's Name/Address)

In force, right now
at no cost to you!

(Bill-Me-Later Offer)

The envelope containing this document was stamped "Handle With Care," which applied to both the policy *and* the customer! Through inserts with premium billing as well as direct mail, Old American Insurance Company customers received a variety of offers designed to increase their existing coverage. They were also provided the opportunity to request information about other Old American Insurance Company products. Using the right offer, targeting the right customers and executing effective attention-getting and direct response–driven creative appeals (the 40-40-20 rule)—can spell great success for any direct marketer. Consumer response to the offers described in this case was outstanding. Old American Insurance Company was highly successful in using the variety of offers to increase both the number of new policyholders and renewals. The objective of each offer was met and exceeded, which is the real measure by which direct marketers gauge success. ■

Case Discussion Questions

1. What variety of offers did Old American Insurance Company use in marketing its Building-a-Customer program? What was the objective of each offer?
2. How were the strategies of cross-selling and continuity selling applied by the company?
3. What other offers could the company have utilized in marketing to the senior citizen market segment? Why do you think these offers would have been successful?
4. Provide a specific example from the case of how the direct marketing 40-40-20 rule is being followed by Old American Insurance Company.

Notes

1. Adapted from Edward L. Nash, *Direct Marketing: Strategy, Planning, Execution*, 2nd ed. (New York: McGraw-Hill, 1986).
2. Ibid., p. 19.
3. Adapted from Lois K. Geller, *Response: The Complete Guide to Profitable Direct Marketing* (New York: The Free Press, 1996).
4. Ibid., 26.
5. Ibid., 27.
6. Adapted from Mary Lou Roberts and Paul D. Berger, *Direct Marketing Management*, 2nd ed. (Upper Saddle River, NJ: Prentice Hall, 1999).
7. Adapted from Donna Baier Stein and Floyd Kemske, *Write On Target* (Lincolnwood, IL: NTC Business Books, 1997).
8. Adapted from Lois K. Geller, *Response: The Complete Guide to Profitable Direct Marketing*, (New York: The Free Press, 1996), 41.

5

CREATIVE STRATEGIES IN DIRECT MARKETING

You receive a direct-mail package from a sporting goods company. As you begin to open the package, a tennis racket and ball pop out of the package with the caption "tennis anyone?" That's creativity! In direct marketing terms, creativity encompasses the *content* of the direct-mail package, direct response advertisement, Web site or whatever media format is being used to convey the direct marketing offer. Creative strategies include decisions about the words, terms, symbols, designs, pictures, image, and media format that will be used in direct marketing activities. The old cliché *"it's not creative unless it sells"* implies that the creative strategies must attain the objectives set forth by the direct marketer. These objectives may be to generate a response, transaction, political vote, or charitable donation. Regardless of the objectives, direct marketers make many decisions about the creative strategies. These decisions include brand and image building, copywriting and graphics, and message creation based on media selection. These are the key topics of this chapter.

OFFERS + DATABASES + PROMOTIONS = CUSTOMERS

Promotion's purpose is to disseminate information that brings responses to an offer from a qualified database. Its intention is to sell something. Its objective is the creation and cultivation of customers. It is an adjunct to an offer targeted to a defined database.

Phrases such as these typify compelling promotional copy:

- "An important message for persons over age 65."
- "Are you tired of the back-breaking work caring for your lawn?"
- "At last . . . a simple, effective way to rid your house of bugs."
- "Do you need more room in your house . . . or a new roof?"
- "Here's good news for taxpayers . . . "

The creative process to develop direct response promotion, in any format or in any medium, begins with research and leads to idea generation and finally copywriting. A successful promotion has at its heart a concept and an offer . . . and blends product, price, and place in a way that *provides benefits to a target market,* as illustrated in the a forementioned copy examples.

Customers will respond to offers if they provide benefits that appeal to them. Such benefits can be the physical attributes of a product, translated into terms that meet customer needs. Customers don't buy quarter-inch drill bits; they buy the ability to make quarter-inch holes! They don't buy power steering; they buy ease in parking a car parallel to a curb. Direct marketers therefore use promotion that is benefit oriented. They sell benefits in a manner that matches a customer's motivation.

Promotion consists of advertising, selling, publicity, and sales support. It is a *means* and not an *end* in and of itself, and it is a vital part of the direct marketing process. Many marketers mistakenly view promotion as the *total* direct marketing process, which it is not. As examples, these marketers refer to the creation of "direct mail," the development of "telemarketing programs," the production of "television commercials," or the building of a "Web site." Creating direct marketing promotion actually encompasses all of these activities and more.

It's especially important for us to recognize the distinguishing characteristics of direct marketing—use of databases, measurement and accountability, and benefit orientation—when creating promotions. Promotions must convey benefits relevant to a database of customers and prospects, not to simply arouse interest. They must be geared to draw a measurable response, and the costs of promotion must be related to the expected results. Creating promotions in direct marketing requires the special kind of creativity with which this chapter is concerned. With emphasis on the "message" aspect of promotion, we will look first at copywriting and graphics techniques and strategies. We will then look at creating messages for specific media. The "media" themselves—printed media (direct mail, magazines, newspapers), broadcast media (television, radio), and interactive electronic media (telephone, Internet)—will be dealt with in turn in later chapters as will the adaptation of messages to these.

Direct marketers relate the costs of promotion to the results achieved from it. Managers need to see costs such as advertising and selling as adding value. Organizations work continually to improve efficiency of direct marketing to measure its costs and its results accurately. It has been said that "if it weren't for advertising, you would pay more for most things you buy." The informational value of promotion makes this so through creation of demand resulting from product awareness by customers.

A goal of marketing is to develop a customer orientation. Thus, it seems reasonable to establish the satisfaction of customer wants and needs as an objective. Given that, we can evaluate direct marketing in terms of satisfied customer wants, as customers themselves express those wants or value their fulfillment. At the same time, the direct marketer needs to be aware of whether the provision of such benefits to customers might have detrimental social impact on others. It is the task of promotion in marketing that accomplishes this. Marketing is not, as Theodore Levitt wrote, "the devious art of separating the unwary consumer from his loose change."[1] It is the fulfilling of needs and wants of customers through the promise of benefits.

BRANDS AND IMAGE BUILDING VERSUS RESPONSE AND TRANSACTIONS

Mindful that a major goal of marketing is to convey product benefits to present and potential customers, advertising professionals have vacillated in recent times between ads that create brand awareness, or are image building, and those more directed to immediate sales.

Direct marketers feel that "it's not creative unless it *sells something!*" While this is likely an exaggeration, we need to distinguish between advertising that promotes brand and builds long-term image and advertising that seeks an immediate response and/or transaction. Those creating direct marketing promotions are more attuned to the latter objectives, but that is not to say they are oblivious to the former.

Some direct marketing firms have built strong brands and images to go with them. L.L. Bean, Amazon.com, Nature Conservancy, Dell Computer, Sharper Image, and Victoria's Secret are just a few of the organizations whose roots lie in mail order and whose immediate objective has been to get responses to their catalogs, Web sites, or retail stores. Ford, Firestone, Arm & Hammer, Tide, Crane's Papers, and Perdue's Chickens are well-known brands that have conjured images as a result of promotion activities intended to achieve brand preferences, not necessarily immediate sales.

Although there has been conflict between the two camps—traditional mass-market advertisers and those whose advertising is targeted to immediate response—in reality, this seeming distinction turns out not to be an "either/or" proposition. Both objectives require healthy doses of know-how and experience in order to create productive promotions. Companies now often pursue the two objectives simultaneously.

Recent promotion strategy employed for the Buick automobile provides a notable example of the melding of image-building advertising with that which seeks an immediate response. Buick provides an example of a long-time and highly-trusted "brand" which, historically, built its image through significant expenditures in mass-market print and broadcast media. Such ads conjured up elegant lifestyles and, ultimately, an older market segment. Most recently, Buick's apparent commitment to database-driven direct marketing has accelerated even as the firm has curtailed its mass-market advertising to audiences as heterogeneous as Super Bowl television viewers. At this writing, Buick has introduced the Rendezvous model whose 7-passenger seating configuration and extensive cargo room, combining the features of a van with those of a sports utility vehicle, offers major appeal to young families. This image has been enhanced by golfer Tiger Woods appearing in recent television advertising for Buick. A year-long direct-mail campaign, geared to those expressing initial interest in the model, included constant benefit-oriented sales pitches to the acquired database, along with attention-getting devices, such as three-dimensional puzzles, golf tees, and Nike golf balls, and culminating with the sending of a "pin number." This code, when presented to the local Buick dealer, assured early delivery of the Rendezvous to interested customers who were also advised that the very first car assembled would go to Tiger Woods himself!

Buick's "image" advertising in a variety of media—most of it now benefit oriented as well as response-driven—reinforces its existing customer relationships at the same time as it seeks to acquire new customers. By coupling ongoing brand and image-building advertising with database refinements, market segmentation, and benefit-oriented promotion offers, Buick's ongoing customer relationship management is sure to create responses and new sales even as it keeps the new customers it acquires.

Creating direct marketing promotions such as that for the Buick Rendezvous calls for special talent in both developing messages and determining appropriate media. The objectives of direct response adverting, not unlike those of image-building advertising, are to get attention, arouse interest, create desire, and compel action as it relates *benefits* to customers. Thus, the direct response copywriter must not only possess skill as a wordsmith but he or she must also possess knowledge of buyer behavior and motivations. Such knowledge is essential in developing a direct marketing creative strategy, as the following section demonstrates.

BUYER BEHAVIOR: THE ABILITY TO BUY VERSUS THE PRONENESS TO SPEND

In the perspective of traditional economics, the demand by individual consumers is often viewed as a function of their money income or their accumulated wealth. In the real world, money income is not the *only* determinant of demand and, in fact, it might not even be the major one. In addition to recognizing the real complexity of demand, the direct marketer also needs to study and understand buyer behavior.

What influences motivate buyers to take action? A buyer's ability to buy can be evaluated by well-understood demographic indicators such as income, wealth, age, gender, and marital status. However, buyer behavior is also influenced by environmental factors, psychographic indicators of lifestyle that are not readily identifiable or easily measurable. Marketers want to measure these environmental factors to determine the proneness to spend, the willingness to buy. To do this they utilize such measurements as income in relation to what others are earning in a particular ZIP code area, they study purchase actions of record, as well as the educational level and the social class of the area. These can be important customer qualifications. As social economist Thorstein Veblen observed,[2] so can the "conspicuous consumption," of a neighborhood.

The basic concept of human ecology that behavior is a response to environmental influences tells us that a household with a $20,000 annual income located in a ZIP code area in which the median household income is $30,000 is likely to emulate that median level. The reverse is also true, with a $50,000 household tending to behave like its $30,000 ZIP code area neighbors. It is this tendency that contributes to homogeneity of behavior within such areas, even though there is a variance of characteristics among and between individual households.

Discretionary household purchases under such circumstances are dependent not just on the *ability to buy* but also on the *proneness to spend*. Because this is such a potentially powerful economic force, direct marketers are well advised to understand it as they study the qualifications available within customer databases, the readership of magazines and newspapers, or the characteristics of television viewers and Internet browsers.

It is imperative for direct marketers to understand the economic and social differences among an infinite variety of consumers in the marketplace. They must also be aware of a vast number of factors motivating these individuals. The challenge to those responsible for direct response creative strategies is to "get inside the head" of a buyer and to know both what the benefits to the customer will be and what will motivate the customer to take action to gain them.

COPYWRITING AND GRAPHICS TECHNIQUES FOR CREATING PROMOTIONS

Charles B. Mills, a direct response copywriter at O. M. Scott's Lawn Products, when asked why he was so adept at writing copy for Scott's grass seed, replied: "Because I like to talk about your lawn, not about my seed." Airlines sell a vacation in some exotic place, not the air trip to get there. Designers sell fashion and acceptance more than the practicality of clothing. Insurance companies sell security and peace of mind, not a paper contract. Elmer Wheeler, sales motivator, summed it up, saying, "Sell the sizzle, not the steak." Direct response advertisers rely on copy which emphasizes such benefits in order to motivate responders.

Vic Schwab, a successful advertising copywriter with such ability, described the copywriting art as "learning to think like a horse." As an illustration, he told the story of a farmer who had lost his horse. "How'd you find him so quickly?" asked a neighbor. To which the farmer replied: "Well, I just asked myself, if I were a horse, where would I go? I went there and there he was!" Schwab used this story to drive home his copywriter's maxim that you have to "show people an advantage." This meant, to Schwab, that *you had to know them!*

Today, a database can provide the knowledge that enables the trained copywriter to "think like a horse," to relate the benefits of offers to customers. Direct response copywriting is an art. Those who have the talent and have achieved a track record of success are much in demand. They have the ability to translate product features into advantages, these into benefits and benefits into words, design, and graphics.

Features Versus Advantages Versus Benefits

Offers incorporating customer benefits are structured to incite action and overcome human inertia. An analytical technique for identifying benefits, FAB (features-advantages-benefits), appears in Figure 5-1.

As demonstrated in Figure 5-1, a washing machine might be of compact size, feature high spin speed, provide a variety of wash temperature choices, accommodate a range of colors, and might include a tumble drier. These are *features* of the washing machine included in its manufacture . . . features often promoted in consumer advertising.

Translating Features of a Washing Machine into Advantages and Then into Benefits

Features (what the product has):
- compact size
- high spin speed
- wash temperature choice
- range of colors
- integrated tumble drier

Advantages (what the features do):
- fits into a smaller space
- clothes dry faster
- accommodates a full range of fabrics
- offers choice to consumer
- moves from wash to dry automatically

Benefits (why customers buy):
- space saving
- time saving
- does a good job
- flexibility
- convenience
- economy
- no more hand washing
- choices

How to get from features to benefits:
- . . . imagination
- . . . technology
- . . . product design
- . . . common sense

FIGURE 5-1   How the Copywriter Translates Features into Benefits and Benefits into Advantages

The direct response advertising copywriter seeks to translate these product features into *advantages* and, then, from these into *benefits*. Compact size, for example, provides the advantage of the machine fitting into a smaller space, the benefit being space saving. High spin, as another example, provides the advantage of clothes drying faster and the resulting benefit to the customer of saving time. Figure 5-1 provides the direct response copywriter with a useful procedure for identifying benefits as a necessary prelude to actual copywriting.

The promotion formats of direct response advertising are virtually unlimited. They can be categorized according to the media in which they are used: direct mail, print (magazines, newspapers), broadcast (television, radio), interactive (telephone, Internet, and salespersons) as well as alternative media, such as point-of-purchase displays and billboards. These formats, grouped by media where used, are shown in Figure 5-2.

FIGURE 5-2   Formats of Direct Response Advertising and Selling

DIRECT MAIL	PRINT	BROADCAST	ELECTRONIC	OTHER
Letters	**Newspapers:**	**Television:**	**Telephone:**	**Point-of-Purchase**
Memorandums	*Display Ads*	*Commercials*	*Scripts*	**Billboards**
Cards	*Inserts*	*Spots*	*Data Support*	**Car Cards**
Self-Mailers	*Supplements*	*Demonstration*	*Outbound*	**Signage**
Circulars	*Sections*	*Infomercials*	*Inbound*	**Exhibits**
Folders	*Topic Pages*	*Programming*	*Customers*	**Sampling**
Broadsides	*Spec Interests*	*Home Shopping*	*Prospects*	**Matchbooks**
Brochures				
Booklets	**Magazines:**	**Cable:**	**Internet:**	**Sales Persons:**
Catalogs	*Display Ads*	*Commercials*	*World Wide Web*	*Database*
Publications	*Inserts*	*Spots*	*Linkages*	*Recruiting*
Bulletins	*Supplements*	*Demonstration*	*Home Pages*	*Training*
Price Lists	*Sections*	*Infomercials*	*Info Support*	*Motivating*
Inserts/Reprints	*Covers*	*Programming*	*Database*	
Phono Records	*Topic Pages*	*Home Shopping*		**Retail Locations:**
Invitations	*Special Interests*			*Database*
Survey Research	*Magalogs*	Radio:		*Traffic Builders*
Coupons		*Commercials*		
Tickets		*Spots*		
Calendars		*Programming*		
Novelties		*Narration*		
Envelopes		*News*		
Statement Inserts				
Package Inserts				
Co-ops				
Syndications				

Writing the Copy

Successful copywriting often follows a writing formula to keep copy flowing in a logical sequence. Several of these formulae, which have been used extensively for many years, are presented here.

Bob Stone's Seven-Step Formula

1. Promise a benefit in your headline or first paragraph, your most important benefit.[3]
2. Immediately enlarge on your most important benefit.
3. Tell the reader exactly what he or she is going to get.
4. Back up your statements with proofs and endorsements.
5. Tell the reader what will be lost by not acting.
6. Rephrase your prominent benefits in the closing offer.
7. Incite action now.

A-I-D-A

Of unknown origin, this formula has been used a great deal by direct response copywriters for many years:

1. Attract *A*ttention
2. Arouse *I*nterest
3. Stimulate *D*esire
4. Call for *A*ction

P-P-P-P

Created by Henry Hoke, Sr., and popularized by Edward N. Mayer, Jr., two pioneer direct marketers, is this tried-and-true formula for direct response copywriting:

1. *Picture*—get attention early in copy to create desire.
2. *Promise*—tell what the product or service will do, describe its benefits to the reader.
3. *Prove*—show value, backed up with personal testimonials or endorsements.
4. *Push*—ask for the order.

Star-Chain-Hook

L. E. "Cy" Frailey, who authored many books on letter writing, described "the Star, the Chain, and the Hook" invented by another professional letter writer, Frank Dignan, as follows:[4]

1. Get the reader's favorable attention. Do it with an opening paragraph which is bright and brisk—*the Star*.
2. Follow quickly with a flow of facts, reasons, and benefits, all selected and placed in the best order to transform attention to interest and finally to desire—*the Chain*.
3. Suggest action and make it easy as possible—*the Hook*.

Using Design and Graphics

Hand in hand with copy—the words, the expressions, the ideas, the meanings—go design and graphics—the art, the layout, the symbols, the effects. Here are included the impact of photographs, illustrations, type styles, paper, inks, size, and a variety of other attention-getting devices. Through design and graphics, the designer, like the copywriter, creates mood and feeling while getting and holding attention. In direct marketing the ultimate goal of the designer, like that of the copywriter, is to stimulate action, to generate measurable response. Thus, design (like copy) becomes a means and not an end . . . another element of the total promotion process.

The designer of direct marketing promotion has available a great many graphic techniques for use in a variety of media: direct mail, print, broadcast, and interactive electronic display as well as posters and billboards. These include the following.

Layouts

A **layout** positions copy and illustrations not only to gain attention but also to direct the reader through the message in the sequence intended by the copywriter. Compelling layouts make optimal use of type as well as white space, photographs along with illustrations, and other graphic techniques, including shapes, sizes, folds, die-cuts, and "pop-ups."

Illustrations and Photographs

A compelling illustration can create attention. Photographs of products in use, especially showing people, can dramatize benefits. The designer, using graphic illustrations, can even extend to designed borders, highlighting of copy elements for prominence, tint blocks, and emphasis of elements such as product features and response forms.

Involvement Devices

Many direct response advertising devices spur action by **involvement devices** that engage the reader in some way. These include tokens, stamps, punch-outs, puzzles, premiums, and gadgets that the reader returns to the seller. Links and click buttons are natural involvement devices of Web sites.

Type

Designers utilize typefaces to suggest boldness or dignity, Old English or Asian, antiquity or space age, movement or emphasis, masculinity or femininity. They know that typefaces need to be relevant to the message but they also need to be easily and instantly readable. Sizes of typefaces are a factor to consider as are the thickness and complexity of the type's structure. When the designer utilizes more than one typeface and/or type size, these should blend and the variety should not become complicated. Sometimes, to create emphasis, typefaces can be overprinted on one another and sometimes they are "reversed," that is, white on color. Certain special designs become recognizable logotypes for organizations, such as the typefaces used in advertising for Sears, Swiss Colony, *Time,* and IBM.

Paper

Here the designer is concerned with substance, texture, and finish as well as color, weight, size, and shape of paper. A linen or laid finish can denote elegance. A parchment stock can denote permanence. Paper can have a high-gloss finish for use in a catalog of up-scale merchandise or it can simulate the look of a newspaper to convey timeliness. Paper can convey the impression of the Yellow Pages of a telephone book or the urgency of a telegram. Paper not only helps set the tone of a direct response advertisement but its texture, weight, and size can have substantial impact on cost.

Ink

Like paper, ink can convey impressions through color, gloss, intensity, and placement. Ink selection must consider the paper and the printing process as well as design. Some inks are even available with fragrances, such as the smell of old lavender or of pine trees. Some can be embossed to simulate gold and silver coins. Some can be scraped off to reveal a printed message underneath. Some can be printed on unusual paper stock such as cellophane, waxed paper, or foil.

Color

Much information has been developed about the physical and psychological effects of color since Sir Isaac Newton first associated basic colors with sunlight. We know that light, heat, and color have much in common. The darker the color, the more light and heat are absorbed. Certain colors, notably yellow, can be seen farther than others; black printed on yellow provides maximum readability. Some colors convey associations: purple implies royalty, red is associated with danger, green denotes safety, and blue is a "health" color (i.e., health insurance provided by Blue Cross). Psychologically, the "warm" colors—yellow, orange, red—stimulate and the "cool" colors—blue, green, violet—sedate. Thus, the former might more likely encourage action if used in a direct response advertisement. Colors have different meanings to various cultures, to various ages, in various geographic locations; the direct response advertising designer needs to be aware of these.

CREATING MESSAGES FOR SPECIFIC MEDIA

The copywriting and graphics techniques discussed in the preceding sections apply to all the media used by direct response advertisers: direct mail, print, broadcast, and electronic. This section is concerned with special considerations when creating messages for each of these media. The characteristics of the media themselves will be discussed in subsequent chapters.

Direct Mail

Compared with other media, direct mail provides considerably more space and opportunity to tell a complete story. It can gain attention and develop an orderly and logical flow of information leading to action by the reader. Direct mail, too, has a unique capability to involve the recipient and faces less competition for attention at the time it is received than other advertising media. It is the most scientifically testable of all media because marketers can control experimentation with variables such as format, copy, and graphics.

Direct mail affords the opportunity for positioning products to specific market segments and can, through computer and printing technology, individualize each piece to each recipient. These inherent advantages of direct mail also give it the highest cost per reader, so that marketers must always seek the highest response rate, when compared with other lower-cost media. There are three basic formats of direct mail: the self-mailer, the classic format, and the catalog.

Self-Mailers

A **self-mailer** is any direct-mail piece mailed without an envelope. Self-mailers can range from simple postcards to tubes to a variety of different sizes and shapes of direct mail. Self-mailers can promote a single product/service or many products/services at one time. Mailing pieces promoting a single product or a limited group of related products are often called **solo mailers.**

Classic Format

The **classic format** consists of these components: a mailing envelope, a letter, a circular, and a return device. Some direct marketers will include an extra enclosure or separate slip of paper that highlights a free gift or some other information, which is often printed on a different color and size of paper to make it stand out from the rest of the mailing package. If there is lack of experience about the promotion format to be used, this is usually the starting point. The components of a classic direct-mail format are visualized in Figure 5-3.

Mailing Envelope   The envelope is a vital component to the success of a direct-mail package, for unless the envelope receives attention and is opened, the contents will never be revealed. For this reason, direct response advertisers often use teaser copy on the outside of a mailing envelope in order to lead the recipient inside; to entice but not reveal. Size, shape, paper, and illustration can provide feelings of importance, urgency, prestige, and bargain.

Letter   The principal element of the direct mail package, the **letter,** provides the primary means for communication and personalization. Marketers frequently ask, "How long should a letter be?" The answer is obvious: *As long as it needs to be;* or, as Abraham Lincoln responded when he was asked how long a man's legs should be,

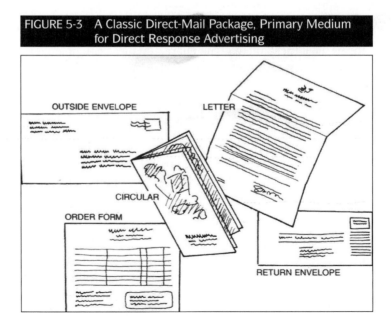

FIGURE 5-3   A Classic Direct-Mail Package, Primary Medium for Direct Response Advertising

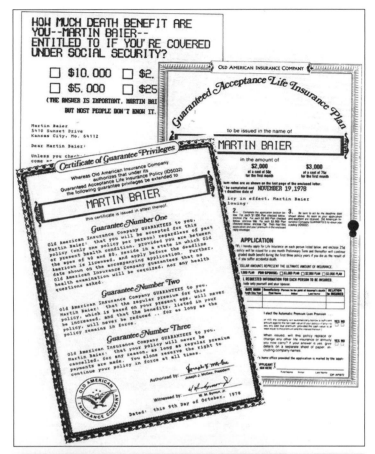

FIGURE 5-4   Direct mail, with computerized databases, can be highly personalized. Laser and ink-jet printing technology makes possible a variety of formats and type styles.

"Long enough to touch the ground." Letters can be narrative and intriguing, such as those setting the scene for books or magazines, or they can be factual and staccato, such as those used for merchandise or insurance.

The P.S. (postscript) at the end of a letter has high visual value. The recipient will frequently read this part of the letter first. For that reason, the copywriter often uses the P.S. to restate the offer, highlight benefits, and direct the reader to another part of the package.

Databases allow for personalization of letters. An example is shown in Figure 5-4.

Circular   The **circular** (often called a folder or brochure) is an optional piece that augments the letter (if needed) to provide product specifications, to cover technical points such as pricing, to provide scene-setting narrative and photographs, and to dramatize and illustrate, while incorporating benefits to the reader. A circular is

FIGURE 5-5   A direct-mail circular created for the Nature Book Club by Donna Baier Stein, visualizing good use of layout, headline, and subheads. Body copy encourages action.

sometimes a physical part of the letter itself, pages two and three of a four-page letter/brochure format, for example. It can be as simple as a single sheet printed on one side only or as complicated as multi-folded brochures, giant broadsides, or multipage booklets.

Headlines and illustrations are vital parts of circulars, along with adequate subheads and body copy to provide full description and to entice action. An example of a circular with many of these elements is shown in Figure 5-5.

Response Device   Once the mailing envelope, letter, and circular have performed their particular functions, the **response device** provides the means for action. This device can be as simple as a postage-paid return card with a mere "check off" of instructions, or it can be an order form providing for remittance or credit instructions along with specific product selections, or it can be as complex as an application for insurance, a credit card, or an investment. In any event, it should be a selling piece. It

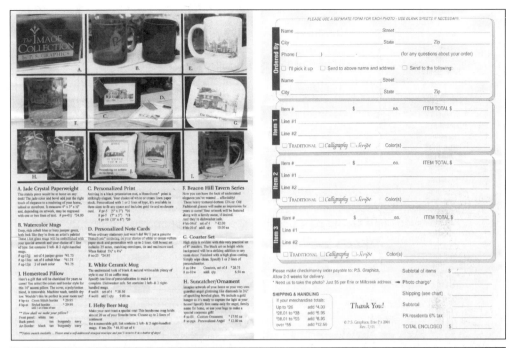

FIGURE 5-6   Example of an Order Form as a Response Device

should have a name to identify it, it should be well designed, and it should contain compelling and clear-cut copy. It should be easy to complete. Figure 5-6 shows an order form used by PS Graphics when marketing Homefronts® personalized stationery. The order form is the response device for the company. Note the adequate amount of space and special instructions to guide the consumer in completing the order form.

The real challenge to the direct response advertiser in developing response devices is to provide, in a condensed format, all the necessary elements of the response/transaction while, at the same time, keeping the form logical, orderly, and simple. Involvement devices should be constructed to lure the reader into action. A signature is often required, such as with a charged merchandise order, an insurance application, a credit authorization, or an investment instruction.

Reply Envelope   Unless a card is used as a response device, a separate reply envelope is usually provided as an incentive and as a convenience and to assure privacy, especially if remittance is requested. Often, depending on the mathematics of the offer and whether or not curiosity seekers are to be discouraged, reply postage is prepaid. Sometimes wallet-flap envelopes incorporate an order form on the seal flap. Specialty envelopes provide an order blank combined with a reply envelope. Examples of such order forms can be found bound, as a convenience, into many mail-order catalogs. Like other elements of the classic direct-mail package, the reply envelope should be designed to encourage action.

Catalogs

Certainly one of the most challenging and popular formats for direct marketers is the catalog. A **catalog** is a multipage format or booklet that displays photographs and/or descriptive details of products/services along with prices and order details. A catalog can have just a few pages or hundreds of pages. Direct marketers may produce their catalogs in-house or by contract with an outside agency or organization. Catalog shopping offers almost every product imaginable, from art supplies to gourmet food and drink, children's clothing, games, toys, home furnishings, perfumes, gear for camping and sporting, automotive supplies, gardening tools, jewelry, and books. You can also find the latest, greatest fashions.

Copy, Design, and Graphics

A notable attribute of catalog copy is succinctness, brevity, and conciseness . . . few words and to the point. Catalog copy goes hand in hand with design, illustration, and graphics. Pictures show it, words describe it. Descriptive words often found in catalog copy include these: *quality, you, genuine, fine, full, comfortable, heavy, natural,* and *best.* Like all direct marketing promotional copy, the words are arranged to spell out benefits. The words *inform* at the same time they *sell.*

Layout, including space allocation, is important. Like the store retailer who allocates shelf space and position according to the potential profitability of products displayed, a catalog retailer allocates space and position in print. Successful catalogers allocate space, including preferred positioning, such as covers, according to a product's potential profitability.

The copywriter must anticipate objections and overcome them in advance, at the same time holding the number of words used to a minimum. The catalog copy must be concise, yet it must be complete and clear.

Print Advertising (Magazines and Newspapers)

A key consideration for direct marketers, in the development of direct response advertisements for use in print media, magazines, and newspapers, is space limitation, when compared to direct mail. And, since print advertisements must compete with other advertisements as well as the editorial content of the print media, the headline is the most important element. Like catalog copy, the headlines of print ads must gain attention quickly and the body copy must tell the story completely, yet concisely. Copy must be benefit oriented and the graphic design should lead the reader through the advertisement's elements in intended sequence. Illustrations augment copy.

Elements of Print Ads

The direct response advertisement selling the product from the Halls Collection shown in Figure 5-7 demonstrates many of the necessary elements. The headline shown consists of an overline over the main headline, a main headline, and a main subhead. The body copy, if it is lengthy, can include additional subheads, such as in Figure 5-7, which describes the product and the crystal from which it is fashioned. Sometimes testimonials or endorsements can lend credence to product claims or report satisfied users. Direct response advertisements often incorporate photographs to convey visually what the words describe. The advertisement presents price and terms along with a gift incentive for ordering. The response coupon provides for ease of ordering and the toll-free

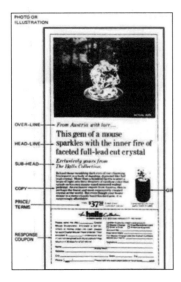

FIGURE 5-7 Direct Response Print Advertisement Selling Product

800 number makes buying even more convenient. Additional graphic design may include copy in a box to call attention of segments to whom the ad is aimed or a contents box (to feature product claims).

Headlines Possibly the most important element of a direct response print advertisement is the headline, and possibly the most famous direct response headline of all times is this one created long ago by John Caples for the U.S. School of Music:

> They Laughed When I Sat Down
> at the Piano . . .
> but When I Started to Play!

Many years after the first appearance of this headline, the following appeared in a business magazine advertisement sponsored by a regional telephone company:

> They Laughed When I Sat Down
> at the Telephone . . .
> but When I Started to Dial!

More recently, this headline appeared in a trade publication advertisement for a high-tech manufacturer, in fact, one that won an advertising industry award for its creator:

> They Laughed When You Sat Down at the Computer . . .
> but Then You Started to Type!

Productive headline ideas are often repeated, as the previous examples above demonstrate. Here are some other effective headlines:

> How to Subscribe to *The Wall Street Journal.* (*The Wall Street Journal*)
> Suddenly I Lost My Memory! (Career Institute)

The Lazy Man's Way to Riches. (Joe Karbo)
Instant Heat Wherever You Want It. (Better Ideas)
How to Save Your Life. (Henniker)
Now . . . $25,000 Term Life Insurance for Only $1.00 a Month. (Allstate Insurance)
What Everyone Ought to Know . . . About This Stock and Bond Business. (Merrill Lynch)

Attention-getting words often found in headlines include:

How	You	Save
New	Free	At Last
Why	Today	Limited Offer

Body Copy   Direct response copy starts with benefits and ends with a request for action. Typical sentences are short and active, including phrases such as these:

Today more than ever . . .	Authorities have proved . . .
Fortunately for you . . .	Try it for 10 days . . .
There's a new way . . .	Judge for yourself . . .

Response Devices   When all is said and done, the time comes to "ask for the order." A good way to determine whether the advertisement can be categorized as "direct response" is to see whether it *asks for action* and how effectively it does so. Remember that a key characteristic of direct marketing is that it is measurable and accountable. Marketers measure transactions, that is orders, inquiries, contributions, or votes. A direct response can be mailing of a coupon or order form, telephoning of an inquiry or an order, browsing and responding to a Web site, a visit to the seller's location, or a request for the seller to come to the buyer's location. Many otherwise good advertisements with effective headlines and compelling body copy fall down when they do not specifically ask the reader to order the product, fill out the coupon, click on the shopping cart, or call 800.

If the designer includes a coupon in the direct response print advertisement, he or she must be careful to provide enough room for the requested fill-in and select paper to take handwriting with ink. This may sound overly basic, but a good designer will, as a test, fill out the coupon to see whether it is adequate.

The terms of the offer, including price, need to be clearly stated. The response mechanism must provide a sense of *action now*. Although layout is not always easy to control, it is desirable to have right-hand coupons on advertisements that run on right-hand pages of print media (especially magazines) and vice versa for left-hand pages. The reason is obvious: It's easier to clip such a coupon if it adjoins an outside edge of the page.

Inserts   A popular form of print advertisement in a magazine or newspaper is an **insert.** Printing technology has made possible a great many variations for such inserts, including folding, gumming, consecutive numbering, die-cutting, and personalization on a printing press. The insert might be a multipage piece or it can be a simple reply card bound next to a full-page advertisement and serving as the response device.

Newspaper inserts abound and appear in a variety of formats, especially on Sundays and midweek, on Wednesdays and Thursdays, which are typically "grocery shopping days" for many newspaper advertisers. Coupons are a major response format used in such inserts. Direct response advertisers using newspaper inserts include insurance companies, land developers, record clubs, trade schools, retail stores, book clubs, magazine publishers, and film processors. A key advantage of newspaper inserts is controlled timing. In many markets, demographic selection often by ZIP code definition makes possible pinpointing messages to market segments.

Copy and format are important considerations for inserts, whether in newspapers or magazines. Single-page or multipage formats are available along with special features, such as perforated coupons and gummed reply envelopes, incorporated right into the format. Inserts offer a chance for unbounded creativity for the writer and designer of direct response print.

Broadcast Advertising (Television and Radio)

Television's limitations for direct response are its high cost and, with the exceptions of programmed infomercials and continuous home shopping, short duration of an individual commercial in which to present a message. The advent of cable and emerging interactive features make possible specifically directed messages and even market segmentation, thus increasing the effectiveness (results vs. costs) of the medium.

Radio has practical limitations, too. Most radio messages reach listeners while they are driving an automobile or otherwise occupied, when telephones or pencil and paper are out of reach. Further, radio does not provide the opportunity to visualize; thus, it is most effective with known products or those which do not require visualization.

Creating Television Commercials

Television is especially suited to visualization of action as well as demonstration. Products appropriate for direct response include these, which often are bought on impulse: recordings, housewares, specialty items such as jewelry, and a variety of services.

A major limitation in creating direct response television commercials is *time*. Commercial time is usually available in multiples of 10, 20, 30, 60, 90, and up to a usual maximum of 120 seconds. A maximum air time of two minutes allows for approximately 200 spoken words. Since audio and visual can be used simultaneously in television, the old adage that "one picture is worth a thousand words" applies *if* the product is one that can be demonstrated, such as the "handy, dandy, utterly amazing kitchen slicer-dicer."

Marketers generally feel they need 20 seconds for attention getting, up to 75 seconds for demonstration, and the remaining 25 seconds of a typical 120-second spot announcement for action such as providing a mailing, Web site address, or telephone number. Because 120 seconds on prime-time television is usually too expensive for the direct response advertiser, most of these commercials appear during low-cost fringe time (early morning, late night, and weekend hours). Often, too, markets can be segmented through specific programs, such as movies or wrestling, usually aired at such other-than-prime times.

Many direct marketers have experienced profitable response rates using infomercials, program-style narrated commercials which may run as long as 30 minutes in other-than-prime time, usually on special-interest cable channels. Featured are products, such as exercisers or nutrition supplements, which can benefit from extensive demonstration and enjoy audience involvement.

Concept   The logical starting point in creating direct response television commercials is determining just what the advertising is about and what it is to do . . . its concept. It might be used as support, to call attention to a newspaper insert or a forthcoming direct-mail package. Or, to get leads for sales follow-up. Or, to generate orders or create store traffic. Unlike the case for direct mail or print media, there is no written record of the product's features and benefits for the audience to refer to at a later time. The television viewer can't be expected to remember too much, so logic and clarity are important.

Storyboards   The visual portion of a television commercial is shown through a series of illustrations called **storyboards,** which demonstrate the continuity, the graphics and photographs, and the video action.

Script   Although a script for a television commercial containing no more than 200 words cannot verbally "explain" as thoroughly as a direct-mail package or print advertisement, the combination of words with pictures and graphics, audio with video, can exert considerable impact. That is why one of the most effective uses of direct response television is to support other direct response advertising media through copy such as "Watch your mailbox for . . . " or "Watch for this offer in next Sunday's *Chicago Tribune*." A visualization of the insert to which attention is being drawn often accompanies this copy. An effective television script needs to be tightly woven and fully coordinated with the visual and graphic elements involved. Like good letter copy or well-written print ads, the television script needs to first get attention, through audio coupled with video and graphics, and then do its job in presenting product features and benefits as it gets the viewer involved and geared to action.

Graphics   Direct response television graphics begin with the words or script coordinated with the other elements that bring the message to life in both audio and video: images, actions, effects, and direction. Actors who deliver the words must be credible, professional, and appropriate to the product. Filming and editing are important so that words are synchronized with pictures. Written words are often superimposed on video to present localized response addresses or telephone numbers. Television graphics are concerned with the interaction of audio and video so that the ultimate effect of the message on the viewer will be maximized.

Production   The production team for a direct response television commercial consists of a variety of highly specialized technicians, coordinated by a producer. Typical concerns at this juncture are whether to use motion-picture film or videotape and live actors, animation, or still illustrations. Directors, actors, and graphic designers become involved as do camera people and film editors. Decisions as to which to employ must relate costs to response.

Creating Radio Commercials

The process of developing radio commercials is less complex than for television. Radio offers the additional advantage of flexibility in that live commercials, often read by a station announcer or known local personality, can be scheduled quickly. If need be, these can be revised right up to air time. Radio commercials are far less expensive than television, too, in air time costs as well as production costs. Through use of particular radio station formats—"easy listening," "rock and roll," or "news/talk" programs—the direct response advertiser can develop a substantial degree of market segmentation. Positioning adjacent to particular programs, such as early-morning farm programs or a popular disc jockey, can further segment markets. Positioning during morning and evening drive times, when office or factory workers are driving to and from their jobs, is another means of market segmentation.

Like other media, radio advertising must first get attention. Sometimes a radio personality reading a script, even in an ad-lib manner, can attract attention. If the product being sold involves music, a few bars can make an effective headline for a radio commercial. Or, a few headline words such as those on page 111.

The close and request for action are of special concern in using radio for direct response. Many times, radio listeners are performing another activity simultaneously, such as driving an automobile, reading a book, taking a shower, or doing household chores. Pencil and paper for writing down addresses and telephone numbers are not readily available nor is it feasible for a listener to stop everything and get them. As a result, the most effective response instruction is one that is easy to remember such as use of a telephone number that spells out a word: "Dial 'Dickens' for your tickets to see *A Christmas Carol*." Or, the use of a post office box with a significant number can be more easily recalled ("Write P.O. Box 1776, Philadelphia, Pennsylvania, to subscribe to *Colonial America*."). Repeating the address or number helps, too.

Telephone Promotion

The telephone, as an alternative to the mail, has become important for *response* in direct marketing, either for ordering or for inquiring . . . often as a result of advertising in another medium. Other interactive electronic communication, the Internet via personal computer and emerging interactive television, perform the same function. In addition, however, the telephone is extensively used by direct marketers as a promotional medium: outbound as well as inbound. Here, the promotion is actually presented via telephone by a sales representative, a fundraiser, or a politician. The intricacies of telephone and Internet marketing will be dealt with in later chapters. Our consideration at this point is concerned with creative strategies applicable to these.

Outbound Calls (WATS)

Outbound telephone calls, often employing Wide Area Telephone Service (WATS) for economical long-distance calling, are used by direct marketers for a variety of purposes.

Well-prepared scripts and well-structured offers can cause telephone promotion to prospective customers to be highly effective, but the medium is usually most efficient if calls are directed to currently active customers or else to prospects that have been pre-qualified in some way. The reason for this is that the cost of an individual telephone call can be as much as four times the cost of an individual direct-mail letter, so it must be four times as productive to be comparable cost-wise.

Pre-qualified outbound calls might include these: inquiry response, upgrade of a new order, new product offering to an existing customer, reactivation of a dormant account, or generation of responses/transactions from a carefully selected list. "Cold calls," when there is no existing relationship with the direct marketer, must be carefully structured in content since, by its very nature, a telephone call often interrupts some other activity of the person being called. Such interruption, in itself, can make the called person angry.

Scripts   Development of scripts for outbound telephone calls offer the dual challenge of maximizing the words to gain a favorable response and, at the same time, minimizing the length and the cost of a call. In some cases a live operator might introduce a call and request permission to play a taped message, often from a celebrity or a personality. At the end of the taped message, the live operator comes back on for close and action.

Automated telephone calls, utilizing automatic dialing together with taped messages and recorded responses, generally have not been effective and they have been met with considerable criticism. Properly used, however, outbound telephone promotion can be well received if the offer is about a specific product, an event, a sale, a theatrical performance, or an election.

Internet Promotion

In developing Web sites on the World Wide Web and creating Internet promotions, the direct marketer must recognize, first of all, a key distinction of this medium. Direct mail and telephones are proactive in that, after a customer or prospect is identified via a database, these media allow the market to send *messages* directly. Print and broadcast media also take the initiative in delivering themselves to readers/viewers/listeners and then providing content or programming attracting them.

In the absence of such motivation, therefore, the first step in creating Internet promotions must be the dissemination of incentives for the prospect to come to the World Wide Web entrepreneur in the first place. This is in contrast to the entrepreneur targeting the prospect, as is the case with direct mail or the telephone, as well as print and broadcast media. This is now typically being done through print, broadcast, and Internet search engines, all of which can let a prospect know the location of the Web direct marketer, as well as benefits to accrue from "browsing."

Having gotten this far, it remains for the copywriter and the graphic designer to structure a Web site, starting with its home page, so that the browser is motivated to becoming a customer. At this stage, everything we've said about creating promotions for all media—direct mail, electronic, print, and broadcast—apply as well to this burgeoning medium. Especially important, however, is the *sequencing* of each visit with "clicks and links." *Information,* as needed, becomes a literal goldmine. And, the logic and convenience of ordering via the World Wide Web is readily apparent. Of course, once a relationship has been established with a customer, then the Internet becomes a way of doing business.

Summary

Offers + Databases + Promotion = Customers. It is the purpose of promotion to provide information which will motivate the recipient to respond to an offer . . . buy, inquire, contribute, vote. It is important to remember that promotion in this context is a *means* and not an *end* in and of itself. The idea of advertising's traditional role to build image and brand recognition is not in conflict with the use of advertising to get immediate response and transactions. Direct response advertisers must distinguish the customer's ability to buy (as measured by income or wealth) from proneness to spend, the willingness to buy (often attributed to lifestyles and preferences).

Direct response copywriting is both art and science, and those who have mastered it are very much in demand. FAB (features-advantages-benefits) analysis is often used by direct response copywriters to position products so that these provide benefits to users. There is a variety of copywriting formulae available to guide creative development and many of these are set forth in the text of this chapter. Design and graphics are important adjuncts to copywriting, used in order to create attention and guide the reader through copy. These include the art, layout, symbols, and effects. Consideration should be given also to such factors as photographs, illustrations, type styles, paper, inks, size, and a variety of attention-getting techniques.

Development of direct response advertising must be concerned with the special characteristics of the medium to be used: direct mail, catalogs, print (magazines and newspapers), broadcast (television and radio), telephone, and the Internet.

Key Terms

- promotion, 111
- layout, 118
- involvement devices, 118
- self-mailer, 120
- solo mailers, 120
- classic format, 120
- letter, 120
- circular, 121
- responsive device, 122
- catalog, 124
- insert, 127
- storyboards, 128

Review Questions

1. Explain why promotion should be viewed as a *means* and not as an *end* in direct marketing.
2. As a promotional strategy in direct marketing, what is the major purpose of advertising?
3. How do measurability and accountability, characteristics key to direct marketing, apply to advertising?
4. What is the meaning of "conspicuous consumption"? What is its relevance to direct marketers?
5. Elaborate on this statement: "Consumer behavior in today's industrial society is interactive and is dependent not so much on income as on the buyer's perception of his or her place in the environment."
6. What, specifically, is *direct response advertising?*
7. How is the cost of promotion justified in our economic system striving for optimum allocation of resources?
8. Distinguish between *"the ability to buy"* and the *"proneness to spend."*
9. Distinguish between print and broadcast advertising media. Give examples of each.
10. Why is an understanding of buyer motivations important in the creation of direct marketing promotions?
11. What is meant by "writing by formula"? Give an example.
12. Why are design and graphics important in the creation of direct response advertising?
13. What are the elements of design?
14. Why is direct mail considered the primary medium for use by direct response advertisers?
15. Of what elements does a "classic" direct mail package consist?
16. What distinguishes direct response advertising in newspapers and magazines?
17. What is the most important element in direct response advertising?
18. In what ways is television used by direct marketers? What are the special advantages of cable? Of radio?
19. How does the telephone differ from other media used by direct response advertisers?
20. How does the Internet differ from other media used by direct response advertisers?

Exercise

Busch Gardens, a well-known amusement park located in Virginia, is holding a contest for college students. The first-place prize is a season passport for two people to enjoy the park for a lifetime for each member of the winning team! The challenge is to identify as many features of the park as possible and their associated advantages. Then, you must convert each advantage into a benefit that the amusement park may use in marketing their park to consumers. You may select your target market customer, either (a) families or (b) young adults. Have fun and good luck!

CASE: EVALUATING BENEFITS VERSUS PERSUASION IN COPY

OVERVIEW

Particularly in the sale of intangible services and especially in fundraising, the direct marketer needs a keen awareness of what motivates response. Donors to worthy causes often contribute for reasons of their own and these reasons may have nothing whatsoever to do with the cause itself. The potential benefits received by such donors are not always readily apparent, which poses a particular challenge to the direct marketer engaged in fundraising.

This case study presents a variety of different copy approaches featured on several mailing envelopes, with each experimentally control-tested against the others. Certain of these copy approaches describe benefits whereas others use persuasion. All are designed to get attention. Discussion should develop the rationale for each copy approach and why it was featured before considering the relative response results. Evaluating the results reported in the case history suggest why the "best" package provided the highest response and why others were "good" or "poor."

CASE

The American Heart Association needed to raise more funds for its health improvement activities at a lower cost. Direct mail had historically been the most important medium for the organization's fundraising and an effort was to be made to improve on current response.

Several new copy approaches were developed. Through scientific experimentation involving test mailings in excess of 200,000 pieces and confirmation with another 200,000 pieces, these copy approaches were tested against each other and against the "control" currently being used. With experimentation, of course, it is necessary to have all aspects of the mailing remain the same except for one variable within each test segment. In this way the change in response can be attributed to change in that variable.

The American Heart Association decided to test six copy approaches in the form of "teasers" displayed on the outside of the mailing envelope. These six envelope "teasers" would be tested against each other and also against the control, the envelope that the fundraiser had been using successfully in the past, but which had no "teaser" at all.

These seven envelope panels, six tests and one control, are visualized in Figure 5-8. A letter, contribution form, and reply envelope, also shown, were enclosed in each mailing envelope. These forms were essentially the same for all seven packages except for the beginning of the letter, which emphasized the "teaser" copy approach that was featured on the outside mailing envelope.

The American Heart Association sent solicitation mailings to their current donors as well as "cold" prospects, those who had not given a contribution before. The response from each group and for each copy approach was tabulated separately through key coding appearing on the contribution form.

These copy approaches were tested, as in Figure 5-8:

Effort	Copy Approach
1	Use the enclosed FREE GIFT.
2	Emergency Heart Attack Card Enclosed.
3	4 years ago Billy Thompson's dad would have died . . .
4	If you have ever worried about having a heart attack . . .
5	You hold lives in your hands . . . TODAY . . . AND THAT'S IMPORTANT!
6	We'd like to show you how you can help save a life. YOURS.
7	(Control) No teaser copy.

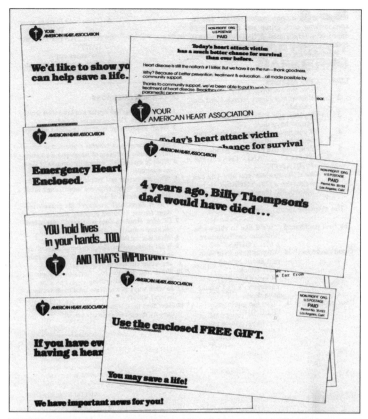

FIGURE 5-8   Copy Approaches Tested by the American Heart Association

The response results were these:

The best package:	6 We'd like to show you how you can help save a life. YOURS.
Good packages:	4 If you have ever worried about having a heart attack . . .
	3 4 years ago Billy Thompson's dad would have died . . . .
Poor packages:	1 Use the enclosed FREE GIFT.
	5 You hold lives in your hands . . . TODAY . . . AND THAT'S IMPORTANT!
	7 No teaser copy.
	2 Emergency Heart Attack Card Enclosed.

Source: This case was originally developed by Freeman F. Gosden, Jr., President of Smith-Hemmings-Gosden, Direct Response Advertising, El Monte, California, who conducted the test from which it was derived. ∎

Case Discussion Questions

1. Review each envelope teaser shown in Figure 5-8 and explain the rationale for each copy approach. Keep in mind, each envelope teaser was created to get attention.
2. Based on the test results, the best package was # 6 "We'd like to show you how you can help save a life. YOURS." Do you personally agree with the test results? Why or why not?
3. Create three additional envelope copy teasers that could be tested against the best package. What is the rationale behind each of your newly created teasers? Why do you think each would be effective?

Notes

1. Theodore Levitt, *The Marketing Mode* (New York: McGraw-Hill, 1969), 1.
2. Thorstein Veblen, *The Theory of the Leisure Class* (London: Macmillan, 1917), 110.
3. Bob Stone, *Successful Direct Marketing Methods,* 7th ed. (New York: McGraw-Hill, 2001), 294–395.
4. L. E. Frailey, *Handbook of Business Letters* (Upper Saddle River, NJ: Prentice Hall, 1948), 110.

CHAPTER

6

DIRECT MAIL AND OTHER PRINT MEDIA

There are two fundamental means of conveying mass communication: printing presses and electronic transmitters. In this chapter we look at print media as direct marketers utilize them for direct response advertising. Electronic media that carry direct response advertising are *broadcast media* such as television and radio, discussed in Chapter 7, and *interactive electronic*

media such as the telephone as well as the Internet and its commerce component, the World Wide Web, discussed in Chapters 8 and 9. Although we don't
discuss them here, salespeople are interactive media, too, either face to face or
with electronic intervention.

Direct mail, in its various formats, is a print medium. Publications, magazines, and newspapers represent another form of printed communication. In
contrast with direct-mail ads, which are delivered individually, magazines and
newspapers convey direct response advertising to groups of readers in a
package along with other advertisements as well as editorial matter. The total
content of these print media largely pre-selects the individual publication's
readers. In most cases, too, the reader subscribes to and pays for the publication's content.

We talked about the promotion *formats* of direct marketing and their creation, categorized by media, in Chapter 5. In this chapter we are concerned with
the print media themselves—direct mail (including self-mailers, classic packages,
and catalogs), newspapers, magazines, and collateral-printed materials—and
their characteristics and advantages and disadvantages. We'll discuss the potential for market segmentation through readership of specific parts of a particular
print medium at a particular time . . . sports or obituaries in today's newspaper,
as examples.

Direct mail has long been the basic promotion format for direct marketers.
It relies on mailing lists and data about the individuals or organizations on such
lists to most effectively reach market segments.

DIRECT MAIL AS A PRINT MEDIUM

Direct marketers use virtually all forms of advertising media to generate measurable
responses, but **direct mail** continues to be the dominant medium they use for direct
response advertising. Not all direct mail is carried by the United States Postal
Service; however, some go by private carriers such as United Parcel Service, and/or
other door-to-door distributors, such as newspaper carriers on their circulation
rounds. Some are enclosed within newspapers and magazines. Sometimes marketers
also combine several offers into a single package, such as coupons or other inserts
into newspapers, or enclose offers with other mail or parcels, such as statement
stuffers or package inserts.

Of all the media available for direct response advertising, direct mail can be the
most selective and offers the most potential for personalization. It is the most flexible (mainly because of the many different formats available) and also the most
suitable for test. Because of these pinpoint attributes of its distribution, it has the
potential for the highest rate of response. Figure 6-1 provides a sample direct-mail
package for a graphic and stationery company. Note how the various elements of
design are used (layout, illustration, type, etc.) to lead up to the all important
request for a response.

Its inherent advantages, however, cause direct mail to be the most expensive
medium per prospect reached. Even with a volume of 100,000 pieces, it may be difficult
to distribute a traditional direct-mail package (mailing envelope, computer-processed

FIGURE 6-1   Homefronts® Direct-Mail Package

four-page letter, circular, order form, and business reply envelope) for less than $1000 per thousand pieces.[1] This is true even though preferential postage rates apply to non-profit organizations and also to those large volume mailers who presort their direct mail by ZIP code or by postal carrier route. Volume mailers can benefit, too, from lower average printing and production costs.

Market Segmentation

Databases are most often the distribution vehicle for direct mail. Sophisticated techniques for compiling, warehousing, and mining such databases—coupled with computer technology for most effectively utilizing transaction, demographic, psychographic, and other data inherent to them—can pinpoint prospects and identify market segments in a highly efficient manner.[2] With such data, the direct marketer can efficiently segment house lists (active and inactive customers as well as inquirers) and compiled databases of other organizations. Figure 6-2 shows a direct-mail piece that was mailed to the "best customers" segment of McDonald Garden Center's three retail locations. The offer states that those customers presenting the mailer along with their loyalty card by a specified date will receive a free gift. This

FIGURE 6-2 A Best Customer Mailing Piece

encourages a timely response and the response device (which is the mailer itself) is both accountable and measurable.

Computer match coding and merge-purge techniques can eliminate duplicate mailings within and between lists, addresses can be standardized to maximize deliverability, and data about buying patterns can help determine customer potential. Databases are at the heart of direct mail as a print medium.

Catalogs

Catalogs have become a vital and productive format of direct mail. Although there is evidence of trade catalogs in mid-fifteenth century Europe and even in pre-Revolution America, the pioneering general merchandise mail-order catalogs were those of Montgomery Ward and Sears Roebuck, which were first issued post-Civil War. The specialty-product catalogs of Joseph Spiegel and L.L. Bean first appeared in the early twentieth century.

While the original Ward and Sears catalogs endeavored to provide all things to all people—and ultimately became too big and prohibitively expensive to circulate—today's successful catalogs rely on databases to target specialized product lines to most-likely-interested market segments. Their fit with the marketplace has made catalogs such as Lands' End, Sharper Image, and Peruvian Connection successful.

Today's catalogs are not confined to consumer products; they also play an important role in business-to-business distribution. Interestingly enough, the office product catalogs of Staples, Office Depot, and others, augmented by extensive in-store distribution, were preceded long ago by similar catalogs which were circulated to offices by salespeople, who then took orders by telephone. John H. Patterson, who founded the National Cash Register Company (today's NCR), used direct-mail catalogs as early as the 1920s to get qualified leads for follow-up by salespeople calling on industrial organizations.

A recent study by the Direct Marketing Association reveals that a majority (89 percent) of consumers has purchased from catalogs and 57 percent have purchased during a preceding year.[3]

Syndication Mailings

Syndication mailings, usually arranged by an intermediary between the producer and the seller called a syndicate, offers a product to an established (and usually credit-approved) customer list. The most common users of syndication are publishers, oil companies, bank credit cards, department stores, catalog merchandisers, and other organizations that have an existing customer relationship. These direct marketers supply the databases of their customers and the goodwill inherent within customer relationships, and assume the accounts receivable after the sale. The producer (of a pair of binoculars, for example) benefits from an efficient and effective distribution system for its products. The syndicate bears promotion costs, supplies and ships merchandise, handles customer service, and pays the direct marketer a sales commission for the use of its databases of customers and their goodwill.

Syndication mailing had its roots in the 1950s when large lists of mail-order buyers and respondents began to proliferate, notably among publishers of encyclopedias and other books, as well as mail-order merchants and those with accounts receivables such as oil companies and credit card organizations. Most of these early syndications moved goods with relatively high unit price, such as a home movie outfit or a power tool, for example.

Whereas the early users of syndication mailings were as much interested in activating their credit customers as they were in earning a profit from the merchandise sale itself, today's direct marketers look on syndication as a profit center and another indication of the inherent value of a customer relationship. Syndication can provide an unusually high rate of return for a nominal investment.

Coupons

As a promotional medium—primarily for grocery, health, and beauty care products—a **coupon** is an offer by a manufacturer or retailer that includes an incentive for purchase of a product or service in the form of a specified price reduction. A major objective of coupons is to motivate buyers to try a new product or to convert occasional users into regular customers. A further objective is to increase sales so the retailer will give the product greater display space.

Coupons distributed by direct mail can be self-mailers for a single brand or they can be enclosed in an envelope with descriptive literature; or, there may be several brands cooperating in a single distribution sponsored by either the manufacturer or a mailing organization. Even cooperative coupon mailings can be directed to specific market segments such as teenagers, senior citizens, professionals, or business organizations. Marketers also place coupons in their company newsletters. Figure 6-3 provides an example of how McDonald Garden Center offers dollar-savings coupons to those regular customers who receive its newsletter.

FIGURE 6-3   Coupon Distribution via a Newsletter

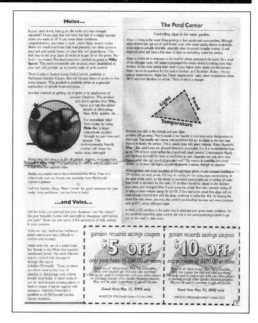

Of the 256 billion coupons distributed during 1999, only 1.84 percent (6.8 billion) were redeemed. Redemption rates have been declining since 1993 when 2.00 percent (6.2 billion) of 309.7 billion coupons distributed were redeemed. Most coupons, 81.3 percent, were distributed through newspapers in 1999 and just 2.1 percent were distributed through direct mail. However, although the cost of direct-mail distribution of coupons is somewhat higher, the redemption rate for these more-targeted coupons was a much higher 3.5 percent.[4]

Fraudulent redemption of coupons, without purchase as intended, is a major problem for manufacturers as well as retailers. Because in direct mail the coupon is enclosed in a sealed envelope addressed to a particular person, making the coupons unavailable in volume for fraudulent redemption, direct mail is probably the safest way to distribute coupons.

Cooperative Mailings

Cooperative mailings provide participants, usually noncompeting direct response advertisers, with opportunities to reduce mailing cost in reaching common prospects. Because the recipient's attention is divided among several advertisers, however, response to cooperative mailings is also lower than direct mailings featuring a single offer. The circulation of cooperative mailings ranges from consumer distribution, which reaches one-half of all U.S. households periodically, to highly pinpointed market segments, such as Doctor's Marketplace. In another form called a "ride-along," a direct marketer might include one or more noncompeting offers with a catalog or individual mailing.

Mass cooperative mailings frequently combine coupon offers with other direct response offers, thus amortizing the total mailing cost among several advertising participants. Although participation in a cooperative mailing can cost $100 or less per thousand, this cost rises according to the degree of selectivity in the mailing.

Some cooperative mailings provide opportunities to reach market segments such as apartment dwellers, Hispanic-speaking households, or consumers in particular ZIP code clusters. As many as a dozen or more offers might be contained in a cooperative mailed to a specific market segment. Such mass cooperatives are sometimes distributed through other print media: newspapers and magazines. A recent Valpak® mailing to a local geographical area contained valuable offers of 23 direct marketers representing a wide variety of businesses and industries. Figure 6-4 provides the list of these different types of organizations.

Statement/Invoice Stuffers

Periodic bills and reminder statements mailed to customers of department stores, utilities, oil companies, publications, and bank credit cards provide an opportunity for merchandising complementary, but not competing, offers of products and services with **stuffers** inserted in the envelope with the invoice or statement. Distribution can be wide and cost is relatively low, ranging from $50 to $100 per thousand. Deliverability is ensured, since most bills travel via first-class mail, and virtually everyone opens their bills. The billing company implies an endorsement of the offer and, in some cases, also offers credit to make the purchase. Marketers can segment these mailings by selecting the organization sending out the bills.

```
┌─────────────────────────────────────────────────────────────────┐
│                       Valpak® Savings Mailing                     │
│                                                                   │
│   Automobile Insurance              Contact Lens Direct           │
│   Personalized Checks               Valpak® Promotion             │
│   Cabinet Re-facing                 Auto Glass Replacement        │
│   Fine China                        Home Security System          │
│   Hotel Accommodations              Automobile Dealership Services │
│   Optical Services                  Child Learning & Development Center │
│   Fast Food Restaurant              Carpet & Upholstery Cleaning  │
│   Maid Services                     Photography Studio            │
│   Dry Cleaner Services              Address Label                 │
│   Automobile Tune & Lube            Storage Space Rental          │
│   Internet Services                 Health Insurance              │
│   Tire Sale Announcement                                          │
│                                                                   │
└─────────────────────────────────────────────────────────────────┘
```

FIGURE 6-4   Contents of a Cooperative Mailing

Package Inserts

Package inserts are related to stuffers but offer the additional advantage of arriving when the recipient has just made a purchase. Certain direct marketers offer the opportunity for one or more direct response advertisers to include inserts with customer shipments. Gourmet meat purveyor Omaha Steaks, for example, might enclose an offer of gourmet coffee from Gevalia in its shipments. Some package shippers may even offer specific selection by product line or geographic location. Inserts might be loose or contained within a separate folder in the package. Cost is about the same as that for billing inserts.

Take-One Racks

Another alternative method of print distribution is the use of **take-one racks** in supermarkets, restaurants, hotels, drug stores, transportation terminals, buses and trains, or other high-traffic locations. These might be placed in a cardboard display container adjacent to a cash register, or could be placed in a wire rack strategically hung on a wall in a supermarket and containing many offers. An advantage of such distribution is that those who voluntarily take a promotion piece from the rack are usually more than casually interested. Thus, the response rate from take-one rack inserts is relatively high when lower cost is considered. Even though distribution within a single rack might be quite low, say, less than 100 per month, the number of potential outlets for racks is quite large and distribution could total into the millions.

Other print media include magazines and newspapers, with which the following sections are concerned.

MAGAZINES AS A PRINT MEDIUM

A major restructuring of the magazine industry in the 1970s changed the way marketers use magazines for direct response advertising. The demise of three mass-circulation magazines—*Life, Look,* and the *Saturday Evening Post*—was followed by the proliferation of smaller-circulation special-interest magazines appealing to well-defined market segments.

Market Segmentation

Special-interest magazines, through their selection of content and resulting readership, serve to define market segments and even psychographic lifestyles for direct response advertisers. Categories of special-interest magazines are today virtually unlimited: class (the *New Yorker, Smithsonian,* and *Museum*); literary (*Atlantic, Harpers,* and the *New York Times Book Review*); sports (*Sports Illustrated, Ski,* and *Golf*); how-to (*Popular Mechanics, Popular Science,* and *Woodworking*); news (*Time, Newsweek,* and *U.S. News*); religious (*Christian Herald* and *Catholic Digest*); and many other diverse titles such as *Entertainment Weekly, Self, Vanity Fair,* and *Playboy*).

Certain magazines—including, among many others, the *New Yorker, Business Week,* and *Newsweek*—are available in demographic editions describing market segments, such as women, college students, and business executives. Some publications, including *TV Guide,* offer geographic editions which are described by ZIP code areas. Some, such as *Time,* combine both demographic and geographic market segmentation, offering selected advertisers access to these selected groupings. Occasionally, using laser printing technology, individual ads are personalized to individual subscribers.

Categories of Magazines

Magazines can be grouped by editorial content into five major categories:

1. ***General Mass:***   Characterized by high circulation and relatively low cost per thousand readers, general mass circulation magazines include *Reader's Digest, TV Guide, People,* and *National Geographic.*
2. ***Women's Service:***   Like the category above, women's service magazines are characterized by heavy circulation and reasonably low cost per thousand readers. Included are magazines such as *McCall's, Good Housekeeping, Family Circle, Seventeen,* and *Ladies Home Journal.*
3. ***Shelter:***   With selected demographics and increased cost, shelter magazines (those that focus on homes, decorating, and gardening) include *Architectural Digest, Better Homes and Gardens, House & Garden,* and *House Beautiful.*
4. ***Business:***   This category includes *Fortune, Forbes, American Banker, Business Week, Nation's Business, Fast Company, Inc.,* and *Black Enterprise.*
5. ***Special Interest:***   With highly selected demographics and even lifestyle definition, this category would include magazines such as *Travel & Leisure, Cosmopolitan, Gourmet, Boys Life, Ski, Golf Digest,* and *Jogging.* Figure 6-5 provides a list of some special-interest magazines.

Advantages and Disadvantages

Magazines can be selected to reach defined market segments: mass or class; rural, urban, or suburban; females or males; senior citizens or teenagers. Modern printing technology permits excellent reproduction at a relatively low cost per thousand circulation. Because magazines usually come out periodically—weekly, monthly, quarterly—they enjoy relatively long life and often many readers will read a single copy. Through split-run techniques in which alternative advertisements are placed in

---

SPECIALTY MAGAZINES

Touring Times–The Travel Magazine of Rural Route Tours
International and American Group Travel

Baker's Digest

Personals–A Magazine for Meeting People

Diversion–The Magazine for Physicians At Leisure

WindRider–The Nations Leading Windsurfing Magazine

The Plate Collector

American Bicyclist and Motorcyclist

The Italians

OffHours–The Physicians' Guide to Leisure and Finance

Chain Saw Industry & Power Equipment Dealer

Physician's Assets

Hobby Merchandiser

The Logger and *Lumberman Magazine*

The Internal Auditor

Twins–The Magazine for Parents of Multiples

Cheerleader Today

Modern Bride

FIGURE 6-5   Unique Special-Interest Magazines

---

every other copy, magazines can be tested relatively inexpensively for ways to maximize direct response.

On the negative side, however, magazines offer direct marketers less space in which to tell their story than direct mail does. Additionally, closing dates for magazines (the date by which the magazine must receive the ad) are often considerably in advance of the issue dates and, because of staggered distribution, over a long period of time, response is usually spread out over time and thus slower.

Relative Cost

Although there are literally thousands of magazines published, the circulation of only a few hundred is audited and authenticated by the Audit Bureau of Circulations. These titles, however, have a combined circulation of hundreds of millions. The cost of one black-and-white advertising page could be in the range of $15 per thousand for large circulation publications and four or five times that for trade or business publications. This is, of course, considerably less than the cost of direct mail at $1000 per thousand pieces, especially when we can obtain a degree of market segmentation by using specific magazines.

These factors influence the cost of magazine advertising: the amount of space purchased; whether the ad is in color or black and white; whether the ink bleeds off the edges of the page; and the use of regional, demographic, or test market selections.

Certain magazines offer discounted rates for direct response advertisers as well as special rates for categories such as publishers or schools. Sometimes, standby or "remnant" space is available at publication deadline and at substantial discounts.

Position and Timing

Although the front and back covers usually get maximum readership in a magazine, many publications do not permit direct response coupons in these preferred positions. The front portion of the magazine, assuming a full page, is preferable. A right-hand page is usually better for direct response than a left-hand page, but there are exceptions, such as the last left-hand page in the book. Whether on a right-hand or left-hand page, the response coupon, if there is one, should always appear on the outside margin and never in the gutter (center fold) of the magazine. Inserts and bind-in response devices, reply cards or envelopes, serve to call attention to the advertisement.

Many magazines offer advertisers an opportunity, along with a special cooperative advertising rate, to have their advertisement listed and highlighted on a bingo card. A **bingo card** (also called an information card) is an insert or page of a magazine that is created by the publisher to provide a numeric listing of advertisers. Bingo cards can be bound into the magazine or loosely inserted and serve as a response mechanism for consumers to request additional information by simply circling or checking the number corresponding to each advertiser. Advertisers will often reference the bingo card in their ad with statements such as "for further information circle item 27." Consumers send completed cards directly to the publisher who, in turn, sends compiled lists of inquiries to the appropriate participating advertiser. Figure 6-6 provides an example of a bingo card.

FIGURE 6-6   Bingo Card Sample

Advertisement

READERS' RESOURCE BOARD

To receive information from the companies listed on the following page, please circle the corresponding numbers below.

1	2	3	4	5	6	7	8	9	10	11	12	13	14	15
16	17	18	19	20	21	22	23	24	25	26	27	28	29	30
31	32	33	34	35	36	37	38	39	40	41	42	43	44	45
46	47	48	49	50	51	52	53	54	55	56	57	58	59	60
61	62	63	64	65	66	67	68	69	70	71				

NAME

ADDRESS

CITY   STATE   ZIP

Offer expires June 23, 1999   0499

Aside from seasonal offers, response from magazine advertisements usually follows the normal direct marketing cycle. The strongest response occurs in January–February and September–October, with the poorest response during June–July. (These are *circulation* dates and not always the dates appearing on the cover of the magazine.)

NEWSPAPERS AS A PRINT MEDIUM

Along with magazines, newspapers represent a major medium for distribution of printed direct response advertising. There are an estimated 1,500 daily newspapers in the United States. A sizable number of weekly and farm newspapers are also available for use by direct marketers.

Market Segmentation

Like magazines, newspapers help segment the market for direct response advertising although not as finely as magazines. National newspapers, such as *The Wall Street Journal, USA Today, Christian Science Monitor, Capper's Weekly,* and *National Enquirer,* are directed to well-defined market segments. Additional opportunities for market segmentation through newspapers include urban vs. rural; dailies vs. weeklies; commuter editions vs. those home-delivered; morning vs. evening editions; tabloids; comic sections; and Sunday supplements. Marketers can also select specific types of readers by choosing the placement of direct response advertisements within the newspaper, such as in the sports, television, comic, or business sections, for example.

Categories of Newspaper Advertising

Aside from type and location of a newspaper's circulation, there are three distinct ways to reach a newspaper's readers: (1) run-of-paper (ROP), (2) preprinted inserts, or (3) syndicated Sunday supplements.

Run-of-Paper Advertisements

Although position in a newspaper can many times be specified and paid for, **run-of-paper (ROP) advertisements**—positioning the ad at the will of the newspaper—do not normally have the visual impact or dominance required for direct response advertisers. Most ROP direct response advertisements are small or appear in specific "mail-order" sections of newspapers. (Full-page direct response advertising in newspapers will, of course, increase dominance wherever placed.)

Preprinted Inserts

Preprinted inserts run typically in Sunday editions or on Wednesday or Thursday mornings. The direct response advertiser usually prints them ahead of time and provides them to the newspaper according to the publication's specifications.

Sunday Supplements

Mass circulation **Sunday supplements,** such as *Parade* and *Family Weekly,* are edited nationally but appear locally in the Sunday editions of many newspapers. They offer large circulation and a great deal of flexibility at a relatively low cost. One variation of the Sunday supplement is the comic section, which reaches as many as 50 million households. Sunday supplements, both magazine and comic sections, have proven successful for many direct response advertisers.

Advantages and Disadvantages

Key advantages of newspapers for direct response advertisers include short closing dates and relatively fast response. A wide variety of formats is available, as well as broad coverage of geographic or demographic areas. A disadvantage is that response from newspaper advertisements is usually short-lived since tomorrow brings another edition.

Newspapers are well known for providing strong market penetration in a local geographical area. Figure 6-7 provides an example of a direct response–space ad from a local newspaper. Note the offer being presented is designed to appeal to the consumers residing in a specific geographical area—Virginia Beach.

Although this is not necessarily true of pre-printed inserts, the print quality of newspapers is generally not as good as that of the other print media, direct mail, and magazines, and there is limited color availability. At times, too, the timeliness of the editorial content of newspapers and the abundance of their advertising content detract from the readership of direct response advertising. Newspapers do not have the degree

FIGURE 6-7   Direct Response–Space Ad Example

FIGURE 6-8   Run-of-Paper Ad Space

of selectivity or market segmentation that direct mail has. Therefore, most direct response ads in newspapers keep the message more generic. As shown in the newspaper ads in Figure 6-8, McDonald Garden Center knows its ad will reach both customers and prospective customers in the local geographical area.

Position and Timing

There are many opportunities for **positioning** in newspapers. An obvious one is placement of a funeral service inquiry ad adjacent to the obituaries. Another is placement of automobile tire and hunting gear ads in the sports section. Most newspapers have food sections—usually on Wednesday or Thursday—and relevant ads are obvious candidates for placement there. Financial advisors and stock brokers are appropriate advertisers in business sections. Coupons, if used, should be positioned on the outside of the page for easy clipping.

Timing can be important, too. Seasonal interests are obvious. Sunday editions typically are read at a more leisurely pace and in a family setting. Morning editions may be more appropriate for retailers than evening editions. As already noted, Wednesday and/or Thursday may be more favorable to grocery shopping ads and weekend sport sections carry a lot of scores and other references for sports fans. Tuesdays may be relatively light days for advertising so ads can be showcased. Friday editions may emphasize weekend activities. And, of course, major news happenings (often unforeseen) can grab attention away from all the other contents.

Summary

Of all the media used by direct marketers, direct mail remains the primary one, relying on databases to most effectively reach market segments. Direct mail is the most selective, the most flexible medium, and it offers the greatest potential for the highest rate of response although it is the most expensive medium per prospect mailed. Variations of direct mail include self-mailers, classic formats, catalogs, syndication mailings, coupons, cooperative mailings, and miscellaneous distribution such as statement/invoice stuffers, package inserts, and take-one racks.

Printed media, other than direct mail, include magazines and newspapers. Magazines, as they have moved away from mass circulation to special interest circulation, offer increased opportunities for market segmentation through definition of content and readership. We generally categorize magazines as general mass, women's service, shelter, business, and special interest. Thus, magazine readership can help describe markets. Although they offer high-quality printing reproduction, magazines provide direct marketers less space for their messages than does direct mail. The cost of circulation of magazines is substantially lower than that of direct mail, but response rates of individual advertisements are also much lower.

Daily newspapers in the United States reach about two-thirds of all households. There are also a good many weekly and farm newspapers, which are also used extensively by direct marketers. Like magazines, newspapers can be segmented for direct response advertisers by geographic location, special positioning within the paper, and other factors such as morning or evening editions, and commuter or home delivery circulation. Response advertisers can use ROP (run-of-paper), pre-printed inserts, or Sunday supplements.

Key Terms

- direct mail, 137
- syndication mailings, 140
- coupon, 141
- cooperative mailings, 142
- stuffers, 142
- package inserts, 143
- take-one racks, 143
- bingo card, 146
- run-of-paper (ROP) advertisements, 147
- preprinted inserts, 147
- Sunday supplements, 147
- positioning, 149

Review Questions

1. What are the two fundamental means of conveying mass communication? What are the media which comprise these two? Give examples of each.
2. Is it appropriate to view the Internet (i.e., the World Wide Web) as a medium? Give reasons for your response.
3. What is the major advantage of direct mail over other media for direct response?
4. Why is direct mail an ideal medium for market segmentation?
5. Discuss the attributes of a database which could be helpful for targeting direct mail to the most likely prospects. How can these be used in developing promotion copy?
6. In what ways do contemporary mailed catalogs differ from those pioneered by Ward, Sears, and Spiegel?
7. What is meant by syndication of direct mail?
8. Why is a coupon considered to be direct response advertising?
9. Evaluation of media for direct response advertising must relate results to costs. How might this be done?
10. Describe and show examples of these alternatives to traditional direct mail: cooperative

mailings, statement/invoice stuffers, package inserts, and take-one racks.

11. Discuss the relative advantages and disadvantages of direct response advertising placed in magazines and/or newspapers.

12. Of what importance are position and timing of direct response advertising placed in magazines and/or newspapers?

Exercise

Congratulations! You have just been hired as a marketing director for a specialty magazine. Your primary responsibility is to increase the number of subscribers to your magazine. Your assignment is to (a) describe the magazine and its target market; (b) create a media plan comprised of only print media; and (c) develop the rough creative materials you plan to use in the execution of the media plan. Your new boss didn't give you a budget, so be creative!

CASE: NEWPORT NEWS, INC.

OVERVIEW

This case investigates a multipage format of direct mail—the catalog. It stimulates thinking about the research and preparation involved in producing and distributing a catalog and, naturally, the costs incurred throughout the process. It also provides an overview of the critical roles that testing and product selection play in the successful execution of a catalog.

In the catalog business, direct marketers are constantly creating new offers to generate consumer purchases at some future time. Catalog development is a detailed process—one requiring much research and testing. Savvy direct marketers utilize their database as a tool to aid in numerous catalog production decisions, such as the product variety to be offered and the teaser copy to be placed on the front page of the catalog.

CASE

A model example of a retail and catalog business is Spiegel, Inc. (The Spiegel Group). The Spiegel Group is comprised of three separate and distinct brands, each uniquely designed to target and sell to different groups of consumers. They are Eddie Bauer (apparel for men and women, and bed and bath décor), Spiegel (women's apparel and home furnishings), and Newport News (moderately priced, trendy women's fashion). Each of these brands has a separate yet effective way of utilizing database marketing in their respective catalog businesses. This case will examine Newport News, which has developed a niche by offering versatile, on-trend, women's fashion at easily affordable prices through direct-mail catalogs and the Internet.

Newport News has been in the direct marketing arena for 30 years. In this time it has learned many valuable lessons about the industry, the strategies of direct mail, and, most importantly, the ever-changing consumer.

The company started as a division of the popular cosmetics brand Avon. On November 6, 1987, the company, then called New Hampton, broke free and declared its independence from Avon, where the catalog was called Avon Fashions. However the company soon faced an uncertain future when in August 1993, it declared bankruptcy (Chapter 11). Spiegel stepped in at the same time and purchased substantially all its assets and the company was officially renamed Newport News, Inc., in 1995. Through 2000 the company continued to grow; however, difficult economic conditions since then have presented challenging times. In March 2003 Spiegel, Inc., along with its principal operating subsidiaries, filed for bankruptcy protection under Chapter 11. This situation has pushed Newport News to focus even more attention on serving its existing customers and identifying prospective customers.

Improved technology has allowed Newport News to store important customer data in its database. Of its roughly eight million customers about three million are considered *active buyers*. An active buyer is defined by Newport News as "a customer who has ordered something from the company within the past 24 months." Active buyers are treated differently from inactive buyers. For example, people on the active buyer list receive more catalogs from Newport News, because these customers have recently shown an interest in its product(s) and are more likely to make a purchase.

Being in the direct mail business is very costly, so effective target marketing is extremely important. Newport News had 89 separate catalog mailings in 2002, an average of two per week, for a total of approximately 248 million pieces.

Companies such as Newport News recognize that customers develop certain perceptions about the product quality based solely on the quality of the catalog. A company with high-quality goods should have a high-quality catalog to project that same image to the consumer. The company must determine the most effective cover that will inspire the prospective customer to open the catalog and look inside. Research has determined that the model on the cover also can make the difference between whether a catalog edition makes a sale or not. Therefore, great care is taken when selecting models for each catalog cover. In addition, the company conducts market tests, not only for the models, but for the many product offerings in each catalog. Each catalog must be considered an asset and treated as such by targeting mailings as efficiently as possible.

In 2003 Newport News introduced a new approach that utilizes a new direct-mail format called a "magalog," a cross between a catalog and a magazine. With this new approach, Newport News is positioning itself as the only fashion catalog that sells on-trend merchandise at great value *and* that shows its customers how to make informed shopping decisions to look their best. The innovative magazine-style format combines fashionable merchandise with authoritative editorial content and a fresh, new layout. The magalog is a larger booklet than a traditional Newport News catalog and has a magazine binding and feel to it. It provides the customer with more copy and fashion tips that would normally be found in a magazine, while still trying to sell products.

Figure 6-9 shows some of the different types of page layouts found in a recent Newport News magalog. So far, the magalog has shown signs of success by generating a response rate that is higher than that of the typical Newport News catalog.

The goal of every direct marketing company is to know exactly who its best customers are, but as of yet no one has determined an exact method of accomplishing this task. Newport News is always looking for ways to maintain and increase its response rate. As shown in Figure 6-10, the company is constantly testing a variety of different teaser copy on the front cover of its catalogs, product offerings, catalog layout, models, props,

and photographs to determine which are the most effective.

Only through testing can the company determine what products and features of each catalog it should continue. The more information the company has, the better it can target customers who are more likely to make a purchase and avoid the extra cost of sending catalogs to those who are not. Newport News rents lists from other companies as well as using in-house lists within The Spiegel Group. The process doesn't end with getting the name, however. That is only the beginning.

Newport News conducts extensive research to determine what other products its customers are purchasing and from what competitors. Newport News takes that data and compares trends to determine where potential customers may be found. It develops customer profiles through market research, and then it finds prospective companies that have current, qualifying customers that fit its desired customer profiles. It rents lists from those companies in order to target potential customers. This strategy enables the company to attract potential customers who may be interested in the products offered by Newport News but have had no previous exposure to the company.

Newport News can actually determine how certain segments and/or certain catalogs are performing simply by looking up the current information in the database. This is especially important because this is how Newport News determines the response rate that each segment and each catalog is generating. In order to provide information for the database, each Newport News catalog has a "campaign" number which identifies the catalog mailing and a "mailkey" number to identify the customer segment. The sales associates ask for these numbers at the start of each order. Some of the metrics Newport News uses include orders generated, gross demand (in dollars) generated, and units generated. Each piece of information is collected for each catalog mailing. Newport News can then begin adjusting its marketing

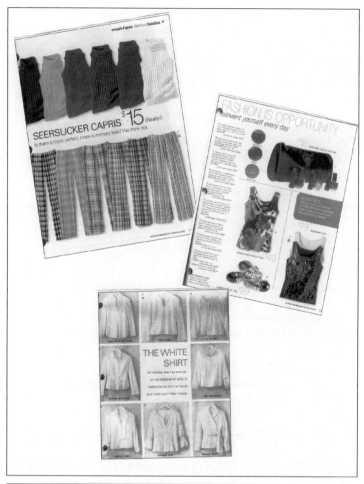

FIGURE 6-9   Page Layouts from a Newport News Magalog

strategy directly toward certain customer segments, which may contain devoted customers who have been historically proven to be a company's best customers.

Newport News does something very interesting with its best customers: it refers to them as "trendsetters" and uses these customers and their preferences to forecast buying trends. These trendsetters may receive catalogs well before other customers, and Newport News will track their purchases, using this information to forecast demand for certain products offered in its catalogs. For example, if the trendsetter group has a high response to a particular leather coat, Newport News may increase the quantity of this coat in its inventory in anticipation of higher sales in the near future. The company also takes items with high trendsetter demand and places them in multiple catalog mailings. Newport News uses its trendsetter forecasts to increase overall productivity as well, by dropping items with low trendsetter demand. These strategies demonstrate the firm's confidence in applying its marketing research to creating successful catalogs.

FIGURE 6-10   Examples of Teaser Copy on Newport News Catalog Covers

The creation of a catalog begins with market research and database analysis. It is a continuous process that utilizes the company's database to track and compare the performance of each catalog mailed to the customer. Overall, Newport News has been successful by understanding its consumers and their buying behavior, creating offers and producing catalogs that appeal to these consumers, and by never losing sight of the most important asset the company has—its customers. ■

Case Discussion Questions

1. Come up with a list of companies you think Newport News should consider for list rental. Why did you choose these companies? Would you consider these firms "like" or "unlike" Newport News?
2. Newport News uses *trendsetters* in an attempt to forecast demand. What factors would you look for when considering someone to be a trendsetter? What factors would make someone not suitable for being a trendsetter?
3. Describe how customer perceptions can be influenced by the *quality* of a direct-mail catalog.
4. Why do you think Newport News implemented the "campaign" and "mailkey" numbers into their business model? What kind of information can these tools provide that is useful to marketers?
5. Describe the new brand positioning for Newport News and its innovative direct mail format. Why do you think this format might be more productive for the company than the typical catalog?

Notes

1. *Statistical Fact Book 2003* (New York: Direct Marketing Association, Inc., 2003), 49.
2. See Chapter 2, which deals with market segmentation strategies, and Chapter 3, which deals with database development.
3. *Statistical Fact Book 2000* (New York: Direct Marketing Association, Inc., 2000), 5.
4. Ibid., 106ff.

7 | BROADCAST AND OTHER ELECTRONIC MEDIA

Broadcast is the most universal of communications media. Unlike print media, broadcast reaches virtually everyone and every location. There are more radios than people in the United States, and most people listen to the radio during some part of each day. Virtually every one of the 102,475,000 households in the United States has at least one television set, and many households have more. Nearly 82 percent of U.S. households are cable subscribers.[1] The average television set is used as much as six hours per day, and television long ago replaced the newspaper as the primary source of news.

With its universality, broadcast reaches the full range of geographic, demographic, and psychographic market segments, which are not always easily separated. Relatively high costs associated with relatively low response rates result from reaching (and paying for) nonqualified prospects. Measurability and accountability, hallmarks of direct marketing, are difficult, if not impossible, with the broadcast media. Still, the potential reach is there, if it can be harnessed.

In spite of their universality, however, broadcast media—television and radio—account for only a small percentage of total expenditures for direct response advertising. Most television advertising creatively emphasizes product brand and image rather than asking for an immediate response, the preferred advertising mode of direct marketers. This, however, is changing as direct marketers experiment with and learn about the broadcast media of television and radio.

In this chapter, we first look at the ramifications of television, such as network, cable, and satellite transmission, as well as forthcoming interactivity. Then, we highlight *other* interactive electronic media: the telephone (more detailed in Chapter 8) and the Internet (more detailed in Chapter 9). As we look at interactivity, we would be remiss not to include a medium which, although not necessarily aided and abetted "electronically," may be the most interactive of all: the living, breathing salesperson.

TELEVISION

When it began, transmitted via established networks and/or local channels, television was not an important medium for direct response advertising. But its value has increased as direct marketers have learned how to use it. Cable and satellite transmission now provide an almost endless variety of programming and special-interest channels, defining the potential for market segmentation. Interactive modes of television provide the immediate response—along with measurability and accountability—on which direct marketers thrive.

Direct response advertisers utilize television in the following three ways, as we will detail in this chapter:

1. To sell products or services . . . or a political candidate.
2. To get inquiries: expressions of interest or sales leads for personal follow-up.
3. To support other media: newspaper inserts or heavy penetration direct mail.

To accomplish these alternatives, direct response advertisers need to be mindful that television viewers have one of two objectives: *entertainment* or *information*. It also is important that advertisers know how to direct their messages to defined market segments so as to minimize the high cost of reaching television audiences.

Market Segmentation

When a farmer "broadcasts" seed, much of that seed lodges in moist, fertile ground and, under ideal growing conditions, it is nurtured into a living plant. Another portion of the seed is borne away by the wind or, for other reasons, fails to achieve the proper conditions for germination. Direct marketers using television are like the farmer sowing seed. Although television has the potential for reaching virtually everyone, it can achieve the objectives of the direct response advertiser only if it is seen in the right place at the right time under the right conditions. Market segmentation, in television as in other media, is one way to maximize direct response.

Television programming plays an important role in defining specific audience segments; sports, news, comedies, westerns, mysteries, variety, documentaries, wrestling, and opera or drama can describe market segments of viewers and thus provide a showcase for a particular direct response offer. Other factors that can help segment markets include time of day or day of the week. Viewers of one of television's most-watched audience events each year, the football Super Bowl, are large in number and broad in characteristics. On the other hand, viewers of an Alfred Hitchcock movie are a more narrowly defined group, and whether they watch late at night or mid-afternoon also can make a difference in the demographic and psychographic characteristics of the audience. The "reach" of a local TV station can itself describe geographic markets differentiated by ZIP code characteristics.

Offering direct response advertisers even greater opportunities for market segmentation is cable television with its hundreds of specialized channels. Cable households have grown both more numerous and more affluent over the past 15 years. From 1985 to 2001 the average cable household income rose 75 percent from $32,182 to $56,172. This is $14,546 more than the average income of noncable households—which was $41,626 in 2001.[2] Highly specialized programming, "live" news, sporting events, and a variety of movie fare can help define desirable segments of cable television audiences as can special-interest channels, such as CNN, ESPN, the History Channel, or the Golf Channel.

Characteristics of Television Time

Like empty seats on a departing airplane, television time is perishable. Furthermore, once 24 hours per day have been used within a market, coverage cannot be extended nor can more time be manufactured or "imported from Japan." Only actual viewing can be increased. It is this penetration of the potential market, the number of viewers, that determines the price of commercial television time.

This price usually peaks during prime time, the early evening hours, and drops to a minimum during the wee hours of the morning. The cost of television time is highest when the viewing audience is the largest, although the cost is often set without regard to audience composition. Prime time may not be the best time for direct response advertising unless an offer appeals to a large and diversified audience. Further, large audiences attracted to a suspense-filled event like the Super Bowl are not inclined to break off watching in order to "call this 800 number *now!*"

The cost of a 120-second selling commercial, as typically used for direct response advertising on television, is not an adequate indication of success unless it is related to anticipated (actual) response to the advertising. The key to maximizing such response lies in market segmentation: Just who are the viewers at a particular time and how receptive are they to a direct offer?

Because television costs as well as audience segments vary, the most valid measurement for the direct marketer is **cost per response (CPR),** not **cost per viewer (CPV).**

Nielsen audience ratings, **gross rating points (GRP),** and areas of dominant influence (ADI)—the glossary of television time buying for the general advertiser—have little or no relevance for the direct marketer who wants somewhat more from direct response advertising than simply "recall." For example, gross rating points are a combination of **reach** and **frequency** measures. GRPs are determined by multiplying *reach* (the number of people exposed to vehicles carrying the ad) by *frequency* (the number of insertions purchased in a specific communication vehicle within a specified time period). GRPs may be able to measure the number of people exposed to an ad, however, they cannot determine whether that ad stimulated any subsequent action (response and/or order). As an example, the CPV of reaching one of television's largest audiences, those watching the Super Bowl might be quite low, but because of the diversity of this audience, the CPR could be prohibitively high.

The acronym that counts is CPR (cost per response), the total cost of a direct marketing campaign divided by the number of responses that campaign generated:

$$CPR = \frac{\text{Total Promotion Budget}}{\text{Total Number of Orders/Inquiries Received}}$$

Direct marketers must always relate advertising results to its costs.

Direct Marketing Uses of Television

We've said that there are three basic ways in which direct marketers use television. Let's now look at each in turn.

The first of these ways is to *sell something:* a recording, a subscription, a kitchen utensil. Consumers are ordering a broad assortment of products/services via direct response television (DRTV). Figure 7-1 provides a list of the top selling DRTV products/services in 2001.

TOP SELLING DIRECT RESPONSE

TELEVISION PURCHASES IN 2001

PRODUCT/SERVICE	2001
Exercise	43%
Diet/Health Weight	33%
Videos	20%
Beauty/Cosmetics	18%
Kitchen/Cookware	18%
Music	17%
Self-Improvement/Education	16%
Jewelry	11%
Electronics	8%
Collectibles and Hobbies	8%
Magazine Subscriptions	6%
Automotive	4%
Financial Services	3%

FIGURE 7-1 Direct Response Television Purchases

Source: Statistical Fact Book 2002 (New York: Direct Marketing Association Inc., 2002), 115.

Direct marketers usually require a 2-minute (120-second) commercial to achieve a direct sale. Customers respond by mail or, more likely, by telephone or through a Web site.

The second purpose of television for direct marketers is to *generate leads* for products or for political candidates seeking votes. These responses require a two-step process in which the television commercial stimulates the original inquiry and the customer follows up by mail, telephone, Web site, or personal visit to a store or a voting booth. Sixty-second television commercials are adequate to generate such leads.

The third direct marketing use of television is as *support* of direct response advertising in another medium, such as a newspaper. *Reader's Digest,* Publishers Clearing House, Time-Life, and others have used television successfully in this way. Usually 10- or 30-second commercials are adequate as reminders, with extensive repetition over a period of several days being the key to success. Support television, often purchased locally, creates interest in the offer and directs the viewer to the printed medium, which, in turn, provides detailed explanations as well as means for response.

Television Home Shopping and Infomercials

Home Shopping Network (HSN) and Quality/Value/Convenience (QVC) are notable examples of television channels devoted to the continuous sale of merchandise. While such programming does not yet provide random access for product selection—as would a printed catalog or a Web site—technology for such interactivity is emerging. For now, these networks primarily offer products such as jewelry, cosmetics, and electronics, which are frequently purchased on impulse. These products are extensively demonstrated, priced for quick sale, and sometimes rely on well-known personalities for credibility. Television home shoppers claim that product demonstrations were the prime motivating factor for their purchasing from television.[3]

So-called **infomercials** have become an important means of demonstrating and selling certain categories of products through television. These ads appear primarily on cable channels and often during early-morning and late-night time slots. They are usually of 30-minute duration. Featured products include exercisers, cookware, weight-loss offers, and sundry cleaning products. The health and fitness category is the most frequently aired type of infomercial—representing five of the top ten infomercial spots aired in 2001. Figure 7-2 lists the most frequently aired types of infomercial. The average cost to produce an infomercial ranges from $126,000 for a low-end production to $636,592 for a high-end production.[4]

Advantages and Disadvantages

Television, when used for direct response advertising, can provide a wide choice of cost alternatives and achieve quick (although short-lived) responses. The combination of video and audio, simultaneously providing a sales message along with a product demonstration, can deliver a lot of impact in a short time. Figure 7-3 provides a script for a television advertisement prior to ad production. Note the coordination necessary between the video and audio components.

Limited time is one of the medium's disadvantages when product descriptions are complex or are not subject to simple demonstration. Another major drawback is lack of a response device that the viewer can reference at a later time.

MOST FREQUENTLY AIRED INFOMERCIALS ON CABLE TV FOR 2001			
RANK	**SHOW TITLE**	**MARKETING COMPANY**	**CATEGORY**
1	Sharper Image	The Sharper Image	Miscellaneous
2	Carleton Sheets	Professional Education	Business & Finance
3	Bun & Thigh Rocker	Lohan Media, LLC	Health & Fitness
4	Proactiv	Guth-Renker Corporation	Beauty
5	Gazelle Freestyle	Fitness Quest	Health & Fitness
6	As See On TV PC	Reliant Interactive Media	Computers & Electronics
7	Ab-Boer	Thane International, Inc.	Health & Fitness
8	Total Gym	American Telecast1	Health & Fitness
9	Principal Secret	Ruth-Renker Corporation	Beauty
10	Chitosol	DMI/Global Marketing Solutions	Education & Self-Help

FIGURE 7-2   The Most Frequently Aired Infomercials

Source: Statistical Fact Book 2002 (New York: Direct Marketing Association, Inc., 2002), 119.

RADIO

When radio broadcasting was still in its infancy in the 1920s, it became a major medium for direct response advertising. It was productive for books and records, as it is today, but also, in that early period, for proprietary medicines and health cures. A powerful radio station in Del Rio, Texas, with the call letters XERA, built its transmitter across the border in Mexico to circumvent curtailment of its power as well as regulation of its direct response advertisements. These advertisements were often "exaggerations of the truth" at best. XERA (and other stations) solicited orders for *"genuine synthetic diamonds"* as well as inquiries for Dr. Brinkley's "goat gland transplants," for those seeking perpetual youth. Mail-order nurseries, pioneers in direct marketing, offered their plants and trees and religious groups raised funds for their evangelists through the medium of radio. Radio is still probably as strong a direct response medium as it was then, although it is minimally used today.

Market Segmentation
Even more than television channels, individual radio stations tend to develop strong images of programming, attracting particular types of listeners. Such program formats can segment markets into an array of specific subgroups that is virtually unlimited: all-music,

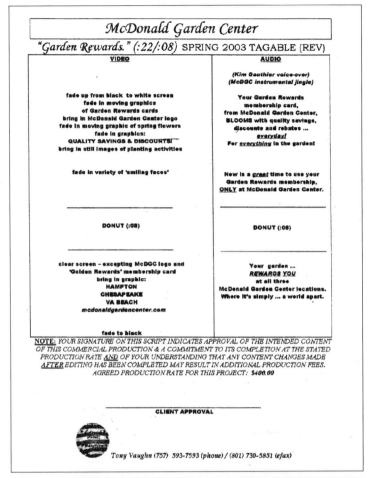

FIGURE 7-3 Script for a McDonald Garden Center Television Advertisement

all-news, and all-talk. Program format doesn't stop with just "music," however. Music can be "rock," "classical," "easy listening," "country/western," "show tunes," or nostalgic "music-of-your-life" programming. Figure 7-4 provides a list of the FM and AM stations in a southeastern metropolitan area of the United States. There are many different formats or programs available to satisfy the listening desires of all consumers.

Listeners are loyal to certain stations, so direct response advertising, presented within an established program format by a well-known personality, derives an air of credibility or even an implied endorsement from the station announcer. (For many years, syndicated radio news commentator Paul Harvey has provided a notable example, with his personally presented commercials for insurance and health products.) Unlike the case in television, in which viewers are constantly surfing among as many as a dozen or more favorite channels, according to the Radio Advertising Bureau, the average radio listener "tunes in regularly to less than three stations—no matter how

FIGURE 7-4 AM and FM Radio Stations for a Local Market

FM and AM Radio Stations
Southeastern Virginia

FM STATIONS	AM STATIONS
88.1 WHOV–Jazz, gospel, Latin	560 WGAI–News, talk, sports
88.5 WOCD–Christian music	670 WRJR–Radio Vida Spanish American
88.7 WFOS–Classical, big band	790 WNIS–News, talk, information
89.5 WHRV–Jazz, folk, public radio	850 WTAR–Talk, information
90.3 WHRO–Classical music	1010 WPMH–Christian talk radio
91.1 WNSB–New adult contemporary	1050 WFOG–Music for Your Life
91.5 WYCS–Religious music	1230 WJOI–Easy listening
92.1 WSW–Urban adult music	1240 WCNC–Adult standards
92.9 WWSO–Oldies	1250 WLQM–Urban gospel
93.7 WKOC–Adult album alternative	1260 WZVO–Nostalgia
94.1 WXEZ–Gospel/Christian	1270 WTJZ–Urban gospel
94.5 WWOC–Country	1310 WGH–Talk, live sports
94.9 WPTE–Modern music	1350 WGPL–Gospel
95.3 WOBR–Classical rock	1400 WPCE–Gospel programming
95.7 WVKL–R&B	1450 WBVA–"The Buzz" Hot Talk, sports
96.1 WROX–Alternative rock music	1490 WBYM–Classic country hits
96.5 WKLR–Classic hits	1550 WVAB–CNN All-News
96.7 WKIX–Country	1600 WCPK–Gospel
97.3 WGH–Modern country	1650 WHKT–Radio Disney, live sports
98.1 WOBX–Hot contemporary	
98.7 WNOR–Contemporary rock	
99.3 WQDK–Contemporary country	
99.7 WYFI–Christian music	
100.5 WCMS–Contemporary country	
101.3 WWDE–Adult contemporary	
101.7 WLQM–Real country, NASCAR	
102.5 WERX–Oldies	
102.9 WOWI–Urban contemporary	
103.3 WESR–Adult contemporary	
104.1 WCXL–Adult contemporary	
104.5 WNVZ–Contemporary hit radio	
105.3 WSVY–Urban adult music	
105.7 WRSF–New country	
106.9 WAFX–Classic rock	
107.5 WKRE–Oldies, adult contemporary	
107.7 WJCD–Smooth jazz, easy listening	

many he can receive." Several thousand radio stations (AM stations as well as FM stations) provide a lot of choices, and there appears to be relatively little switching!

In addition to program format and station loyalty, another means of market segmentation through radio is by its use during particular times of the day or even days of the week. Unlike most television viewers, radio listeners can be involved in another activity while listening to the radio and so direct marketers can reach them in an automobile, on arising, or in front of a mirror while shaving. Of course, the listener's attention is not always undivided at these times, and the real challenge to the direct marketer is to deliver a direct response instruction that the listener will recall later.

Rate Structure

A major boost for radio in direct response advertising is its relatively low cost. Whereas the economics of television dictate a maximum commercial length of 2 minutes, commercial messages on the radio can be melded with disc jockey chatter. Entire 15-minute information radio programs have been built around the content of a magazine, such as *Kiplinger,* for which subscriptions are being simultaneously solicited. The same format has also been applied to advice for household repairs at the same time as orders are solicited for a *Home Handyman's Guide.*

Some radio stations accept per inquiry (PI) arrangements under which the station runs commercial messages, at its own discretion, in return for remuneration from a direct response advertiser for each sale or inquiry produced in this manner.

Advantages and Disadvantages

Radio is the most flexible of all response media in that it requires relatively little in the way of preparation . . . and it can be scheduled or the copy can be changed right up to the time the message is aired. In contrast with the cost of direct mail or other print media and the high preparatory cost of television video, radio has minimal production costs. In fact, the direct response advertiser accrues virtually no production cost if the message can be typed for reading by a local station announcer. Because the various program formats of radio are conducive to testing, the direct response advertiser can readily test alternative copy and formats at relatively low cost.

A major disadvantage of radio, like that of television, is absence of a response device that can be referenced at some later time. Radio, too, lacks the visual impact afforded by direct mail and the other print media as well as by television.

INTERACTIVE ELECTRONIC MEDIA

The interactive media of direct marketing encompass the electronic capabilities of the telephone (both outbound *and* inbound), and the computer (for accessing the Internet and the World Wide Web) as well as the emerging technology of interactive television (for viewing and then responding through a "black box" integrated with a cable system). Under certain conditions direct marketing also embraces the interaction of a salesperson, occurring when direct response advertising results in a salesperson's visit to a buyer's location; or, it can entail a buyer's visit to a retail location as a result of a direct response offer in any medium.

Telemarketing

The telephone occupies a dual position in direct marketing.[5] Like print or broadcast media, it is outbound, a conduit for direct response advertising. It also is inbound, as an alternative to mail, fax, or Web site for the response itself. Thus, **telemarketing,** the use of the telephone in direct marketing, can also be inbound or outbound. The telephone is an interactive medium, which provides the flexibility and immediate response of a personal conversation. It can be especially effective when used in concert with other direct response media, such as direct mail or a Web site.

Experienced telemarketers report that, used correctly and often in tandem with other media, the telephone can generate three to seven times the response achieved by mail alone. The cost of a telemarketing call averages $4.00 and the average cost of a direct mailing piece is $1.00; this difference means that to be cost effective a telemarketing call must be at least four times as effective as a mailing piece.

When calculating telemarketing costs, the direct marketer needs to consider not only the line and hardware, but also the program design, creative development, as well as labor costs. The latter should include supervisory as well as clerical support costs. If the telephone is used as an alternative to a personal visit by a salesperson, as is often the case, the telephone can be tremendously more efficient.

Telemarketing has been woven into the planning of most direct marketers. To those who know how to use them, the interactive features of the telephone are, in many cases, replacing the face-to-face contact of a salesperson's visit to a prospect or a buyer's visit to a retail location. The telephone obviates the need for travel and makes it possible to talk *with* and not just *to* customers and prospects.

Personal Computers

The future is *now* insofar as personal computer applications for direct response advertising are concerned.[6] The World Wide Web offers consumers access to advertisers such as Lands' End, Nordstrom's, Amazon.com, Ford, and American Express. Consumers can also make travel bookings and investment transactions as well as purchase automobiles, computers, and a host of other consumer products.

Technology has advanced rapidly to allow sophisticated graphic presentations, browsing, and downloading of information. Once confined to e-mail, special-interest forums, and service offers, the Internet now emphasizes electronic shopping.

But, even though the advertising pages of the Internet are information laden, it is still up to prospects to seek them out and then to self-identify as market segments. It is thus the prospect that must be *pro-active,* as well as technically inclined, in the search for benefits to fulfill needs—rather than the advertiser, whose objective it is to *sell something through benefit-oriented offers targeted to database-qualified prospects*. Some have described the Internet as a classified directory badly in need of a Dewey Decimal System!

TELEVISION/TELEPHONE HOOKUPS

The history of interactive television/telephone hookups has been spotty, as experiment after experiment has been boldly launched and quietly withdrawn. Interactive technology, fiber-optic transmission, and wireless are now advancing rapidly. Cable TV home shopping, under these conditions, could one day become a video extension of direct mail, utilizing the telephone or a cable network for response. Still to come, of course, is customer acceptance of the process.

Direct marketers' interest in the new electronic media is in its ability to allow for shopping, responding, and ordering. Their watchword is *interactivity*. They are looking forward to letting customers respond instantly through personal computers and television sets just as they are already doing with telephones.

Even as the use of telephones and personal computers is burgeoning as interactive electronic media for direct marketers, another form of interactive telecommunications is emerging that combines the capabilities of television, cable, telephone, and computer networks. Under the broad heading of "interactive television" the system culminates in a home installation that looks like a standard television set merged with a standard telephone and connected with a black box microprocessor. With the addition of a small television camera and microphone, the video-audio receiving unit can become a sending unit as well. If the user wants hard copy, the system provides that along with display on the video screen.

Broadcasting thus becomes "narrow casting" and the ultimate individual selectivity sought by direct marketers is at hand. In *The Third Wave,* a good many years ago, Alvin Toffler prophetically wrote, "Thus begins a truly new era—the age of the de-massified media. A new info-sphere is emerging alongside the new techno-sphere . . . instead of masses of people all receiving the same messages, smaller de-massified groups receive and send large amounts of their imagery to one another."[7]

Actually, the first interactive "videotext" system, called Prestel, was started in England in 1979. Beginning service with about 1,500 viewers, Prestel had about 12,000 viewers by 1982, heavily weighted to business users. Products and information provided by Prestel included transportation timetables, shopping guides, classified ads, news, touring guides, financial data, and an encyclopedia. The amount of data on the screen at one time (that is, per frame) was a maximum of 960 characters, equivalent to about two or three paragraphs of newsprint. Simple graphics were reproduced using small color blocks. Still photos or moving pictures were not yet in use.[8]

A system, similar to Prestel, but with better resolution and graphics, was developed originally in France and called Teletel. In early 1982, about 2,500 French households in the Velizy suburb of Paris were participating in an imaginative experiment of the Teletel system under the auspices of the French government. Direct marketers in the experiment included three giant catalog firms: Les Trois Suisses, La Redoute, and Camif. Teletel users could book railway tickets, consult bank accounts, dispatch and receive written messages, play video games, and consult classified advertising. They could also send orders to mail-order firms or to local shopkeepers. The French government believed, too, that it could save money by providing a terminal permitting citizens to access telephone numbers nationwide, and it ultimately did this, thus saving the cost of the printed telephone directory.

Canada developed its own high-resolution system called Telidon, while in the United States Knight-Ridder completed—and then disbanded—market trials in Coral Gables, Florida, using a system called Viewtron. AT&T undertook a joint venture with CBS for a failed experiment in New Jersey; a videotext system called Bildschirmtext that was developed in Germany.

In June 1979, Digital Broadcasting Telecomputing Corporation of America, McLean, Virginia, unveiled The Source, which later became a subsidiary of a direct marketer,

Reader's Digest. The Source was the first information and service network to be offered to personal computer owners in the United States. Users could make airline reservations, buy and sell real estate, get instant news, sports, and weather reports from UPI or access the *New York Times* Information Bank. An interactive system, The Source provided information by either video display screen or hard copy printed on a silver-coated paper.

The Source also allowed for the sending of electronic mail. Later, electronic computer originated mail (E-COM) was instituted by the Postal Service, but for a short time only.

The application of videodiscs (today's laser discs) to direct marketing was pioneered by Sears Roebuck & Company with its 236-page Summer 1981 catalog. This basic experiment was conducted in nine stores and 1,000 households. Recipients of a videodisc catalog required a videodisc player to display it.

SALESPEOPLE

Our discussion of interactive media concludes with reference to the place of personal selling in direct marketing. Salespeople work, in an electronic sense, in telemarketing. They also conduct face-to-face contact if a direct response advertising offer brings a buyer into a retail location to be served by a salesperson. Or, conversely, an inquiry resulting from a direct response advertisement could cause a salesperson to call on the buyer. In each instance, direct marketing has brought in the interactive salesperson in closing the sale . . . often aided and abetted by electronic intervention. There are other opportunities for salespeople, such as at displays, exhibits, or fairs. In any event, the salesperson becomes an important adjunct of the direct marketing process, often used as an interactive medium as the occasion warrants.

Summary

Direct response advertising in broadcast media involves electronic transmission through television or radio and utilization of these media is increasing as direct marketers learn how to use them. Both these media are virtually universal in their reach. But, specific programming of individual television channels or radio stations makes these media capable of market segmentation based on demographics of their viewers/listeners. The cost of television without such segmentation is typically too high for direct response advertisers. Implementation in broadcast television or radio involves specific programming, timing, and positioning as well as geographic location of market segments.

Direct marketers use television to sell directly, to get inquiries, and to give support to other media. Expanded use of home shopping networks and lengthy infomercials has enhanced the viability of television as a selling, as well as an advertising medium.

Telephones have become important not only as direct response advertising (outbound calls) but also as a response device (inbound calls). And, the advent of the Internet has presented direct marketers with a major new interactive medium.

The emerging technology of interactive television, coupled with telephone or cable systems to provide two-way communication, is of special interest to direct marketers. Another interactive medium, not always electronic, is the salesperson. Not only is personal selling many times involved on the telephone or at a Web site, but salespeople often respond to inquiries or serve customers visiting a retail location as a result of direct response advertising in any medium.

Key Terms

- broadcast, 157
- cost per response (CPR), 159
- cost per viewer (CPV), 159
- gross rating points (GRP), 160
- reach, 160
- frequency, 160
- infomercials, 161
- telemarketing, 166

Review Questions

1. Broadcast media (television and radio) are the most universal of all media, but what limits their effectiveness for direct response advertising?
2. Suggest ways to segment markets through broadcast media: television and radio.
3. How does the cost of television relate to its availability?
4. Discuss "recall" as a measurement tool used by general television advertisers and relate this to "response" as a measurement tool used by direct marketers.
5. In what ways do direct marketers use television as a medium?
6. What is an *infomercial* on television? How do these differ from the programming of home shopping channels?
7. What are the advantages and disadvantages of utilizing radio for direct response advertising?
8. What are the interactive electronic media?
9. Distinguish between inbound and outbound telemarketing and describe both inbound and outbound uses of the telephone.
10. Under what circumstances is the telephone more cost efficient than direct mail?
11. Is it correct to view the Internet as a medium? Give reasons for your opinion.
12. Explain the technology of interactive television. What are implications of this emerging medium for direct marketers?
13. Discuss Alvin Toffler's 1981 prediction that broadcasting would become "narrow casting."
14. Discuss the historical emergence of videotext, notably in Britain, France, and Canada, prior to innovation in the United States.
15. Is it correct to view salespeople as a medium? Give reasons for your opinion.

Exercise

Have you ever wanted to be a "couch potato" – even for a little while? Go ahead. Sit down this evening or weekend and watch television for a couple of hours. While you're watching, write down all of the television commercials you view. How many of them are direct response ads? What makes each advertisement a direct response ad? For those ads that are not, identify how you could convert three into direct response ads that are measurable and accountable.

CASE: GEICO DIRECT

OVERVIEW

This case explains the various types of message appeals available to marketers. It also explores the benefits associated with innovative media buys for direct response television (DRTV) campaigns. This case enables the student to appreciate the risk and value associated with a unique positioning strategy implemented by a direct marketer.

What you are about to read is a success story about a well-known direct response television (DRTV) campaign that uses humorous ad appeals and innovative media buys to sell a commodity—automobile insurance. The DRTV campaign is the brainchild of the creative minds at The Martin Agency, located in Richmond, Virginia. This campaign and case study are a testament to the great things that can occur when a client and an agency have a collaborative relationship. It also affirms the fact that being different and trying new things with an established medium can really pay off. Are you ready to read, learn, and think "out-of-the-box"? If so, we'd like to introduce you to the client, GEICO Direct.

CASE

GEICO (which stands for Government Employees Insurance Company) was founded in 1936. Today the GEICO companies insure over 7 million drivers and have assets over $11 billion. GEICO is ranked the fifth largest in the auto insurance market behind State Farm, Allstate, Progressive, and Farmers. It is one of the fastest growing auto insurers and has over 5 million policyholders.

GEICO's success has been largely attributed to its widespread television and radio direct response advertising campaigns. However, before we present the direct response television campaign, some background information about television advertising and advertising appeals in general is warranted.

Advertising on television presents strengths and weaknesses. As a marketing medium, it is often seen as an intrusion, an unwanted interruption. The ability of advertisements to attract attention and engage the viewer's senses is unique.

Creating and producing direct response ads for television is a laborious and expensive process, however. The objective of DRTV commercials is to break through the high degree of clutter associated with television and evoke action from the audience. Of course, before any DRTV ad can ever hope to generate a response, it must grab the viewer's attention and then maintain it. This is no small task since most people do not view television ads while sitting idle without distraction. In an attempt to obtain the viewer's attention and subsequent action, direct marketers such as GEICO may use any number of different advertising appeals in developing the message strategy. There are two broad categories of message appeals—rational appeals and emotional appeals.

Rational appeals present facts or information to the consumer in a logical manner. These appeals focus on the consumer's practical need for the product or service. Rational appeals aim at the logical buying motives of a consumer. While rational appeals can be very effective, they can also be viewed as boring or dull. In contrast, emotional appeals are seen as more exciting and are more effective in attracting the attention of most consumers. Emotional appeals focus on the wants or desires of consumers as opposed to their basic needs. Emotional appeals target consumer feelings or social and psychological needs. Humorous messages are one form of emotional appeal. Humorous ads have strong message permanence (the amount of time the ad remains in the consumer's memory). Humor is most effectively used with the media formats of television and radio. When used appropriately (tastefully) and in the right circumstances, humor has been found to be an extremely effective advertising technique.

Indeed, this is the case with GEICO Direct and their "A 15-minute call could save you 15% or more on car insurance" DRTV advertising campaign.

The GEICO "15-minute call" campaign took the idea of buying automobile insurance (which doesn't seem very exciting and the insurance product itself is probably considered an unsought good by most consumers) and turned it into a personalized, quick process with a worry-free consequence. The Martin Agency's work with this campaign was among the more innovative direct marketing campaigns of the 1990s. At the time, 60-second and 120-second spots were the standard TV media buys in direct marketing. Instead, GEICO ran back-to-back 15-second spots in a 30-second media buy. This media strategy of pairing two 15-second DRTV spots did a number of smart things for GEICO, including the following:

- First, it allowed smaller, customized messages to be tailored to individual market needs, creating a cafeteria menu of creative options. For example, a new market might get a spot with a message about how many new drivers sign up with GEICO every day paired with a spot focusing on price. In Washington, D.C., GEICO's hometown, a different pair of service and savings messages was teamed to address specific needs in that market. Thus, segmented messages were relatively easy to execute with this new media format.
- Second, it provided two opportunities for the toll-free telephone number to appear in the 30-second media buy. This longer exposure allowed the number to make a better impression, while still leaving room for the creative work to stress the brand. Most importantly, it contributed to the ability of each DRTV spot to generate a consumer response—the ultimate goal of a DRTV campaign.
- Third, it permitted years of creative inventory to be mixed and matched for years to

come, with less creative wear-out. This strategy offered significant savings for GEICO in the long term.
- Fourth, it enabled the message to break through. Different was good, especially when battling against giants who had worked for years to build their brands. Most insurance companies' ads were similar, many incorporating "scare tactics" in their messages. However, there was no confusing a GEICO ad with another insurance company's. GEICO's unique positioning strategy effectively generated consumer awareness and placed GEICO in the minds of millions of consumers as an exciting and easy-to-deal-with insurance company.
- Fifth, the media strategy proved you should never underestimate the value of a strong call to action. And never change it if it's working. The modular media and messaging needed glue to hold it all together and keep the telephones ringing. The glue for this campaign was a strong call to action that remained constant in every spot—"A 15-minute call could save you 15% or more on car insurance."

GEICO does not have insurance agents so the DRTV spots themselves needed to have personality. They were in fact the human voice for the company until the call was made and a real voice could answer. The fact that the GEICO marketing group understood this and was brave enough to be different from their competitors and embrace a humorous tone is another reason this brand made its mark so effectively. Consumers were pleasantly surprised that an insurance company could make them smile. Humor can be a fine line to walk and consumers' perceptions of humor can vary. The humor in GEICO ads pokes fun or makes light of the human condition but does not belittle the serious nature of the product. The campaign includes everything from snappy one-liners to buttons at the end and over-the-top

FIGURE 7-5   GEICO "Coffee Cups" TV Spot

visual exaggeration. An example of a GEICO advertisement is provided in Figure 7-5.

In conclusion, GEICO now owns its look, tone, and feel. No other name in the business can be substituted for what GEICO does. That has been the goal for the GEICO marketing group from the very first batch of creative work that The Martin Agency produced to the present. Indeed, the GEICO story is an impressive one—and one that most direct response advertisers would like to emulate. So, the next time you are faced with the task of creating a DRTV campaign—think about doing something different. Think about GEICO.

Source: This case is based on information provided by The Martin Agency, Richmond, Virginia. ∎

Case Discussion Questions

1. GEICO's marketing team took great risk in agreeing to a new approach to direct response advertising. How did their approach set them apart from other insurance companies?
2. With its heavy emphasis on humor GEICO has managed to gain the attention of many prospective customers. Was this risky? Why or why not? Could GEICO have achieved the same success without the use of humor?
3. How did GEICO differ from the norm of television advertising and was it effective?
4. Has the use of emotional appeals been successful for GEICO? In your opinion, would the use of rational appeals be as successful based on what you know about this company and the industry? Why?
5. In your opinion, what could GEICO do to maintain such a spectacular marketing performance in the future?

Notes

1. *Statistical Fact Book 2002* (New York: Direct Marketing Association, Inc., 2002), 118.
2. Ibid.
3. *Statistical Fact Book 2002* (New York: Direct Marketing Association, Inc., 2002), 116.
4. Ibid., 114.
5. Much more detail on this subject appears in Chapter 8. This section is included here so as to point out the telephone as an interactive electronic medium.
6. More on the subject of the Internet as a medium appears in Chapter 9. This section is included here so as to point out the Internet as an electronic medium.
7. Alvin Toffler, *The Third Wave* (New York: William Morrow & Co., Bantam Book ed., 1981), 165.
8. Patricia K. McCarthy, "Interactive Television: A Direct Marketing Tool," *Direct Marketing* (February 1980): 30ff.

CHAPTER
8 | TELEMARKETING

The telephone occupies a dual position in direct marketing. Like print or broadcast media, it is a conduit for direct response advertising, and like mail or the Internet, it can carry the response itself. Thus, telephone marketing, or telemarketing, is both a marketing medium *and* a response mechanism. **Telemarketing** has been defined as a medium that uses sophisticated telecommunications and information systems combined with personal selling and servicing skills to help companies keep in close contact with present and potential customers, increase sales, and enhance business productivity.[1]

The objective of telemarketing is to reach customers in a personalized interaction that meets customer needs and improves cost effectiveness for the organization. Its scope is limited only by the imagination of the direct marketer, who can use it both for-profit and non-profit organizations as well as for individuals (such as political candidates), alone or with other marketing media, and targeted to both businesses (B-2-B) and final consumers (B-2-C).

THE TELEPHONE AS A MARKETING MEDIUM

The application of the telephone to direct marketing efforts is a most powerful combination. No other direct marketing medium can match its effectiveness. Telemarketing is actually a form of personal selling, since it occurs on a person-to-person basis but without the face-to-face aspect. Telephone marketing is projected as the leader of the direct marketing labor force in 2003 by employing 6.4 million workers or 29 percent of all direct marketing employees.[2] Outbound telephone marketing expenditures represents the largest category of direct marketing media spending–by a large margin. Telephone ad expenditures are expected to grow to $79.7 billion in 2003, which represents 39 percent of all direct marketing expenditures.[3] In addition, telephone marketing represents the largest category of direct marketing sales for both business and final consumers. It accounted for $764.9 billion in 2003.[4] The DMA expects consumer telephone marketing to account for $315.3 billion in 2003 projected sales and expects it to grow by 8.0 percent per year to reach $435.4 billion in 2007.[5]

However, the DMA made all of these predictions prior to the proposed National Do Not Call Registry became effective on October 1, 2003. The Federal Communication Commission and the Federal Trade Commission have been charged with enforcing this new legislation. These new federal regulations stand to drastically restrict the number of consumers direct marketers will be legally able to call. It will also reduce the number of people employed in this sector of the direct marketing industry. The new FCC/FTC Do Not Call Registry will be discussed in greater detail later in this chapter. For now, keep in mind that as the FTC enforces these new regulations, the future of some telephone marketing activities will be greatly affected. Let's take a closer look at the two basic ways direct marketers use the telephone.

Inbound Versus Outbound Calls

Telemarketing applications may be categorized as **inbound calls,** where customers are calling to place an order, to request more information, or for customer service, and **outbound calls,** where firms call to make a sale or to offer information hoping for a later sale. Let's discuss each application of telemarketing in greater detail.

Inbound Calls

Inbound calls are also referred to as **reactive telemarketing** in that the initiator of the marketing communications is the customer. The customer places that call at his or her convenience to obtain information or to place an order, often using a toll-free number provided by the organization. The Federal Communications Commission has designated not only 800 numbers as *toll-free* but also the area codes 888, 877, and 866.

Customers are increasingly using the telephone to place orders today. Catalog direct marketers report an increasing percentage of orders reaching them by phone, especially during holiday seasons. The recent surge of the World Wide Web and Internet marketing strategies has also increased the number of inbound calls to marketers. Consumers have used the Internet to search for product or service information, and then have turned to the telephone to place orders for products and services that were presented in a company's Web site.

Toll-free telephone service has itself been a tremendous incentive to the use of inbound telephone calls to respond to offers or transact an order. The marketer's direct response advertising in other media must provide incentives as well by appealing to the emotions, pointing out the advantages of personal service, or highlighting the convenience of having a telephone order-taker on-hand 24 hours a day to answer questions and ensure faster deliveries or services.

The applications of inbound telemarketing generally include the following:

- Ordering or inquiring
- Clarifying or requesting assistance
- Responding immediately to an advertisement
- Expediting processing
- Locating a dealer or a product servicing location
- Making reservations for travel accommodations, hotel rooms, conferences
- Obtaining financial data, stock prices, yields, etc.
- Making pledges or contributions
- Obtaining warranty information

Outbound Calls

Outbound calls are also referred to as **proactive telemarketing** because the company is the initiator of the marketing communications. Outbound calls are generally longer in duration and require more experienced higher-paid personnel.

Savvy direct marketers employ **Wide Area Telephone Service (WATS)** for economical long-distance calling, since a WATS line can handle a large volume of calls for a set fee. In essence, the company receives a volume discount on its telephone service. The large outbound telemarketers are now using T1 service. A **T1** is a giant pipeline or conduit through which a user may send multiple voice, data, or even video signals. It supports simultaneous voice/Internet connectivity, enabling telephone sales reps, or telereps, to speak to customers while also participating in their Internet session. Instead of simply carrying one voice conversation at a time, a T1 can carry almost 100 conversations or data connections simultaneously.

Although well-prepared scripts and well-structured offers can make telephone promotion highly effective, the medium is usually most efficient if calls are directed to persons who have been pre-qualified in some way. The reason is that the cost of an individual telephone call can be as much as four times the cost of an individual direct-mail letter and thus it must be four times as productive to justify the expense of the call. Therefore, when telemarketers properly segment the market (according to a wide variety of segmentation variables) and pre-qualify prospects the length of the call may be reduced and the number of positive consumer responses may be increased.

Pre-qualified outbound calls might include response to an inquiry, a new product offer to an existing customer, or generation of responses/transactions from a carefully selected list. **"Cold calls"** (which are calls made when there is no existing relationship with, or recognition of, the direct marketer) must be carefully structured in content since, by their very nature, they usually interrupt some other activity of the person being called and can create a negative response.

Direct marketers use the telephone for a great variety of outbound call applications, including the following:

- Generating new sales, including reorders and new product introductions
- Generating leads and qualifying inquiries for personal sales follow-up
- Serving present accounts
- Reactivating old customers
- Upgrading and increasing incoming orders
- Validating the legitimacy of orders before shipping
- Responding to customer service needs, including customer complaints
- Surveying customers, members, donors, voters
- Substituting for a personal sales call
- Expressing thanks to a customer, donor, or voter
- Credit screening and checking as well as collection
- Performing research and gathering or disseminating information

An example of one company experiencing great success with outbound telemarketing is Merrimack, New Hampshire-based computer cataloger "PC Connection". It increased their outbound sales staff by 75 percent in 1999 and in 2000 their first-quarter outbound sales revenue increased 45 percent to $326.1 million. Moreover, their earnings soared 61 percent to $7.1 million and the average order size increased from $626 to $926 in a one-year period.[6] Needless to say, outbound calls have the ability to generate great profit when executed properly.

Advantages and Disadvantages of Telemarketing

Some of the specific advantages of using the telephone as a marketing medium include

- It provides *two-way communication,* and provides *immediate feedback.* This quick feedback, often in response to a test campaign, can be of great assistance to the direct marketer in making any needed changes before the entire marketing campaign is executed.
- It is a *very flexible medium.* Although the telerep may use a prepared script, this doesn't limit the number of changes you can make to that script as needed. You may also change the message for each caller.
- It is a *most productive medium.* The telephone is actually more productive than traditional personal selling when you consider the sheer number of sales calls that a rep can make by phone on a daily or weekly basis. According to Bob Stone, a member in the Direct Marketing Hall of Fame, a traditional field salesperson can make 5 or 6 sales calls per day, which would compute to 25 to 30 sales calls per week; whereas, a telemarketer can make 25 to 30 sales calls per day, which translates into 125 to 150 sales calls per week.[7] Therefore, the telephone as a marketing medium is considered to be five times more productive in

Approximate Inbound Cost per Call	
Category	Range of Cost
Business	$2.50 to $7.00
Consumer	$1.50 to $3.00

Approximate Outbound Cost per Decision-Maker Contact	
Category	Range of Cost
Business	$6.00 to $16.00
Consumer	$1.15 to $4.00

FIGURE 8-1   Average Cost per Call

Source: Bob Stone and John Wyman, *Successful Telemarketing*, 2nd ed. (Lincolnwood, IL: NTC Business Books, 1992), 152.

reaching prospects or customers than traditional personal selling. For example, during the time a field salesperson wines and dines a client over a three-hour lunch, a telemarketing representative can contact about 10 customers—and the company won't have to pay for an expensive meal.

- Telemarketing is a ***cost-effective medium.*** Although the exact costs vary depending upon the type of call being placed, the average cost per call is far lower for telephone selling than for traditional personal selling. See Figure 8-1 for an overview of the average costs per call.

Some of the distinct disadvantages of telemarketing include

- It is by far the most ***intrusive marketing medium*** used by direct marketers. Telemarketing has a poor image among people who dislike the intrusion of marketers' outbound calling.
- Telemarketing ***lacks visual enhancement.*** It is not a visual medium and thus its power is often related to its being integrated with other media.
- Telemarketing ***does not provide a permanent tangible response device.*** Once again, it must be coupled with other media in order to provide a physical form for the customer to sign or a brochure to keep on hand to review at a later time.
- Its effectiveness depends on ***retaining highly trained telephone operators.*** It can be difficult to hire, train, and keep telephone operators because the operators must be able to handle intense personal interaction and frequent rejection.

Most direct marketers have concluded that although telemarketing has its share of disadvantages, it is a highly effective medium. Here's a brief overview of the history of how the telephone became the largest direct marketing medium in the United States.

History

In 1957, the first outbound telephone service agencies, Corporate Communications, Inc., (CCI) and Dial America Marketing, were born. These companies were the first of their kind to offer outbound telemarketing services to magazine publishers to increase subscriptions. In 1968, AT&T introduced toll-free service, promoted the use of inbound telephone marketing, and basically introduced the concept of *non*–face-to-face customer service. During the 1970s, outbound telephone marketing was promoted by AT&T to businesses as a solution to offset the rising cost of field sales calls.

It is estimated that more than 17 million toll-free 800-number calls are made every day.[8] Some of the largest teleservice outsourcing firms (e.g., airlines and credit card companies) can handle in excess of 100,000 calls per hour. A survey conducted by Deloitte and Touche (D&T) found that the toll-free call has become a standard for customer acquisition and customer service. It was used by 80 percent of business-to-consumer marketers, 66 percent of business-to-business marketers, and 50 percent of non-profit organizations surveyed.[9]

In 1980, the 900 number or "pay-per-call" was introduced. Inaugurated by AT&T as a polling device during the 1980 Carter/Reagan presidential debates, pay-per-call programs were developed as revenue businesses, largely by entertainment companies.[10] For example, years ago Dick Clark's "30 years of Rock 'n Roll" attracted 1.8 million 900-number calls in a single day as people voted for their favorite songs.[11]

Throughout the 1980s most large corporations established formal inbound telemarketing programs offering their customers the ability to do business with them in a variety of new ways. Today, telemarketing is utilized by virtually every industry in the United States. The dramatic increase in the use of the telephone for marketing purposes is partially due to the driving force of technology. New sophistication in call handling technologies is partly behind the industry's explosion. Over the past two decades there have been tremendous changes in telephone technology. Let's look at some of the technological breakthroughs in the telecommunications industry.

Telemarketing Technology

Major telecommunications technologies have been developed to support the call handling industry made possible by 800 and 900 numbers. Telecommunications network suppliers including MCI, AT&T, Sprint Telemedia, and Telesphere now support two critical systems that permit more efficient and effective call handling. These are Dialed Number Identification System (DNIS) and Automated Numbering Identification (ANI).

Dialed Number Identification System (DNIS)

The Dialed Number Identification System (DNIS) allows any organization that has multiple 800 or 900 numbers to differentiate incoming calls based on the number dialed by the caller. Marketers can also track media performance by placing different 800 or 900 numbers in ads run in different media and then analyzing the DNIS records to trace which callers responded to which ads. This accountability allows marketing managers to better allocate their media resources.

Automated Numbering Identification (ANI)

Automated Numbering Identification (ANI) identifies the telephone number of the person calling. Marketers can match the phone number against a name and address database, and the caller's name, address, and account history will be displayed on the screen of the telephone operator receiving the call. This enables the company to shorten the length of each call by eliminating repetitive information gathering. Marketers can also use ANI to place callbacks on abandoned calls and to give priority handling to preferred customers.

Other Technologies for Incoming Calls

Today there are three basic types of voice technology to handle incoming calls. These have either replaced or complemented live telephone operators in reducing costs and improving customer service. The three methods are:

1. *Audiotex*—plays a prerecorded message on request. Passive audiotext simply plays the message. Active audiotext lets callers respond to a recorded menu, using the telephone's touchtone keypad to select recorded messages of their choice.
2. *Voice Messaging*—stores and retrieves voice mail from mailboxes.
3. *Interactive Voice Response (IVR)*—enables callers to access and update a database using their touchtone keypads.

Technologies for Outbound Calls

Predictive dialers are becoming the standard in business-to-consumer telemarketing. **Predictive dialers** are advanced hardware systems that use machines to dial and connect the call only when the computer detects a live human voice on the other end of the line. These devices increase the amount of time that telephone sales representatives spend talking with live prospects (as opposed to fruitlessly calling answering machines or untended phones) from 20 minutes per hour to nearly 50 minutes.[12] The way predictive dialers work is simple. Using a specified database, the predictive dialer automatically enters phone numbers on the extra phone lines. When someone picks up the phone, the server automatically routes the call to an unoccupied telerep. A well-designed system is staffed and timed so that the gap between the prospect's hello and a friendly response from the agent is minimal, as is the rate of abandoned calls.

Short messaging service (SMS) is a service that provides alerts by delivering a text message to cellular telephones of users who have signed up for the service. The retailer logs on to a secure Web site and enters a message, specifying the band of users he or she wishes to reach. Users are segmented by gender and age—information they provided when they first subscribed to the service. However, the challenge is the large universe of pre-paid cellular telephone users about whom marketers know very little. In conclusion, one of the greatest challenges in communication technology is just to keep up with the rate of change. Regardless of the type of communication technology used, all direct marketers must carefully create telemarketing programs if they want to use this medium to interact with their consumers. Let's examine what is involved in planning a telemarketing program.

PLANNING A TELEMARKETING PROGRAM

To be successful in telemarketing, telephone operators must convey a trustworthy, reliable telephone image to the customer. Companies must train their telephone operators to develop these telephone skills and provide them with well-conceived scripts.

Preparing the Telephone Scripts

A **telephone script** is a call guide to assist the telephone operator in communicating effectively with the prospect or customer. Most do not have to be read word for word; in fact, the most effective scripts are more like a detailed outline that provides structure to the conversation. Each *outbound* telemarketing call aims to deliver a sales presentation to the potential customer or client. The purpose of each *inbound* call is to deliver information to the customer and/or receive the customer's order information. Thus, different types of telephone scripts are needed for different types of telemarketing calls. In either case, developing scripts offers the dual challenge of determining the right words to gain a favorable customer response or impression and, at the same time, minimizing the length and the cost of a call.

Writing a telephone script is both an art and a science. One valuable asset of a telemarketing script is the *flexibility* it provides allowing the telemarketer to change or experiment. While most marketing media call for copy to be finalized by a certain date, telemarketing scripts can be revised after a few or a few dozen calls.

Many copywriters have developed strategies for successful script writing. Jim Kobs has offered the following seven principles for successful telephone script writing:[13]

1. ***Know the target audience.*** You must know who you are trying to reach and for what purpose.
2. ***Get off on the right foot or you might as well get off the phone.*** Everyone has heard of the old cliché "the first impression is a lasting one" or "you never get a second chance to make a first impression." However worn out these phrases may be, they are true, especially when it comes to telemarketing scripts.
3. ***Develop the basic copy story in a natural style.*** In other words, write the telemarketing script for the ear, not the eye. Select the tone and words of the message to reflect how a person would speak, not write. Most people speak in a more friendly, low-key, and less professional manner than they write. They don't use long sentences; in fact, they often use sentence fragments. A good script must include good dialog for a telephone call.
4. ***Encourage dialog.*** A good script should talk *with* someone, not *at* them. The script should have areas where natural pauses would take place, giving the prospect or customer a chance to respond.
5. ***Anticipate questions and objections.*** *Objections* are reasons why the customer or prospect thinks he or she cannot complete the action that your offer is requesting. Another familiar saying is appropriate here: "The best defense is a strong offense." So, anticipate those various objections and be prepared with answers that will capitalize on those objections.
6. ***Close, close, close.*** The chief objective of the personal selling process is to close the sale and create a customer. This principle applies to telephone selling as well. Though you can use many tactics to close a sale, the key thing to remember is that it often takes a minimum of three attempts, so you often have to help the customer agree to purchase a product or place an order.
7. ***Don't wear out your welcome.*** This is especially true of outbound calling, since the operator might be calling a customer at a less than convenient moment.

In creating persuasive telephone scripts, Aldyn McKean, telephone consultant, has suggested that a good script is composed of at least the following 11 parts:[14]

1. ***Opening:*** Greet the person being called; identify caller.
2. ***Empathy/involvement stage:*** Establish rapport, emphasize common concerns, and create involvement.
3. ***Product information:*** Describe the product/service and its benefits.
4. ***Offer:*** Explain and clarify terms.

5. *Close:*　Request action(s).
6. *Reconfirmation:*　Repeat the terms agreed to.
7. *Probe:*　Inject a query designed to prompt negative or undecided prospects into asking questions or offering objections.
8. *Answers to questions:*　These answers should lead back to the close.
9. *Responses to objections:*　Commonly raised objections should have pre-scripted responses, also leading back to the close.
10. *Second effort:*　An additional short presentation should be made whenever a prospect is undecided or is negative without offering specific objections.
11. *Farewell:*　No matter what, the telephone call should always end on a reassuring, friendly, and polite note.

Training Telephone Operators

Many people might think that the best way to develop an effective telephone operator is to take someone with field sales experience and transfer that sales knowledge to the telephone. However, in reality, this rarely works. One of the reasons field sales people often do not make good telephone operators is that they are accustomed to face-to-face interaction with their customers and dislike working behind a desk. These work qualities are the exact opposite of the requirements of a telemarketing representative.

When hiring a telephone operator, companies normally look for the following six qualities:[15]

1. *Experience*—primarily in a call center or customer service situation. Prior experience may aid the telerep in being persistent and able to handle rejection and continue on.
2. *Interpersonal skills*—an outgoing personality, good communication skills, articulate speech, and good voice quality—one that is clear and pleasant.
3. *Computer literacy*—including typing and word processing skills and being able to navigate through various computer menus and screens.
4. *Basic reliability*—since telephone operator turnover is so high, reliability and stability are important qualities. Employee turnover in call centers throughout the retail industry averages more than 30 percent and often exceeds 60 percent.[16]
5. *Problem-solving skills*—ability to deal with complaints, handle irate customers, and field difficult questions. Telephone reps need the ability to remain calm and polite under fire and to interpret company policies in order to provide customers with quick and accurate answers. They must be flexible and adapt to different clients and different situations.
6. *Good organizational skills*—including good time-management skills.

Finding and retaining good telephone operators is a constant challenge for telemarketers. In addition to high turnover rates, there has been a shrinking employment pool for this industry. A recent survey conducted in the teleservices industry found that compensation varied widely depending on such variables as industry sector, product prices, and the complexity of the sale. Although in one instance annual teleservice representative compensation of $75,996 was reported, the annual *median pay* for teleservice representatives was $24,744 for those employed in a service agency, and $33,456 for those employed in the company's own call center.[17] Most companies believe developing a mixture of base salary, commissions, and bonuses is most effective for retaining teleservice representatives.

Integrating with Other Media

Telemarketing is most effective in conjunction with other direct marketing media. Each medium supports the other and creates a synergistic effect while conveying the message in a different manner. For example, a printed advertisement has maximum visual impact, while the telephone is concentrated on the auditory senses. Let's discuss each complementary medium separately.

Television

Television would not be a direct response medium without the telephone. Most direct response advertisements on television provide a toll-free number for the customer or prospect to use in responding to the ad. Television can convey a message that appeals to both visual and auditory senses at the same time. Additionally, it is very powerful for testimonials and can aid in reducing the risk customers sometimes feel when making direct marketing purchases.

Direct Mail

Telemarketing and direct mail enjoy a close and versatile relationship. Most direct-mail packages allow the recipient to order the product or obtain additional information by calling a toll-free 800number. In addition, direct mail is an effective follow-up to outbound calls. For example, telemarketing operators can qualify a prospect to determine whether he or she is interested in receiving additional information about a product or service or interact with a customer who has an inquiry and is in need of more information.

Catalogs

The telephone provides customers with easy access, often 24 hours a day, 7 days a week, to most catalog direct marketers. Most catalogs present a toll-free number on every other page. Therefore, many catalog orders are placed via the telephone.

Print

Toll-free inbound calling, along with credit cards, have been partially responsible for the growth of direct response ads placed in newspapers and magazines. Direct marketers that use other direct response mechanisms are often used in conjunction with newspaper and magazine ads. Consumers can clip coupons, access Internet sites, and clip complete and return forms via direct mail.

Radio

Like the telephone, radio is an auditory medium. Telephone is primarily a response mechanism for radio ads since many of them provide a number that consumers may call to place an order, make a request, or obtain additional information.

Yellow Pages

Unlike other media, Yellow Page advertisements promote only the telephone as a response mechanism. According to Stone and Wyman, there are more than 6,400 Yellow Pages directories published each year in the United States. In addition, approximately $8.3 billion is spent in Yellow Pages advertising each year.[18] Most businesses place local numbers in their Yellow Pages ads, while many companies also include toll-free numbers in their ads to encourage inbound calls.

Internet

The Internet is the only medium that actually competes with the telephone as a marketing medium. Unlike the other media, the Internet offers both the speed and the convenience of the telephone. However, as a response mechanism, it is presently trailing behind the telephone primarily due to the following three reasons: (a) many customers are reluctant to submit credit card numbers over the Internet; (b) Internet navigation to locate desired products and services is often more time consuming than placing a telephone call; and (c) many customers still like to interact with a "live" voice. The Internet currently feeds the telephone as a response mechanism where customers may call the company to either place an order or obtain additional information that is not available on the company's Web site.

A great example of how to successfully integrate the telephone with other media is illustrated in the following case of Lens Express.

Lens Express, a Deerfield Beach, Florida, marketer of contact lenses advertised in *Cosmopolitan* magazine and on television. Its ads featured "Wonder Woman" Lynda Carter. Lens Express tagged ads in each medium in which they advertised with a designated toll-free telephone number so that when calls came into the service agency handling its incoming telephone traffic, management could see which ads were most effective. WATS forwards the leads to Lens Express electronically overnight, and the company mails a brochure to each prospect.

Whenever a prescription was required, Lens Express referred someone to a local provider, usually a doctor participating in its Preferred Eye Care program. Otherwise, the customer responded by merely calling another toll-free number to reach one of the company's own telephone reps, all of whom have been trained in the art of relationship selling. The rep took the order and encouraged the caller to sign up for a Lens Express membership that entitles her or him to professional eye care services at set rates plus discounts on replacement lenses.

Besides handling this level of cross-selling, Lens Express reps were trained to get the most out of all responses lodged in the company's rapidly expanding database. For example, an automated call-center system from Electronic Information Systems, Stamford, Connecticut, automatically dialed customers every six months and, on hearing someone on the line, instantly switched the call to a rep who reminded the party that it was time for new lenses. Similarly, people who received brochures but didn't order were dialed automatically in three to six months to requalify their interest.

Source: Adapted from Martin Everett, "Your Job Is on the (Phone) Line," *Sales & Marketing Management* 145, no. 5 (May 1993): 67–68.

CALL CENTERS

A **call center** is a dedicated team supported by various telephone technological resources to provide responses to customer inquiries.[19] Some marketers think of call centers as the "telephonic front door" to the company or the main access point for obtaining information or placing an order. In essence, the call center is the formal entity of an organization, or representing an organization, that handles communication with any type of stakeholder. Regardless of whether a customer is placing an order, calling to check on the status of an order, inquiring about new products or services, seeking technical support, or placing a complaint, the call center should provide a seamless communication process and quality service. Following is an example of an organization effectively carrying out this communication and service.

Pittsburgh-based PNC Bank has devised a customer rating program that automatically activates when customers contact its National Financial Services Center. It uses software that requires customers to enter their PIN or Social Security number. The bank determines the customer's identity and analyzes that person's past transactions with the bank and places the customer into one of several preset "needs-based segments."

Callers with basic transactions are transferred to an entry-level telephone representative. Callers with complex financial histories are given to handlers with a specific expertise. And, a "most valuable customer" is routed to a relationship consultant—one of 30 or 40 service representatives deemed the bank's very best.

Source: Adapted from Don Peppers & Martha Rogers, "Don't Put Customer Relationships On Hold," *Sales & Marketing Management* 151, no. 9 (September 1999): 26.

Call centers can operate (a) within the company or in-house, (b) outside the company, when calls are made or taken by a teleservice outsourcing firm, or (c) a combination of both. According to a recent study conducted by the Direct Marketing Association and PriceWaterhouseCoopers, more companies own their call center operations than outsource them; however a sizeable number do both.[20] See Figure 8-2 for a breakdown of call center operations.

Each type of call center organization has similar functions, yet all have unique features and challenges. The decision about how to carry out telemarketing activities ultimately is a function of company's financial situation and the nature of its telemarketing program. A major factor in determining whether to establish the call center in-house or outsource it is the expected pattern of calls. When customer orders are expected to come into the company all at once (or within a relatively short time interval), it becomes difficult to staff the call center to receive and process each order on a timely basis. This is when outsourcing begins to look attractive because nothing is worse than putting your customers "on hold." Only outsourcers with thousands of positions can handle such call volume effectively. According to Peppers and Rogers,

PriceWaterhouseCoopers and the DMA conducted a survey of 159 senior marketing executives from companies with revenue of $100 million and higher. The survey, "Customer Relationship Management Technology Enabled Marketing," was conducted from March to May 1999.

OWNERSHIP OF CALL CENTERS
59% of companies who responded own call centers operations.

Outsource call center operations: 11%
Own call center operations: 59%
Both own and outsource call center operations: 30%

FIGURE 8-2   Customer Relationship Management Technology Enabled Market
Source: Statistical Fact Book 2000 (New York: Direct Marketing Association, Inc., 2000), 228.

"Customers today are accustomed to having their needs met immediately, completely, conveniently, and inexpensively."[21]

The retail industry measures the level of customer dissatisfaction by calculating the rate of **call abandonment,** the number of callers who hang-up before being served by a telephone sales representative. Many telemarketing companies strive to keep this rate below 2 to 3 percent.[22] However, during peak calling times, consumers may abandon 20 to 30 percent of the calls. To reduce customer frustration, many companies route incoming calls through interactive voice response equipment to capture preliminary information and balance the workload among teleservice agents. Nonetheless, even one missed call can lead to the loss of a sale and more importantly, the loss of a customer. At these times outside service centers should handle customer orders. Let's examine both in-house and outsourced call centers.

In-House Call Center

In-house call centers require substantial investment in facilities and equipment. Direct marketers can place outbound calls or receive inbound calls from the same call center due to advances in telephone and computer technology. According to Roberts and Berger, setting up an in-house call center and managing an ongoing program entail the following 11 activities:[23]

1. Obtaining the support of top management
2. Setting goals and objectives
3. Integrating telephone marketing with other promotional activities, including the field sales force
4. Developing telephone scripts and guides
5. Recruiting and training telephone personnel
6. Supervising and motivating telephone representatives
7. Integrating telephone and computer systems
8. Designing a productive work environment
9. Developing measurement systems
10. Testing systems and procedures
11. Reporting and controlling the operation

The biggest advantage of establishing an in-house call center is the degree of control the company has over the telemarketing operations. The biggest disadvantages of an in-house call center are the time it takes to properly train telemarketing representatives and the large financial burden. Many in-house call centers, especially those B-2-C organizations that offer seasonal products, rely on a large number of seasonal, part-time or flex-time employees. For example, Lillian Vernon Corporation hires 1,350 seasonal employees each year to assist in handling the 5.3 million inbound calls from customers. While many of these employees may be returning for a second, third, fourth, or fifth year, the expenses of retraining them is enormous. Thus, farming out a company's telemarketing activities can cut costs and eliminate a large portion of the company's personnel load. We'll talk more about in-house call center operations in Chapter 10, "Customer Service and Fulfillment."

Outside (Outsourcing) Call Centers

Outsourcing formally refers to the process of having all call center activities handled by an outside organization or a teleservice outsourcer. The primary advantage of outsourcing for the marketer is a reduction in expenses and capital outlays. Most call center outsourcers are larger than in-house call centers and can more easily accommodate a large volume of seasonal orders. Additionally, because of their size, they offer lower costs and provide better formal training for telephone operators than in-house call centers. In addition, most call center outsourcers tend to utilize the most advanced technology available to stay efficient.

There are four main advantages to using an outside service bureau to conduct a company's telemarketing program:[24]

1. *Low initial investment*—marketers pay for the telemarketing program on a short-term basis only
2. *Fixed operating costs*—with a defined rate schedule provided by the call center outsourcer
3. *Quick start-up*—shorter lead times for implementing the telemarketing program
4. *Time flexibility*—24-hour, seven-day-a-week service for inbound calling and, as required by the Federal Trade Commission, restricted hours for outbound calling

There are also disadvantages associated with call center outsourcers:[25]

1. *Lack of direct control*—the company does not have the same degree of control over an external organization.
2. *Lack of direct security*—because of the remote location of the call center outsourcer, the company cannot keep its customer information in its exclusive possession. However, most call center outsourcers take great security measures.
3. *Lack of employee loyalty*—employees possess greater loyalty to the call center outsourcer than to the company that they are representing on the telephone.
4. *Mass-market approach*—service bureaus are high volume businesses, thus the quality of the sales pitch for any single company could suffer.
5. *Caliber of personnel*—often call center outsourcers pay less than in-house call centers, thus the quality of personnel is affected.

Regardless of the aforementioned disadvantages, many telemarketing companies successfully outsource their call center activities to service bureaus. An example of a successful business relationship with an outside call center can be seen below in the case of Delta Airlines Employee Credit Union.

Delta Employees Employee Credit Union has outsourced most of its call center functions to AnyTime Access, Sacramento, California. With a loyal membership—76% consider the credit union to be their primary financial institution—Atlanta-based Delta wanted to grow its loan portfolio while maintaining high levels of member service and satisfaction. The $1.5 billion institution, which serves Delta Airlines employees and their families, has a limited branch network and a global clientele of 140,000, who transact primarily via phone, fax, mail, and the Internet.

Although there was great opportunity to generate loan growth, Delta did not have the personnel to process the loan applications quickly enough. That led Delta to AnyTime Access, which handles a 24-hour call center operation on a pay-per transaction basis.

AnyTime Access processed all calls, including general inquiry calls, to a Delta employees-branded 800-telephone line, marketed by LoanLine. AnyTime also processed all loan applications submitted via the credit union's Web site. Outsourcing the loan application process has reduced processing time from around 18 minutes to between seven and ten minutes. Additionally, two weeks after being rolled out, the new call center set up and processed 1,200 loan applications. Soon after that, AnyTime was processing about 3,100 loans a month, plus Delta saw a 59 percentage gain in loan center production, with only three employees added to its staff.

Source: Adapted from *Kenneth Kiesnoski, "Credit Unions Embrace Electronic Delivery,"* Bank Systems & Technology, Vol. 36, Iss. 8, August, 1999, pp. 31–32.

MEDIA MEASUREMENT

Inbound calls are generally less expensive than outbound calls. This is due in part to the fact that inbound calls are generally shorter in duration than outbound calls. Inbound calls generally cost $1.50 to $7.00 per call depending on the type of call, duration, and complexity of the call. Outbound calls placed to final consumers (also called business-to-consumer or B-2-C) range between $1.15 to $4.00 per call. Outbound calls placed to businesses (also called business-to-business or B-2-B) typically range between $6.00 and $16.00.[26] The average range of costs for inbound and outbound calls are just some of the many costs involved in telemarketing.

The three components that make up the cost of a telemarketing call are (1) personnel, (2) equipment and overhead, and (3) telecommunications service. The breakdown of telemarketing expenditures for both in-house operations and outsourced firms is normally as follows: personnel accounts for 50 percent of the costs; overhead is responsible for 30 percent; and telecommunications service accounts for 20 percent of total costs.[27] Direct marketers incur substantial costs in the hiring, training, and maintaining of personnel needed to staff an in-house call center. Also, companies that extensively use Interactive Voice Response instead of live agents have reduced

The following is a breakdown of costs for operating a B-to-B telemarketing center.

8 Representatives @ 230 days and 1,610 hours per rep.

STAFF

(1) Manager/Supervisor @ $48,000 base plus commissions, incentives, and 30% tax and fringe.
(8) Representatives @ $32,000 base plus commissions, incentives, and 30% tax and fringe.
(1) Admin/Asst. @ $24,000 base plus 30% tax and fringe.
Commissions: at 100% of target
-Manager/Supervisor $5,000
-Reps $2,000 each

TELEPHONE
Network @ .05/minute of connect time for 24.5 connect minutes per hour.
Equipment: $13,000 (from capital expense statement).

AUTOMATION
H/W: $11,333 (from capital expense statement)
S/W: $22,000 (from capital expense statement)

RENT
$22,800 (from capital expense statement)

WORKSTATIONS & OTHER FURNISHINGS AND OFFICE EQUIPMENT
(from capital expense statement)
Workstations: $4,650
Furnishings: $1,300
Office Equipment: $4,375

MAIL, CATALOG, FAXES
Sent as a direct result of phone activity, estimated @ $3.00 per rep phone hour.

FIGURE 8-3   Outbound Business-to-Business Sales Operation Annual Costs

personnel costs but raised equipment and overhead costs. The costs vary due to the fact that many organizations do not operate their own call center, but outsource these duties to an external agency. However, numerous costs are incurred in either kind of call handling procedure.

The DMA estimates that it costs close to $865,000 per year to operate an eight-person outbound business-to-business call center. These costs are summarized in Figure 8-3. Similarly, the DMA estimates that it costs approximately $1,262,139 to operate an outbound consumer sales operation based on a call schedule of Monday through Thursday from 9:00 A.M. to 9:00 P.M. and Friday and Saturday from 9:00 A.M. to 5:00 P.M. Although the total annual costs are greater for consumer than business-to-business, the cost per representative hour is greater for business-to-business ($67.14 vs. $27.09).[28]

Finally, the geographic location of a call center has an impact on its operating costs. For example, as shown in Figure 8-4, San Francisco, California, is the most expensive geographic location in the United States for operating a call center, while New Brunswick, Canada, is one of the least costly.

In conclusion, although it is a very cost-effective medium compared with personal selling, there are many costs involved in using the telephone as both a marketing medium and a response mechanism. Each must be calculated and monitored. Direct

	ANNUAL COSTS		
	ANNUAL	**REP HOUR**	**REP DAY**
8 reps @ 230 days each	1,840		
8 reps @ 1,610 hours each	12,880		
STAFF			
Manager/Supervisor (1)	$ 48,000	$ 3.73	
Representatives (8)	256,000	19.88	
Administrative Assistant (1)	24,000	1.86	
Commissions	151,000	11.72	
Incentives	21,000	1.63	
30% Tax and Fringe	150,000	11.65	
SUBTOTAL	$ 650,000	$ 50.47	$ 353.26
TELEPHONE			
Network @.08 min.	18,032	1.40	
Equipment	13,000	1.01	
SUBTOTAL	$ 31,032	$ 2.41	$ 16.87
AUTOMATION			
H/W:	11,333	.88	
S/W:	22,000	1.71	
SUBTOTAL	$ 33,333	$ 2.59	$ 18.12
RENT & OTHER	33,125	2.57	18.00
MAIL, CATALOG & FAXES	38,640	3.00	21.00
TOTAL DIRECT EXPENSES	$ 786,130	$ 61.03	$ 427.24
Plus			
CORP. GENERAL & ADMINISTRATION (10%)	78,613	6.10	42.73
GRAND TOTAL	**$864,743**	**$67.14**	**$469.97**

FIGURE 8-3   Outbound Business-to-Business Sales Operation Annual Costs (continued)

Source: "Oetting & Company, Inc.," in *Statistical Fact Book 2003* (New York: Costs Direct Marketing Association, Inc., 2003), 96–97.

marketers must also address other issues regarding telemarketing. These include ethical and legal issues. Let's take a closer look at each.

ETHICAL AND LEGAL ASPECTS OF TELEMARKETING

Unfortunately, select ethical abuses have tarnished telemarketing's reputation and created an environment where legal regulations must now be imposed. There are many ethical and legal issues involved with using the telephone as a marketing medium. The Direct Marketing Association (DMA) and the Telemarketing Task Force of the Electronic Retailing Association (ERA) has addressed the ethical aspects of telephone marketing and issued ethical guidelines. The Federal Communications

GEOGRAPHICALLY-VARIABLE CENTER OPERATING COST RANKINGS

This report,prepared by the Boyd Company, Inc., location consultants of Princeton, NJ, features a factor-by-factor comparative operating cost analysis of a series of North American call center locations. Annual operating costs in the study are scaled to a representative 800-number customer service center employing 200 hourly workers, occupying some 30,000 sq. ft. of office space, and having a monthly call volume of 1.5 million minutes of billable inbound toll-free service. Total annual operating costs for 45 leading U.S. and Canadian call center locations are detailed below.

Call Center Location	Total Annual Operating Cost
San Francisco, CA	$10,722,275
New York, NY	$10,436,521
Jersey City, NJ	$10,151,988
Stamford, CT	$10,046,902
Los Angeles, CA	$10,019,594
Boston, MA	$9,970,278
Denver, CO	$9,720,896
Chicago, IL	$9,694,287
Philadelphia, PA	$9,570,754
Wilmington, DE	$9,499,287
Dallas, TX	$9,420,779
Toronto, CAN	$9,311,849
Atlanta, GA	$9,219,562
Charlotte, NC	$9,215,750
Miami, FL	$9,105,585
Providence, RI	$9,083,588
Salt Lake City, UT	$9,079,332
Allentown/Bethlehem/Easton, PA	$9,051,905
Buffalo, NY	$9,012,771
Cincinnati, OH	$8,980,999
Provo, UT	$8,962,526
Tampa/St. Petersburg, FL	$8,945,985
Orlando, FL	$8,912,765
Dover, DE	$8,895,887
Raleigh/Durham, NC	$8,894,785
Delray Beach, FL	$8,860,040
Camp Hill, PA	$8,839,158
Omaha, NE	$8,813,037
Portland, ME	$8,721,971
Scranton/Wilkes-Barre/Hazleton, PA	$8,694,153
Jacksonville, FL	$8,676,034
Ft. Lauderdale/Hollywood, FL	$8,646,810
Grand Rapids, MI	$8,604,212
Richmond, VA	$8,568,664
Charleston, SC	$8,541,051
Norfolk/Virginia Beach, VA	$8,524,285
Columbia, SC	$8,438,623
St. Cloud, MN	$8,412,504
Savannah, GA	$8,294,389
Hartford, CT	$8,251,533
Knoxville, TN	$8,216,741
Jacksonville, NC	$8,114,139
Augusta, GA	$8,109,977
Mobile, AL	$7,924,384
New Brunswick, CAN	$7,804,477

FIGURE 8-4   Geographically Variable Center

Commission (FCC) implements the rules of the Telephone Consumer Protection Act of 1991, and the Federal Trade Commission (FTC) has also issued a comprehensive set of telemarketing rules that organizations must follow in order to conform to the legal constraints of using the telephone as a marketing medium. The most recent federal regulations that may be enforced by both the FCC and the FTC include the National Do Not Call Registry.

We will review the DMA and ERA guidelines along with the FCC and the FTC regulations including the National Do Not Call Registry in this chapter. In Chapter 12, "Ethical and Legal Issues in Direct Marketing," we'll expand on the legal regulations and address the laws pertaining to wireless devices and facsimile machines.

Direct Marketing Association Guidelines

The DMA guidelines are accepted principles of conduct consistent with the ethical guidelines provided for other marketing media. Keep in mind the DMA has created these guidelines to self-regulate the industry. Telemarketers are urged, not legally bound, to honor them. For more information about DMA telemarketing guidelines visit the DMA Web site at www.the-dma.org/guidelines/ethicalguidelines.pdf. Briefly, these are the guidelines:

Prompt Disclosure/Identity of Seller—Telephone representatives must promptly disclose the name of the sponsor, the name of the individual caller, and the primary purposes of the contact.

Honesty—All offers must be clear, honest, and complete so that the recipient of the call will know the exact nature of what is being offered and the commitment involved in the placing of an order. Telephone offers should not be made under the guise of research or a survey when the real intent is to sell products or services or to raise funds.

Terms of the Offer—Telephone marketers should disclose the cost of the merchandise or service, all terms, and conditions, including payment plans, refund policies, and the amount or existence of any extra charges such as shipping, handling, or insurance.

Reasonable Hours—Telephone marketers should avoid making calls during hours that are unreasonable to the recipients of the calls.

Use of Automatic Equipment—When using automatic dialing equipment, telephone marketers should only use equipment that allows the telephone to release the line immediately when the called party disconnects.

Taping of Conversations—Taping of telephone conversations made for telephone marketing purposes should not be conducted without legal notice to or consent of all parties or the use of a beeping device. A beeping device alerts the caller to the fact that the telephone call is being recorded.

Name Removal—Telephone marketers should remove the name of any individual from their telephone lists when requested directly by the customer to do so by using the DMA Telephone Preference Service name-removal list.

Minors—Telephone marketers should be especially sensitive to the obligations and responsibilities of dealing with minors since they are generally less experienced in their rights as consumers.

Monitoring—Telephone operators should be informed of all call monitoring practices prior to the use of any telephone monitoring activities.

Prompt Delivery—Telephone marketers should abide by the FTC's Mail or Telephone Order Merchandise (30-Day) Rule when shipping pre-paid merchandise and are urged to ship orders as promptly as possible. This 30-Day Rule requires direct marketers to ship merchandise within 30 days from the time an order was received *unless* their advertisement states the timeframe within which an order will be delivered.

Cooling-Off Period—Telephone marketers should honor cancellation requests which originate within three days of sales agreement.

Restricted Contracts—A telephone marketer should not knowingly call anyone who has an unlisted or unpublished telephone number except in instances where the telephone number was given to the marketer directly by the customer.

Transfer of Customer Data—Telephone marketers who receive or collect customer data as a result of telephone marketing contact and who intend to rent, sell, or exchange that data for direct marketing purposes should inform the customer of this practice.

Laws, Codes, and Regulations—Telephone marketers should operate in accordance with the laws and regulations of the United States Postal Service, the Federal Communications Commission, the Federal Trade Commission, the Federal Reserve Board, and other applicable federal, state, and local laws governing advertising, marketing practices, and the transaction of business by mail, telephone, and the print and broadcast media.

ERA Telemarketing Guidelines

The Electronic Retailing Association (ERA) is a group of 24 association members that includes retailers, telemarketing companies, and membership club companies. A Telemarketing Task Force of the ERA has created a set of telemarketing guidelines. These guidelines have been accepted and approved by the Federal Trade Commission. Some key components of these guidelines include[29]

- All statements made during a telemarketing call must be truthful and not misleading.
- Members should ensure that the billing methods they use are clearly disclosed to consumers before completing a telephone sale.
- Members should maintain, and require their telemarketing service providers to maintain, a list of consumers who ask not to receive telemarketing calls as required by the Federal Trade Commission and the Federal Communications Commission regulations.
- For all calls, before taking consumers' credit card or bankcard information, members should disclose the nature of the goods or services being offered; the total cost and quantity being ordered, limitations, or conditions to obtain or use the goods or services; and the terms of their refund policy.
- Members engaged in telemarketing, or those who provide assistance to others who are engaged in telemarketing, should conduct a reasonable inquiry into the experience, background, and practices of those with whom they work in connection with a telemarketing campaign.

Let's now look at the federal regulations affecting telephone marketers.

Federal Communication Commission Rules

The Telephone Consumer Protection Act (TCPA) was passed in 1991. The FCC implemented the rules and regulations of the Act in 1992.[30] From a telephone marketer's point of view, the most significant part of the TCPA regulations concern commercial solicitation calls made to residences. Direct marketers making those calls are required to

- Limit the calls to the period between 8 A.M. and 9 P.M.
- Maintain a do-not-call list and honor any consumer request to not be called again. The FCC permits one error in a twelve-month period. The FCC will work closely with the FTC in enforcing the new National Do Not Call Registry.
- Have a clearly written policy, available to anyone upon request.
- If you are a Service Bureau, forward all requests to be removed from a list to the company on whose behalf you are calling.

A call is exempt from the TCPA if the call

- Is made on behalf of a tax-exempt non-profit organization.
- Is not made for a commercial purpose.
- Does not include an unsolicited advertisement, even if it is made for a commercial purpose.
- Is made to a consumer with whom the calling company has an "established business relationship."

Other important provisions of the TCPA include

- A ban on autodialers and artificial or pre-recorded voice messages programmed to call any emergency phone lines, pagers, or cellular phones, or a call for which a charge is made to the calling party.
- A prohibition against the use of artificial or pre-recorded voice messages to call a residence except in cases of emergency or if the caller has received prior express consent.
- A prohibition against the use of an autodialer to engage two or more lines of a multi-line business.
- A requirement that anyone using an autodialer or an artificial or pre-recorded voice message to call any number must state the identity of the caller at the beginning of the message and give the address and phone number of the caller during the call.
- A ban on sending unsolicited advertisements by fax to anyone without prior express consent.

The TCPA can be enforced in at least three different ways:

1. The individual who receives a call after a name removal request has been given to the caller is granted a private right of action in a local court and may sue for $500 in damages for each violation.
2. States may initiate civil action against offending companies on behalf of their citizens.
3. Complaints may be filed with the FCC, which has the power to assess penalties against parties in violation of the TCPA.

Federal Trade Commission Rules

In 1995, the Federal Trade Commission issued a comprehensive set of rules that affect not only all telemarketers, but those marketing by computer modem as well. These rules affect all outbound calls and those inbound calls that occur in response to any direct mail or targeted solicitation, with the exception of catalogs. Inbound calls from customers desiring to place an order from a catalog are exempt, providing the telephone operator does not engage in any further solicitation on the phone. The following is a brief overview of each FTC regulation rule.

> ***Disclosure Requirements***—At the beginning of each call, the caller's first and last name and the fact that it is a sales call must be disclosed. If the solicitation is for a charitable donation, the telemarketer's status as a paid professional fundraiser and the purpose of the call must be disclosed.
>
> ***Prohibited Misrepresentation***—The FTC rules clearly prohibit misrepresentation of any information required to be disclosed by the rule and any material aspects about the solicitation or the offered goods or services.
>
> ***Assisting Telemarketing Fraud***—The FTC has ruled that anyone who provides substantial assistance to telemarketers may be potentially liable if the program is ultimately found to be unlawful.
>
> ***The FCC/FTC Do Not Call (DNC) Registry***—The FTC was planning to enforce the new DNC Registry on October 1, 2003. Consumers began signing up for the registry during Summer 2003. The FTC has indicated that the national DNC list could contain 40 to 60 million consumer telephone numbers.[31] Consumers are allowed to sign up via the telephone by calling (888) 382–1222 or online at www.donotcall.gov. AT&T has been awarded the contract to administer the registry.

Section 310.2 of this new federal DNC legislation provides for an Established Business Relationship (EBR) exemption. Thus, direct marketers may still call customers who appear on the registry providing they are calling on them

- Within 18 months of their last purchase, transaction, shipment, end of subscription/membership, or
- Within 3 months of their last inquiry or application.

Exemptions to the DNC legislation have also been made for most business-to-business calls, common carriers, airlines, some financial institutions, and insurance companies to the extent regulated under state law; intrastate calls; and non-profit organizations, and third-party marketers calling on their behalf, are required to honor in-house suppress requests.[32] However, federal judges have found these exemptions in the proposed DNC Registry legislation to be "unconstitutional" on the grounds of freedom of speech because it would have allowed telemarketers for charitable organizations to continue to call numbers on the list, even though commercial firms would be barred from doing so. In essence, federal judges ruled that the FTC has imposed a content-based limitation on what the consumer may ban from his or her home ... thereby involving the government in deciding what speech consumers should hear. It is expected that the law will require the FTC to make modifications in the DNC legislation prior to FTC enforcement. Therefore, FTC enforcement of the DNC Registry has been postponed beyond the original October 1, 2003, date while the FTC appeals the judges ruling and modifies the proposed DNC legislation.

However, despite two court rulings against the FTC, the FCC will enforce its do-not-call rules against telemarketers who call numbers on the National DNC Registry beginning on October 1, 2003. The FCC legislation has not been disturbed by the rulings of the federal judges on the DNC Registry. The FCC joined the FTC in 2002 to ensure the DNC Registry applies to all industries. The FCC's do-not-call regulations mirror and expand upon those of the FTC. The FCC has the power to penalize telemarketers up to $120,000 depending on their industry.

How does the National DNC Registry work? Telephone marketers are required to "scrub" its lists (which means they must search the registry) at least every three months and eliminate from their call lists phone numbers of prospects who have registered. Each company accessing the registry data is required to pay an annual fee based on the number of area codes the company accesses. The DNC list will cost telemarketers $25 per area code—up to a maximum of $7,375 for the entire country. The first five area codes are free.[33] The bottom line for direct marketers is that they cannot contact prospects who are on the National DNC Registry unless they receive the prospect's written and signed permission to do so.

In addition to the new federal regulations, many states are adopting local legislation regarding outbound telephone marketing activities. As of July 28, 2003, 39 states across the United States of America have adopted state no-call list laws, although, many state laws will use the FTC National DNC list.[34]

In conclusion, the regulatory environment is one that is always changing. Direct marketers, especially telephone marketers, need to be constantly and closely monitoring the rules and regulations set forth by the FCC, the FTC and other regulatory agencies. We will discuss the legal environment and the regulatory agencies in greater detail in Chapter 12.

Summary

The telephone is an important and highly productive direct marketing medium. It encompasses both inbound calls (consumers calling into the company) and outbound calls (companies calling out to consumers) and has a wealth of technology to support the many applications of both types of calls. Advances in telephone technology have included Dialed Number Identification System, Automated Numbering Identification, Audiotex, Voice Messaging, Interactive Voice Response, Predictive Dialers, and Short Messaging Service.

Much planning goes into the preparation of a telemarketing program, including preparing the telephone script, training the telephone operators, and integrating the campaign with other media. Telemarketing program operations can be conducted from either in-house call centers or an outside agency. There are distinct advantages and disadvantages associated with each location—including costs and quality of control issues.

There are many ethical and legal aspects affecting telemarketing activities. As presented in this chapter, these guidelines and regulations primarily come from the Direct Marketing Association, Electronic Retailing Association, the Federal Communication Commission, and the Federal Trade Commission. Each addresses important issues concerning telemarketing.

Key Terms

- telemarketing, 174
- inbound calls, 175
- outbound calls, 175
- reactive telemarketing, 175
- proactive telemarketing, 176
- T1, 176

- Wide Area Telephone Service (WATS), 176
- "cold calls", 177
- predictive dialers, 180
- short messaging service, (SMS) 180

- telephone script, 180
- call center, 185
- call abandonment, 186
- outsourcing, 187

Review Questions

1. Explain the difference between inbound versus outbound calls as they are related to tele-marketing.
2. List a few advantages and disadvantages of tele-marketing.
3. How has technology changed telemarketing?
4. Why is it necessary for telemarketers to have a telephone script to follow when communicating with customers or prospects?
5. List the seven principles for successful tele-phone script writing as offered by Jim Kobs.
6. Explain how each medium interacts with the telephone for marketing purposes. Be sure to identify the only medium that actually competes with telephone as a marketing medium.
7. Provide a brief update on the status of the pro-posed FCC/FTC Do Not Call Registry.
8. What is the function of a call center? How are telemarketing activities carried out via call centers?
9. Explain the Direct Marketing Association's Guidelines for individuals and organizations that are involved in direct telephone marketing.
10. In addition to the Direct Marketing Association, explain the other organizations regulating tele-marketing practices.

Exercise

Think of your favorite product and the company that owns that product. Would you recommend to their marketing department that they use telemarketing as a marketing medium to sell their product, assuming they do not already? Explain the possible advantages and disadvantages of selling this product via telemarketing. If you would suggest selling the product using telemar-keting as a medium, what category of telemarketing would be most useful, outbound calls or inbound calls, or a combination of both? Explain your answer.

CASE: 1-800-FLOWERS

OVERVIEW

This case provides real stories of how 1-800-FLOWERS has made its customers the top priority and how it has been able to motivate its telemarketing representatives to embrace this customer orientation. The roles of changing technology and changing consumer needs have lead the company to become a successful multichannel direct marketer. This case illustrates the important role that high-quality customer service and employee motivation play in building a successful telemarketing operation. Jim McCann, owner of 1-800-FLOWERS, demonstrates how his company combines recognition of people with technology to build a highly profitable direct marketing business.

CASE

The original 1-800-FLOWERS was started by a group of successful businessmen from Dallas, Texas. The founders spent $30 million during their first year of business and built the world's largest telemarketing center. This call center consisted of million-dollar telephone switches, state-of-the-art IBM computer systems, 700 workstations, and a detailed bridge command to oversee the entire operation. The operation was housed in 55,000 square feet of office space. A network of 6,800 "fulfilling florists" were paid on a commission basis to create, package, and deliver the orders received by the 1-800-FLOWERS telecommunications call center.

Sound great? You bet! Was it profitable? No way! With that kind of killer overhead and nobody with a burning desire to manage the business on a daily basis, the company lost money right from the start. What was missing in the business start-up was a focus on the customer. The original owners failed to establish relationships with their customers.

Then, one day, in walks Jim McCann, then owner of Flora Plenty, a successful 14-store

retail chain of florists in New York. Flora Plenty was doing extensive telemarketing for its retail chain, plus it was one of the "fulfilling florists" for 1-800-FLOWERS. McCann had a passion for serving the customer and he sincerely believed in the 1-800-FLOWERS concept. He thought the company could be highly successful if managed properly. Thus, on November 6, 1984, after a few years of negotiation, McCann bought 1-800-FLOWERS for $7 million, and managed it first as a partnership, then later as sole proprietor. The acquisition gave McCann the right to use the 1-800-FLOWERS' telephone number but left him buried in debt and scrambling to create a makeshift operation for the new company with very little overhead. In the beginning McCann himself went back to answering the phone: "Thank you for calling 1-800-FLOWERS, how can we help you today?"

McCann knew the three big challenges that were ahead for this troubled business:

1. At that time, 1-800 numbers were still new to most consumers and it was going to take time to build consumer confidence in purchasing via 1-800 technology.
2. Most consumers were not aware of 1-800-FLOWERS yet often had a need to purchase flowers. Thus, brand awareness would need to be developed such that consumers thought about 1-800-FLOWERS whenever they had the urge to buy flowers.
3. And most importantly, there was the challenge of building relationships with customers—one at a time—to gain their loyalty for a lifetime. McCann realized that if he were going to make a business out of something impersonal like buying flowers over the telephone, he would have to create a personal relationship with EVERY caller. The sale would be almost secondary.

FIGURE 8-5   1-800-Flowers Web site

When McCann first bought the business, it was a lousy deal: several million dollars of debt and a telephone number, a telephone number with a not very good track record at that. One of the keys in turning 1-800-FLOWERS into a success story in the world of telemarketing has been getting people to want to buy flowers over the telephone for someone they really care about. In 1992, as 1-800-FLOWERS entered on-line commerce (www.1800flowers.com), the company had to give people a reason to want to be in its virtual store. See Figure 8-5 for the company's Web site.

The company added personal contact and entertainment to the value equation to make people want to visit its site. McCann credits the fact that 1-800-FLOWERS was named the single most successful business operation on the World Wide Web in 1996 to the lessons he learned 10 years earlier in telemarketing. He believes the Internet fulfills the same functions as any other retail system, so the jump from telemarketing to modem marketing was a natural one for 1-800-FLOWERS. On the Internet, as with telemarketing, a company must have strong infrastructure to keep track of inventory, process orders, secure billing, and deliver the product. And, above all, the business must focus on people.

At 1-800-FLOWERS, people are the priority. Here are a few examples of what this means:

- It is not uncommon for managers to place smiley face stickers on a telerep's computer whenever the telerep has been seen smiling while on the telephone with a customer. Customers can tell a smiling, happy person over the phone and it will make the customer experience more enjoyable. Thus, the telerep is rewarded simply for smiling.
- Like many companies, 1-800-FLOWERS monitors telerep phone calls. However, the primary reason for the monitoring is to reveal strengths to be shared with others. This ensures the quality control of telereps and provides clues on how to sharpen the telephone script and improve customer service.
- Public praise of the telerep is also commonplace at 1-800-FLOWERS. In fact, the company purchased a refrigerator door and mounted it on the wall at the entrance to the telecenter. Whenever a telerep was found doing something noteworthy, the manager wrote it up and stuck it to the refrigerator door with a magnet.
- There is a "Legends" book at 1-800-FLOWERS. This book is filled with stories of associates going the extra mile to please a customer. This book is given to new service telereps as a part of their training—it provides the rules for working in customer service. The new employees are told that if what they are doing to serve a customer is not worthy of being included in the Legends book, then they are probably not doing enough.

In summary, good old-fashioned rules have been the guiding light to McCann in building 1-800-FLOWERS into a successful business. McCann believes in putting a premium on people and making an emotional contact—by planting emotional seeds that will yield sales and build customer relationships far in excess of a simple sale. The company tries to please each and every customer. If a customer isn't happy, company policy is to "find out what it will take to make the unsatisfied customer happy, then do it." The 1-800-FLOWERS "Absolute Guarantee" policy is unique to the floral industry: "If at any time, you are not satisfied with the product you ordered, we will replace it. Or refund your money. Or do whatever it takes to ensure that you, the customer, are happy and will continue to be a customer of ours in the future."

Technology also plays a key role in the success of 1-800-FLOWERS. The company uses technology to

1. process orders more quickly;
2. confirm product delivery more accurately;
3. remind customers of birthdays and anniversaries more faithfully; and
4. free employees to devote themselves to creating customer relationships.

As McCann puts it, "computers aren't friendly, people are." Technology is very effective at improving a business, but too much technology can depersonalize a business—which is a bad thing. Over the years, 1-800-FLOWERS has investigated new telephone technology and has experienced both positive and negative outcomes.

Technology allowed the company to adjust the length of the phone ring. During the busiest times (Mother's Day, Valentines Day, and Christmas) telereps had the alternatives of putting people on hold with canned music or letting the phone ring. Since it was already established that people like to have their telephone call answered by the third ring, 1-800-FLOWERS simply extended each ring from six seconds to nine seconds. The company found that there was no perception of a longer wait, so with the same number of rings, 1-800-FLOWERS was able to serve customers during peak seasons without turning them off with too many rings or too much "elevator music." This same technology enabled the company to pick up the phone before the caller even heard a ring—but callers thought it was downright creepy, as if the company knew what the customer was doing before they did it. Therefore, although technology would allow the company to eliminate telephone rings, 1-800-FLOWERS chose to stay with the old-fashioned ring cycle because people felt comfortable with it.

What was once a simple, toll-free number is now a well-established brand. 1-800-FLOWERS has blossomed into a successful direct marketer with a database of loyal customers and a nationwide network of 2,500 "Bloom Net" florists who have been handpicked to fulfill orders for 1-800-FLOWERS. The company has become a multichannel direct marketer. It now sells its products via telephone, Internet, on-site retail stores, and even catalogs. Figure 8-6 shows a couple of 1-800-FLOWERS catalogs.

The 1-800-FLOWERS call center, once a bunch of crates and boards and telephones down in the basement of a Queens, New York, floral shop, now has the capability to handle millions of calls a week from its present location in Westbury, Long Island. With unparalleled attention to customers, motivated employees, and modern technology, 1-800-FLOWERS, the world's largest florist, is poised to continue its direct marketing success story well into the future. In fact, combined on-line and telephonic revenues increased 9.9 percent to $73.3 million for the first quarter in 2002 compared with $66.7 million in the prior year period. In addition, customers continue to embrace the company's expanded non-floral gift offerings, which represented 38.2 percent of total combined on line and telephonic revenues, compared with 34.9 percent in the prior year period.*

*2001 Business Wire/NewsBank, Inc., 1-800-FLOWERS.COM, (NASDAW: FLWS), Record Number: 094930EF6A50141235A64.

FIGURE 8-6   1-800-Flowers Catalog Covers

In conclusion, according to Jim McCann, "today 740,000 people are celebrating their birthdays, tomorrow another 740,000 will be celebrating theirs. If you'd like to make one or two of them feel terrific on their special day . . . I know a 1-800 number you can call!"

Source: Adapted from Jim McCann and Peter Kaminsky, *Stop and Sell the Roses: Lessons from Business & Life* (New York: Ballantine Books, 1998). ■

Case Discussion Questions

1. Discuss how 1-800-FLOWERS became a telemarketing success story. What were the main ingredients in its success?
2. Why did 1-800-FLOWERS become a multichannel direct marketer, instead of specializing solely in telemarketing? How should the company use these channels to support one another?
3. What role did technology play in assisting the company in achieving its goals? Has improved technology always lead to success for 1-800-FLOWERS? Support your answer with specific details and examples.

Notes

1. Bob Stone and John Wyman, *Successful Telemarketing*, 2nd ed. (Lincolnwood, IL: NTC Business Books, 1992.)
2. Direct Marketing Association, *Economic Impact U.S. Direct Marketing Today* (New York: Direct Marketing Association, 2003), 23.
3. Ibid., 17.
4. Ibid., 18.
5. Ibid., 19.
6. Mark DelFranco, "Outbound Efforts Pay Off," *Catalog Age* 17, no. 8 (July, 2000): 8.
7. Bob Stone, *Successful Direct Marketing Methods*, 6th ed. (Lincolnwood, IL: NTC Business Books, 1997).
8. Jim Kobs, *Profitable Direct Marketing*, 2nd ed. (Lincolnwood, IL: NTC Publishing Group, 1993), 175.
9. Janet A Smith, "The New Frontier," *Direct Marketing* (July 1991): 61.
10. Ibid.
11. N.R. Kleinfeld, "Business Dials 1–900 Profits," *New York Times*, May 8, 1988, sec. 3, p. 4.
12. Kelly J. Andrews, "Predictive Dialers: Better Dialing Through Technology," *Target Marketing* 21, no. 11 (1998): 30.
13. Jim Kobs, *Profitable Direct Marketing*, 2nd ed. (Lincolnwood, IL: NTC Business Books, 1993), 171–174.
14. Adapted from Aldyn McKean, "Promotinal Techniques in Telephone Advertising," in *DMA Fact Book* (New York: Direct Marketing Association, Inc., 1983), 127–131.
15. Adapted from Steve Jarvis, "Call Centers Raise Bar On Hiring Criteria," *Marketing News* 34, no. 19 (September 11, 2000); adapted from Bob Stone, *Successful Direct Marketing Methods*, 6th ed. (Lincolnwood, IL: NTC Business Books, 1997), 147.
16. Bobette M. Gustafson, "A Well-staffed PFS Call Center Can Improve Patient Satisfaction," *Healthcare Financial Management* 53, no. 7 (July 1999): 64.
17. Chad Kaydo, "Compensation in the Call Center," *Sales & Marketing Management* 151, no. 8 (August 1999): 75.

18. Bob Stone and John Wyman, *Successful Telemarketing*, 2nd ed. (Lincolnwood, IL: NTC Business Books, 1992), 5.

19. Bobette M. Gustafson, "A Well-Staffed PFS Call Center Can Improve Patient Satisfaction," *Healthcare Financial Management* 53, no. 7 (July 1999): 64.

20. *Statistical Fact Book 2000* (New York: Direct Marketing Association, Inc., 2000), 228.

21. Don Peppers and Martha Rogers, "Don't Put Customer Relationships on Hold," *Sales & Marketing Management* 151, no 9 (September 1999): 26.

22. Bobette M. Gustafson, "A Well-Staffed PFS Call Center Can Improve Patient Satisfaction," *Healthcare Financial Management* 53, no. 7 (July 1999): 64.

23. Adapted from Mary Lou Roberts and Paul D. Berger, *Direct Marketing Management*, 2nd ed. (Upper Saddle River, NJ: Prentice Hall, 1999), 345–346.

24. Adapted from Stanley Leo Fidel, *Startup Telemarketing* (New York: John Wiley & Sons, 1987), 35–38.

25. Ibid., 39–40.

26. Bob Stone and Ron Jacobs, *Successful Direct Marketing Methods*, 7th ed. (Lincolnwood, IL: NTC Business Books, 2001), 143.

27. Carol J. Scovotti, telemarketing expert, interview by author, September, 2003.

28. *Statistical Fact Book 2003* (New York: Direct Marketing Association, Inc., 2003), 97–99.

29. "ERA Approves Telemarketing Guidelines," *Direct Marketing* 63, no. 5 (September 2000): 19.

30. Adapted from the Direct Marketing Association, *Telephone Consumer Protection Act (TCPA)*, <http://www.the-dma.org/guidelines/tcpa.shtml> (September 17, 2003).

31. Direct Marketing Association, *The FTC's New Telemarketing Sales Rule: Q & A's*, DMA Telemarketing Resource Center, <http://www.the-dma.org/government/teleresourcecenter.shtml> (September 12, 2003).

32. Direct Marketing Asociation, *10 Steps to Making a Sale Under the FTC's New Telemarketing Sales Rule*, DMA Telemarketing Resource Center, <http://www.the-dma.org/government/teleresourcecenter.shtml> (September 12, 2003).

33. Direct Marketing Association, *FAQ Regarding: New National Do-Not-Call System & Regulations*. DMA Telemarketing Resource Center, <http://www.the-dma.org/government/teleresourcecenter.shtml> (August 25, 2003).

34. Direct Marketing Association, *State Telephone Compliance Guide: State Do-Not-Call Lists*, DMA Telemarketing Resource Center, <http://www.the-dma.org/government/teleresourcecenter.shtml> (September 12, 2003).

CHAPTER

9

THE INTERNET

THE NEWEST INTERACTIVE MARKETING MEDIUM

The Internet is the newest interactive marketing medium for direct marketers offering information access and two-way communication with customers in real-time via the computer. Interactivity is what makes marketing on the Internet different from other forms of direct marketing media. According to the DMA, in order to be considered "interactive" a new medium must meet the following three criteria:[1]

1. Consumers must be able to control when they view the products, and which types of products they are viewing.
2. Consumers must be able to control the pace at which they review products. They must be able to review the product content at their leisure, reading the product literature at a pace that is convenient to them, rather than being forced to progress to the next product.
3. Consumers must be able to place an order or request additional information directly via the medium rather than having to order through another method.

If one or more of these characteristics is missing, then the medium cannot be considered "interactive." Thus, infomercials and television home shopping are not considered interactive media at the present time since they present product information in a predetermined order and according to a set time frame. We cannot predict how technology will change in the future to enable more media to meet the interactive criteria. However, at present, the Internet (which includes the World Wide Web and e-mail) is the only medium that is considered to be truly interactive according to the DMA.

There has been a great deal of hype about interactive media and many new buzzwords have emerged. Keep in mind as you read this chapter that interactive media simply provide another means for reaching consumers directly in their homes and offices. "Technology and marketing have coexisted—generally to the benefit of each—for hundreds of years. In this sense, the Internet is merely the most recent technology for the delivery of marketing."[2] Let's take a look at the growth of this new interactive medium.

Growth of Internet Marketing

In 2003 advertising expenditures for interactive marketing will total $4.6 billion. That number is expected to grow by 18.5 percent annually to reach $8.8 billion in 2007. Interactive media direct marketing sales will reach $41.5 billion in 2003 and are expected to grow annually by 21 percent per year to reach $87.5 billion in 2007.[3] In 2001, about 205,686 workers were employed in interactive marketing. Interactive marketing is estimated to grow 18 percent per year to reach 501,766 workers by 2007.[4]

The Internet also has the fastest growth and acceptance rates of all other technological media. Consider the time is has taken these technologies to reach 50 million users: telephone—40 years; radio—38 years; cable television—10 years; the Internet—5 years.[5] However, several factors affect the rate of growth of this new medium for global interactions. These include computer access and/or ownership; computer literacy, an understanding of both hardware and software; network availability, especially in developing nations; language differences; cultural differences; and governmental

By the year 2006, it is estimated that the average U.S. adult will spend 213 hours per year online.

- **1997** **26 hours**
- **1998** **54 hours**
- **1999** **82 hours**
- **2000** **106 hours**
- **2001** **134 hours**
- **2002** **157 hours**
- **2003** **174 hours**
- **2004** **189 hours**
- **2005** **199 hours**
- **2006** **213 hours**

FIGURE 9-1 Hours Per Year Using Consumer On-line/Internet Access Services

Source: Veronis Suhler, "Stevenson Communications Industry Forecast, 2002," in *The Statistical Fact Book 2003,* 25th ed. (New York: The Direct Marketing Association, Inc., 2003), p. 126.

regulations.[6] Finally, although it is a global medium, most of what has been written about the Internet is based on experiences of companies and consumers in the United States and other highly developed nations.

Other statistics documenting the explosion of interactive media include the following:

- According to the DMA, by the year 2006, each U.S. consumer will spend a projected $122.32 per year in on-line/Internet access services—almost 63 percent more than what was spent in 2002.[7] In addition, it is estimated that by the year 2006 the average U.S. adult will spend 213 hours per year on-line.[8] Figure 9-1 shows the growth in the number of hours each person spends online.
- Researchers predict that business-to-business e-commerce will grow from $147 billion in 1999 to $7.2 trillion in 2004.[9]
- Research shows that by 2005 total spending on e-mail marketing services should reach $3.5 billion, which is an annual growth rate of 40%.[10]
- Consumer on-line shopping has grown each year, from $8.5 billion in 1998 to $23 billion in 2000. It is expected to increase to $64.1 billion by 2006.[11]

These statistics underscore the importance of the Internet to marketers. Marketers must clearly understand all aspects of the Internet if they are going to be successful in taking full advantage of this new enabling technology and integrating it into their promotional mix.

Internet marketing campaigns targeted to final consumers have received a great deal of publicity, however, using interactive media for business consumers is a common and profitable strategy as well. The next section will provide details about the growth of the Internet for business consumers.

Business-to-Business Internet Transactions

The use of interactive media for business-to-business (B2B) interactions is on the rise. B2B on-line sales revenues are expected to grow at a similar rate (21 percent annually) to on-line business-to-consumer (B2C) revenue. It is estimated that B2B on-line sales revenue will increase to $52.8 billion in 2007.[12]

Most B2B Web sites should contain the following information:

- Company name
- Company logo
- Company history
- Listing of sales offices
- Listing of corporate offices
- New products
- Product ordering information
- Catalogs
- Product specifications
- Listing of distributors
- Listing of repair facilities
- Listing of clients/customers

In addition, many companies include a company catalog on their Web site.

Like B2C interactions, B2B interactions aim to produce a measurable transaction. Business consumers select which Web sites they want to visit, just as final consumers do. However, unlike final consumers, business consumers normally have a specific task—locating information or purchasing products/services—to complete in a specified period of time. Thus, B2B interactions may be subject to greater time constraints than B2C interactions. Another difference is that B2B interactions often lead to a repeat purchase, thus, the possibility of establishing an ongoing customer relationship is greater than with B2C interactions. Regardless of the type of customer to be served by a company's interactive media campaign, both marketers and consumers must first understand the differences between the Internet and the World Wide Web (WWW). The next section will allow you to check your understanding of these terms.

Differences Between the Internet and the World Wide Web
The Internet ("Net")

The term "Internet" is actually a combination of the words, international and network. The **Internet** is literally a worldwide network of computers connected to one another to enable rapid transmission of data from one point to another. For direct marketers, the Internet is a means of communication between consumers and millions of other organizations. The Internet is more than computers and their contents. The Internet is a social space where users communicate with each other via e-mail, Usenet (consisting of over 50,000 discussion groups arranged hierarchically by topic), and the WWW, the Web. This global network includes millions of corporate, government, organizational, and private networks, as well as e-mail, newsgroups, and the Web.[13] It is similar to the telephone in that just as telephone calls can be made anywhere in the world, a computer can link up to anywhere in the world, provided it is connected to the Internet. The Internet has over 2.2 million public Web sites containing over 300 million Web pages, and 400,000 private sites accessible only with prior authorization.[14]

The Internet began as a high-tech tool for facilitating communication between scientists developed under the sponsorship of the Defense Department's Advanced Research Projects Agency (DARPA). In 1969, the network, then called DARPAnet became a reality when two nodes were linked together. By 1989, the National

Science Foundation had replaced the Defense Department as the chief source of support for the network of networks, re-named "NSFnet." Originally intended to facilitate research and communication within the scientific community, the Internet has grown to include networks and users across a wide variety of backgrounds and interests. The first widespread interest in the Internet as a vehicle for commerce occurred in 1993.

The World Wide Web ("WWW" or "Web")

The WWW began as a very small part of the Internet. However, because the Web has had such strong appeal, it is now the dominant part and is what most people think about when they think of the Internet. The **World Wide Web (WWW)** is the portion of the Internet that has color, sound, graphics, animation, video, interactivity, and ways to move from one Web page to another.[15] It is made up of millions of individual pages that are linked to other pages. The Web received its name because the many interconnections between Web pages evoke the image of a spider web. The links that enable the user to move from one Web site to another are called **hypertext.** Hypertext links often are recognizable by their underline. The software that enables one to view the pages on the WWW is called a **browser.**

Given the differences between the Internet and the WWW, can you explain how the concept of e-commerce fits in? Many business strategies that involve the Internet are commonly referred to as "electronic commerce." **Electronic commerce** is the completion of buying and selling transactions online.[16] E-commerce is a label that encompasses a wide variety of business activities, including those most typically associated with marketing. Electronic commerce had its start in corporations and banks, primarily as a means of facilitating business transactions electronically. Two of these early applications of electronic commerce were electronic data interchange (EDI) and electronic funds transfer (EFT). Now that you have reviewed the key concepts associated with the Internet, let's examine some of the advantages and disadvantages associated with this new marketing medium.

Advantages and Disadvantages

As a medium, the Internet offers the following advantages:

- *Wide Reach.*   The Internet reaches a worldwide audience of millions of consumers and enables small companies and entrepreneurs to be transformed into global entities instantaneously.
- *Convenience.*   The Internet is almost like a global trade show that is open 24 hours a day, 7 days a week. Consumers can shop from their homes at any time of the day or night.
- *Selective Communication.*   The Internet enables marketers to target and communicate with customers and interested prospects, both locally and globally, and offers instant worldwide access with 24 hours per day, 7 days per week, 365 days per year.
- *Low Cost.*   Direct marketers pay for the Internet based on local telephone access, not on how widely they distribute their message. Thus, the Internet offers a near zero incremental contact cost and worldwide access without long-distance charges.

- *Creative Variety.* Direct marketers can select from an endless array of creative formats and options, including, animation, sound, text, graphics, and video. Just check out the Web sites of 1-800-FLOWERS (www.1800flowers.com) or the Gap (www.gap.com) and see for yourself.
- *Inbound Transmission Ease.* The Internet enables quick and easy inbound transmissions and replies, since systems now exist which will automatically fulfill information requests from visitors to the direct marketers homepage. Just check out any of the airline Web sites, such as Delta (www.delta.com), and you can obtain flight schedule information and availability along with airfares with just a few clicks of your mouse.
- *Flexibility.* The Internet offers great flexibility and permits changes in offers and direct response communications instantly, instead of waiting until the next printed catalog is published to change prices or other features.

The Internet also possesses several disadvantages.

- *Unregulated.* The Internet is still evolving and is unregulated at the present time. Many uncontrollable variables, such as legal aspects, must be constantly monitored.
- *Lack of Control.* The Internet is difficult to control—anyone can click on a Web site and obtain information. In addition, it is driven by the end-user—since the end-user must seek out what he or she wants and when he or she wants it. Thus, direct marketers cannot control who visits their Web site or when consumers visit their Web site.
- *Limited Reach.* The Internet can only reach certain consumer types—omitting anyone who does not have computer access, and failing to reach those who have computer access but opt not to spend time on-line.
- *Lack of Privacy.* Privacy concerns are on the rise—once again marketers must keep abreast of changing policies.
- *Lack of Technical Support.* Internet users often need technical support for their on-line activities. This is a deterrent for some prospective Internet users, especially those in other countries where technology and technological support lags behind that of the United States.

Regardless of its disadvantages, the Internet is an important direct marketing channel and can provide support to and be supported by other channels. In fact, cross-channel influence has become so important that direct marketers are beginning to measure the percentage of customers that looked for or purchased something previously seen in another channel. Research has shown that 68 percent of all on-line customers who received a catalog, first shopped the catalog, then bought on-line. Similarly, 25 percent of all on-line shoppers first shopped in a retail store.[17] The next section will explain the many applications of the Internet—beyond consummating purchases.

APPLICATIONS OF INTERACTIVE MEDIA

Some companies use the Internet to provide customer service, while others use it to sell goods and services. However, most companies have established a Web site with the primary purpose of disseminating product/service information. Three primary marketing activities are well suited to the Web. They include[18]

- making information available to prospective customers
- providing customer support and service
- enabling transactions to occur

Direct marketers have been performing the above marketing activities for decades without the Internet, but now due to technological advances, they are able to transfer their knowledge and experience to this new, interactive marketing medium. It is also clear to many companies that merely having a "Web presence" is not enough. What it takes to succeed in this electronic marketplace is a clear plan for the organization to follow and execute, along with a strong commitment of both human resources and capital for the technological infrastructure to support the various on-line marketing activities.

The popularity of personal computers combined with the development of the WWW has spawned the growth of electronic technology. Most companies have followed a natural pattern of evolution in their e-business initiatives. This evolution can be summarized in the following six stages:[19]

> *Stage 1:*   Brochureware—In this stage organizations began to use the Internet as a bulleting board for brochures, employee telephone directories, and, over time, for more critical documents such as catalogs and price lists.
> *Stage 2:*   Customer Interactivity—This next phase is when companies created an interactive dialogue with their customers, encouraging them to inquire, request, register, etc. on-line.
> *Stage 3:*   Transaction Enabler—In this stage companies began using the Internet to expand transactions (selling products, procuring supplies, enabling internal processes such as human resources activities).
> *Stage 4:*   One-to-One Relationships—This is when the Internet began to be used to create customized silos of interactivity. Because Web technology allows companies to deal with customers on a one-to-one basis, product pricing became fluid, dictated by individual customers, often in an auction process.
> *Stage 5:*   Real-Time Organizations—Zero latency organizations are able to plan, execute, and aggregate buyers and sellers in a virtual arena. These companies understand customer needs and deliver value in real-time.
> *Stage 6:*   Communities of Interests (COINs)—The Internet helps companies create communities of common interests (by content, by community, and/or by type of commerce) that closely link various partners in a value chain. Examples of this stage of involvement include marketing companies such as eBay where consumers who possess common needs or interests can competitively bid on a given product.

Although marketing on the Web is the primary use of interactive media for direct marketers, e-mail marketing, on-line market research, Web advertising, and e-branding are other tasks effectively conducted on the Internet. Let's look briefly at each.

E-Mail Marketing

E-mail is a part of the Internet that is separate from the Web. It is electronic communication that travels all over the world via the Internet, but is not a part of the World Wide Web. There are three types of e-mail of interest to marketers:[20]

1. ***E-mail from companies targeting promotions to specific consumers.*** This method is most effective when it is database-driven and customized to match the needs of specific market segments of consumers.
2. ***E-mail from the consumer to the company,*** often placing an inquiry or a request for additional information.
3. ***E-mail from the consumer to another consumer.*** This is the electronic version of word of mouth. This form of e-mail has also been referred to as **viral marketing** where e-mail messages are forwarded to other consumers by a consumer. In fact, the term "viralocity" has been coined to measure both the number of messages and the rate of speed by which e-mail messages are forwarded by a consumer to other consumers.

E-mail is similar to traditional direct mail in that it is conducted on a one-to-one, personal basis. However, e-mail costs a lot less than traditional mail and, therefore, enables companies to communicate on a more frequent basis. Research shows that 80 percent of Internet users respond to e-mail, compared with a 2-percent response rate for the average direct-mail campaign.[21] In addition, consumers respond more quickly to e-mail than to direct mail, with replies normally coming from consumers within 36 hours from the time they received the message. Consumer response for an average direct-mail campaign will take weeks. E-mail direct marketing is most productive when companies use their own customer lists instead of lists generated by third parties. Many companies have developed an e-mail list of their customers and send each customer newsletters and other communication on a regular basis. For example, New England Business Service, the Groton, Massachusetts-based manufacturer of forms and supplies started an e-mail newsletter. Their customers must register to receive the newsletter, which includes tips for business owners and special offers. Their current circulation list is about 6,000 customers and is growing.[22]

E-mail is also an effective means of distributing special promotional information to customers. In Figure 9-2, Lillian Vernon Corporation offers its valued customers an opportunity to receive e-mails on new products and special promotions.

Another example of effective e-mail marketing is a well-known hotel that recently sent an e-mail message offering discounted hotel rooms to about 8,000 customers who agreed to be put on its mailing list; the offer received a 45-percent response and resulted in the sale of 2,000 rooms.[23]

According to Boldfish, Inc., a well-known e-mail marketing company, there are 10 strategies direct marketers should follow in order to achieve direct e-mail success.

Because sending e-mail messages is easy, cheap, and fast, some companies have misused this medium. **Spam** is the term for unsolicited e-mail messages. Spam is considered the "junk mail" of the Internet. Direct marketers can avoid sending spam by handling customer information carefully and adhering to ethical e-mail marketing practices. Providing a way for consumers to "opt-in" to a mailing list is a starting point for practicing ethical e-mail marketing. Direct marketers must follow the established rules for using e-mail. One commandment with which direct marketers must comply is "Thou shalt NOT send e-mails to consumers without obtaining their permission."

According to Hans Peter Brondmo, founder of Post Communications, a company that creates customized e-mail marketing programs, there are many rules that marketers should follow when conducting e-mail marketing.

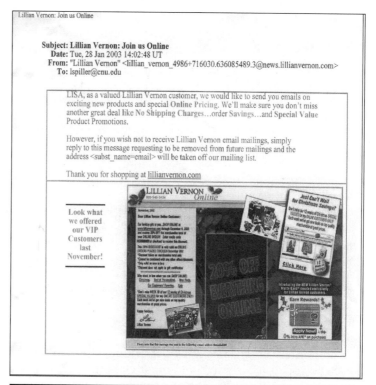

FIGURE 9-2   Lillian Vernon Corporation On-line Offer Request

When done right, an e-mail campaign can build profitable customer relationships at a fraction of the cost of other direct marketing methods. There are new regulatory issues affecting e-mail marketing activities and direct marketers must keep abreast of the changes occurring in this area. Once an abstract concept, permission-based marketing is quickly becoming a reality.

On-line Market Research

Technology has made marketing information readily available, easy to access, current, and affordable. It has transformed secondary data collection into a highly effective and relevant marketing activity. Much of the information available on-line, such as government reports, is free of charge which enables marketers of any size to access and obtain this valuable market data. The main cost involved in conducting on-line market research is the human resource costs, since it requires manpower to surf the Net and identify and download relevant information.

Primary data collection has also been enhanced by technological progress. Consumers seem to be more receptive to participating in surveys conducted via the Internet as opposed to mail and telephone surveys. Thus, the Internet offers an alternative medium for executing marketing research studies on a one-to-one basis with customers. On the other hand, with the number of Internet users approaching 50 percent of the U.S. population, an estimated 30 to 40 percent of marketers will use on-line primary research in 2005, and on-line methods are projected to generate $3.1 billion (50 percent) of revenue for marketing research firms.[24] Some of the more common primary data collection techniques being implemented on-line include on-line surveys and on-line panels.

On-line Surveys

On-line survey research is carried out by either sending electronic questionnaires to customers via individual e-mails or by posting a survey on a company's Web site. Sending questions via e-mail allows for personalization and control over the timing of and distribution of the on-line survey. E-mail surveys are also the preferred method of data collection in countries where users must pay by the hour for Internet connection since e-mail may be answered off-line while a respondent must be on-line to complete a survey on the Web.

However, Web surveys can be written in a more "user-friendly" fashion than e-mail, with radio buttons, drop-down menus, and blank spaces for each customer to record their responses. Although Web surveys are not as easy to create as most other types of Web pages, Web surveys are converted to hypertext markup language (HTML) files and do not need lengthy printing, collating, and mailing time. **HTML** is a simple coding system used to format documents for viewing by Web clients. Web pages are usually written in this standard specification. Among its other advantages, on-line survey research is still relatively fast and inexpensive and can be conducted nearly instantaneously on a worldwide basis.

On-line Panels

On-line panels overcome the sampling and response problems associated with on-line surveys. **On-line panels,** which are similar to focus group interviews, are discussions marketers conduct with people who have agreed to talk about a selected topic over a period of time. For example, a fitness magazine might conduct an on-line panel to discuss the latest available fitness equipment and to obtain feedback as to the ease and effectiveness of the equipment. Normally, panelists receive a fee or gifts for their participation. Each person must complete a comprehensive survey after being accepted to participate as a panelist so that researchers have data about their characteristics and behavior. On-line panels provide marketers with a supply of willing respondents about whom they already have extensive data. Thus, there is no need to ask demographic questions each time. Marketers contact panelists on a regular basis with high expectations for a positive response to their request for information. Many publishers have on-line panels to assist in the development of magazine content. For example, *Working Mother* magazine has an on-line reader advisory panel. Digital Marketing Services (DMS) has exclusive rights to millions of America Online (AOL) members for marketing research purposes. DMS provides survey opportunities to AOL members and gives respondents credits on their monthly AOL bill for participating in market research activities.[25]

Web Advertising

Web advertising is highly versatile. It can be as simple as text (a few paragraphs or literally pages of text), or highly detailed to include graphics, sound, animation, and hyperlinks. Check out the Web sites of Starbucks (www.starbucks.com) and

Ben & Jerry's (www.benjerrys.com) to enjoy the colors, animation, and sound they provide. The most common form of Web advertising is banner ads.

Banner Advertising

"Banners" and "buttons" basically occupy designated space that is available for rent on Web pages. Banners are rectangular in shape and buttons are either square or round. **Banner advertising** is the digital analog to print ads, targeting a broad audience with the goal of creating awareness about the product or service being promoted. Banner ads are similar to space ads used in print media; however, they have video and audio capabilities because they are designed for interactive media.

Because banner ads request an immediate action from the viewer, they are a direct-response ad. The goal of banner ads is two-fold: first, to increase brand awareness by exposing consumers to the banner ad, and second, to maximize the "*click-through*" rates or "ad clicks." **Click-through rates,** also called **ad clicks,** are defined as the number of times a user "clicks" on an on-line ad, often measured as a function of time ("ad clicks per day"). Typically, click-through rates are relatively low, less than 2 percent in most cases.[26] Direct marketers must be creative to increase these rates.

Here are four strategies to maximize click-through rates:[27]

- *Ask for the click-through action.* The easiest way to increase click-through is to simply ask for it. A research study found a 44-percent improvement in click-through rates just from providing visual or text cues that a banner leads to more information.[28]
- *Animate a banner advertisement.* Animation increases the likelihood that the ad will draw the user's attention and also generates more clicks than static banners all else being equal.
- *Involve the audience.* The third generation of banner ads is interactive. Engage the viewers to allow them to personalize ads to their needs. Involving the viewer allows the advertiser to get to know them better . . . one of the primary goals of direct marketing!
- *Change creative messages frequently.* The nature of the Internet means that responses occur quickly, on the first few impressions. Therefore, creative wears out more quickly than with traditional media. Research indicates that the appeal of banners wear out after about 200,000 to 400,000 impressions.[29]

The first banner ad appeared on Hot Wired in 1994. Since that time, banner advertising has progressed through the following three stages:[30]

Stage 1: In the beginning, banner ads featured the words "click here," "free," and "download" in bright colors. These words were used to train users that banners were interactive and that by clicking on them the user would be transported to another Web site.

Stage 2: This stage featured banners with animation. Movement captured consumers attention on an otherwise static Web page. Many banner ads used today still feature animation.

Stage 3: This final stage produced the interactive banner. Some banner ads feature drop-down menus, built-in games, check boxes, and search boxes to engage the user.

According to AdKnowledge (www.adknowledge.com), the three most common sizes of banner ads are 480 X 60 pixels, 120 X 60 pixels, and 88 X 31 pixels.[31] **Pixel** stands for picture element. It is a tiny dot of light on a computer screen. A computer screen is divided into tiny little pixels. The color of a pixel is partly determined by how many "bits" (on/off units) are used to store the pixel. A bit is the smallest unit of information that a computer understands. A **bit** is one electronic pulse.[32]

Banner advertising is not the only advertising tool available on the Web, although it is the dominant form. "Embedded ads" are gaining attention, too. **Embedded ads** allow the viewer to receive more information without having to link to other Web sites. These ads are designed to overcome the space limitations of banners. Other forms of Web advertising are being investigated and will likely change the nature of Web advertising in the near future as this dynamic new medium evolves. Savvy marketers are incorporating Web advertising in their promotional mix, but not replacing traditional media. The effectiveness of combining Web ads with other promotional strategies is illustrated in the following Oldsmobile example.

In an effort to attract younger customers, Oldsmobile launched a Web campaign in 1997. It placed banner ads on Web sites, sponsored contests on partner Web sites such as Launch.com and ETRADE.com, and utilized print and television advertising. During a Super Bowl game, Oldsmobile gave away thousands of autographed footballs to fans who visited and registered on the Oldsmobile Web site. Additionally, Oldsmobile partnered with Blockbuster Video where those individuals who registered on-line and test drove a Silhouette would earn a $50 gift certificate to Blockbuster. How well did the promotional mix work? Quite well. In 18 months, the age of the average Oldsmobile buyer dropped from 60 to 48, while at the same time the average income and educational level of its customers increased.

Source: Adapted from Mark McMaster, "Reinventing an Old Brand Online," *Sales & Marketing Management* Vol: 152, no. 11, (November 2000): pp 25–26.

E-Branding

Using the Web to provide customer service and support while maintaining customer awareness of a company's brand is an increasingly popular marketing strategy. **Branding** refers to the use of a name, term, symbol, or design (or a combination of these) to identify a company's goods and services and to distinguish them from their competitors. **E-branding** refers to carrying out branding strategies electronically. The benefits of branding include the customer's recognition of the brand and the ultimate trust the customer places in the brand name (and parent company). Remember that on the Internet the customer is in the driver's seat and can select which Web sites to visit. Without name-brand familiarity, the customer will likely fail to click on a Web site that could contain needed information and/or need-satisfying products and services.

Using one of the company's brand names in the Web address will help the consumer quickly find the site and will also serve to reinforce the brand name.

When consumers go to a company's Web site, they are looking primarily for product and business information. Thus, marketers should use the Web for more than traditional advertising and entertainment, they should use it as a forum to communicate a company's brand and its benefits to consumers. The Web is one of the places where one can effectively combine branding and direct marketing.

General Mills, Inc. provides a good example of how branding on the Web may be executed. The Web site for its Betty Crocker brand (www.bettycrocker.com) is extremely service and relationship-oriented, offering recipes, menus, and more. The Web site, shown in Figure 9-3, attracts approximately 400,000 visitors a month, for 9-million page impressions. Consumers have downloaded over 5 million Betty Crocker recipes from the site.[33]

FIGURE 9-3   Betty Crocker Web Site

MEASURING AND INCREASING SITE TRAFFIC AND STICKINESS

In the above section you reviewed the many applications of the Internet. Now let's discuss how direct marketers make these applications work effectively to meet marketing goals and objectives. One of the primary goals of using interactive media is to communicate and interact with consumers and prospects on a one-to-one basis. But unlike most traditional media which flows from the company to the customer or prospect, interactive media relies on consumers to locate the Web site and click on it to receive the message. This dynamic is an example of the **pull strategy** in which consumers must seek out and demand information and/or products and services from the producer. The opposite is a **push strategy** where information and marketing activities follow the normal path of distribution of a product (from the producer to the consumer). Therefore, promoting a Web site is a critical part of successfully marketing via interactive media.

Web Site Promotion

For decades the advertising community has argued that if consumers are not aware of a company's products or services, they cannot purchase them. The same is true for a company's web site. The theory that if you "build a better mousetrap," consumers will beat a path to your door doesn't work. Investing thousands of dollars into developing the most creative Web site means nothing if potential customers don't know it exists.

Here are ten strategies designed to promote a Web site to increase site traffic:[34]

- Put the **URL** (universal resource locator, otherwise known as the Internet address) *everywhere*. All promotional literature should contain the URL, including business cards, letterhead, print and other advertisements, direct-mail packages, etc.
- Ask and you shall receive. Ask visitors to bookmark the Web site.
- Give customers a *reason* to bookmark the Web site. Give away free stuff such as advice, contests, premiums, etc. Be creative and be sure to promote the fact that the Web site offers free stuff. By providing value to the customer you give them a reason to click, stick, and come back.
- Offer a chat room or provide a bulletin board to open communication among consumers and give them a reason to come back.
- Create an e-business card that accompanies each e-mail messages. Be sure to include the URL in hyperlink format.
- Establish a reciprocal Web linking program. Most people find Web sites by following links from other sites. For example, go to Apartments.com and not only an you view apartments for rent throughout the United States, but you can link to many services commonly related to apartment rental. The Web site provides links to moving companies, truck rental companies, banks, insurance companies, storage facilities, utility connections, furniture for rent, and much more. A good way to add links to a Web site is to explore competitor's URLs and develop a list of sites from which you should be linked.
- Use search engines and register the site at other Web sites. A **search engine** is similar to a library card catalog. It is an index of key words that enables Web browsers to find what they are looking for. Some search engines such as Yahoo! will search the entire Web, making them more powerful than those that only search by category type and a site description.

- Promote the site in mailings and newsgroups. Be sure to offer useful advice in a news group related to the business and discretely add your short e-business card at the end of the message.
- Create a banner ad. In return for showing banners on your Web site, bannerexchange.com will place your banner on the Banner Exchange Network of Web pages. For more information go to http://www.bannerexchange.com.
- Promote the site using good ole' word-of-mouth advertising. Tell everyone about your Web site.

Creating Web Site Stickiness

Once consumers "click" on a company's site, they want them to "stick" or, at the very least, bookmark the site for easy navigation in returning to it. It is well known that when surfing the Web, consumers may "click" on many Web sites, but only stay or "stick" for 15 seconds to 2 minutes, depending on the visitor's objectives.[35]

Some strategies to get consumers to "stick" on a particular Web site include:

- Make the Web site easy to navigate—consumers should not and will not work to make sense of the Web site.
- Offer free giveaways.
- Provide relevant, timely news and information.
- Create dynamic Web pages—ones that change every time the customer revisits.
- Offer chat rooms.
- Personalize the Web page.
- Be sure to establish necessary links for the consumer to pull in relevant data from other sites to create a "one-stop shopping" effect, thus, there will be no need to go to other Web sites. For example, if you go to www.hotels.com you can make reservations from 6,500 hotels in over 300 cities. In addition, the Web site enables you to link to rental car companies, such as Alamo Rental Car, and reserve an automobile for your trip or vacation. You can even plan a vacation package complete with hotel, airline, and automobile reservations directly from the Web site. That's one-stop shopping!

Media Measurement—"E-Metrics"

The above section described a variety of ways direct marketers can make Internet applications effective. This section explains how direct marketers measure that effectiveness. All direct marketing activities must be accountable and measurable, and those carried out on interactive media are no different. They provide direct response advertising opportunities whose effectiveness we can measure. However, since consumers initiate most of the interactions on the Internet and not the marketer, the measurement tactics are different from those used for traditional media.

The most common interactive measurement technique is based on a "clickstream" model. A **clickstream** is "the database created by the date-stamped and time-stamped, coded/interpreted, button-pushing events enacted by users of interactive media."[36] The following five elements make up the clickstream and provide direct marketers with the measurement needed to determine the effectiveness of Internet applications:[37]

- **Hits** are basically the equivalent of an advertising impression; that is, given that a person is viewing a particular page at a particular time. A hit is Web terminology for any request for data from a Web page or file. It is often used to compare popularity/traffic of a site in the context of getting so many "hits" during a given period. Regardless of how long or short the visit to a Web page, each link on the page counts as a hit. For this reason, hits are easily measured, but may provide little real information to the direct marketer.

- **Pages** are a measure of the number of pages downloaded from a specific site at a particular time. One link may allow the viewer access to many pages, but too often the viewer may not scroll through all of them and therefore may not see all the material contained in the Web site. Thus, a count of pages also may not provide meaningful measurement.
- **Visits** count the total number of times a user accessed a particular site during a given period of time. This measure is similar to "frequency" in mass media advertising. Visits are different from hits. A single visit is usually recorded as several hits and, depending on the browser, the page size, and other factors, the number of hits per page can vary widely.
- **Users** measure the number of different people, that is "unique visitors," who visit a particular site during a given period of time. This measure is similar to "reach" in mass media advertising.
- **Identified users** is the demographic profile of either visits or users of a site during a specified period of time. It is similar to the demographic profiles of readers, listeners, or viewers that mass media provides to their advertisers.

Other forms of measurement include tracking or measuring capabilities that enable companies to follow and document the Web surfing habits of consumers. The process is simple. When a consumer visits a Web site, the site plants a **cookie** (an electronic tag) on the consumer's computer. The cookie enables the Web site to follow consumers as they shop and recognize them on return visits. Cookies can reveal how long the consumer stays at a page, which products the consumer likes, and which other sites the consumer visits. Although it is possible to program a computer to reject cookies, cookies allow personalized information to be stored at the consumer's favorite Web sites, making shopping and other on-line transactions more convenient.

Marketers can also track how many people have received the company's e-mails, how many people have opened them, how many people have responded by clicking on the link in the e-mail, and how many people have taken the action the e-mail has requested. Direct marketers demand measurability and accountability, and interactive media delivers it in real-time.

REGULATORY ISSUES

On-line Privacy Issues

While millions of consumers have been quick to embrace technology, consumers have called for regulation. Some consumers view on-line data collection as an invasion of privacy that, at best, inundates them with spam, and at worst, risks putting their financial or personal information in the hands of potential employers, lenders, or insurance companies. Most consumers freely provide their e-mail address or shopping preferences in exchange for better customer service. However, they don't expect marketers to share the information without their consent and use it to target them for other offers (especially from other companies).

DMA On-line Privacy Principles

The DMA provides direct marketers with ethical principles of conduct in order to establish a self-regulating function rather than accept broad governmental intervention. DMA On-line Privacy Principles state that all marketers operating on-line sites should

1. make available their information practices to consumers in a *prominent place* on their Web site; and
2. furnish consumers with the opportunity to opt out of the disclosure of such information. An example of an opt-out notice is shown in Figure 9-4.

In addition, the on-line notice should be easy to find, easy to read, and easy to understand. As shown in Figure 9-5, the DMA itself is following these privacy principles by disclosing its own information practices and offering Web site visitors an opportunity to opt out of receiving future marketing communications from the organization.

The DMA privacy policy specifically expects the *on-line notice* to perform the following seven tasks:[38]

1. Identify the marketer.
2. Disclose their e-mail and postal addresses.
3. State whether the marketer collects personal information on-line from individuals.
4. Contain a disclosure statement regarding the *information collected* (see Figure 9-6 for examples of disclosure statements for information collected).
5. Contain a disclosure statement regarding the *uses of such information* (see Figure 9-7 for examples of disclosure statements for information uses).
6. State the nature and purpose of disclosures of such information and the types of persons to which disclosures may be made.
7. Explain the mechanism by which the individual may limit the disclosure of such information.

In addition, the DMA privacy principles address *unsolicited advertising e-mail* and *marketing on-line to children.* Regarding unsolicited marketing e-mail, the DMA offers the following four principles:[39]

1. On-line solicitations should be posted to newsgroups, bulleting boards, and chat rooms only when consistent with the forum's stated policies.

FIGURE 9-4 Example of Opt-Out Notice

> *"I do not want (please check all that apply):*
>
> ___ *Transfer of information to third parties*
> ___ *Contact by third parties*
> ___ *Future offers from us*

Source: The Direct-Marketing Association, Inc., "Online Privacy Principles & Guidelines, (Direct Marketing Association, New York, NY, July 1997, p. 5). Reproduced with permission.

FIGURE 9-5   DMA Web Site Privacy Policy

This is the web site of The Direct Marketing Association (The DMA).

Our postal address is:

1120 Avenue of the Americas
New York, NY 10036-6700

We can be reached via e-mail at dma@the-dma.org or you can reach us by telephone at 212.768.7277.

For years The DMA has developed guidelines and programs to help marketers meet consumer privacy expectations. By providing consumers with notice of information practices ad the ability to remove their names from lists, marketers have demonstrated their commitment to protecting consumer privacy. As interactive media evolve, The DMA and its membership renew their commitment to offer notice and opt-out in this new medium.

Note: The DMA does not compile, buy, sell, rent or trade consumer mailing lists. All marketing efforts we undertake are targeted toward a business audience only.

For each visitor to our Web page, our Web server does not recognize information regarding the domain or e-mail address.

We collect the e-mail addresses of those who communicate with us via e-mail, and any information volunteered by the customer, such as survey information and/or site registrations. The information we collect is used to improve the content of our Web page and to contact customers for marketing purposes.

If you do not want to receive e-mail from the DMA in the future, please let us know by sending us an e-mail, calling or writing us at the above address.

Marketers that supply The DMA with their postal address on-line may receive periodic mailings from us with information on new DMA products and services or upcoming DMA events. They may also receive mailings from other reputable companies.

If you do not wish to receive such mailings, please let us know by sending an e-mail, calling or writing us at the above address. Please provide us with your exact name and address and we will be sure your name is removed from our marketing list and/or the list we share with other organizations. Persons who supply The DMA with their telephone numbers on-line may receive telephone contact from us with information regarding orders they have placed on-line, new products and services or upcoming events. They may also receive periodic telemarketing calls from other carefully screened business-to-business marketers.

If you do not wish to receive such telephone calls, please let us know by sending e-mail to us at the above address, or calling us at the above telephone number or writing to us at the above address. Please provide your correct phone number and we will be sure your name is removed from our marketing list and/or the list we share with other organizations.

Companies that wish to create a privacy policy page and post it to their Web site can use *The DMA's Privacy Policy Creation Tool.*

Source: The Direct Marketing Association, Inc., "Web site Privacy Policy," <http://www.the-dma.org/policy.html> (August 2001). Reprinted with permission.

"We collect information on the times and ways you use our Web site."

"We keep the information you provide in responding to our questionnaire."

"We maintain your name, postal, and e-mail addresses, telephone number, and payment and order processing information. We also may keep information on your communications with our customer service representatives."

FIGURE 9-6   Examples of Information Collected Disclosure Statement

Source: The Direct-Marketing Association, Inc., "Online Privacy Principles & Guidelines, (Direct Marketing Association, New York, NY, July 1997, p. 4). Reproduced with permission.

2. Online e-mail solicitations should be clearly identified as solicitations and should disclose the marketer's identity.

3. Consumers should be given an opportunity to opt out prior to marketers using the information for on-line solicitations or at least have the their on-line information suppressed. Marketers who operate chat areas, newsgroups, and other public forums should use these spaces to inform individuals that information they voluntarily disclose in these areas may result in unsolicited messages by others.

4. Marketers should take reasonable steps to ensure that they meet the industry principles for sharing of lists and data about consumers.

DMA Guidelines for on-line data collection from or about children include:[40]

- Marketers should take into consideration the age, knowledge, sophistication, and maturity of the intended audiences.
- Marketers should be sensitive to parents' concerns about the collection of their children's names, addresses, or other similar information, and should support the ability of parents to limit the collection of such data for marketing purposes through the notice and opt out.
- Marketers should limit the use of data collected from children in the course of their on-line activities to the promotion, sale, and delivery of goods and services the provision of all necessary customer services, the performance of market research, and other appropriate marketing activities.
- Marketers should also effectively explain that the information is being requested for marketing purposes.
- Marketers should implement strict security measures to ensure against unauthorized access, alteration, or dissemination of the data collected on-line from children.

FIGURE 9-7   Examples of Information Uses Disclosure Statement

---

"We will use your e-mail address only to contact you about merchandise or services you have indicated are of interest to you."

"We use information for billing purposes and to measure consumer interest in our various services or pages."

Source: The Direct-Marketing Association, Inc., "Online Privacy Principles & Guidelines, (Direct Marketing Association, New York, NY, July 1997, p. 4). Reproduced with permission.

With these privacy principles for on-line marketing activities in place, it is up to direct marketers to ensure that their marketing programs include responsive personal information protection practices.

Third Party Intervention: Infomediaries

Infomediaires are companies that act as intermediaries or third parties by gathering personal information from a user and providing it to other sites *with* the user's approval. These companies vary in their methods, but each attempts to provide consumers with a type of privacy assistance by enabling consumers to control and limit access to their personal information when shopping online. An overview of such firms, including Enonymous, PrivaSeek, and Zero-Knowledge Systems, is given in Figure 9-8.

Critics of infomediaries claim that these companies fail to provide enough protection and that they have the potential to exploit what they claim to protect. The World Wide Web Consortium, the Washington-based organization that sets standards for the Internet, has been working on the Platform for Privacy Preferences initiative (called P3P). The

---

FIGURE 9-8   A Description of Select Infomediaries

Enonymous
This web site rating service enables web surfers to go to enonymous.com and download a software program called Enonymous Adviser. When installed, the program asks the user to provide information including name, date of birth, shipping and billing addresses, telephone number, e-mail address, credit card number and preferred method of contact. Then when the user goes shopping online or visits a portal or other site that requires registration, Enonymous checks to see what rating it has given the site's privacy policy—whether and under what circumstances it will share information it receives with third parties. If the site has a low rating or has not been rated, the Enonymous Advisor sends a pop up message alerting the user. However, if the site has an adequate privacy policy, the software retrieves the necessary data from the user's hard drive and fills in the blank fields when the user registers or makes a purchase. This service has evaluated more 30,000 web sites and has assigned each a one-four star privacy rating.

PrivaSeek
This company's Persona Valet program functions like a digital wallet and stores user information at a data center (not on the user's hard drive). The service then allows the user to pick and choose what data a site can have. Privaseek does not rate sites, assuming that users will read a site's privacy policy. Once a user sets up an account, Persona Valet maintains for the user a record of sites visited, when, and what personal information was submitted. The company has formed partnerships with several online merchants. In return for PrivaSeek's services, users will see advertisements and special offers geared to their interests and shopping tastes when they visit partner sites, based on the information they have given to PrivaSeek.

Zero-Knowledge Systems
This organization offers consumers a service called the "Freedom Program." This service gives Web surfers anonymity by protecting identifiable information within the network of the company's servers. The way this service works is that people who download the Freedom software can create several user identities, or pseudonyms. In addition to encrypting data so that a person or another computer cannot read it, Freedom routes the information through the company's network of servers so that it cannot be traced to a user's computer. At present, a pseudonym costs $10 per year and the software can be downloaded at www.freedom.net

Source: Catherine Greenman, "Efforts to Keep the Web from Getting Too Personal," *New York Times,* April 27, 2000, Sec. G, p. 6.

initiative calls for the development of a software program that enables Web browsers to read a Web site's privacy policy automatically and compare it with the user's privacy preferences. What is unclear, at present, is how the P3P will work with existing informediary programs, and whether browser companies and Web developers will incorporate it into their products. Most recently, Microsoft's Director of Corporate Privacy said the company was working toward developing a P3P compliance program for businesses and consumers. This program would automatically compare a Web site operator's privacy practices to the consumer's preferences, and inform the consumer of any nonconformance or mismatch. Direct marketers need to stay abreast of infomediaries and the role they may play in the future as gatekeepers to consumers. They certainly could become a third-party regulator of many on-line marketing activities.

Summary

The Internet is the newest interactive medium in direct marketing. It is "interactive" because it meets the three criteria established by the DMA where consumers must be able to have control over the information being presented, the pace at which the products are reviewed, and the ability to place an order or request additional information directly from the medium itself. Direct marketers use the Internet to communicate with both final consumers as well as business consumers. This chapter details the importance of business-to-business Internet transactions. The chapter also explains the differences between the Internet and the World Wide Web.

The Internet offers direct marketers a number of advantages over other media channels and yet it also has distinct disadvantages. Some of the advantages include cost, speed and ease of communications, great flexibility in creative formats, and effective targeting of messages to consumers. Some of the disadvantages include limited reach, lack of control, and lack of regulation. There are many applications of interactive media—e-mail marketing, on-line market research, Web advertising, and e-branding are some of the chief applications. Each of these applications along with strategies to maximize their effectiveness are explained in this chapter. As with any direct marketing medium, accountability and measurability are important characteristics. Strategies for increasing Web site traffic and stickiness are presented in the chapter, along with how to measure the effectiveness of this new direct marketing medium. There are many regulatory issues affecting this new medium. On-line privacy issues, the DMA On-line Privacy Principles, and third-party infomediaries are included among these important regulatory issues.

Key Terms

- Internet, 207
- World Wide Web (WWW), 208
- hypertext, 208
- browser, 208
- electronic commerce, 208
- e-mail, 210
- viral marketing, 211
- spam, 211
- HTML, 213
- on-line panels, 213

- banner advertising, 214
- click-through rates, 214
- ad clicks, 214
- pixel, 215
- bit, 215
- embedded ads, 215
- branding, 215
- e-branding, 215
- pull strategy, 217
- push strategy, 217

- URL, 217
- search engine, 217
- clickstream, 218
- hits, 218
- pages, 219
- visits, 219
- users, 219
- identified users, 219
- cookie, 219
- infomediaries, 223

Review Questions

1. What makes marketing on the Internet different from other forms of direct marketing media?
2. What are some advantages of interactive media?
3. What does the term *Internet* mean?
4. Explain the evolution of e-business.
5. What are the requirements of interactive media?
6. What is *e-mail marketing?*
7. How has technology changed marketing research?
8. What are five strategies to maximizing "click-through" rates?
9. What are some of the on-line privacy principles that the Direct Marketing Association (DMA) suggests all marketers operating on-line sites honor?
10. What are infomediaries, what do they do, and what are some of the objections that have been raised about them?

Exercise

The company you work for has recently hired a new member to your direct marketing team. This person was a direct marketing whiz, 20 years ago, when the age of the Internet had not yet changed the face of business. For the past 20 years, this person has been living in a very obscure and isolated country where the Internet has not even been introduced yet. It is your job to bring this person back up to speed. How will you transform her knowledge of the activities of the Internet? Create a communication outline to be used as a training guide to bring this individual up to date on how marketing is taking place in the twenty-first century. Be sure to address the key aspects of the Internet as presented throughout this chapter.

CASE: DELL COMPUTER CORPORATION

OVERVIEW

The Dell Inc. is an American success story and is an example of how an entrepreneur can build a company using a strategy of direct marketing. Illustrating the use of the Internet as a direct marketing medium, Dell allows customers to customize their orders in order to maximize customer value and customer satisfaction. This case demonstrates the power of the Internet as a direct marketing method. It also shows how this new medium is focused on developing relationships with each customer on a one-to-one basis.

CASE

In 1984 Michael Dell started the Dell Inc. from his college dorm room in Texas. Today, Dell is located in Round Rock, Texas, and is the world's largest direct computer systems company. Dell is a very profitable company. In May 2002 it reported profits of $457 million and revenues of $8.1 billion. Dell has achieved great success by delivering great customer value coupled with excellent customer service and fast delivery. It is not unusual for a customer to place an order for a customer-made computer on Monday and take delivery of his new computer by mid-week.

Direct Marketing Channels
Dell Inc. utilizes two main direct marketing channels in selling its computers and related products. One method is telemarketing via inbound calling. Dell was the first company in the industry to offer direct, toll-free, 24-hour technical support services. This method allows consumers to speak with an actual representative to place their order. Providing one-on-one interaction with customers has proven to be a successful method for Dell as well as various other companies. This method also provides an avenue for both up-selling and cross-selling opportunities. Once the telephone representative has sold the customer a personal computer

they are then able to suggest all the necessary accessories as well as warranty options to accompany their product.

Dell's Web Site
The second direct marketing channel utilized by Dell Inc. is its Web site. Currently consumers are able to visit www.dell.com to obtain information about Dell's many products and services. Some of these include servers, storage, workstations, notebook computers, and desktop computers. After clicking the "Buy a Dell" icon on Dell's Web site, the consumer can select and customize a computer system to meet his specific needs. Consumers are then able to place their order with a simple click of the "purchase" button on the Dell Web site and within five minutes the customer receives an electronic order confirmation. At that point, consumers can begin tracking their order status via Internet links that Dell has created to allow customers to track shipments online via Airborne Express, Fed Exp, United Parcel Service, or their preferred shipper. In addition, within 48 hours from the time the order was placed, Dell sends each customer a detailed manufacturing update. That's customer service! And that is why the Internet has become Dell's number one direct marketing channel.

The Web site, as shown in Figure 9-9, allows customers to experience Dell's "build to order" process. While placing an order on its Web site you are able to view the products and accessories you wish to order. These pictures are also accompanied by prices to provide the customers with a visual of the purchase that they are about to make. The Internet is a prime medium for cross-selling as well. How does Dell make use of this capability? The Dell Web site provides an area where customers are able to log in. This allows the computer to identify the user and all the products that they have previously purchased. At that point the customer is able to view and determine which

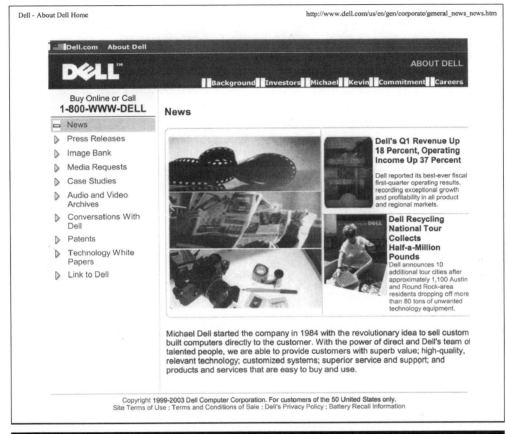

Dell - About Dell Home
http://www.dell.com/us/en/gen/corporate/general_news_news.htm

FIGURE 9-9 Dell Web Site Homepage

products complement the ones they have previously purchased.

Dell started selling computers via its Web site in 1996. Today they sell more than $30 million worth of computers daily from the Web site, accounting for over almost half its revenues. The Web site receives millions of visits at more than 50 country-specific sites, and on-line buyers range from individual consumers to large corporations.

Customer Service
Dell provides its business-to-business (B2B) customers an added service. In addition to offering each of them customized computers, Dell offers to pre-configure each computer to

meet the exact specifications of each business customer. Dell often preloads computers with a company's own software and can even affix inventory tags onto each machine so that computers can be delivered directly to an employee's desk. That kind of service saves the business customer a great deal of time and money. As you might expect based on this kind of superior service, Dell's B2B sales have skyrocketed—now accounting for nearly two-thirds of Dell's business.

In addition to receiving excellent customer service, Dell's customers enjoy lower prices as well. How is that possible? Dell's direct marketing methods translate into lower costs and greater efficiency for the company, advantages that, in turn, are passed on to Dell customers. Dell carries no inventory other than work in progress. It builds only the exact systems customers order and thus can avoid storing parts and finished systems. The firm also requires suppliers to keep stock no more than an hour's drive from the Dell manufacturing plant—and most suppliers are located less than 20 minutes away. Because Dell doesn't use any middlemen, it avoids added distribution costs. Like all direct marketers, it interacts with each customer on a person-to-person basis, to better detect changes in consumer demand and strengthen customer relationships.

Dell Inc.'s distinct competency is its ability to conduct direct selling methods and offer innovative ideas. Whether a customer is placing their order on the Internet or by telephone, their computers are personalized to their specific needs. One of the keys to enhancing customer relationships is allowing the customer to have an individual identity. This is one of the many Customer Relationship Management (CRM) techniques that Dell has in place. CRM has also allowed Dell representatives to call a customer by his name when answering inbound calls and enabled the Dell Web site to refer to customer's usernames while they are browsing the company Web site.

To ensure the survival of any company, marketing and advertising must be carried out effectively. Dell Inc. has chosen to create brand awareness through e-mails sent to existing and potential customers, as well as advertisements placed on various related Web sites. In order to ensure ultimate customer satisfaction, Dell conducts surveys via e-mail, which include questions about customer satisfaction, customer demographics, psychographics, market trends, and preferences. This allows customers to voice their opinions and to provide Dell with crucial information to better market its products to its target markets.

The latest evolution in Dell's Internet strategy is to provide Web sites customized for particular consumer market segments (e.g., small, medium, or large businesses, education, etc.) or for a specific country or region to give each market segment better customer service.

SUMMARY AND CONCLUSION

Dell Inc. has built its business empire via direct marketing. Much of Dell's success has come from constant improvements and innovations in its direct marketing methods. The Internet has not only been used to sell computers, it has also been used to keep Dell's shareholders and customers informed of the latest news within Dell Inc. Brochures, press releases, technical reports, and other documents may be accessed on the Internet. This method is convenient for customers as well as cost efficient for Dell. Allowing its shareholders and customers to have timely access to special documents gives them a sense of importance. Dell Inc. is leveraging the power of direct marketing on the Internet. It has become very profitable in its on-line direct selling efforts and have quickly become the leader in the personal computer supplier market.

Sources: Dell Inc., Dell Home and Home Office, <http://www.dell.com/us/en/dhs/default.htm?rpo=true> May, 2002; Dell Inc., Dell Investor Relations, <http://www.dell.com/us/en/gen/corporate/investor/investor/.htm>, May, 2002; Dell Inc., Dell Financial Fact Sheet for FY '02–'04 <http://www.dell.com/us/en/gen/corporate/investor/investor_000_q4fy02fs.htm>, May, 2002; Roger A. Kerin and Robert A. Peterson, *Strategic Marketing Problems* (Upper Saddle River, NJ: Prentice Hall, 2001); Philip Kotler and Gary Armstrong, *Principles of Marketing,* 9th ed. (Upper Saddle River, NJ: Prentice Hall, 2001), 615–621; Joseph E. Maglitta, "Special Dell-ivery," *Electronic Business* 23, no. 12 (1997): 43–47; and Gary McWilliams, "Whirlwind on the Web," *Business Week,* April 7, 1997, 132–36. ■

Case Discussion Questions

1. What are the advantages and disadvantages associated with Dell Inc.'s two methods of receiving orders? Why have these methods provided Dell with a distinct competitive advantage?
2. Browse the Dell Web site at www.dell.com and make a list of the innovations Dell has used to differentiates itself as an on-line marketer.
3. What forms of marketing research does Dell currently conduct? What additional forms of market research could they use? How would they carry out these suggested research activities?
4. Based on this case and your visit to Dell's Web site, what are the primary advantages/disadvantages of utilizing the Internet as an advertising medium?

Notes

1. *Interactive Direct Marketing: A DMA Guide to New Media Opportunities,* Introduction Section, (New York, The Direct Marketing Association, Inc., 2000), 5.
2. Eloise Coupey, *Marketing and the Internet,* (Upper Saddle River, NJ: Prentice Hall, 2001), 7.
3. *Economic Impact: U.S. Direct & Interactive Marketing Today,* 8th ed. (New York: The Direct Marketing Association, Inc., 2003,) 35–36.
4. Ibid., 36.
5. Eloise Coupey, *Marketing and the Internet* (Upper Saddle River, NJ: Prentice Hall, 2001), 5.
6. Saeed Samiee, "The Internet and International Marketing: Is There a Fit?" *Journal of Interactive Marketing* (1998), Vol. 12, Issue 4, pp. 5–21.
7. Veronis Suhler, "Stevenson Communications Industry Forecast, 2002," in *The Statistical Fact Book 2003,* 25th ed. (New York: The Direct Marketing Association, Inc., 2003), 125.
8. Ibid., 126.
9. Melinda Ligos, "Clicks & Misses," *Sales & Marketing Management* (June 2000), 68.
10. *The Statistical Fact Book 2002,* 24th ed. (New York: The Direct Marketing Association, Inc., 2002), 132.
11. Veronis Suhler, "The Publishing & Media Group, Forrester Reseacher, Paul Kagan Associates, Kelsey Group, 2001," in *The Statistical Fact Book 2002,* 24th ed. (New York: The Direct Marketing Association), 135.
12. *Economic Impact: U.S. Direct & Interactive Marketing Today,* 8th ed. (New York: The Direct Marketing Association, Inc., 2003), 36.
13. Judy Strauss and Raymond Frost, *E-Marketing,* 2nd ed. (Upper Saddle River, NJ: Prentice Hall, 2001), 9.
14. Ibid., 10.
15. Robin Williams and John Tollett, *The Non-Designer's Web Book,* 2nd ed. (Berkeley, CA: Peachpit Press, 2000), 21.
16. Eloise Coupey, *Marketing and the Internet* (Upper Saddle River, NJ: Prentice Hall, 2001), 17.
17. "The Multi-Channel Retail Report," J.C. Williams Group; Shop.org; and BizRate.com; *The Statistical Fact Book 2002,* 24th ed. (New York: The Direct Marketing Association, 2002), 154.
18. Mary Lou Roberts and Paul D. Berger, *Direct Marketing Management,* 2nd ed. (Upper Saddle River, NJ: Prentice Hall, 1999), 414.
19. Adapted from Amir Hartman and John Sifonis, with John Kador, *Net Ready: Strategies for Success in the E-Conomy* (New York: McGraw-Hill, 2000), xviii–xix.
20. Judy Strauss and Raymond Frost, *E-Marketing,* 2nd ed. (Upper Saddle River, NJ: Prentice Hall, 2001), 21.

21. Roberta Rusaro, "More Sites Use E-Mail for Marketing," *Computerworld,* October 19, 1998, 51–54.

22. Sarah Lorge, "Banner Ads vs. E-Mail Marketing," *Sales & Marketing Management* 151, no. 8 (August 1999): 15.

23. BoldFish, "Top Ten Stratetgies for Direct Email Success," BoldFish, Inc., Santa Clara, CA, obtained in August, 2002 <www.boldfish.com>.

24. Dana James, "The Future of Online Research," *Marketing News,* January 3, 2000, 1–11.

25. Maryann Jones Thompson, "When Market Research Turns into Marketing," *The Industry Standard* (August 30, 1999), 68–76.

26. Tracy L. Tuten, Michael Bosnjak, and Wolfgang Bandilla, "Banner-Advertised Web Surveys," *Marketing Research* 11, no. 4 (Winter 1999/Spring, 2000): 18.

27. "Tips to Make Your Internet Advertisements More Effective," *Mediaweek,* May 5, 1997, 46–50.

28. Ibid.

29. Ibid.

30. Judy Strauss and Raymond Frost, *E-Marketing,* 2nd ed. (Upper Saddle River, NJ: Prentice Hall, 2001), 227.

31. Ibid., 226.

32. Robin Williams & John Tollett, *The Non-Designer's Web Book,* 2nd ed. (Berkeley, CA: Peachpit Press, 2000), 162.

33. David Klein, "Advertisers Should Invest in Sites, Not Just Banner Ads," *Advertising Age* 68, no. 43 (October 27, 1997): 52.

34. Adapted from Michelle Carpenter, Electronic Commerce Education and Training Services Manager, "The Virginia Electronic Commerce Technology Center" (unpublished presentation presented at Christopher Newport University, Newport News, Virginia June 13, 2001).

35. Horacio D. Rozanski, Gerry Bollman, and Martin Lipman, "Seize the Occasion: Usage-Based Segmentation for Internet Marketers," *e-INSIGHTS* (2001), 7.

36. Mary Lou Roberts and Paul D. Berger, *Direct Marketing Management,* 2nd ed. (Upper Saddle River, NJ: Prentice Hall, 1999), 426.

37. Ibid., 426–427.

38. The Direct Marketing Association, Inc., "Online Marketing Privacy Principles and Guidelines," July Direct Marketing Associations, New York, NY, July 1997, pp. 3–9.

39. Ibid.

40. Ibid.

CHAPTER

10

CUSTOMER SERVICE AND FULFILLMENT

This chapter discusses what many professionals refer to as the "back-end" of the direct marketing process—the customer service and fulfillment operations. Many experts contend that back-end functions alone cannot make a sale but certainly can break one. More importantly, the lack of good customer service and efficient fulfillment operations can injure the relationship the direct marketer has with the customer and ultimately lead to the loss of that customer. As we'll see later in the chapter with a simple order from Lillian Vernon Online, business does not end when the firm receives an order. We'll also discuss the components of customer service and fulfillment along with strategies to help direct marketers maximize their customer's satisfaction level. Finally, we'll look at delivery options.

THE IMPORTANCE OF CUSTOMER SERVICE

Each customer wants to be satisfied. **Customer satisfaction** has been defined as the extent to which a firm fulfills a consumer's needs, desires, and expectations.[1] Contrary to what many believe, the customer doesn't care about what has to happen behind the scenes to get the product or service delivered on time. The customer is primarily interested in what the marketer can do to satisfy her needs.

Direct marketers know that simply providing a quality product or service is not enough. So they have begun to create strategies designed to move goods from factories and warehouses directly to the customer in the shortest possible time and at the lowest possible cost, using the level of service to differentiate their organization from others. It is also customer service that enables the organization to exceed rather than simply meet the customer's expectations. Delivering high-quality customer service can enable the direct marketer to develop a long-term relationship with each customer, which is, after all, the ultimate goal of direct marketing.

Customer Relationship Management

Customer relationship management (CRM) is a business strategy designed to identify and maximize customer value. This strategy requires a customer-centric business philosophy and culture to support effective marketing services processes. It is about developing and implementing business strategies and supporting technologies that close the gaps between an organization's current and potential performance in customer acquisition, growth, and retention. In essence, CRM is a big picture approach that integrates sales, order fulfillment and customer service, and coordinates and unifies all points of interaction with the customer, throughout the customer life cycle and across multiple channels.

Business doesn't end when an order is received. In fact, most direct marketers believe that is when it begins. Let's take a look at all the CRM strategies direct marketers implement before and after a customer places an order. What does a customer experience when shopping on-line?

Imagine a customer sitting at a personal computer in the comforts of their home. They have just connected to Lillian Vernon Online (www.lillianvernon.com). Figure 10-1 shows the homepage of the Lillian Vernon Online Web site. Stop there

FIGURE 10-1   Lillian Vernon Corporation Web Site

for a moment. How the customer or prospective customer got to this point is also a part of CRM—since CRM begins with prospecting for new customers. Researching and analyzing the purchasing history of current customers enables the direct marketer to more effectively prospect for new customers. So once a prospect or customer is interested in the products and services offered by Lillian Vernon Corporation the customer becomes a likely candidate to go to Lillian Vernon Online. A great deal of business planning, consumer research, and historical sales analysis has gone into determining which products are displayed on the homepage. In addition, great care has been put forth to organize and design the Web site so the customer can easily navigate and shop from it. This is just the beginning of CRM.

Once the customer makes a product selection (such as a leather handbag, as shown in Figure 10-2) the Web site automatically offers additional related products or services (e.g., matching leather organizers). This is an example of up-selling, cross-selling, and suggestive selling. Any of these suggested items may be added to the customer's shopping cart with a simple *click*. Then the Web site visually displays the updated shopping cart to the customer as shown in Figure 10-3. This point provides another cross-selling opportunity with an offer to purchase some inexpensive unrelated items (e.g., a small box of candy). Think of this as offering impulse items—similar to those that are located near the checkout counters in traditional retail stores. Once the customer makes her final selections, the customer proceeds to a checkout stage where the Web site totals the order, adds shipping and handling fees, and verifies personalization (if applicable). Figure 10-4 shows a sample customer checkout form for a customer purchasing three personalized leather bags. The shipping and billing addresses are determined as is the method of payment. Most direct marketers offer several payment methods to enable each customer to select the preferred method. Next, Lillian Vernon sends the customer an order confirmation.

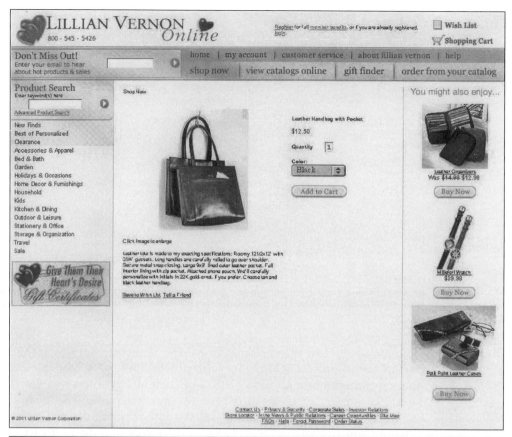

FIGURE 10-2   Lillian Vernon Online Up-Selling and Cross-Selling Opportunities

Figure 10-5, shows that this is an opportunity for the company to thank the customer and to provide the order number in case the customer has an inquiry about that particular order. In this example, Lillian Vernon Corporation also confirms the customer's gift message.

What happens next? A few days later Lillian Vernon Corporation may send the customer an e-mail providing details about the status of the on-line order. This is an additional opportunity for the direct marketer to thank the customer for her order and to provide an order update. In addition, it allows the company to remind the customer about their customer service priority and how their products carry a 100-percent money-back guarantee. In sum, it enables the direct marketer to strengthen the relationship it has with that customer.

Lillian Vernon Corporation enters the information collected about the customer and her transaction data into the Lillian Vernon customer database. The company will use this information to target future direct response communications to that customer. From this point on, the direct marketer will communicate with that customer on a regular basis. Each time Lillian Vernon Corporation contacts the customer via some direct response media (e.g., an on-line message, telephone call, or catalog) the contact and

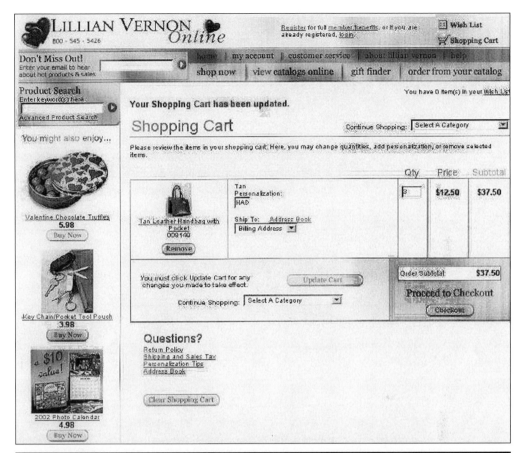

FIGURE 10-3   Sample On-Line Shopping Cart of a Lillian Vernon Customer with Additional Cross-Selling Effort

response (if applicable) will help to further that customer relationship. Although we've used an on-line example above, all CRM activities at Lillian Vernon Corporation are similar, whether on-line or through a catalog or a telephone contact. The case provided at the end of this chapter details what happens on the company side of the Lillian Vernon Corporation CRM.

The main purpose of all back-end functions is to build and maintain a better relationship with the customer. When carried out effectively, the back-end functions can strengthen customer relationships and encourage the customer to continue to purchase from the organization.

Beyond waiting for the customer to repeat purchase, how do direct marketers determine the strength of their relationship with the customer? How does a direct marketer assess the level of service the customer is receiving from their organization? How will direct marketers determine whether their relationship with each customer can be improved? How can they know what is best for the customer? The next section details how direct marketers can evaluate CRM.

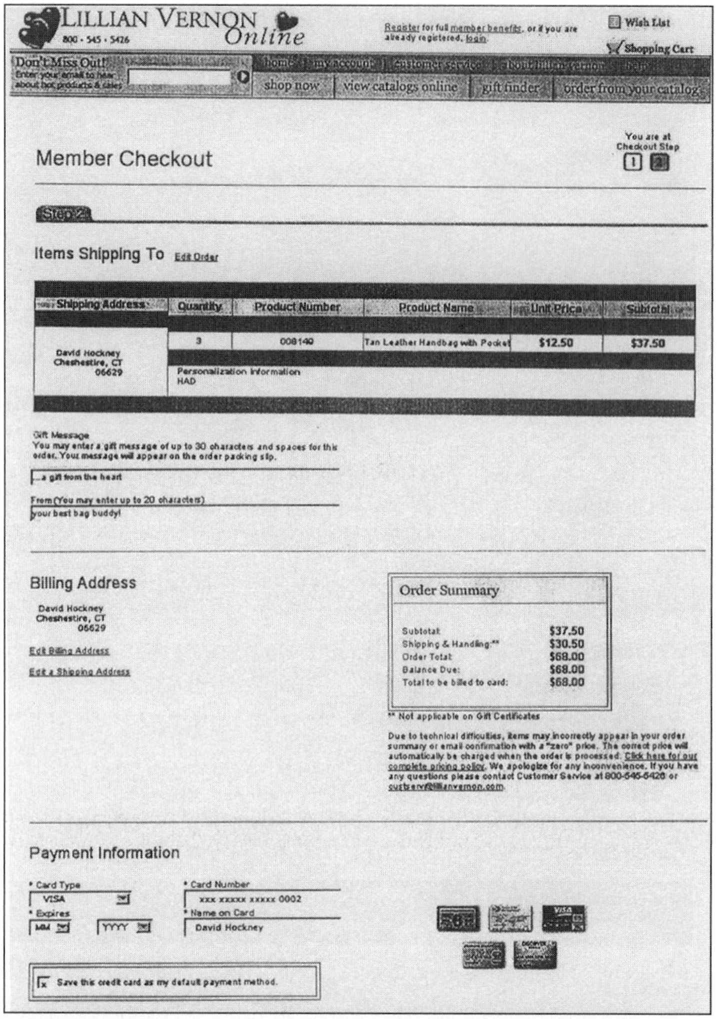

FIGURE 10-4   Sample On-Line Order Form for a Lillian Vernon Customer

Evaluating CRM

Direct marketers can evaluate CRM strength in a number of ways. First, they might begin by pretending they are the customer. Every organization likes to think they are doing a good job of serving their customers. But savvy direct marketers investigate this from both sides of the relationship. Are inquiries processed in a timely manner? Are customer complaints addressed as quickly and as professionally as they should be? Is delivery time as expedient as you promised the customer it would be? Direct marketers determine the answers to these questions in two ways:

1. Place an inquiry, order, or a complaint with the organization under a fictitious name and experience first hand the level of customer service your organization really delivers.

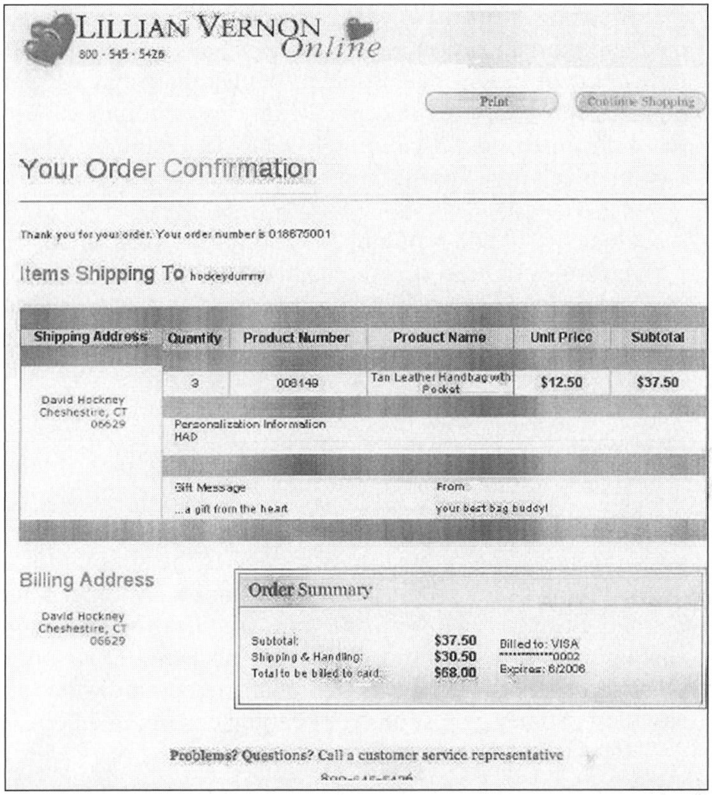

FIGURE 10-5   On-Line Customer Order Confirmation Notice

2. Send periodic follow-up surveys consisting of only a few questions designed to address the customer's fulfillment experience. Questions might address the speed, accuracy, and degree of staff friendliness the customer experienced when interacting with the organization. An example of a brief customer survey designed for assessing the fulfillment experience is shown in Figure 10-6.

Regardless of the manner in which you obtain this information, it is critical to perceive the fulfillment experience from the customer's point of view. This experience and any subsequent action you take should lead to an improved relationship with the customer.

FIGURE 10-6   Sample Customer Survey

Please tell us how we rated:	Excellent	Good	Fair	Poor
Knowledgeable Phone Operators	❏	❏	❏	❏
Promptness of Delivery	❏	❏	❏	❏
Overall Impression of Service	❏	❏	❏	❏
Other Comments:				

A strong focus on CRM is crucial to the success and profitability of every direct marketing organization. Many professionals believe that it may be necessary to make CRM part of the broader concept of customer management because the whole organization must support and participate in customer relationship maintenance. These words from Robert McKim, CEO of MS Database Marketing sum up the value of customer relationship marketing:

> Gone are the days of empty 'customer is king' lip service. The key to the new rules of success is the ability to address each customer's idiosyncrasies and needs, balanced with their current and future value to the company. Firms that do this can differentiate themselves from the competition, forge long-term customer relationships, engender customer loyalty, stop attrition and enjoy success in the 21st century.[2]

The next section provides suggestions and examples of how to keep customers happy.

Keeping Customers Happy

At the foundation of customer service is the simple notion of *keeping the customer happy*. Only a satisfied customer is a happy customer. Only a satisfied customer will come back and purchase from your organization again and again. However, keeping customers happy does not happen by accident. Direct marketers need to constantly keep abreast of the customer's changing needs and wants and must always strive to satisfy these. Some suggestions for keeping customers happy are shown here.

TIPS FOR KEEPING CUSTOMERS HAPPY

- Remember that the customer is always right.
- Don't promise something you cannot deliver.
- Inform your customers about how to return products.
- Inform your customers about how to complain.

- Test your own service.
- Date and record all customer correspondence.
- Investigate your competitor's offerings on a regular basis.
- Exercise care in billing and collection.

Source: Adapted from Stanley J. Fenvessy, "Introduction to Fulfillment," in *Direct Marketing Manual* (New York: Direct Marketing Association, Inc., October 1979), p. 500: 1.

Many companies go out of their way to exceed customer expectations and delight the customer. Let's look at some examples of great customer service.

SubmitOrder.com, an outside fulfillment center, recently handled a customer service incident for Limited Too. The dimensions of a toy were missing in the catalog and the customer called to get assistance prior to placing an order. The SubmitOrder representative checked both the Limited Too Web site and the store catalog, but was unable to locate the needed information. Eventually, the employee put the customer on hold and went and measured the toy himself. After taking the customer's order, the employee notified Limited Too executives that the toy dimensions should be added to the catalog along with the product description.[3] That's good customer service.

Let's look at another example. One holiday season a customer ordered two "Towers of Treats" from the Harry and David Specialty Foods and Gifts catalog to have delivered to two neighbors. The customer had placed the order in time to have the packages arrive the day or two prior to seeing the neighbors at a dinner party. The packages didn't arrive before the date of the dinner, nor did they arrive before the holiday. When the customer found this out, she telephoned the company. The customer service department was very professional and apologetic and offered to re-send the ordered items that had not arrived. Within a week the packages were received by each of the neighbors and the customer received a note of thanks for both her order and her patience, another apology for the inconvenience, *and* a free gift. Mistakes happen . . . but how they are handled can either contribute to a positive customer experience or reinforce a negative one.

Providing good customer service can sometimes be just a simple response to a customer's suggestion. For example, Lillian Vernon Corporation once received a letter from a customer who explained that while she purchased a lot of presents from their catalog for her nieces and nephews, she sometimes had trouble figuring out what present was suitable for which age group. Since the time of that letter, Lillian Vernon catalog copy includes age guidelines to assist customers with making those purchase decisions.[4] Good customer service is an important part of fulfilling the customer's expectations. The next section details what else is involved in the direct marketing fulfillment process.

FULFILLMENT

What Is Fulfillment?

Fulfillment is the act of carrying out a customer's expectations. Strictly defined, fulfillment means sending the product to the customer or delivering the service agreed upon. Loosely defined, it includes the entire dialogue (all interactions with the customer) and delivery functions. Marketers also see fulfillment as a part of the "extended product," or the intangible part of the product. For example, think in terms of the dialogue that a customer has with an organization. A customer or potential customer may communicate with the direct marketer by making an inquiry or placing an order and then expects to receive a response in a timely fashion. Likewise, customers expect their orders to be filled and delivered in a timely fashion. These dialogue and delivery activities are fulfillment.

Adequate fulfillment, by minimizing the time between ordering and receiving, can alleviate two distinct handicaps inherent in direct marketing: (1) a time lag between placing an order and receiving it; and (2) a lack of familiarity with the actual product, which has been purchased remotely by mail, telephone, or on-line. Ultimate success in direct marketing depends on adequate fulfillment. It has been said that "The best copy, the best graphics, and the wisest choice of lists are all a sheer waste of money, time, and talent if they are not followed through with really outstanding fulfillment."[5] Let's investigate the standards direct marketers must meet in order to provide really outstanding fulfillment.

Traditional Fulfillment Standards

Fulfillment standards have changed over the past couple of decades. The consumer is increasingly desiring, demanding, and expecting faster turnaround times on orders and all forms of communication with companies. This is especially true of those orders and inquiries that come to the organization via the Internet. Consumers are busier today, they are more astute, and they procrastinate. With overnight delivery, 800 numbers, fax machines, and the Internet, direct marketers have inadvertently encouraged customers to wait longer before placing an order because the consumer expects an immediate delivery services from the direct marketer.[6] While not every direct marketer can provide immediate delivery services, all direct marketers must uphold certain delivery standards. The following are some basic fulfillment standards that direct marketing organizations should follow to ensure excellent customer service.[7]

BASIC FULFILLMENT STANDARDS

1. Orders should be shipped between 48 to 72 hours of placement.

2. Organizations should strive for an 85 to 90 percent rate on shipment, where 85 to 90 percent of the products are available in the warehouse to be shipped upon receipt of the order. If the product is not available, the customer should be informed of that at the time of order, and given the option either to wait for the back order or to select a different item.

3. Customer refunds should be processed within 72 hours, or at least acknowledged, so that an already dissatisfied customer is not further inconvenienced.

4. Ninety percent of all telephone calls placed to the organization should be answered without a holding delay. This requires good operational planning on behalf of the organization.

5. Customers should receive a response to any inquiry they place to the organization within one calendar week from the time of receipt of the inquiry.

Source: Adapted from Heather Thiermann, "Fulfillment: Do It Right," *Target Marketing* Vol 9, no. 11 (November 1986).

THE FULFILLMENT PROCESS

The fulfillment process consists of the following six basic elements: offer, response, processing, shipping, billing, and customer service. Figure 10-7 shows a model of the elements involved in the fulfillment process. Let us now take a closer look at each element.

FIGURE 10-7 The Fulfillment Process

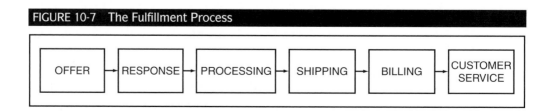

The Offer

We saw in Chapter 4 that the **offer** is the terms under which a direct marketer promotes a specific product or service to the customer. To create an offer the direct marketers first undertakes a number of activities, such as a close examination of the target customer, market segmentation, product or service research, database analysis, price determination, packaging requirements, and others. Direct marketers should properly address and direct the product/service offer and ensure that it is relevant to the needs of the addressee. This description should be adequate and fair and communicate the offer's relevance to the prospect's needs. Direct marketers should clearly state all disclosures and all options, such as sizes and colors. Direct marketers must specify credit terms. They should leave nothing to the imagination of the consumer during this initial stage.

A relevant product offering is timely and clear. Since an order form is an essential contractual document, it should be legally correct as well as distinct, simply stated, and easy to follow. When creating the order form, the direct marketer may use check-off boxes, or something equally easy to identify, for allowing customers to select size, color, or style variations and any other specialized information, such as personalization.

The Response

Direct marketers generally receive consumer responses (inquiries) or transactions (orders) via mail, telephone, fax, or the Internet. If an order or inquiry is placed through the mail, by fax or via the Internet, it is critical that the consumer completes the order form in a full and accurate manner. The consumer must provide all information necessary for the direct marketer to fill the order. If the order or inquiry is placed via telephone, then telephone operators need to be especially diligent in collecting order information. The way an organization handles the receipt of an order or inquiry is a critical juncture in the fulfillment process

Processing

After the direct marketer receives an order, the marketer undertakes editing and coding as well as credit checking and capturing of vital data for updating the database. The seller also prepares a series of documents such as shipping labels, billing notifications, and inventory instructions. At this stage, if there might be a delay in shipping an order, the marketer lets the customer know and anticipates any possible complaints.

Inventory control is another critical part of fulfillment operations. Direct marketers must examine inventory for quality checks prior to packaging and, if possible, after packaging, as well. Computer technology can be of great assistance in processing orders. For example, at Lillian Vernon Corporation, computers are programmed to catch errors such as an invalid address or an invalid credit card. Further, if an item can be personalized and the order information provided by the customer does not include personalization information, the computer flags the order and alerts the employee of the situation.[8]

Shipping

A computerized inventory control system is often the key to proper and timely shipment. Out-of-stock and back orders, requiring separate shipments later, are costly to the direct marketer and frustrating to the customer.

Back orders may even result in corrective action by governmental agencies. The Federal Trade Commission (FTC) trade regulations require all direct marketers to comply with strict guidelines in out-of-stock situations by notifying the customer if an item cannot be shipped within 30 days of the time it was placed. In addition, the customer must have the opportunity to cancel the order because of the out-of-stock condition. Direct marketers should not substitute a similar item to try to fulfill the sale, nor send a different color or size without explicit authorization from the customer. If these FTC guidelines are not followed, direct marketers may incur punitive actions, such as fines.

Billing

Once an order is on its way, the organization should receive payment as expeditiously as possible. If the customer did not use a credit or debit card and payment did not accompany the order, then clear billing instructions, with appropriate follow-up, are vital to ensure not only payment but also customer goodwill.

This need for clarity and accuracy also extends to proper receipt and posting of the payment, especially with extended-pay options. We often hear of computer errors, such as incorrect billings and incorrect postings, but more than likely these are human instruction errors.

Customer Service

The customer service function of the fulfillment process specifically refers to the handling of complaints, inquiries, replacements, and special problems. The high costs associated with this kind of customer service should be one of the incentives to getting it right the first time. Another more important incentive is, of course, that only a satisfied customer comes back. Therefore, since direct marketers place great importance on repeat business, they should pay great attention to detail in all aspects of the fulfillment process so as to eliminate the need to handle complaints and special problems. This care will also eliminate the risk of losing a valued customer.

However, since 100-percent quality control is often unattainable, shipping and billing errors inevitably occur and only prompt handling and adjustment can overcome these. A customer might receive an incorrect shipment, be erroneously billed for a product that has been paid for, or be billed incessantly for a product that was returned. Though such occurrences can become extremely complicated, all should be meticulously adjusted as soon as possible.

Not all communications from customers relevant to fulfillment are complaints—many are inquiries. Many seek further information and some request additional orders. These, too, are a proper concern of the fulfillment operation and properly fall under the heading of customer service. Good customer service is simply good business. Some tips for providing excellent customer service are presented in Figure 10-8.

FULFILLMENT OPTIONS

Options for fulfilling a customer's order include handling all of the processing within the company (in-house), outsourcing the fulfillment activities to an outside fulfillment service, and handling the fulfillment activities online, either in-house or with an outside agency. Let's see what each of these entails and how marketers choose among them.

FIGURE 10-8   Tips for Providing Excellent Customer Service

TIPS FOR PROVIDING EXCELLENT CUSTOMER SERVICE

1. *Conduct Customer Satisfaction Research.* A simple survey asking customers to indicate how well the company and its competitors are performing should be conducted on a regular basis.

2. *Simplify Your Guarantee.* Omit the confusing legal jargon and explain the refund and replacement policy in simple everyday language.

3. *Acknowledge Orders.* If merchandise cannot be shipped immediately, send a postcard acknowledgment. Many customers probably won't mind waiting a short time period for their order if they know that their order has been received and is getting careful attention by the direct marketer.

4. *Ship Merchandise More Promptly.* Most professionals believe that order turn-around time should be one week. Thus, the product should be in the customer's hands the week following the one in which the order was placed.

5. *Don't Bill Before You Ship.* Customers should be told that payment is not necessary until after the order has been received—just in case they receive an invoice prior to the merchandise they order.

6. *Acknowledge Returns and Cancellations.* When customers return merchandise, they want to be assured that the direct marketer has received it. Send a simple acknowledgment card telling the customer you received the returned goods or cancellation request, explain that it may take a couple of weeks to process it, and to disregard any invoice for the product(s) that they may receive in the interim.

7. *Answer Correspondence Promptly.* Nothing is more bothersome to the customer than having to write multiple letters or make multiple calls to get a problem straightened out with the direct marketer. Direct marketers can use a form with check-off boxes, if necessary, to make it easier for the customer to reply. Most importantly, follow through to get the problem straightened out to minimize the inconvenience of the customer.

8. *Make Complaint Resolution a Priority.* Recent research points to the fact that customers who have a complaint or problem satisfactorily resolved become *better* long-term customers than those who never had a problem. In addition, it is well documented that an unhappy customer tells many more people about their dissatisfaction than does a happy customer.

9. *Appoint Your Own Consumer Affairs Manager.* This person might be called the "customer service manager." Their job is to keep customers happy, seeing that orders go out promptly and that complaints are handled properly. This person should be empowered by the organization to make changes in policy and procedures.

10. *Make Customers Your Top Priority.* Everyone within an organization should understand the value of keeping customers satisfied and happy. Train and reward employees for good customer service.

Sources: Adapted from Jim Kobs, *Profitable Direct Marketing* (Lincolnwood, IL: NTC Business Books, 1993); and Bob Stone, *Successful Direct Marketing Methods* (Lincolnwood, IL: NTC Business Books, 1994).

In-House Fulfillment

Many traditional direct marketing organizations (L.L. Bean, Lands' End, Lillian Vernon, Speigel, Inc., Williams-Sonoma, Orvis, Avon, etc.) operate their own fulfillment centers. Most of these direct marketers have invested heavily in automation and bar code systems to make their fulfillment centers more efficient and improve customer service. However, as many professionals agree, automation in a fulfillment operation warehouse must benefit the customer as well as the company. Some direct marketers believe that the ability of an organization to deliver good customer service is *not* dependent on automation alone. They believe that new technology, coupled with a well-trained staff, can create good customer service.

The In-House Warehouse Process

While some in-house fulfillment centers may differ, most traditional fulfillment warehouses operate in a similar manner. The fulfillment warehouse process normally follows the steps presented in Figure 10-9. Let's walk through the process step by step:

1. The direct marketer receives the customer's order via mail, telephone, fax, or the Internet.
2. The direct marketer processes the order and checks inventory levels (if they have not already been checked while receiving the order).
3. The direct marketer sends several documents per order to the warehouse, including the packing slip and the picking list. The **packing slip** identifies the products to be included with the order and the **picking list** normally provides routing information regarding the most efficient way to physically move through the warehouse and assemble the items ordered by the customer.
4. Fulfillment center personnel, often called *pickers,* physically move through the warehouse and as items are picked, the items are merged with the packing slip. The pickers check the picked items against the packing slip and indicate a correct match with his or her initials. The picker is responsible for order accuracy. Figure 10-10 shows employees picking merchandise from the warehouse of Lillian Vernon Corporation's National Distribution Center.
5. The order then moves to a packing area—where the *packer* rechecks the products picked against the order and initials the packing slip before boxing the order. This is a second quality control checkpoint.
6. The packer packs the items into an appropriately sized carton enclosing a variety of materials, including a catalog, gift boxes, dunnage material (like foam or bubble wrap to protect products during shipment), and promotional inserts.

FIGURE 10-9   Flow Chart of Warehouse Process

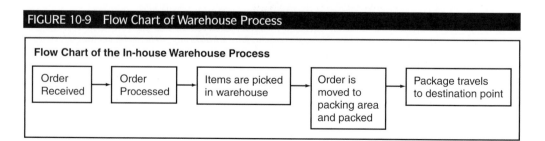

Flow Chart of the In-house Warehouse Process

Order Received → Order Processed → Items are picked in warehouse → Order is moved to packing area and packed → Package travels to destination point

FIGURE 10-10   Lillian Vernon Corporation National Distribution Center Employee Picks Merchandise from the Warehouse Shelves

These materials are within an arm's reach of the packer to ensure high productivity levels. As shown in Figure 10-11, warehouse employees must inspect, weigh, and scan each package before it is shipped to the customer.

7. Finally, as shown in Figure 10-12, the package moves via conveyor belt to the appropriate truck for transportation to its destination. Often, prior to the package leaving the warehouse, a warehouse supervisor randomly opens packages to check for order accuracy. This is the third quality control checkpoint.

Other warehouse activities occur simultaneously. For example, the warehouse is receiving shipments of products and warehouse employees are responsible for restocking the inventory as well as replenishing the packaging stations with packing materials, such as tissue paper, inserts, and bulk packing material called "peanuts." Some employees may be applying personalization to products if requested by the customer. And of course, the direct marketer is collecting customer database information and updating customer records. Inventory availability drives the efficiency and success of this fulfillment process. Occasionally a customer will not be shipped their complete order due to the inventory not being in stock. In this situation, the customer is informed that the product is on back order and will be shipped by a specified date.

However, some direct marketers do not believe in this traditional fulfillment process. They do not support the storage of products and having inventories sitting in a warehouse waiting for an order to be placed by the customer. They support the concept referred to as "integrated order fulfillment."

FIGURE 10-11   Lillian Vernon Corporation National Distribution Center Employee Scans a Package

Integrated Order Fulfillment

Integrated order fulfillment is an emerging business concept based on the idea that the process of building and delivering products should not begin until after the firm receives an order for them. This is a sharp contrast to the traditional fulfillment model in which assorted products are collected and stored in the distribution center warehouse until an order arrives.

The following eight steps describe the process of integrated order fulfillment:[9]

Step 1.   The direct marketer receives a customer's order via mail, telephone, fax, or the Internet.

Step 2.   The direct marketer processes the order. This includes logging the order into the computer system and determining whether any special promotions or discounts should be noted on the customer's invoice.

Step 3.   Next, sourcing occurs. This is where the direct marketer determines where the individual products or components needed to fill the order will come from. The primary choices are the company's own production lines or an outside, contract manufacturer.

Step 4.   Now it is time for the direct marketer to store the product. This is the brief holding of products or components in a warehouse until their scheduled delivery or manufacture times.

Step 5.   The direct marketer assembles the product. Product assembly includes the gathering of parts in a central place where they are put together to form the finished product.

FIGURE 10-12 Lillian Vernon Corporation National Distribution Center Operations

Step 6. Next, the direct marketer ships the product to the customer.
Step 7. The direct marketer tracks the distribution of the product and fulfills any after-sale service needs.
Step 8. Finally, the customer grades the company on how well it performs the entire process on each individual order.

Integrated order fulfillment will not work for every organization. It is primarily designed for those direct marketers who manufacture custom-made products on a customer-by-customer basis. According to Stig Durlow, Chairman and Chief Executive Officer of the Swedish Software Company Industrial Matematik International (IMI), who manufactures a popular fulfillment software system called System ESS, "Integrated order fulfillment helps companies make the jump from the industrial age to the information age by forcing everyone within the enterprise—including outside contractors—to think first about exactly what the customer has asked for before taking any action toward fulfilling a particular order."[10]
Integrated order fulfillment is carried out at the fulfillment center of the well-known direct marketer and personal computer manufacturer, Gateway.

GATEWAY INTEGRATED ORDER FULFILLMENT

Gateway's business model may be described as the following: Except for a few retail outlets, or showrooms, Gateway gets the word out about their product via advertising, a lot of advertising. The customer decides what computer they want and what features they want on their computer. They then call Gateway and custom build their computer over the telephone with a representative. In about five days the computer is built and shipped to the customer in Gateway's trademark white boxes with black cow spots.

When a consumer places an order, Gateway builds the computer to the customer's specification. Gateway often changes product configurations every three days. Probably the most valuable thing Gateway offers its customers is a customer-oriented approach to product customization that carries over to a comprehensive approach to customer service.

As you can already guess, Gateway has no inventory to speak of. The computers they sell are built when a consumer places an order, not before. There are several advantages of this integrated fulfillment system. For example, Gateway can change the price of the computers whenever a price change is needed. They can also give customers a better price on the computer since there is no middleman. Ted Waitt, Gateway's founder, calls this the "value equation." Companies like Gateway, who primarily base their business on a direct marketing model—blending marketing and manufacturing—are far ahead of most other companies in meeting the needs of individual customers.

Sources: Denise Duclaux, "Gateway Casually Builds Booming Business in Direct Sales," *DM News*, February 17, 1997; Michael Warshaw, "Guts and Glory: From Farm Boy to Billionaire," *Success*, March 28, 1997.

Outside Fulfillment Centers

Once upon a time, most traditional direct marketers had their own fulfillment or distribution center to warehouse products until picked and packed for shipment to customers. However, this traditional fulfillment model is changing. Today, many direct marketers are extending their businesses to the Web and are realizing their need to quickly convert their operating models from shipping in bulk to processing thousands of daily on-line orders consisting of just a few items.[11] So they are outsourcing their fulfillment operations to third-party fulfillment centers or on-line fulfillment providers in order to obtain the customer service expertise they need. Many direct marketers are moving toward the business model that management experts have dubbed the **virtual enterprise.** According to this model, the company whose name appears on any given product is primarily a marketing and customer service entity, with actual product development and distribution being handled by a broad—and sometimes far flung—network of subcontractors.[12]

Advantages of an Outside Fulfillment Service

There are certain distinct advantages of hiring an outside contractor to provide back-end support versus handling fulfillment in-house. Some of those advantages include the ability of the company to focus more specifically on marketing and sales activities, opposed to warehousing and distributing tasks. Another advantage is that outside fulfillment companies are likely to have state-of-the-art fulfillment software that most direct marketers would otherwise find too expensive to acquire. A third advantage concerns financial risk. By contracting outside fulfillment services, direct marketers can treat fulfillment costs as variable costs. Thus, there will be less financial risk because fulfillment costs will be more predictable. A final advantage is that the direct marketer may receive equivalent fulfillment services at a lower cost per order than the in-house cost per order.

Some traditional retailers just getting started in direct marketing activities, especially those planning to utilize electronic media, have also decided to outsource their fulfillment operations to a third party. Some quickly realize that fulfillment capabilities are outside their general core competencies. Many other direct marketers are outsourcing fulfillment operations so that they may concentrate on multichannel marketing activities, especially those tasks associated with the Web.

An Example of an Outside Fulfillment Company

The executives of Limited Too, a fashion leader in pre-teen clothing and accessories, decided to outsource e-fulfillment to SubmitOrder.com, a Dublin, Ohio-based firm. What attracted Limited Too executives to contract SubmitOrder.com was the broad range of services they offered beyond on-line order fulfillment. Dennis Spina, CEO of SubmitOrder.com, believes that what separates them from many outside fulfillment companies are their comprehensive services. SubmitOrder.com can do everything from setting up the information technology system to integrating the front-end sales and marketing activities with the back-end order processing and order fulfillment activities.[13] In addition, SubmitOrder.com has an IT system that can be easily linked with retailers' systems and its distribution facilities are designed to quickly move products—more than 99 percent of orders are shipped the same day they are received.[14] It was that quick order turnaround time that attracted Limited Too executives to partner with SubmitOrder.com because in the trendy fad business, you can never deliver too quickly. In addition, the customer base of Limited Too is primarily pre-teens who both demand and are accustomed to receiving instant gratification.

On-line Fulfillment

Of all the changes that computers and information technology have brought to our modern society, few are more visible than the change in the way products and services are bought and sold. ActivMedia projects that by 2005, sales of consumable items over the Internet will approach $119 billion. The entire e-retail market is projected to be more than $2 trillion.[15] Consumers have signaled acceptance of purchasing products and services over the World Wide Web.

Electronic media raise new managerial and customer service challenges for direct marketing organizations. Many organizations have learned the hard way that there is more to e-commerce than opening a Web site and inviting consumers to come and shop. It is well established that the primary problem with e-commerce customer satisfaction is *fulfillment*. According to the Better Business Bureau, botched orders topped the list of customer complaints for organizations doing business over the Internet during 1999, with problems in as many as 1 in 20 orders.[16] In addition, the Federal Trade Commission announced in August 2000 that it was imposing fines on seven companies, including Macys.com and Toysrus.com, for failing to ship products to customers as promised during the 1999 Christmas season.[17]

Fulfillment guru Bill Kuipers sees little change in fulfillment as a result of electronic media. "You still have to warehouse, pack, and ship."[18] However, Kuipers does believe that companies need to plan for the fulfillment process when they use the Internet. Customers shopping on-line have higher expectations and service standards than do their off-line counterparts.

Customers are looking for a quicker response to their order or inquiry. They often expect to receive a response to their on-line communication the same day—and no later than the next day, and they like to be able to investigate the shipping status of their orders on-line. These high consumer expectations can be a real fulfillment nightmare for the on-line direct marketer who isn't able to meet them.

E-Fulfillment

E-fulfillment refers to the integration of people, processes, and technology to ensure customer satisfaction before, during, and after the on-line buying experience.[19] It is another way of referring to fulfillment strategies for on-line orders. The term was developed by Dennis Spina, Chief Executive Officer of SubmitOrder.com. On-line retailers have what may be the unique ability to extend the interaction with their customers by creating a memorable and distinct fulfillment experience. Unlike passive traditional media, interactive media put the consumer in control, with both positive and negative consequences. The positive include the great opportunity for building brand awareness and enhancing the relationship with the customer. The organization's Web site might earn that all-important "bookmark" status on the consumer's computer. However, just one poor on-line experience can have disturbing effects. Not only will the consumer not purchase from your organization again, they are likely to tell many friends about their bad experience . . . leading to brand image deterioration.

The major problem with many e-commerce organizations is that they lack the needed focus and emphasis on e-fulfillment. According to Kuipers, e-commerce organizations treat fulfillment and customer service as incidental rather than fundamental. They're interested in technical capabilities—instant messages, e-mail, click to talk, etc.—and they don't realize that what they need most to satisfy the customer and keep the customer coming back is a polished customer fulfillment infrastructure.[20] However, that may be in part due to the fact that most organizations wanting to attract and obtain customer orders electronically don't have the fulfillment systems or infrastructures and don't want to be in the warehousing business. Therefore, these organizations normally outsource or hire third-party service bureaus to sort, pick, pack, and ship the product.

DELIVERY OPTIONS

Since the delivery of products is such a vital part of the fulfillment operations of direct marketers, we should look at the alternative delivery options that are available, especially those that provide individual delivery to households and businesses rather than those that handle bulk shipments. Direct marketers are concerned with product delivery, but also with the delivery of advertising and other promotion materials.

Multichannel Distribution

Multichannel distribution (also called dual distribution) refers to a marketer using several (two or more) competing channels of distribution to reach the same target consumer. By practicing dual distribution, direct marketers may incur greater expense, but normally yield greater customer satisfaction by enabling the customer to select their preferred shopping channel. Some customers prefer product delivery to their doorstep and others won't purchase the product without careful personal examination of the product, including trying it on for size and style decisions.

An example of multichannel distribution is Victoria's Secret, the well-known marketer of women's fashions and lingerie. They use the following three competing channels of distribution: first, their catalogs are mailed to their database of customers and prospective customers; second, their Web site encourages consumers to shop on-line at www.VictoriasSecret.com; and, third, their retail stores are located in most major shopping malls enabling consumers to come into the store to browse and purchase the merchandise in person. These channels of promotion and distribution compete with one another for the same target consumer's order, and yet, if it didn't offer all these options, the company might lose potential consumers to other marketers. Multichannel distribution offers multiple options for today's increasingly demanding consumer.

United States Postal Service

The volume and scope of operations of the United States Postal Service (USPS) is mind-boggling.[21] The USPS handled over 207 billion pieces of mail during 2001. In 2001, the growth rate of domestic mail volume was 2.1 percent, slightly lower than the growth rates for 2000 (3.1 percent) and 1999 (2.4 percent). Much of the recent growth in mail volume is attributable to direct marketing.

The total number of direct mail pieces in 2001 was 93.8 billion, and the 1996 reclassification of mail categories reflects direct mail's importance. Effective July 1, 1996, there are three categories of business mail: first-class mail, periodicals (previously second-class mail), and standard mail, the category into which direct response advertising falls (previously third- and fourth-class mail).

First-Class Mail

Accounting for 50 percent of all mailed pieces during fiscal year 2001 were more than 103 billion first-class mail pieces. This category includes business reply envelopes and cards. The postage rate is higher than for the other classes but so is the cost of priority handling and individual sorting. This category of mail is the largest source of mail revenue for the USPS, although that percentage has been steadily shrinking over the past few decades. It generated 70 percent of USPS revenue in 1977, 64.6 percent in 1987, and 56.6 percent in 2001.

Periodicals

The periodicals category consists of publications. It includes magazines, newspapers, and miscellaneous periodicals, such as classroom publications. It accounts for slightly over 10 billion mailed pieces a year. This category of mail showed a decrease in the mail volume over the years. It accounted for almost 10 percent of all mail delivered in 1977. It dropped to only 6.5 percent of mail in 1987, and continued to decline to only 5.0 percent in 2001.

Standard Mail

Standard mail is the category mainly used for the distribution of direct response advertising. Although postage rates are lower per piece, mailers of this class must ZIP code their mail, sort and bundle, tie, bag, and personally deliver the sacks of mail to the post office. Thus, the direct mailer performs up to one-half the basic tasks normally performed by the postal service for first-class mail. Delivery is also deferred. This class accounted for 43.4 percent of total mail revenue in 2001, which is an increase from 15.2 percent in 1977 and 21.1 percent in 1987. This class represents the second largest source of revenue for the USPS. Standard mail accounted for 89.9 billion pieces of mail in 2001, a decrease of 1 percent over the previous year's standard mail volume.

Special Mail Services

There are certain alternatives for expedited mail service of special interest to direct marketers. These include

- *Express Mail*—Overnight service to designated destinations for items mailed prior to 5:00 P.M. is guaranteed.
- *Mailgram*—A joint offering of the Western Union computer system and the USPS, who delivers the mailgram the next day by a postal carrier.
- *Electronic Computer Originated Mail Service (E-COM)*—Permits volume mailers to transmit computer-generated messages via certain telecommunications carriers to 25 serving post offices throughout the continental United States for further postal delivery to businesses and households. This service began in January 1982.
- *On-line Services*—As the Internet gains popularity, the United States Postal Services continues to offer more and more on-line services such as Mailing Online, Card Store, Certified Mail, and Postecs. Using NetPost™, for instance, you can send professionally printed letters, postcards, and booklets that have been created on a personal computer. NetPost also offers CardStore, an ideal way to customize your business or personal message. The United States Postal Services says, "It's like having a Post Office and a professional printing and mailing service inside your personal computer 24 hours a day, 7 days a week." Mailing Online™ allows you to print and send your mail anywhere, anytime. PosteCS™ allows you to send your files securely on-line using Post Electronic Courier Service. All these services are ideal for direct marketers, saving time and creating efficiency.

Alternative Delivery Systems

Although the Private Express Statutes grant the United States Postal Service a form of monopoly over first-class mail delivery, they have been in transition and, now make private delivery services possible under certain conditions. Alternatives to first-class mail, permitted under the Private Express Statutes provided they meet certain criteria, include FedEx and major airlines. (Other alternatives of course are the telephone and the Internet, as well as additional emerging forms of electronic message transmission.)

Certain publications, including *Better Homes and Gardens* and the *Wall Street Journal*, among others, have been experimenting with delivery alternatives to the periodicals category of mail. These alternatives have been increasing as have the number of private firms distributing direct mail advertising, including samples, in selected markets.

According to the Direct Marketing Association (DMA), the United Parcel Service (UPS) is the most popular method to handle shipments among catalogers. UPS handled 41 percent of all shipments in 2001, while USPS Priority Mail handled 21.3 percent, USPS Parcel Post handled 13.9 percent, and UPS Expedited accounted for 5.9 percent. Although UPS is the best known of the private parcel services, FedEx (Two-Day and Overnight combined) also accounted for 3.7 percent of all shipments, while "other carriers," including most airlines, Emery Air freight, and selected bus lines and trucking firms, accounted for 5.2 percent of parcel shipments in 2001.[22]

FULFILLMENT PROBLEMS

Everybody makes mistakes—and fulfillment centers are no exception. The crucial point for the direct marketer is becoming aware of the mistake and fixing it promptly—making it right for the customer so that the final impression is a positive one. Keep in mind that the fulfillment experience often determines whether or not the customer will respond to the next sales offer.

What are some common sources of fulfillment problems and how can direct marketers attempt to avoid these mistakes? Let's examine these two important issues.

Sources of Fulfillment Problems

Many of the most common fulfillment problems originate in the warehouse. These problems can occur in many ways. Let's look at some of the potential sources of fulfillment problems:

- *Accuracy of the order*—Delivering the wrong product to the customer is a costly mistake. It may result in losing the customer's future business as the customer has lost a certain degree of confidence in the direct marketer.
- *Package presentation*—Packaging is an extension of the company's image and sloppy packaging communicates a poor image. Small details like the correct position of the label on the mailing carton and the neatness of the outer carton seal are important. Even more important is the product placement within the package—making sure that the product is upright or positioned the best way to ensure it reaches the customer in good condition.
- *Speed of delivery*—In today's electronic age customers demand faster delivery than ever before. However, accuracy cannot be sacrificed for speed. Therefore, the fulfillment challenge is to process and fill orders as efficiently as possible.
- *Stock availability*—Delivering what you offer is the ultimate role of fulfillment. Maintaining an accurate inventory system and an adequate amount of inventory is crucial to fulfillment success. Back orders commonly result not only in the loss of a sale, but also in the loss of a customer.
- *Return processing*—It would be wonderful if every product a customer ordered was received and kept. The fact is that many products get returned for many different reasons and direct marketers must process these returns in a timely and professional manner.

Other common fulfillment problems come from areas outside the warehouse and are commonly related to customer database files. Included in this category of fulfillment mistakes are: not thanking the customer for the order; sending the customer an invoice *after* payment has already been sent; misspelling the customer's name; and using the incorrect prefix (for example, using "Mr."or "Ms." instead of "Dr."). Mistakes like these can make the customer skeptical and could result in the loss of future business.

Ways to Avoid Fulfillment Problems

Fortunately, direct marketers can take many simple steps to avoid fulfillment problems and actually assist the organization in exceeding consumer expectations. Although many of these may seem like commonsense marketing, all direct marketers do not exercise these steps. The ways to avoid fulfillment problems include the following:

- Pay careful attention to the packing slips and picking lists to ensure that orders get filled accurately and expediently. The packing slip identifies the items ordered by each customer. The picking list also identifies each item on the order and serves as a routing guide to move the picker efficiently through the warehouse.
- Include a toll-free number for customer service in a prominent place on the catalog, direct-mail piece, Internet site, or packing slip with the order. If your toll-free phone line is too expensive because too many calls are coming in, then maybe you've got too many service problems. So fix them.[23] However, you should encourage your customers to call you even if the problem is small.
- Hire a professional, well-trained customer service staff. If your customers are important to you, make sure their interaction with your organization is a positive experience. Nothing is more frustrating for a consumer than dealing with an inept customer service representative. The more positive you can make the customer experience the greater the probability the customer will return and purchase from your organization again. Smart direct marketers ensure repeat business by establishing customer service standards and monitoring customer service representatives (often via tape-recorded telephone calls) to measure and control the service level.
- Establish quality control measures for each phase of the fulfillment process. From order receiving to warehousing, from order processing to shipping and delivery, from picking and packing to handling customer complaints . . . each part of the fulfillment process is important and you should establish and monitor quality control standards that focus on the customer. Service levels are shaped by the needs of the target audience, the desired image of the company, and management's ability to define and implement the necessary programs and systems in the operation.[24] Setting up these quality control standards, communicating them to all employees, and monitoring their performance and ultimate effect on customer satisfaction is a proactive approach to delivering quality service and to avoiding fulfillment problems before they begin.

Summary

In summary, fulfillment is the final impression left with the customer. It is also a chance to communicate with the customer by enclosing additional promotional materials and/or new catalogs. Being attentive to detail in the fulfillment process should generate satisfied customers and future business for the organization. This chapter has discussed how customer service and fulfillment activities are vital to the success of any direct marketing organization. They may not be glamorous, but they are the guts of direct marketing. The importance of customer service begins with an understanding of customer satisfaction and customer relationship management. Direct marketers follow a step-by-step process to ensure customer relationships are managed properly. Direct marketers use personal experience and surveys to determine whether or not the organization is providing good customer service and keeping customers happy. Good customer service, correct order entry, and prompt order delivery generates satisfied customers and repeat buyers. There are six steps in fulfillment process — offer, response, processing, shipping, billing, and customer service. Direct marketers may select from various fulfillment options, including in-house fulfillment, outside fulfillment centers, and on-line fulfillment, in order to serve its customers. In addition, direct marketers must select from the various delivery options, available for shipping products to consumers. These delivery options include multi-channel distribution, United States Postal Service and alternative delivery systems. The chapter concludes by providing an overview of some of the most common fulfillment problems along with ways to avoid these problems.

Key Terms

- customer satisfaction, 232
- customer relationship management (CRM), 232
- fulfillment, 239
- offer, 241
- packing slip, 244
- picking list, 244
- integrated order fulfillment, 246
- virtual enterprise, 248
- e-fulfillment, 250
- multichannel distribution, 251

Review Questions

1. Explain the term *customer satisfaction.* What is its relationship to direct marketing?
2. How does a direct marker determine how strong their relationship is with their customers?
3. What are some of the ways a firm can keep their customers happy? Describe from your own personal experience the actions direct marketers have taken to keep you happy.
4. Describe the relationship between fulfillment and customer service.
5. List and describe the six steps of the fulfillment process.
6. What is *multichannel distribution?* What are some of the advantages of multichannel distribution?
7. Discuss some common fulfillment problems along with actions direct marketers may take to avoid future fulfillment problems. Why don't all direct marketers exercise these preventative measures?
8. Describe how the traditional fulfillment model is changing.
9. Compare the advantages and disadvantages between in-house fulfillment and outside fulfillment services. Name some companies that are using the different types of fulfillment services.
10. List and explain the eight steps of the integrated order fulfillment concept.

Exercise

You are an employee of a small clothing boutique that also distributes a catalog. You work in the fulfillment department. Currently the company uses in-house fulfillment, but you learn that your boss is considering using an outside fulfillment service to meet demand. Business has grown rapidly since the company has gone online and is now receiving on-line orders. He is also suggesting that the boutique may save money by using an outside fulfillment service. Voice your opinion on the matter. Should the company keep fulfilling orders in-house or should they use an outside fulfillment source? What variables would impact your decision? Be sure to give specific reasons to support your position on the matter.

CASE: LILLIAN VERNON CORPORATION NATIONAL DISTRIBUTION CENTER

OVERVIEW

In a crowded and extremely competitive marketplace, the leading direct marketers know they must serve and satisfy their customers. Lillian Vernon Corporation serves its customers in a courteous manner by an efficient and effective fulfillment operation. This operation is housed at the National Distribution Center in Virginia Beach, Virginia. The complexity of fulfillment operations demonstrates how a computerized warehouse system is imperative in ensuring quality control and customer satisfaction for Lillian Vernon customers. This case study focuses on the back-end of the direct marketing industry—customer service and fulfillment. It demonstrates the importance of serving customers via multichannel marketing. It also examines the fulfillment process from the moment a customer places an order to when the product is delivered.

CASE

Today, the company is a sophisticated operation, using state-of-the-art technologies and computer systems all guided by the same fundamental business principles—100-percent customer satisfaction guaranteed. Lillian Vernon Corporation offers many products that customers cannot easily find elsewhere. Personalization is always free of charge. The company takes great pride in the unique products, affordable prices, and outstanding customer service it provides each customer. Lillian Vernon Corporation produces seven catalog titles that offer a wide variety of gifts, housewares, decorative items, gardening, and children's products. Lillian Vernon Corporation's continued success can be attributed to the corporation's efforts to gain and keep the trust and loyalty of its customers. It achieves this by providing quality service and merchandise, which in return meets customer expectations and earns lasting customer loyalty.

Lillian Vernon Corporation National Distribution Center

"Customer Service: the Cornerstone of our Business" is carved on the cornerstone of the National Distribution Center in Virginia Beach, Virginia. Opened in 1998, the distribution center is one of the largest in the industry with 850,000 square feet, an area the size of 18 football fields! The National Distribution Center is highly computerized and automated and is the heart of the company. It is the hub for the company's fulfillment, storage, and call center operations.

Order Fulfillment Process. According to David Hochberg, Vice-President of Public Affairs at Lillian Vernon Corporation, "Fulfillment is the backbone of our business."* During the Christmas season, Lillian Vernon Corporation processes over 50,000 orders a day and employs more than 5,300 employees to ensure good customer service and quick order processing. Customers can order by mail, telephone, fax, or on-line 24 hours a day, 7 days a week, 365 days a year. At the present time, Lillian Vernon Corporation receives 50 percent of all orders via telephone, 23 percent by postal mail, and 27 percent on-line via its Web site, www.lillianvernon.com. On-line business has surged since opening their first Web site in 1995. Lillian Vernon Corporation downloads on-line orders directly into the computer system for order fulfillment processing. With the rapid increase in on-line shopping, the company has created an interactive Web site that generates offers based on the customer's purchase behavior. For example, when a customer orders a particular

*Personal Interview with David C. Hochberg, Lillian Vernon Corporation, 2003.

item on-line, the Web site automatically offers an item that corresponds to that order, taking advantage of up-selling and cross-selling opportunities. If a customer orders a set of stars and stripes serving bowls, the Web site recommends to the customer that they may also enjoy the stars and stripes cake stand and server or chip and dip bowl. Usually the offer includes a "two-for" discount (purchase two items to obtain a discount) enticing the customer into placing a larger order. Customers placing orders by telephone receive similar up-selling and cross-selling efforts from trained call center associates. A series of pop-up windows on the computer screen in front each call center associate are designed to prompt cross-selling and up-selling activities. The average acceptance rate to these suggestive selling efforts is 15 percent.

Before each Lillian Vernon catalog is mailed, the company receives and stocks all products in the National Distribution Center's eight-tiered storage facility. Forklift trucks on the receiving docks receive products and teams unload, check, and warehouse the merchandise. Material handlers check the merchandise and load it onto pallets for the next step in the process—quality assurance. Inspectors then check the merchandise for the correct quantity and quality and send it to the storage facility. When the merchandise is needed, lift operators take it from storage to the replenishing area where material handlers take it to the pick areas.

The order fulfillment process begins when an order is placed with the company. When orders arrive by mail, mail processors open the envelopes, review the order for completeness, verify payments, and batch the orders for entry into computers. The mail processors then forward the order to mail-order entry employees who use a keyboard to enter orders into the computer system. Once these employees complete this order entry process, the order is ready to be filled by staff in the distribution center.

The entire merchandise receipt, storage, retrieval, and picking system is bar code driven. Distribution center staff continuously update inventory situations through radio-frequency systems ensuring the accuracy and timeliness of inventory status. The shipping label for each individual package includes a bar code that contains the customer order number and the first three-digits of the "ship-to" address. With the system of checks and balances, the company is able to increase customer satisfaction and avoid gridlock. The system allows the company to know at any given time where a package is and at what stage of the process the order is in "real-time."

Free personalization of Lillian Vernon merchandise is popular with many customers. Approximately 65 percent of the packages that leave the distribution center include personalized items. Personalization operators must carefully read the packing slip to ensure accuracy in the personalization process. Lillian Vernon Corporation offers many personalization processes. Figure 10-13 overviews these processes.

It takes skill and two weeks of training to learn to operate the high-tech computerized machines used to personalize the company's items. While computers run many of the personalization machines, operators are responsible for ensuring accuracy and preventing malfunction. Figure 10-14 shows some of the personalization processes being applied at Lillian Vernon Corporation.

Once the operators personalize the product, the fulfillment process continues on to order processors in the picking department. Order processors (also called "pickers") select the merchandise ordered by a customer from pick racks to prepare it for shipment. Order processors read each computerized packing list and pick items accordingly. The order processor then places the items in boxes on a large cart. It takes approximately 17 to 20 minutes for order processors to pick the items off of the racks for one cart—which contains up to 16 orders. The order processors walk approximately 10 miles a day picking merchandise off of the pick floor. The pick completion area is where outbound quality assurance personnel check the merchandise to ensure that the order is correct prior to shipment. The computer chooses the appropriate size box in which to

---

LILLIAN VERNON CORPORATION PERSONALIZATION PROCESSES

Engraving – A mechanical diamond chip used on steel, silver, gold, Lucite, and plastic.

Gold Stamp – A heat transfer of pressure sensitive gold foil on leather.

Sandblast – An etching system using silica carbide pressure to personalize on glass, metal, ceramic, resin, stone and plastic.

Heat Press – A heat transfer of pressure sensitive vinyl or felt letters used on textiles.

YAG-based Lasers – Light lasers that burn into ceramic, plastic, resin, and metal.

Epilog, LMI and Meistergram Lasers – Lasers that burn on wood, plastic, leather and resins.

Embroidery – A computerized sewing machine that embroiders or sews names, initials, monograms and graphics primarily on textiles.

Multi-Head Embroidery – A computerized sewing machine with multiple embroidery heads that embroiders several products at once.

Linotype – A linotype machine that makes dies and imprints foil onto pencils and greeting cards.

Sublimation – A thermal transfer which can be applied to textiles, metals, ceramics and plastics.

FIGURE 10-13   Personalization Processes

Source: Personal Communication from David Hochberg. V.P. Public Affairs, Lillian Vernon Corporation: Rye, NY; March, 2003.

---

package and ship the order for greater efficiency. Lillian Vernon Corporation never sends its customers a package with just the ordered item in it. The packing slip will also indicate the collateral material that should be added to the box. These package inserts may include another Lillian Vernon catalog, cross-selling promotions, a free gift, and/or other company's inserts, such as a book offer from a publishing company. The book publisher would pay a fee to Lillian Vernon Corporation to distribute their literature. Once fulfillment personnel include the appropriate inserts, they add protective packing material. The personnel then tape the box shut and attach the mailing label. Once the order is ready for shipment, the conveyor belt scans, weighs, and sorts the order to the correct shipping door. As shown in Figure 10-15, the unique system of "smart" conveyers allows the company to offer the most cost effective order fulfillment, which improves the level of service Lillian Vernon Corporation is able to provide its customers. The order is then on its way to the customer!

Customer Service Operations

Also located at the national distribution center is a 400-seat call center. In addition to receiving telephone orders, the Lillian Vernon Corporation call center provides answers for customers who call with questions or problems they may have concerning a product or an order. Each Customer service associate receives 60 hours of classroom training. They also receive after-training support from "aisle buddies," "group leaders," and "coaches." Customer service representatives are taught that the call they answer is *their* call and they are responsible for assisting that customer. This is the Lillian Vernon Corporation concept of "One Call, Once Person," which means customer service associates at Lillian Vernon are given tiered authority and can resolve most problems without supervisor intervention or assistance. Experienced customer service associates can handle upset customers with refunds and replacements without management approval up to a certain level and that level increases with experience.

FIGURE 10-14   Personalization Operators at Lillian Vernon Corporation

Lillian Vernon Corporation's 100-percent customer satisfaction guarantee reassures the customer that if, for any reason they are not satisfied with a product, it can be returned for a refund at any time. The returned merchandise is sent to the returns area, where returns adjustors unpack it and handle the return. Lillian Vernon Corporation disposes of returns through its outlet stores, returns to stock, or donations to charities.

"Under Promise, Over Deliver" is just another slogan Lillian Vernon Corporation uses to ensure the best possible customer service in their fulfillment process. Good customer service and accurate and efficient fulfillment are two key ingredients that guarantee that Lillian Vernon Corporation will remain one of America's largest specialty catalog companies for years to come.

Source: This case is based on information provided from David Hochberg, Vice-President of Public Affairs, Lillian Vernon Corporation; Lillian Vernon National Distribution Center representatives; and *Lillian Vernon: An Eye for Winners* (New York: Harper-Collins Publishers, Inc., 1996). ■

FIGURE 10-15   Conveyor Belts Moves Packages Through the Lillian Vernon Corporation Distribution Process

Case Discussion Questions

1. Discuss the many ways Lillian Vernon Corporation practices good customer service.
2. Illustrate the steps involved in the Lillian Vernon Corporation fulfillment process. Is the flow of this process efficient? How might it be improved?
3. How does the bar code system facilitate and expedite order processing at the Lillian Vernon Distribution Center?
4. What vendors might be interested in having their promotional material included as a package insert along with Lillian Vernon order? Why?

Notes

1. William D. Perreault, Jr., and E. Jerome McCarthy, *Basic Marketing: A Global Managerial Approach,* 13th ed. (CITY: Irwin McGraw-Hill, 1999), 5.
2. Robert McKim, "Is CRM Part of Customer Management," dmnews.com Monday, March 13, 2000, <http://www.dmnews.com/archive/2000-03/7058.html> (May 10, 2000).
3. Susan Reda, "Customer Service, Brand Management Seen as Key Aspects of On-Line Fulfillment," *Stores* (October, 2000), 44.
4. *Lillian Vernon: An Eye For Winners* (New York: HarperCollins Publishers, Inc., 1996).
5. Robert D. Downey, "Proper Fulfillment—Image with the Proper Stuff," *Direct Marketing* (July 1985), 28.

6. Jack Schmid, "How the Back End Drives the Bottom Line," *Target Marketing* 13, no. 5 (May 1990).

7. Heather Thiermann, "Fulfillment: Do It Right," *Target Marketing* 9, no. 11 (November 1986).

8. *Lillian Vernon: An Eye For Winners* (New York: HarperCollins Publishers, Inc., 1996).

9. Sidney Hill, "Integrated Order Fulfillment for the Virtual Enterprise," dmnews.com, February 1998, <http://www.manufacturingsystems.com> (May 10, 2000).

10. Ibid., 3A.

11. Susan Reda, "Customer Service, Brand Management Seen as Key Aspects of On-Line Fulfillment," *Stores* (October 2000), 44.

12. Sidney Hill, "Integrated Order Fulfillment for the Virtual Enterprise," dmnews.com, February 1998, <http://www.manufacturingsystems.com> (May 10, 2000).

13. Ibid., 42.

14. Ibid., 42.

15. Mike Littell, "Keep an Eye on the Back End, CRM," dmnews.com February 25, 2000, <http://www.dmnews.com/archive/2000-02-21/6675.html> (May 10, 2000).

16. Ibid.

17. Susan Reda, "Customer Service, Brand Management Seen as Key Aspects of On-Line Fulfillment," *Stores* (October 2000), 44.

18. Jonathan Boorstein, "Customer Service: Fulfillment 101," *Direct*, May 2, 2000, <http://www.directmag.com/Content/monthly/200/2000050119.htm> May, 2000.

19. Susan Reda, "Customer Service, Brand Management Seen as Key Aspects of On Line Fulfillment, *Stores* (Vol. 82, Issue 10 October 2000), pp. 40–44.

20. Jonathan Boorstein, "Customer Service: Fulfillment 101," May 1, 2000, <http://www.directmag.com/Content/monthly/s222/2000050119.htm> May, 2000.

21. All statistics are based on *The Statistical Fact Book 2002*, 24th ed. (New York: The Direct Marketing Association, Inc., 2002), 254–272.

22. Ibid., 75.

23. John M. Chilson, "The Top 10 Fulfillment Mistakes," *Folio: The Magazine for Magazine Management* 27, no. 7 (May 1998): 61–62.

24. Jeffrey A. Coopersmith, "Customer Service: The Final Link," *Catalog Age* 5, no. 7 (July 1988): 76.

Many marketers, citing their "years of experience," utilize what has been aptly termed "seat-of-the-pants" judgment, relying on their own intuition for making decisions. They are inclined to feeling "my mind is made up, don't confuse me with the facts." Direct marketers, however, are more inclined to make their decisions scientifically, turning to objective research as well as statistical tools and techniques to guide them.

Research in direct marketing serves direct marketers in both fact finding and information gathering. They also use it for problem solving and decision making. In fact, given the huge amount of market information available and the need to make decisions quickly, marketing managers rely on both basic and advanced research techniques utilizing *surveys* as well as *experiments*.

THE NATURE OF RESEARCH

Shown in Figure 11-1 is a listing of definitions of commonly used statistical terms, presented here as a refresher for students as well as a reference for the technical discussions which appear throughout this chapter.

The result of research is often **quantitative,** that is, it is expressed in terms of numbers: population sizes, income levels, housing values, and the like. Beyond the rigor of numbers, though, we often need **qualitative** information about consumer behavior and the reasons people buy, not just data about who or how many buy. We need to know, for example, about their lifestyles and how these motivate their buying decisions.

Research, utilizing both surveys and experiments, enables direct marketers to obtain both quantitative and qualitative data. The most valid research, moreover, measures *results* and not *opinions,* because what survey respondents *say* and what they *do* are frequently quite dissimilar. In one study by a life insurance direct marketer, for example, in which the company remained anonymous during interviewing, the majority of the respondents said they would not purchase life insurance by mail. Yet, every one of them had purchased life insurance by mail from the company conducting the survey!

A better alternative is to experimentally offer the product or service for sale and count those who actually buy and not, as in a survey, count those who say they would buy if given the opportunity. Experimentation is a key characteristic of direct marketing.

Surveys Versus Experiments

As the title of this chapter conveys, direct marketing research is comprised of *surveys* and *experiments*. Determining the response rates to various offerings involves survey research; determining which advertising strategy resulted in more responses involves experimentation research.

A **survey** looks at things the way they are; for example, a mailed questionnaire tries to profile respondents to an offer or to measure product preferences or to determine future buying intentions. An **experiment,** often called a **test** by direct marketers, is designed to measure the effect of change. What happens, for example, when we raise or lower a price level? What is the result of selective promotion to specific market segments? What is the influence on response of one particular promotional strategy versus another? Direct marketers, like traditional marketers, have many ways to conduct

FIGURE 11-1   Definitions of Statistical Terms

Accuracy – The difference between the sample statistic and the actual population parameter.

Alternative Hypothesis – Determined when a null hypothesis is proven wrong (i.e., the hypothesis is shown to be true).

A Priori – In statistical analysis, before the fact.

A Posteriori – In statistical analysis, after the fact.

Bias – A methodical error that occurs in selection of respondents or measurement (i.e., the difference between the expected value of a statistic and the population parameter estimated by the statistic).

Breakeven – The point at which the gross profit on a unit of sale equates to the cost of making that unit sale.

Central Limit Theorem – Assures us that, in a number of random samples taken from a population, the sample means tend to be normally distributed. The shape of such a normal distribution – the so-called "bell-shaped curve" – is completely determined by its two parameters: mean and standard deviation.

Central Tendency – Adherence to the Central Limit Theorem.

Chi-Square Test – One technique for determining whether an observed difference between the test and the control in an experiment is (or is not) *statistically significant*.

Confidence Level – Is the area of the estimated values of the sample within which the true value lies within a predetermined probability, as measured by the number of standard deviations from the mean in a normal distribution.

Control Group – A group on which the experiment is not conducted but that is otherwise identical to the test group.

Dependent Variable – A variable which is influenced by independent variables.

Degree of Freedom – The number of observations that are allowed to vary in a numerical system without changing associated constraints or assumptions.

Dry Testing – An experimental technique used to test a new product not yet available in the marketplace.

Experimentation – A testing process in which events occur randomly in a setting at the discretion of the experimenter and controls are used to identify sources of variation in subjects' response.

Focus Group Interview – Unstructured small group, representative of an appropriate market segment, under skilled leadership, converses in a relaxed environment about the subject of the research.

Hypothesis – An assertion about the value of a variable.

Independent Variable – A variable that exerts influence on various events or outcomes called dependent variables.

Key Code – A unique number or other identifier placed on the order form or other response device so as to identify source of the response.

Law of Large Numbers – Assures us that, as sample size increases, the distribution of sample means concentrates closer to the true mean of the total population.

Limit of Error – Describes the number of percentage points by which the researcher is allowed to comfortably miscalculate the actual value.

Mean – Arithmetic average; a measure of central tendency in a normal distribution.

Median – An average, the mid-point of values; also a measure of central tendency.

(*continued*)

FIGURE 11-1   Continued

Mode – An average, the value that occurs most frequently; also a measure of central tendency.

Normal Distribution – The so-called "bell-shaped curve," whose shape is completely determined by its two parameters: mean and standard deviation.

Null Hypothesis – The statistical hypothesis that the result of an experiment is due only to chance.

Parameter – A characteristic of a population.

Population – The total domain or group of items being considered.

Primary Data – Those data collected specifically for the current research need.

Response Rate – The percentage of those who respond to an offer.

Qualitative Research – That which deals with behavior.

Quantitative Research – That which deals with numbers.

Random Event – An occurrence which has several possible values and occurs with some definable frequency if many repetitions are undertaken.

Random Assignment – Random assignment of subjects to both test and control groups so that differences between groups occur by chance alone.

Random Sample – A sample in which every element of a population has an equal chance of being selected and differences occur by chance only.

Reliability – Standard error of a statistic; its precision.

Sample – Subsets of the total population, for which data are available.

Sample Size – The number of observations in a sample, determined by first looking at two major considerations: (1) the cost of reaching the sample and (2) the amount of information we need to make an efficient decision.

Sampling – A method of choosing observations from which we can predict estimations

Sampling Error – The difference between sample result and the population parameter (which most often is unknown). Sampling error declines as the sample size increases, assuming an unbiased sampling procedure.

Sampling Method – The means of obtaining a sample from a population.

Secondary Data – Those data originally collected for another purpose, that have relevance to, and are available for, the research needs of others.

Simple Random Sample – A sample drawn from a population in a manner in which every possible sample of equal size has the same probability of selection.

Standard Deviation – A measure of dispersion; square root of the variance about a mean.

Statistic – A characteristic of a sample.

Survey – A research method in which hypotheses are tested using questionnaires.

Test – What direct marketers call an experiment.

Type I Error – Occurs when the decision maker rejects the null hypothesis even though it is, in fact, true.

Type II Error – Occurs when the decision maker accepts the null hypothesis when it is, in fact, not true.

Valid – A valid statistic is one without bias.

Variance – A measure of variability from the mean.

surveys. When it comes to experimentation, however, they have become adept with the statistical tools and techniques of such testing and they are thus inclined to use experiments much more often than they use surveys.

Apart from knowing the mechanics of conducting surveys and experiments, direct marketers also need to know how to define people, things, and events in quantitative as well as qualitative terms. Where do they obtain what kinds of information and what do they do with it? How do they design research and how do they structure problems? How do they conduct valid experiments, through proper sampling and estimation techniques? How do they present findings, evaluate them, and then benefit from them? The tools and techniques of research enable them to do all these things.

Problem Structure

How do direct marketing researchers define and structure problems? First, let's consider typical problem areas, such as

- *How much advertising is needed?*   How is an answer determined in dollars and cents? Is the amount of advertising going to be a *result* (of, say, past sales) or a *cause* (of, say, expected future sales)? Do expected results warrant estimated costs? Do anticipated rewards outweigh potential risks?
- *How will the direct marketing mix be selected?*   Once determined, how will the budget be allocated? What products will be offered and at what prices? What market segments will be solicited? And, certainly a major area for testing, what is the most productive promotional strategy: offer, copy, graphics? What media should be used? Will the Internet be used?
- *How will our resources be utilized?*   Should promotional efforts be concentrated in one geographic area, considering its climate and the logistics of distribution? Should resources be allocated over time taking into account potential seasonal or cyclical variations or the stage of the product's life cycle?

There is an art as well as a science to defining marketing challenges such as these, and not all the solutions are derived from challenges, of course. Sometimes direct marketing researchers are trying to fulfill specific objectives. Research is simply the way in which direct marketing managers seek solutions to problems or become knowledgeable about objectives so that they can find solutions or new opportunities.

Marketers must remember, of course, that they can influence their definition of the research goal by researcher/experimenter bias, especially when trying to justify our actions. The findings are also subject to **sampling errors** when the respondents are nonrepresentative, or there is error either in the randomness of the sample or in the sampling process. Asking an apartment dweller what type of lawnmower he or she intends to purchase is an obvious example of a sampling error. Furthermore, "people are human" and their behavior as consumers cannot always be measured precisely.

What to Test

There is virtually no limit to the possibilities for conducting surveys or experiments. So, it is exceedingly important to research only the *important* things and to do this *adequately*. "Adequately" refers not only to the size of the research sample but also to the nature of the sample. "Important" things are, for instance, products/services, media, offers, formats, and timing. Direct marketers of an earlier era tested a host of relatively insignificant things, such as the manner of addressing (typing versus handwriting versus computer labels); the manner of paying postage (postage stamps versus meter imprints versus printed indicia); the covering of the window in a mailing envelope (glassine versus cellophane versus an open window); or the color of ink used for the signature reproduction on a letter. None of these had much impact on the results of the direct marketing effort.

Today's direct marketers test in a manner that will provide statistically valid results that they can project to a larger sample. To ensure control, they test one variable at a time or else they test everything, such as a complete package or a new product. Even though the tools are there, they try not to become "test happy." Later in this chapter, we will cover in detail the tools and techniques of conducting both surveys and experiments.

DATA: TYPES, SOURCES, AND COLLECTION

The goal of research is the acquisition of data from which we derive information. After determining what information is needed, the direct marketer must determine where and how to obtain it and what to do with it. Information is all around us, if we would but recognize it, collect it, catalog it, and refer to it.

Data can be characterized as either primary or secondary. **Secondary data** are those originally collected for another purpose that have relevance to and are available for the research needs of others. **Primary data** are those collected specifically for the current research need. Direct marketers try to collect primary data only when secondary data are not readily available from outside sources or the organization's own internal records, including its own prior experimentation.

Primary data can be collected through survey research as well as experimental research. Surveys are usually conducted by personal interview, by mail, by telephone, via a Web site, or by on-site observation. Experiments are conducted in either a field or a laboratory environment.

Secondary Data

Figure 11-2 lists a variety of sources of secondary data. Digging for and obtaining information that is already available, as contrasted to survey or experimental testing, doesn't appear to be a very exciting activity. Still, one of the most costly mistakes researchers make is literally "reinventing the wheel." It is quite likely that someone has already traveled your road, *including yourself*. The use of secondary data, when available, can save valuable time and is usually less costly. (Secondary data might well have been primary data for the organization originally gathering them.) The volume of secondary data is virtually limitless. The problem, actually, is how to manage the derived information. Where is it? How do you find it? How do you get it? What do you do with it? How do you analyze and evaluate it? How reliable and relevant is it?

The first source to consider for secondary data, although not always realized, is the internal records of your business or organization itself. For example, there is no need for a life insurance company to conduct survey research to determine the average age

A. The Organization's Own Internal Records

B. Government Sources: Federal, State, Local

   1. U.S. Department of Commerce
     -- Bureau of the Census

   2. U.S. Department of Labor
     -- Bureau of Labor Statistics

   3. U.S. Department of Agriculture

   4. Other U.S. Government Sources
     -- President's Office
     -- Congress
     -- Treasury Department
     -- Interior Department
     -- Health & Human Services Department

   5. State and Local Governments
     -- Economic Surveys
     -- License Registrations
     -- Tax Records

C. Trade, Technical, Professional & Business Associations

D. Private Research Organizations

E. Foundations, Universities and Other Nonprofits

F. Libraries, Public and Private

G. Advertising Media

H. Financial Institutions, Utilities, Service Organizations

FIGURE 11-2   Some Sources of Secondary Data

of its policyholders; a quicker and easier way is to look at its own policy records already on file.

Traditionally, organizations have collected and used little internal marketing information. Although costs of advertising, for example, are duly recorded on a typical accounting statement, there is little or no allocation of advertising costs to media or results on that statement. Typically, accounting approaches and operating statements are not adequate nor have they been designed to provide the information needed by marketing decision makers.

Decision makers go to great lengths to measure and predict direct marketing results but they expend only a fraction of their effort on the matter of costs. Usually, such costs appear on accounting statements according to the objective of the expenditure; that is, advertising, printing, postage, mailing list rental, and Web site development. From a manager's standpoint, it would be more appropriate to look at these by products, price level, type/size of customer, market segment, and/or promotion effort.

As Figure 11-2 shows, there is also a great variety of potential sources of secondary data outside the organization's own records. In addition to the government and other public sources listed, there are many private organizations, including research firms, as well as communications media that provide syndicated or custom-designed data on a periodic or one-time basis. The A. C. Nielsen Company, for example, provides an ongoing stream of information about food and drug purchasing and the automobile aftermarket. Daniel Starch monitors magazine readership and advertising recall. Other organizations, such as the Yankelovich Group, George Gallup, the Harris Poll, and the Roper Poll, monitor social, economic, and political changes. Other types of information come from consumer panels, diary groups, store audits, and field enumerations.

Primary Data

Marketers gather primary data specifically for current needs, usually from respondents. The data include

- *Behavior:* what respondents have done or are doing
- *Intentions:* anticipated or expected future behavior
- *Knowledge:* how respondents perceive specific offerings
- *Socioeconomic status:* age, income, education, occupation, gender, marital status
- *Attitudes and opinions:* respondents' views or feelings
- *Motivations:* reasons for respondents' behavior
- *Psychological traits:* respondents' state of mind; that is, personality

There are five major survey methods for collecting primary data:

Personal Interview

The personal interview is the most costly method of survey but it has several advantages: it provides the opportunity for a more complete and accurate sample; it provides the opportunity for more complete information; it offers greater flexibility in structuring questions to the situation; and it ensures a high response rate. Its major disadvantage, besides cost, is the possibility of bias created by the interviewer along with the need for extensive interviewer supervision and control in order to standardize the interview and avoid cheating.

Telephone Interview

The advantages of telephone interviews are economy, speed, representative sampling, minimal nonresponse, simple callbacks, and the ability to make the interview coincide with other activities, such as television viewing. The disadvantages include limited availability of information at the time of contact, and the fact that those without telephone service are not included. Certain types of questions, such as those which require demonstration or visualization, cannot be used. The public also is becoming increasingly resistant to intrusive telephone calls and those with unlisted numbers can be reached only through random-digit dialing.

Mail Questionnaire

Mail questionnaires provide great versatility at low cost. There is no interviewer bias, no field staff is needed, and some respondents are easier to approach by mail and therefore more likely to respond. The respondent may reply at leisure and without interruption; replies may remain confidential as well. Disadvantages include the relatively high rate of nonresponse; the need for follow-up; response bias introduced by the fact that those with strong feeling (either way) tend to respond in greater numbers;

the time required to develop the questionnaire; the lack of assurance that respondents clearly understand the questions.

On-line Surveys

Web-based research, using on-line survey techniques, offers the major advantage of reaching potential respondents at the most opportune time. Many Web sites have incorporated surveys into the process of registering to visit and/or conduct transactions at the site . . . thus targeting their questionnaires to those who have already expressed some degree of interest in them. Potential respondents can also be directed to Web sites to retrieve survey questionnaires and respond to them while on-line. Speed and convenience help increase the response rate.

Observation

The key advantage of observation is that it removes respondent bias. Johnson Wax found that reported usage of its products by respondents differed as much as 50 percent from reality when compared with the actual brand the consumer had at the time of an in-home interview. The major observation methods include in-store and in-home audits, recording devices, and direct observations at the point of purchase, such as a shopping mall. An automobile dealer wanting to know what radio stations prospects for service listen to didn't ask them; its employees observed the dial settings on radios in cars brought in by customers.

EXPERIMENTATION AS TESTING

Many equate marketing research with survey research, but they are not the same. Survey research attempts to observe and record various activities as they naturally arise in the environment. Experimentation, on the other hand, manipulates one or more controllable factors called **independent variables,** to determine their influence on various events or outcomes called **dependent variables.** Experimentation, often called testing, is especially prevalent in direct marketing. In experimentation the experimenter creates an environment in which controls serve to pinpoint the causes of behavior differences among respondents. This method of gathering data requires close adherence to statistical techniques to ensure validity. Because direct marketing researchers rely heavily on experimentation, we will look closely at certain relevant tools and techniques of statistics in this chapter. Some examples of direct marketing questions that call for experimentation are the following:

- How does frequency of mailing to a particular record on a database affect total response?
- How can direct marketers benefit from the World Wide Web?
- Is it possible to increase profits by servicing small industrial accounts totally by mail, telephone, or on-line, rather than using personal salespeople?
- How productive are various segments of a total market?
- Is a newspaper advertisement more effective in color than in black and white?
- What is the best season to offer spring-blooming bulbs, to be planted in the fall?
- What is the most profitable pricing strategy?

Independent variables could be the product or service offered, its price structure, or some attribute of the promotional strategy used in the offer. They can also describe the demography or geography of a market. Independent variables should reflect the situation in the real world, for example, the age, gender, marital status, or ZIP code of residence of a respondent. Marketers should generally evaluate only one independent variable at a time. Certain advanced statistical techniques, however, such as multivariate correlation and regression analysis, offer the opportunity to measure the interaction of many independent variables simultaneously.

In direct marketing, the number of responses and/or transactions is often the dependent variable. In other research situations the dependent variable could be favorable or unfavorable reactions to a product or overall rating of a brand preference. At least three levels of observation are needed for measurement.

Experiments usually take place in a field setting, but marketers do sometimes conduct them under laboratory conditions. In a laboratory, marketers must be sure that the setting is realistic and that the subjects are representative. It would not be appropriate for example, to use college students in a laboratory setting to test a product geared to the senior citizen market. Laboratory experiments can also measure the impact of particular advertisements through such devices as eye motion cameras and mechanical devices that gauge emotional reactions by measuring dilation of the pupil of the eye.

Design of the Experiment

Valid experiments are characterized by (1) the presence of a **control group** on which the experiment is not conducted but that is otherwise identical to the test group and (2) **random assignment** of subjects to both test and control groups so that differences between groups occur by chance alone.

It is naïve to compare responses from two groups that are not randomly selected but also may not be similar in their composition. Consider, for example, the oft-repeated statement that those who receive a college education earn more in their lifetimes than those who do not. The two groups are not comparable and thus it would be foolish to draw a conclusion that college education in and of itself causes higher lifetime income. It is conceivable that the drive that caused the student to enter college in the first place also affects lifetime income.

Common forms of experimental design measure the effect of an experiment as the difference between what is observed about the dependent variable of the test group and what is observed about the dependent variable of the control group. But even with control and randomization, there is still no guarantee that the two groups are identical. Differences between them that arise by chance alone may be substantial.

Adequate scheduling of experiments, their timely release, and key coding are vital. Marketers should devise a comprehensive schedule to describe the purpose of the experiment and also its various components, costs, and expected results for the test segment as well as the control.

Tracking Responses

Obviously, response differences to a product offering—between tests and control—cannot be measured unless there is a complete record of results for all segments of the experiment. And, there must be a means to identify the sources of these results. This is accomplished through **key codes** placed on each response device, such as an order form, to make it easy for us to record results. In direct mail, the key code can be a unique number or other identifier placed on the order form. When the telephone is used for response, the key code can be a unique telephone number, a departmental number, or an individual's name. Many direct marketers using the telephone, or a Web site, ask respondents for the key code printed in the advertisement or on the label of a catalog to which they are responding.

Response Rate and Break-Even Analysis

Possibly the most frequently asked question in direct marketing is, "What response rate should I expect to my offer?" In reality, there is no universal or "normal" response rate. The rate can vary relative to such important considerations as the product itself as well as the demand for it, price competition, market preference, and the nature of the promotional offer. Response will also vary widely according to pre-qualification of the mailing list or the narrowness and appropriateness of market segments tested. Typically, all other factors being equal, present customers will respond to an offer for a new product at a much higher level than will nonqualified prospects. A preprinted circular inserted in a Sunday newspaper will generate more response if there are no directly competitive offers in the same issue. A product in the early stages of its life cycle will create more attention and more interest than one that is generally available and displays little if any differentiation.

A more realistic question to be asked in evaluating the response to an offer is probably, "What response do I *need?*" What would it take to just **break even** on a particular offering?

Here is the formula for determining break-even point for a single sale to a new customer:

$$\frac{Promotion\ cost}{Unit\ profit\ per\ sale} = Break\text{-}even\ number\ of\ sales$$

That is, if the marketer recovers promotion cost from the gross profit (beyond cost-of-goods sold and overhead) of the total number of units sold, he or she breaks even *on those sales*.

Figure 11-3 provides a worksheet for calculating the break-even point and profit at various levels of unit sales per thousand pieces of direct mail promotion. A variation of this worksheet can be used for print, broadcast, or electronic promotion.

Lines 2 through 8 of the break-even calculation in Figure 11-3 represent production costs, totaling $17.69 (line 9) per copy of a book, *Practical Mathematics*. Order processing/collection costs (line 5) and costs of returns (line 6) are amortized and allocated to net sales, in the manner shown at the top of Figure 11-3.

Unit profit, calculated by subtracting $17.69 (line 9) from the selling price of $39.95 (line 1) is $22.26 (line 10). Unit profit divided into total promotion costs of $345.83 per thousand pieces mailed (line 11) provides break-even net sales (line 12). This is 15.54 units per thousand (M), or 1.55 percent. And, that is the answer to our earlier question: "What advertising response is *needed . . . to just break-even?*" Having calculated a break-even response rate of 1.55 percent, lines 13 to 20 of Figure 11-3 present alternative profit amounts at assumed alternative levels of net sales.

The calculation assumes the offering of only a single item and anticipates a desirable net profit at various levels of response beyond the break-even point. However, a

Product/Offer: *Practical Mathematics* @$39.95, net 30 days

Assumptions:		
# Promotions Mail'd	9,508	
Shipments Return'd	8%	
Sales Uncollectable	6%	

Order Processing/Collection Costs:		
Gross Orders	100@$1.80=	$180.00
Less: Returns	8@8% of 100	
Net Sales (A)	92@$0.50=$	46.00
Total	(B)	$226.00
Cost Per Net Sale (B/A) =		$2.46

Cost of Returns:	
Return Servicing	$1.30
Shipping/Delivery	$2.20
Total (C)	$3.50
ReturnsProject'd(D)	8%
CostPerNetSale	$0.30
(CxD/1.00-D)	

Break-Even Calculation:

Line	Description		
1	Selling Price		$39.95
2	Cost-of-Goods Sold	$5.99	
3	G&A Allocation	$3.80	
4	Shipping/Delivery Costs	$2.20	
5	Processing/Collection Costs	$2.46	
6	Cost of Returns	$0.30	
7	Sales Uncollectable	$2.40	
8	Premium Gift Cost	$0.54	
9	Total Production Costs		$17.69
10	UNIT PROFIT (Line 1-Line 9)		$22.26
11	Total Promotion Costs per M Pieces Mailed (includes database, print, mail, postage, overhead)		$345.83
12	BreakevenNtSales/M PiecesMailed(Line11/Line10)		15.54

Total Profit at Alternative Levels of Net Sales:

Line	Description							
13	Projected Net Sales per M Pieces Mailed	17	20	25	30	35	40	45
14	Less: Break-even Sales (Line 12)	15.54	15.54	15.54	15.54	15.54	15.54	15.54
15	Net Sales Earning Full Unit Pro (Line 13- Line 14)	1.46	4.46	9.46	14.46	19.46	24.46	29.46
16	Unit Profit (Line 10)	$22.26	$22.26	$22.26	$22.26	$22.26	$22.26	$22.26
17	Net Profit per M Pieces Mailed (Line 15 x Line 16)	32.61	99.39	210.69	322.00	433.30	544.61	655.91
18	M Pieces Mailed	9,508	9,508	9,508	9,508	9,508	9,508	9,508
19	Total Net Profit (Line17xLine 18/1000)	$310.01	$944.98	$2,003.26	$3,061.55	$4,119.83	$5,178.11	$6,236.40
20	NtPr'fit%NtSales:Line19/Line1xLine13xLine18/1000	4.80%	12.44%	21.10%	26.87%	30.99%	34.08%	36.49%

FIGURE 11-3   Direct Marketing Break-Even Worksheet

more likely and realistic calculation for direct marketers uses continuity, and is applicable to long-term recovery of future time periods . . . such as that experienced by magazine publishers, insurance companies, fundraisers, and catalog merchandisers who expect repeat orders from new customers.

Marketers in these firms compute the lifetime value of a customer in the same way as the break-even rate of a single sale with two critical adjustments. First, they calculate a customer attrition rate. Second, they determine a periodic contribution to cover acquisition cost and then discount it to its present value to provide an acceptable return on investment. This procedure was explained in the section on lifetime value of a customer (LTV) in Chapter 3.

SAMPLES AND ESTIMATIONS

Sampling is a method of choosing observations from which one can predict estimations. In experimentation, without properly selected samples, the resultant estimations and predictions will be invalid. Direct marketers must know the major means of selecting samples from a population, and they need insight into sampling problems and opportunities.

Note that statistical methods, no matter how sophisticated, are not useful for inferring any traits of a larger population if the sample itself is bad. Direct marketing researchers should be able, at least, to obtain adequate samples from a population, to compute sample sizes and confidence intervals, and to know what is there and why. They should also understand the key terms presented at the start of this chapter in Figure 11-1.

Random Samples

To ensure that experimental and control groups are as nearly alike as possible, marketers work to make any differences between the two attributable only to chance. There are a variety of ways to obtain **random samples** from a total population:

- *Simple random samples:*   To construct a simple random sample, select each subject randomly from a population from which the preceding selection has been removed. Preprinted tables or computer-generated lists of random numbers help ensure that all members of the population are equally likely to be chosen.
- *Systematic random samples:*   Systematic random samples are technically not pure random samples, but, since they require only one pass through a large mailing list, they are the type direct marketers most frequently use. Starting with a random number *n,* the marketer selects every *n*th name until the sample is the size desired as a percentage of the entire population.
- *Stratified random samples:*   In stratified random samples, names are drawn in proportion to a particular parameter of a population. For example, the distribution of the sample can be set by age to be proportional to the known age distribution of the population.
- *Cluster samples:*   Marketers can select an entire cluster at random to create a cluster sample, such as the entire ZIP code in an *n*th selection of all ZIP codes.
- *Replicated samples:*   Replicated samples can be created by taking several independent random samples in turn. For example, a direct marketing researcher might first choose a stratum from among all 50 of the United States, then a stratum of counties within these states, then a stratum of census tracts within the selected counties. The direct marketing researcher would vary the choices over a period of time.
- *Sequential samples:*   For a sequential sample the selection of names is based on progressive data; that is, on prior predictions of an outcome, in much the same way television networks predict election outcomes.

In their quest for randomness marketers should remember that the arrangement of the list from which they draw their sample could itself bias the selection. Alphabetic arrangement of a list, for example, could result in ethnic concentrations within certain letters that would not be present if names were not alphabetized. A similar problem could occur when a list is geographically arranged so that location differences are concentrated. Most large lists today are arranged in ZIP code sequence, numerically from East Coast to West Coast, and this form of arrangement is probably as conducive as any to *n*th name selection without bias.

Sampling error (that is, lack of randomness) can also arise when not everyone in the population of interest is included, such as when selections are made from a telephone directory that includes neither households without telephones nor those with unlisted numbers. Another instance of sampling error is the inclusion of nonprospects; for instance, a direct marketing researcher would not use a list that includes apartment dwellers to test an offering of lawn furniture. Another form of error, *nonresponse error,* occurs when an individual is included in the sample but, for one reason or another, is not reached or refuses to respond.

Determining the Sample Size

The proper **sample size** is determined by first looking at two major considerations: (1) the cost of reaching the sample and (2) the amount of information needed to make an efficient decision; that is, the number of responses that will enable a direct marketer to predict a future response rate within a comfortable limit of certainty. A judgment call can be made about samples size, such as "test 5,000" or "test 10 percent," or a calculation can be used. The basis for the formula for sample-size calculation lies in a determination of probabilities. In the paragraphs which follow, we will show all the individual elements in the formula for calculating sample size and then we will put these together into the formula. This formula tells us how many pieces are needed to mail (or calls needed to be made, or Web site visits, or whatever) to get back a certain number of responses and have a certain degree of confidence in those responses.

The **law of large numbers** assures that, as sample size increases, the distribution of sample means (in this case, response rates) concentrates closer to the true mean of the total population. In other words, the more names in a sample, generally, the closer the response is to the response of the total population. Further, the **central limit theorem** assures that, in a number of random samples taken from a population, the sample means (response rates) tend to be normally distributed. The shape of such a **normal distribution**—the so-called "bell-shaped curve"—is completely determined by its two parameters: **mean** (average response rate) and **standard deviation** (variance from the mean).

Statistical evaluation helps the direct marketing researcher arrive at conclusions that are reassuring. Having determined a *confidence level* that is satisfactory, as well as an acceptable *limit of error,* the researcher can estimate the *response rate* to calculate an appropriate *sample size.* Or, after the fact, knowing the actual response rate, he or she can calculate the limit of error. All four elements—*confidence level, limit of error, expected (or actual) response rate,* and *sample size*—enter into this calculation. We should define these terms:

- *Confidence level:*   The **confidence level,** as expressed in our formula, is the number of standard deviations from the mean in a normal distribution; for example, 1.96 standard deviations from the mean contain 95% of the area under a normal curve. (Published statistical tables provide standard deviations for confidence levels (i.e., 99%, 90%, 85%, etc.)) The expressed level denotes the number of times in 100 attempts that the resultant predictions must be correct. At a confidence level of 95%, for example, it can be concluded that 95 times out of 100 attempts, the prediction will be correct.
- *Limit of error:*   **Limit of error** describes the number of percentage points by which the researcher is allowed to comfortably miscalculate the actual response rate. In other words, if a 1-percent response is expected, by how much can be miscalculated and still be in an acceptable, or at least a safe, position?

A 20-percent limit of error, for example, assuming a 1-percent response rate, could result in a range of actual response as low as 8/10th of 1 percent to as high as 1.2 percent; that is, 1 percent ± 20 percent of 1 percent.

- *Expected (actual) response rate:* The response rate (*estimated,* before conduct of an experiment; actual, after conduct of an experiment) represents the number of positive responses expressed as a percentage of the total. In terms of the toss of a coin, how often will "heads" appear? In terms of a direct mailing, how many positive responses will be received? The difference between this positive response and the total quantity mailed describes the percentage of nonresponse, or negative response. If there is 1-percent response, then R (for "response") would equal 0.01 (expressed as a decimal) and 1 minus R (the negative responses) would equal 0.99.

- *Sample size:* The determined sample size is the number of observations in our experiment. This is, as example, the number of individual pieces of direct mail sent out in a test from which will be determined, ultimately, the percentage of response and the percentage of nonresponse. The formula for determining sample size is

$$N = \frac{(R)(1 - R)(C)^2}{E^2}$$

where (R) is the frequency of response, a percentage expressed as a decimal; $(1 - R)$ is the frequency of nonresponse, also a percentage expressed as a decimal; (C) is the confidence level, expressed as a number of standard deviations; (E) is the limit of error expressed as a decimal; and (N) is the sample size, the number of pieces to be mailed.

To illustrate the use of the a forementioned formula, one determines the sample size required in terms of mailing pieces when the expected response is 1 percent and the desired limit of error is ± 0.2 percent at a confidence level of 95 percent. Thus,

$$R = 1\% \ldots \text{ or } 0.01, \text{ expressed as a decimal}$$
$$1 - R = 99\% \ldots \text{ or } 0.99, \text{ expressed as a decimal}$$
$$C = 1.96 \text{ standard deviations, if a 95\% confidence level is accepted}$$
$$E = 0.2\% \ldots \text{ or } 0.002, \text{ expressed as a decimal}$$
$$N = \text{to be determined}$$

Substituting the above values into the formula, there is

$$N = \frac{(0.01)(0.99)(1.96)^2}{(0.002)^2}$$
$$= \frac{(0.01)(0.99)(3.8416)}{(0.000004)}$$
$$= \frac{0.03803184}{0.000004}$$
$$N = 9,508 \text{ pieces to be mailed}$$

Suppose that, in the above experiment, 9,508 pieces had been mailed, and the actual response rate turned out to be 1.5 percent, rather than 1 percent. Still, at a 95-percent confidence level, what would be the limit of error if, on the basis of the 1.5-percent response rate predicted from this mailing, further mailings were sent out? The formula for determining limit of error is

$$E = \sqrt{(R)(1 - R)/N \times C}$$

Substituting the new values (with the same notation as before) into this formula and solving for limit of error, there is

$$E = \sqrt{(0.015)(0.985)/9580} \times 1.96$$
$$E = \sqrt{0.000001554} \times 1.96$$
$$E = 0.00124 \times 1.96$$
$$E = 0.00243 \ldots \text{ or, } 0.243\% \text{ limit of error}$$

These two examples illustrate, first, the statistical importance of setting up direct mail experiments in such a manner as to ensure a sample size adequate for meaningful projection of response within acceptable tolerances. Second, they demonstrate the need for accurate determination of the limit of error, the variation that could occur by chance alone and not as a result of significant differences in particular direct marketing efforts. When comparing the response from two diverse market segments, for example, such "error by chance" difference during the evaluation process must be recognized.

In this example, in which the actual response was 1.5 percent and the error limit was calculated to be 0.243 percent, any response from continuation mailings or comparative tests within the range of 1.257 and 1.743 percent would be statistically "the same as" 1.5 percent, and such variation could have occurred by statistical chance alone at a 95-percent level of confidence.

MEASUREMENT OF DIFFERENCE

Assuming that the direct marketer has properly selected a sample of adequate size and designed and conducted the experiment itself in a valid manner, he or she must also know how to validate the difference between the results of the experiment group and its control group. Only by understanding this can direct marketers decide to change from one promotional strategy to another or from one market segment to another or to adopt a new product in place of an old one.

Typically, in direct marketing experimentation the mean response to a direct mail solicitation is expressed as the average number of responses for each 1,000 pieces of mail sent out, and attributable to the test (in which a single variable has been injected) in relationship to the control. That variable could be the mailing list used. Or, it could be a pricing variance or a product difference. When we compare, the test and the control, we must determine whether, in fact, the difference is real, in a statistical sense, or whether it might have occurred through chance alone. The difference in results must be further related to difference in cost, if there is any. In effect, one tests the hypothesis that there is no difference between the test and the control.

Hypothesis Testing

In testing a **hypothesis**—an assertion about the value of the parameter of a variable—the researcher decides, on the basis of observed facts such as the relative response to a test of variation in advertising copy, for example, whether an assumption seems to be valid. The assumption is called the **null hypothesis** and the researcher must state it in such a way that it can be proved wrong. Assuming that the null hypothesis is in fact true, we can determine the probability to assign to an **alternative hypothesis.** Hypotheses are typically stated in negative terms; that is, a null hypothesis (H_0) versus an alternative hypothesis (H_a) in a form such as the following:

> H_0: Direct mail response from the test promotion is at or below direct mail response from the control promotion.
> H_a: Direct mail response from the test promotion is above direct mail response from the control promotion.

The null hypothesis then states that direct mail response *will not* be better than the control. Measurement sets out to *disprove* this null hypothesis. The probability of this happening might be very small, considering that the experiment involves new and untried copy intended to outperform the control, which presumably is the best copy now available.

In the event it is decided to *reject the null hypothesis,* it is rejected in favor of the alternative. In this instance, if the null hypothesis is rejected, it is because that test response is at or below the control response, it is done in favor of the alternative hypothesis because that test response is significantly better than the control response.

Some results, obviously, are more "significant" than others. A statistician puts a special interpretation on the word "significant" associating it with a specific probability, often denoted by the Greek letter alpha (α), which is decided on prior to testing the hypothesis. The researcher might state that the null hypothesis will be rejected only if the result is significant at a level of, say, 0.05 (5 percent). That is, the test result must diverge enough from the control result so that such result would occur with the probability of 0.05 or less if the hypothesis were true. The statement of a level of significance should be made *prior* to testing the hypothesis to avoid vacillation on the part of the researcher when the actual response is observed.

Types of Errors in Hypothesis Testing

Two types of error can occur in tests of hypotheses. A **Type I error** results when the decision maker rejects the null hypothesis even though it is, in fact, true. In this instance the "wrong" decision allows an action when it should not. The probability of doing this is fixed and equal to α. Note that α determines a critical result so rare that it is preferred to reject the null hypothesis rather than believe an event that rare actually occurred. Thus, α measures the probability of committing a Type I error.

A **Type II error** occurs when the decision maker accepts the null hypothesis when it is, in fact, not true. In this instance the "wrong" decision is to not do something when something should be done. The probability associated with a Type II error is called beta (β) and it is more difficult to measure than α, prior to conducting an experiment, since it requires a fixed value, other than the one assumed within the null hypothesis, around which confidence intervals associated with an alternative hypothesis can be based.

Although researchers are not as concerned with Type II errors in evaluating the results of an experiment, these can be every bit as expensive in opportunity costs as Type I errors. We usually think of "wrong" decisions in terms of doing something when we should not, but there is a lost "opportunity" cost associated with *not* doing something when we should!

This examination of risks should have even the diehard nonbeliever convinced that probability theory is a way of *measuring risk and assessing uncertainly, not a way of eliminating either!* To make an adequate decision, the direct marketing researcher must sample a population, measure relevant variables (one at a time), compute statistics using these variables, infer something about the probability distributions that exist in the population, and, finally, make a decision based on the chance of incurring either a Type I or Type II error.

Statistical Evaluation of Differences

Frequently, when evaluating the results of an experiment and comparing the response from a test with the response from a control, we need to know whether a difference is (or is not) *statistically significant.* The **chi-square (χ^2) test** is one way to determine such a difference.[1] The null hypothesis offered in making the determination is that there is, in fact, no difference between the response from the test and the response from the control. A statistic χ^2 is computed from the observed samples and compared with a chi-square distribution table that lists probabilities for a theoretical sampling distribution.

The shape of a χ^2 distribution varies according to the number of **degrees of freedom,** defined as the number of observations that are allowed to vary. The number of degrees of freedom is determined by multiplying the number of observations in a row (minus 1) times the number of observations in a column (minus 1), thus, $(r-1)(c-1)$, where r is the number of rows and c is the number of columns. For example, the contingency table in Figure 11-4, expressed as "2 × 2" (and read "2 by 2") would involve just one degree of freedom, $(2-1) \times (2-1) = 1$. A table of this form can be used for evaluating the significance of the difference between a test and its control in an experiment.

The typical chi-square table, found in most statistical textbooks, will show critical values for 30 (or more) degrees of freedom for reference when as many as 30 observations are measured *against one another.* Since direct marketers are urged to test just one variable at a time (i.e., a single test against a single control, only the top row of the table)—that for one degree of freedom—needs to be referenced. Here, then, are the critical values of a chi-square distribution for one degree of freedom along with associated probabilities:

Chi-Square Critical Value of .00016 = .99 *probability;* .00063 = .98; .0039 = .95; .016 = 90; .064 = .80; .15 = .70; .46 = .50; 1.07 = .30; 1.64 = .20; 2.71 = .10; .3.84 = .05; 5.41 = .02; 6.64 = .01; 10.83 = .001.

A Priori Versus A Posteriori Analysis

A differentiation should be made between the statistical analysis used in setting up an experiment, particularly the choice of sample size, *before the fact,* ***a priori,*** and the statistical analysis used in evaluating a test for significant differences *after the fact,* ***a posteriori.***

	Test	Control	Totals
Response	A	C	$A + C$
Nonresponse	B	D	$B + D$
Total mailed	$A + B$	$C + D$	$A + B + C + D = N$

The statistic χ^2 is computed as follows:

$$\chi^2 = \frac{N[/(A \times D) - (C \times B)/ - N/2]^2}{(A + B) \times (C + D) \times (A + C) \times (B + D)}$$

Here is a sample calculation:

	Test	Control	Totals
Response	200	100	300
Nonresponse	800	900	1700
Total mailed	1000	1000	2000

$$\chi^2 = \frac{2,000 \times [|180,000 - 80,000| - 1,000]^2}{1,000 \times 1,000 \times 300 \times 1,700}$$

$\chi^2 = 38.4\ldots$ which is significant at the 99 ++ % level since it exceeds the critical value in the χ^2 table for one degree of freedom for a significance level of 0.001, given as 10.83

FIGURE 11-4   Example of Chi-Square Measurement of Difference in an Experiment Between a Test and a Control

In our discussion of sampling earlier, *a priori* analysis assumes (1) a response level, (2) a confidence level, and (3) an acceptable variation for limit of error to be deemed significant. Based on these three assumptions, sample size can be determined by formula. *A posteriori* analysis, performed after the test versus control experiment has been conducted, uses the *known* sample size and *known* response level as inputs to a calculation of confidence intervals; that is, the degree of variation or limit of error associated with varying levels of significance. For an $\alpha = 0.05$, there is one set of very broad limits; for an $\alpha = 0.10$, there is a set of different, more narrowly defined limits; for an $\alpha = 0.25$, there is a set of even more narrowly defined limits.

In *a priori* analysis the decision maker is asked to use his or her best judgment in arriving at three assumptions: expected response, confidence level, and acceptable limit of error. In *a posteriori* analysis, having established a confidence level in the *a priori* setting, and having the willingness to live with the choice after the fact, together with known sample size and response level, the limit of error around the known response level becomes a simple mechanical calculation.

Note that *a posteriori* analysis is possible regardless of the level of response; the analysis can be made even if the actual level achieved differs widely from the level assumed in the *a priori* analysis. The important point is test results must be read and calculations must be made in relation to what actually occurred, irrespective of what was assumed would occur at the time the test was initiated.

Direct marketers do not, however, enjoy a completely pure laboratory environment; rather, it is a marketplace environment. These two environments differ widely in the degree of control that can be exercised over the exogenous factors affecting the realities of the marketplace environment. A few examples will accentuate this point.

- Does seasonality affect results?
- Is the list used in the continuation mailing to the total population derived from the same group as the test sample?
- How does the environment in which the experiment was conducted compare with that of the continuation; that is, current economic conditions, consumer optimism, and world events? All can be significantly different.
- At what stage is the product in its life cycle; that is, have new models been developed and is there increasing competition?

Put simply, the actual level of response of even a meticulously controlled experiment may not always be projected into the future. Conditions might be different. Thus, whereas the relationship between a test and its control may be the same, that is, one is still better than the other, the entire level of response for both might be either higher or lower than that originally experienced.

STRUCTURING AND EVALUATING AN EXPERIMENT

We conduct an experiment in order to make an adequate decision. To do this, the direct marketing researcher must

- Sample a population
- Measure relevant variables, ideally one at a time
- Compute statistics using these measurements
- Infer something about the probability distributions that exist in the population
- Make a decision mindful of the chance of incurring a Type I error (when the decision maker rejects the "null" hypothesis even though it is true) or a Type II error (when the decision maker accepts the null hypothesis when it is *not* true).

Let's say that a direct marketing researcher wants to test a new promotion strategy against his or her present strategy, to be offered to the control group in the experiment. Past experience indicates that he or she can expect a 2-percent response rate from the present promotion.

Here is a framework for implementation of the experiment:

1. State the hypothesis
2. Develop, by *a priori* analysis, the assumptions required and compute the appropriate sample size
3. Structure and perform the experiment
4. Develop, by *a posteriori* analysis, statistics for judging hypothesis validity
5. Make the decision

This procedure sounds simple and appears to be reasonable. Let's follow it step by step.

Step 1.   State the Hypothesis. The null hypothesis is

H_0: Direct mail response from the test promotion is at or below direct mail response from the control promotion.

Although it is not necessary to state an alternative hypothesis at this stage, doing so could imply that he or she is hoping to reject the null hypothesis in favor of the alternative; that is, the test promotion would be better than the control, so that

H_a: Direct mail response from the test promotion is above direct mail response from the control promotion.

Step 2. *A Priori* Analysis. The response level of 2 percent is the first of three assumptions. The second assumption is the significance level, which, when $\alpha = 0.05$, describes a confidence level of 95 percent. (The confidence level is equal to 1.0 minus α, thus $1.0 - 0.05 = 0.95$, or 95 percent.) The final assumption relates to "limit of error" or "variation around the mean" or, more descriptively, the error limit we wish to maintain around the assumed level of response. In this example, we will assume 15 percent. Having established figures for our three assumptions, 2-percent response, 95-percent confidence level, and 15-percent limit of error, we can use the formula given earlier in this chapter to establish the sample size. The three assumptions and resultant sample size are summarized in Figure 11-5. Figure 11-5 shows the effect of the 15-percent error limit. At a 95-percent confidence level, any response below 2.3 percent would not be better than a control response (as assumed) of 2.0 percent.

Step 3. Structure of the Test. Having determined (in the manner demonstrated earlier in this chapter) an objective sample size of 8,365 pieces to be mailed for the control and a comparable volume for the test promotion and having obtained the sample in a valid manner, he or she conducts the experiment through release of the test mailing versus the control mailing.

Step 4. *A Posteriori* Analysis. When all results are in, the direct marketing research examines the response from both the test and the control promotions. One evaluation procedure for determining whether an observed difference is (or is not) statistically significant is the chi-square (χ^2) test, as demonstrated earlier in this chapter.

Step 5. Make the Decision. The decision to accept or reject the promotion tested in the experiment should be clear-cut, based on the *a posteriori* analysis.

Expected (Assumed) Response Rate: 2%, 20/M pieces mailed.

Significance Level (α): .05

Confidence Level $(1.0 - \alpha)$: 95%

Limits of Error:

    Percent Response/M Pieces Mailed

      +15% 20/M + 3/M = 23/M (2.3%)

      −15% 20/M − 3/M = 17/M (1.7%)

Sample Size: 8,365 mailing pieces (determined separately)

FIGURE 11-5 *A Priori* Assumptions and Sample-Size Determination

OPPORTUNITIES FOR EXPERIMENTATION

Under rigidly controlled conditions, direct marketing offers a great deal of opportunity for experimentation. It is this opportunity that provides an environment susceptible to measurement and accountability. The availability of lists and data about these lists also provide populations from which scientifically determined samples can be drawn in order to properly conduct experiments: within lists or within segments of them. The profiling of these lists also makes it possible to further describe market segments for prospecting whether the medium is direct mail, magazines, or newspapers; television or radio; or telephone or the World Wide Web. Within such list refinements, described as market segments, one can test product and price variations and the multitude of variables that compose promotional strategies: copy, art, graphics, color, format, and the offer itself. Individual components of ads or the effort itself, such as a completely new direct mail package can also be tested. With this limitless array of possibilities, however, it is exceedingly important, as noted earlier, to *test only the important things and to test them adequately*.

Direct marketers favor experimentation research over survey research because they can translate many of the techniques used to ask prospects whether they *intend to buy* into direct marketing offers actually *asking them to buy*. One happy compromise of survey research with experimental research, used to test a new product not yet available in the marketplace, is called **dry testing.** Those who use the dry-testing technique must be meticulously careful not to misrepresent the offering. Payment in advance should not be requested and remittances, if received, should be returned promptly; and, those who respond should receive first priority if and when the product ordered becomes a reality.

Another survey research tool is the **focus group interview,** wherein unstructured small groups, representative of appropriate market segments, under skilled leadership, converse in a relaxed environment about the subject of the research, which is often not specifically identified. Although marketers can use such groups for creative stimulation or evaluation, they cannot scientifically control them, so it is not really possible to make scientific projections from the results of a focus group.

Research, utilizing the tools and techniques of both survey and experimentation, as highlighted in this chapter, is a key requirement of the science of direct marketing. While those steeped in the creativity of the arts, who put their emphasis on promotion, often shy away from the rigors of numbers, a healthy respect for statistics is essential to the professional direct marketer. That is why a course in basic statistics must be a prerequisite to a basic course in direct marketing.

Summary

Direct marketing is research oriented and is especially susceptible to the tools and techniques of experimentation. Such experimentation is called "testing" by practitioners and usually measures the impact of changing a variable within product, price, place, or promotion. Although research is concerned with fact finding and information gathering, it has as its objective problem solving or action recommending. Research enables the collection of data, from which information can be derived. Data are categorized as *secondary,* collected originally for another purpose, and *primary,* collected specifically for the research need. Collection of primary data involves either survey or experimentation, the latter most often is utilized in testing by direct marketers. Survey research observes various activities as they naturally arise in the environment whereas experimentation involves the manipulation of one or more independent variables to determine their influence on an outcome, which is the dependent variable.

Valid experiments require controls and randomized samples. In designing experiments it is important to understand the methods for obtaining samples and determining sample sizes. Otherwise, resultant estimations and predictions will not be helpful. Samples may be obtained in many ways. Determination of sample size is concerned with confidence level, error limit, and expected (or actual) percent of response. Sample size and error limit can be calculated statistically, with tables readily available for such determination. Direct marketers must evaluate statistically significant differences in observed responses between test and control. The chi-square distribution describes one statistical tool for analyzing the significance of such differences.

Experiments must be designed and sampling must be controlled so that results are measurable and accountable. Hypothesis testing enables such measurement. It is important to schedule experiments carefully and to record results utilizing key codes to identify sources of response for accurate evaluation.

Key Terms

- quantitative, 263
- qualitative, 263
- survey, 263
- experiment, 263
- test, 263
- sampling errors, 266
- secondary data, 267
- primary data, 267
- independent variables, 270
- dependent variables, 270
- control group, 271
- random assignment, 271

- key codes, 271
- break even, 272
- sampling, 273
- random samples, 274
- sample size, 275
- law of large numbers, 275
- central limit theorem, 275
- normal distribution, 275
- mean, 275
- standard deviation, 275
- confidence level, 275
- limit of error, 275

- hypothesis, 278
- null hypothesis, 278
- alternative hypothesis, 278
- Type I error, 278
- Type II error, 278
- chi-square (χ^2) test, 279
- degrees of freedom, 279
- a priori, 279
- a posteriori, 279
- dry testing, 283
- focus group interview, 283

Review Questions

1. Why might a survey of buying expectations not be a valid indication of actual behavior in the marketplace?
2. Distinguish between surveys and experiments. Which is more used by direct marketers and why?
3. Where might a direct marketer obtain secondary data about
   a. age distribution of a population?
   b. number of corrugated carton manufacturers in a city?
   c. number of households in a ZIP code area?
   d. retail sales of shopping goods in a county?

4. What are the advantages and disadvantages of seeking primary data by each of these survey methods?
   a. personal interview
   b. telephone interview
   c. mail questionnaire
   d. Web site registration
   e. observation
5. Give examples of some questions to which a direct marketer might seek answers through experimentation.
6. What is the ideal way for a direct marketer to structure an experiment?

7. Why is the determination of a proper sample size important in an experiment? What factors must marketers consider in setting sample size?

8. In testing a hypothesis, is a Type I or Type II error more serious? That is, are there greater consequences in (I) "doing something when you shouldn't," or (II) "not doing something when you should"?

9. Why is it important in measuring an experiment that the researcher determine the statistical significance level of observed differences?

10. Does the direct marketing researcher have absolute and complete control over an experiment? Discuss possible situations in which the researcher may not.

11. Why should direct marketers confine experimentation to only those tests that have high consequences?

Exercise

Congratulations! You have just been hired as an associate for a well-known advertising agency. Your first task is to assist a client in determining which of the four direct mail packages they have been using is the most productive. Structure a test to investigate the two different offers the firm has been using along with the four different direct mail formats.

CASE: AN ILLUSTRATIVE EXPERIMENT

OVERVIEW

Experimentation, or testing, as it is usually called by direct marketers, is second nature to them. All too often, however, such experimentation is conducted under the guise of scientific procedure, but the sample selected is not representative, the test structure is faulty, and the sample size is inadequate. The resultant measurement of differences between the test and control reveals differences that are not significant.

True experimentation, if it is to be accomplished properly, should be structured in a valid manner. The results, when measured statistically, should be at an acceptable level of significance so as to provide a prediction with which the researcher can be comfortable. This case provides a means for evaluating a typical direct marketing test structure, one intended to measure the response differences among five advertisements run in a national newspaper.

The purpose of this case study is to stimulate consideration of key elements that determine the adequacy and validity of a direct marketing experiment: sample design, sample size, conduct

FIGURE 11-6   Alternative Print Advertisements (Control Plus Four Experiments) Tested by Omaha Steaks International

Advertising Copy	Circulation	Ad Cost	Results Index
(A) "Try a Little Tenderness" *(Control)*	367,000	$ 578	100%
(B) "Perfect Steaks" *(Experiment 1)*	634,000	$ 824	28%
(C) "Journal" *(Experiment 2)*	652,000	$ 863	29%
(D) "Love at First Bite" *(Experiment 3)*	458,000	$ 721	74%
(E) "Attention Steak Lovers" *(Experiment 4)*	652,000	$1,027	76%

FIGURE 11-7   Results of Omaha Steaks International Experiment

of the experiment, and measurement of difference. Consider, too, the *need for experimentation* and the *importance of control.*

CASE

Omaha Steaks International has long offered six 6-ounce filet mignons, 1–1/4 inch thick, for $29.95 (plus $2.00 shipping/handling) through space advertising in print media. In an October issue of the *Wall Street Journal,* the direct marketer scheduled an experiment of a control advertisement (A) against four test advertisements (B), (C), (D), (E), all of which are illustrated in Figure 11-6. In testing the existing control advertisement against the four alternatives, each of which had a particular promotional theme, management wanted to find out which ad, the existing control or any of the four new advertisements, would produce better response and more sales. After experimentation, management determined that the control advertisement did, in fact, produce orders at a lower cost per sale than did any of the alternatives tested. This determination was based on the results shown in Figure 11-7.

Source: This case was developed from data provided by Fred Simon, Omaha Steaks International, Omaha, NE 68127. ■

Case Discussion Questions

Be prepared to discuss the validity of the following elements of this experiment: (1) objective of the test; (2) design of the test and the determination of the sample; (3) adequacy of sample size; (4) measurement and significance of differences; (5) adequacy of the resultant prediction; and (6) explanation of why the response differences occurred.

Note

1. Other statistical techniques used for measuring significant differences include ANOVA (analysis of variance, the F-test), the T-test (for sample sizes through 30), and the Z-test (for sample sizes larger than 30).

REGULATORY ENVIRONMENT: THE ETHICAL AND LEGAL ISSUES IN DIRECT MARKETING

The regulatory environment of direct marketing includes the two very important areas of ethical and legal issues. **Ethics** are the moral principles of conduct governing the behavior of an individual or a group. **Morals** are often described in terms of good or bad. To be *ethical* in marketing means to conform to the accepted professional standards of conduct. However, you might ask, what exactly are the "accepted professional standards of conduct"?

This chapter will discuss ethics and the ethical behavior expected of direct marketers as set forth by the Direct Marketing Association (DMA) along with the law as it pertains to direct marketing activities. The legal regulations affecting direct marketing activities on the federal, state, and local levels primarily deal with three broad legal issues: intellectual property, security, and privacy. We'll detail the legal issues in each of these three areas in this chapter, after an overview of the ethical aspects of direct marketing.

ETHICS OF DIRECT MARKETING

A different kind of e-business is receiving an increasing amount of attention from the direct marketing community. In this case, the "e" doesn't stand for electronic, it stands for "ethics" and direct marketers are paying close attention. Ethics is concerned with morality: the rightness and wrongness of individual actions or deeds. As former Supreme Court Justice Potter Stewart once said, "Ethics is knowing the difference between what you have a right to do and what is the right thing to do." A **code of ethics** is a set of guideline for making ethical decisions.

DMA's Guidelines for Ethical Business Practices
The Direct Marketing Association has established a detailed code of ethics for direct marketers. These guidelines are intended to provide individuals and organizations in direct marketing in all media with generally accepted principles of conduct. These are self-regulatory measures as opposed to governmental mandates. As shown in Figure 12-1 these ethical guidelines address 10 key areas.

FIGURE 12-1   The DMA's Guidelines for Ethical Business Practices

1. The Terms of the Offer
Article #1:   Honesty and Clarity of Offer
Article #2:   Accuracy and Consistency
Article #3:   Clarity of Representations
Article #4:   Actual Conditions
Article #5:   Disparagement
Article #6:   Decency
Article #7:   Photographs and Artwork
Article #8:   Disclosure of Sponsor and Intent
Article #9:   Accessibility
Article #10: Solicitation in the Guise of an Invoice or Governmental Notification
Article #11: Postage, Shipping, or Handling

2. Marketing to Children
Article #12: Marketing to Children
Article #13: Parental Responsibility and Choice
Article #14: Information from or About Children
Article #15: Marketing Online to Children Under 13 Years of Age

3. Special Offers and Claims
Article #16: Use of the Word "Free" and Other Similar Representations
Article #17: Price Comparisons
Article #18: Guarantees
Article #19: Use of Test or Survey Data
Article #20: Testimonials and Endorsements

4. Sweepstakes
Article #21: Use of the Term "Sweepstakes"
Article #22: No Purchase Option
Article #23: Chances of Winning
Article #24: Prizes
Article #25: Premiums
Article #26: Disclosure of Rules

5. Fulfillment
Article #27: Unordered Merchandise
Article #28: Product Availability and Shipments
Article #29: Dry Testing

6. Collection, Use, and Maintenance of Marketing Data
Article #30: Collection, Use, and Transfer of Personally Identifiable Data
Article #31: Personal Data
Article #32: Collection, Use, and Transfer of Health Related Data
Article #33: Promotion of Marketing Lists
Article #34: Marketing List Usage

7. On-line Marketing
Article #35: On-line Information
Article #36: Commercial Solicitations Online

8. Telephone Marketing
Article #37: Reasonable Hours
Article #38: Taping of Conversations
Article #39: Restricted Contacts
Article #40: Use of Automated Dialing Equipment
Article #41: Use of Predictive Auto Dialing Equipment
Article #42: Use of Telephone Facsimile Machines
Article #43: Promotions for Response by Toll-Free and Pay-Per-Call Numbers
Article #44: Disclosure and Tactics

9. Fundraising
Article #45: Fundraising

10. Laws, Codes, and Regulations
Article #46: Laws, Codes, and Regulations

Note: The above is an overview of the articles that are addressed in each area, however, to receive a complete *Ethical Business Practice* guide, contact the Direct Marketing Association at www.the-dma.org or call (212) 768-7277.

Facts for Business: A Business Checklist for Direct Marketers
(A guide to all Federal Trade Commission Regulations)

A Business Guide to the Federal Trade Commission's Mail or Telephone Order Merchandise Rule
Complying with the FTC Telemarketing Sales Rule

DMA Fair Information Practices Manual
(A guide to assist direct marketers in developing a corporate fair information policy statement)

The DMA Washington Report

The DMA Compendium of Government Issues Affecting Direct Marketers

FIGURE 12-2   DMA Publications and Information Sources

Note: For further information about the activities and services of the DMA Ethics and Consumer Affairs Department contact the DMA's Washington DC office at consumer@the-dma.org or call (202) 955-5030.

The DMA Ethics and Consumer Affairs Department

In addition to providing guidelines for ethical business practices, the DMA sponsors several activities in its Ethics and Consumer Affairs Department. The Mail Preference Service (MPS) offers consumers assistance in decreasing the volume of national advertising mail they receive at home. The Telephone Preference Service (TPS) offers consumers assistance in decreasing the number of national telephone calls received at home. The E-Mail Preference Service (EMPS) is the DMA's most recent service designed to assist consumers in decreasing the number of unsolicited e-mail offers received. In essence, the DMA supports a consumer's right to choose the channel by which he or she would prefer to shop. Thus, a national do not call list has actually existed since 1985 when the DMA established its national Telephone Preference Service.[1] Consumers can register with the TPS by clicking www.dma-consumers.org.

The DMA also publishes a variety of publications designed to assist direct marketers in complying with federal and state regulations. See Figure 12-2 for a list of such DMA publications and information sources. The DMA has established both the guidelines for ethical business practices and an office of Ethics and Consumer Affairs to assist direct marketers in developing and maintaining consumer relationships that are based on fair and ethical principles. To view the DMA's ethical guidelines go to www.the-dma.org/library/guidelines/ethicalguidelines.shtml and browse through the various categories. With these ethical guidelines, the DMA is encouraging all direct marketers to act in a morally correct business manner and to safeguard basic consumer rights.

BASIC CONSUMER RIGHTS

Consumers possess the following basic human rights: (1) the right to safety; (2) the right to be informed; (3) the right to selection; (4) the right to confidentiality; and (5) the right to privacy.[2] Direct marketers should respect and safeguard these rights. Let's look at each.

The Right to Safety

The **right to safety** allows consumers to be safe from both physical and psychological harm. They cannot be harassed or made to feel bad if, for example, they declined a telephone request to purchase a product or service. These circumstances may cause the consumer to experience undue stress.

The Right to Be Informed

The **right to be informed** includes the consumer's right to receive any and all pertinent or requested information. This includes the right to be informed about all stages of the direct marketing process. It is an obligation of direct marketers to fully disclose what they intend to do with the consumer's name and address once it is put onto a mailing list. In addition, direct marketers should provide the consumer with an explanation of why they collect information about consumers and their lifestyles.

The Right to Selection

The **right to selection** includes a consumer's right to choose or make decisions about his or her buying behavior. In other words, to the consumer can accept or reject any offer from a direct marketer or a telemarketer, be it a request to purchase a product or service, subscribe to a magazine, attend a meeting, donate to a charitable organization, or vote for a political candidate. Consumers cannot be made to feel forced into taking an action against their wishes.

The Right to Confidentiality

The **right to confidentiality** is a consumer's right to specify to a given company that information that they freely provide should not be shared. Like information disclosed in a physician–patient or attorney–client relationship, information a consumer provides to direct marketing organization with expressed confidentiality must not be shared. Savvy direct marketers know to be successful they must build long-term relationships with their customers based on trust. This trust must not be betrayed. Direct marketers can uphold the consumer's right to confidentiality by developing proper security measures (electronic watermarks, firewalls, digital signatures, authentication, data integrity, encryption, etc.) to protect the security of the proprietary data the direct marketer has promised to safeguard.

Suppose a nonprofit organization specifically stated in its printed materials that it will not share the names of donors with other charitable organizations . . . and then it turns around and rents its donor lists! This is unethical and constitutes a "breach of confidentiality."

The Right to Privacy

The final basic consumer right, the right to privacy, is probably the most noteworthy consumer right affecting direct marketers. The **right to privacy** has been defined as the ability of an individual to control the access others have to personal information. Because of the heightened awareness and controversy over the matter, along with the legal ramifications of the consumer's right to privacy, we'll discuss privacy issues later in the chapter in more detail than the other four basic consumer rights.

LEGISLATIVE ISSUES

The three primary legislative areas designed to safeguard consumer rights are intellectual property, security, and privacy.

Intellectual Property

Intellectual property is defined as products of the mind or ideas.[3] Some examples include books, music, computer software, designs, and technological know-how. The protection of intellectual property afforded by copyrights, patents, trademarks, and databases is the province of several governmental agencies. Under copyright laws, a copyright owner has the exclusive right to distribute copies of the protected work. Thus, third parties are not permitted to sell, rent, transfer, or otherwise distribute copies of the work without the express permission of the copyright owner. Several channels currently exist for businesses to prevent unauthorized usage of protected material.

Given the freedom of the Internet, protection of trademarks has recently become even more difficult. The Internet's focus on visual advertisements will increase the likelihood of a conflict over trademark rights as more company logos, slogans, brand names, and trademarks are appearing in Web sites. Therefore, this area of intellectual property protection must also be one of the top concerns for direct marketers.

With the introduction of faster computer applications and hard drives with larger capacity for data storage, a new kind of intellectual property has emerged—a database. Data collection, both on-line and off-line, has soared in the past decade. It is now estimated the global market for database software and services is around $9 billion.[4] However, intellectual property protection of an organization's database is a volatile area. Businesses are being caught between the threats of unauthorized access by hackers (which we will discuss with regard to "security" in the next section), requirements to disclose certain data collected to law enforcement agencies, and consumer privacy concerns about data collection (which we will discuss later in the "privacy" section).

Security

In addition to creating and storing databases, companies must also secure their databases from unauthorized access and outside damage. Failure to do so may cause the direct marketer much embarrassment, pain, and potential liability for breaches in security. While technology exists to provide security via password controls and firewalls, these are not completely dependable and security breaches may still occur.

For example, Carmichael Lynch, a public relations and advertising firm, accidentally published its administration password on its Web site. The slip-up went undetected for six months. During that time, unauthorized visitors could have accessed e-mail addresses and passwords for almost 12,000 people who had just registered on the American Standard Web site, or the names, addresses, and vehicle information of 75,000 luxury car and SUV owners.[5]

Another security incident involved a government agency. On April 5, 2002, hackers broke into the payroll database for the State of California. The database contained personal information about the state's 265,000 employees, including names, home addresses, Social Security numbers, and bank account information.

In another recent mishap the publishing giant, Ziff-Davis Media, Inc., suffered a security lapse that exposed the personal data of thousands of magazine subscribers. In restitution, the company agreed to pay $100,000 to the New York State Department of Law and $500 each to the 50 customers whose credit card information had been disclosed.[6]

In response to these types of incidents, a California law known as SB 1386, became the first state law to address security breaches. It requires any person or business that conducts business in California to publicly disclose any security breaches that concerned personal information. That law was scheduled to take effect on July 1, 2003.[7]

Privacy

Consumers are more concerned about privacy today than ever before. However, privacy legislation has existed for a long time. Let's review the history of this important legislation.

PRIVACY LEGISLATION

Privacy legislation actually began over a century ago in 1890 when Samuel Warren and Justice Brandeis wrote a law review article advocating that a person should be protected from having personal matters reported by the press for commercial reasons. That marked the beginning of what many know today as a "consumer's right to privacy." In 1950, laws protected citizens from allowing public organizations to intrude on their private matters. However, these laws did not protect consumers against a private organization's use of personal information. Still, it wasn't until recent years that privacy issues became increasingly visible.

From the explosion of credit cards to the advent of personal computers to the new marketing realities in cyberspace today, the process of direct marketing has attained new heights of marketing success. With this phenomenal success, businesses have also faced scrutiny on numerous aspects of the privacy issue. Whatever the root, the concern over information privacy has been going on for decades. Back in the late 1970s, prior to most technological advances, the following appeared in a newspaper:[8]

> They know about you. They know how old you are.
> They know if you have children. They know about your job.
> They know how much money you make, what kind of car you drive,
> what sort of house you live in and whether you are likely to prefer paté
> de foie gras and champagne or hot dogs and a cold beer.
> They know all this and much, much more.
> And you know how?
> They know your name.
> What they have done with it is very simple:
> they have added it to a mailing list

Though it was an exaggeration (at the time), this excerpt is evidence of a widely held concern that a list is a conduit through which personal information is transferred from one direct marketer to another. While this may be true, as you should realize from the material contained in Chapters 2 and 3, to a direct marketer, a list is an instrument for describing a market segment. Market segments enable direct marketers to target appropriate promotional offers to consumers, thus reducing the amount of irrelevant marketing communication each consumer receives. This is good for both direct marketers and consumers. Information technology has made it possible for marketers, armed with customer information, to design promotional campaigns directed at different segments of prospective and current customers. From a marketing and customer service perspective, the purpose of gathering consumer information is to achieve greater selectivity and to make direct response advertising more relevant to the recipient. The use of personal information enables marketers to develop closer relationships with customers that foster brand loyalty and better customer service. However, regardless of the noble purpose information serves for direct marketers, privacy issues have now become legal matters.

Marketers have always had an interest in knowing consumer information, dating back to the days of corner "mom and pop" stores when everyone knew everyone else and their families and their business. Today is no different. Marketers still want to know about their customers in order to serve them better. Technology makes it easier to do just that. With the swipe of customer loyalty card, consumers receive discounts on purchases or earn bonus points toward free gifts while retailers download information about customer purchasing preferences and habits. From there . . . with a few clicks of the mouse or strokes on the keyboard, the purchase information can be shared with any number of interested parties—for a fee. Technology has made direct marketing list rental activities easier and more efficient. However, before direct marketers start thinking beyond this, they have to realize that along with advances in technology come additional legislative regulations. Perhaps the best-known legislation regarding privacy has come from the Privacy Protection Study Commission.

Privacy Protection Study Commission

The concern of the U.S. consumer and Congress over the broad issue of privacy, including the subject of mailing lists and databases, culminated in the **Privacy Act of 1974.** This act established a Privacy Protection Study Commission to determine whether the various restrictions on what the federal government could do with personal information, as provided in the Privacy Act, should also be applied to the private sector. Significantly for direct marketers, Section V (c), B (i) of the act directed the commission to report to the president and Congress on whether an organization engaged in interstate commerce should be required to remove from its mailing list the name of an individual who does not want to be on it.

In July of 1977, after months of hearing testimony and studying the issues, the commission issued its 618-page *Report from the Privacy Protection Study Commission.* Chapter 4 of this report was devoted entirely to the subject of mailing lists. The commission basically concluded that the appearance of an individual's name on a mailing list, so long as that individual has the prerogative to remove it from that list, was not in and of itself an invasion of privacy. In reaching this conclusion, the commission observed "that the balance that must be struck between the interests of individuals and the interests of direct marketers is an especially delicate one." The commission also noted the economic importance of direct mail "to nonprofit organizations, to the champions of unpopular causes, and to many of the organizations that create diversity in American society."

Agreeing that the *receipt* of direct mail is not really the issue but rather how the mailing list record of an individual is used, the commission further recommended that a private sector organization which rents, sells, exchanges, or otherwise makes the addresses or names and addresses of its customers, members, or donors available to any other person for use in direct mail marketing or solicitation, should adopt a procedure whereby each customer, member, or donor is informed of the organization's list practice. In addition, each consumer should be given an opportunity to indicate to the organization that he or she does not wish to have his or her address or name and address made available for such purposes.[9]

These were the privacy issues of the past. Now direct marketers must prepare for handling the privacy issues of the future. Let's take a look at privacy today.

Privacy Today—Anti-Spam Laws

Spam is unwanted, unsolicited bulk commercial e-mail messages. It has also been referred to as "junk e-mail." Most people today complain about spam. Recipients find it annoying, Internet service providers say it clogs up and slows down the online systems, and many direct marketers claim it is ruining e-mail as a legitimate media channel. The minutes e-mail recipients spend clicking through unwanted e-mail messages add up quickly in a nation with over 160 million Internet users.[10] America Online reports that 70 percent of the e-mail its users receive is now spam, and that the quantity has doubled since January 2003.[11] However, spam is a worldwide issue. According to a study conducted by the European Union, the total cost of spam worldwide is $9.4 billion. In the United States, spam costs the average Internet user $1.00 a month because the sheer volume of messages requires increased network capacity.[12] Internet providers have tools for blocking spam, however, these filtering programs are often time-consuming and ineffective. Senders of spam are finding ways to defeat the filtering software simply by misspelling key words that trigger the filters.

In order to get consumers to open these e-mail messages, the senders of spam also use a variety of attention-getting subject lines and sender names in the "from" field of the e-mail message. Some examples include: "Claim Your Prize" or "Payment Past Due" or "You Have Won." This is where the law comes into play. When the subject line of an e-mail message misrepresents its point of origin or the nature of the message itself, it is considered deceptive.

Although there has been no federal spam legislation enacted, nine spam bills have been introduced in the 108th Congress.[13] The most recent is the Anti-Spam Act of 2003 (H.R. 2515) that was introduced on June 18, 2003. If passed, the Spam Act of 2003 would prohibit commercial e-mail messages with false or misleading message headers or misleading subject lines.[14] The bill would require all *commercial* e-mail messages to be identified as such, and to include a viable return address so recipients can write back and request to be removed from the sender's e-mail list. However, some people say that it is better not to reply at all, not even to ask for removal from the list. Apparently, any kind of transmission only alerts the spammer that your e-mail address is "live" and so they just keep using it.

Federal legislation is inevitable in the future and will likely deal with three spam issues: (1) notice; (2) choice; and (3) fraud. It is probable that the FTC will be active in enforcing future spam regulations and that Internet Service Providers will lead a search for and deployment of technical solutions. Meanwhile, states will continue to pass anti-spam laws. As of August 27, 2003, 35 states have passed anti-spam laws.[15] See Figure 12-3 for a listing of these states and their respective laws.

FIGURE 12-3   State Spam Laws

STATE	LAW	EFFECTIVE DATE
Alaska	HB82	August 1, 2003
Arizona	SB 1280	June 16, 2003
Arkansas	Act 1496 Act 1019	April, 2001 July, 2003
California	Business & Professions Code Section 17538.4	1998
Colorado	Title 6 Chapter 388, Article 2.5	June, 2000
Connecticut	Public Act 03-128	June, 2003
Delaware	Code Title 11, Sections 931, 937 & 938	July, 1999
Idaho	Code Title 48, Chapter 6, Section 48-603E	July, 2000
Illinois	Public Act 91-0233 HB 2972	July, 1999 July, 2003
Indiana	HB 1083	July 1, 2003
Iowa	Section 714E	May, 1999
Kansas	---	May, 2002
Louisiana	Title 14 273.1 HB 2015 SB 863	July, 1999 August 15, 2003 August 15, 2003
Maine	HB 210	May, 2003
Maryland	SB 538 HB 915	May, 2002 May, 2002
Michigan	HB 4519	September 1, 2003
Minnesota	SF 2908	March, 2003
Missouri	RFMO 407.020 HB 228	June, 2000 July, 2003
Nevada	Statute 41.705-735 AB 93	July, 1997 October 1, 2003
New Mexico	SB 699	June 20, 2003
North Carolina	S14-453	June, 1999
North Dakota	HB 1399	April, 2003
Ohio	SB 8	2002
Oklahoma	Title 15, Section 776 SB 660	June, 1999 November 1, 2003
Pennsylvania	Statutes 18:5903	June, 2000
Rhode Island	Title 11, Section 52 Title 6, Chapter 47	July, 1999 July, 1999
South Dakota	SB 180 SB 183	2002 2002
Tennessee	Title 47, Chapter 18	April, 2002
Texas	HB 1292	June, 2003
Utah	HB 80 HB 143	2002 2002
Virginia	Chapter 886 SB 1139	March, 1999 July 1, 2003
Washington	Title 19.190.020 SB 5574	March, 1998 July 27, 2003
West Virginia	Chapter 46A	March, 1999
Wisconsin	Statute 947.0125	June, 2001
Wyoming	SB 41	July 1, 2003

Source: Internet Alliance, *Spam White Paper Addendum,* August, 2003, <www.internetalliance.org.> (as of August 27, 2003).

---

http://www.law.com

American Lawyer Media's law.com is the Web's leading legal news and information network. Law.com connects to 20 award-winning national and regional legal publications on-line. Law.com's Supreme Court Monitor provides information on the "hot topic" legislative issues.

http://www.lexis-nexis.com

LEXIS-NEXIS is a leading on-line provider of market information. The LEXIS-NEXIS database of full-text news reports from around the world is updated continuously.

http://www.fcc.gov

The Federal Communication Commission regulates interstate and international communications. Its Web site provides information and updates concerning related services and legislation.

http://www.ftc.gov

The Federal Trade Commission enforces a variety of federal antitrust and consumer protection laws. Their Web site provides information and updates concerning related laws.

http://www.the.dma.org

The Direct Marketing Association has created the DMA Ethics and Consumer Affairs Department to assist direct marketers in understanding and complying with ethical and legal regulations applicable to the direct marketing industry.

FIGURE 12-4   Legal On-line Sources of Information

In addition, on September 12, 2003, there were 20 spam bills on the state legislative chart.[16] Each bill attempts to protect consumers by proposing to severely limit or eliminate spam. Many of these bills provide criminal penalties for spam transmissions. The Commonwealth of Virginia is one of these states. On April 29, 2003, the Commonwealth of Virginia enacted a law imposing harsh felony penalties for sending unsolicited bulk commercial e-mail messages to or from Virginia. Those found guilty of sending more than 10,000 such deceptive e-mail messages in one day would be subject to a prison term of up to five years.[17] This is a significant legal development since approximately half of all Internet traffic flows through Virginia, the home state and headquarters of a number of major Internet providers, including the nation's largest—America Online.[18]

Federal and state legislation covering the broad range of privacy issues today is rapidly changing. The legal environment concerning spam is also constantly changing. For updated legislative information contact the Internet Alliance at www.internetalliance.org. Direct marketers must constantly monitor key information sources. Figure 12-4 provides a list of some of these.

PRIVACY ISSUES

Annoyance and Violation

To get at the heart of privacy concerns, you have to understand two basic consumer perceptions: **annoyance** and **violation**.[19] People feel annoyed because they receive too much unsolicited marketing communications, and they feel violated because they believe too much information about their personal lives is being exchanged between marketers without their knowledge and/or consent. Many consumers want to place restrictions on the amount of information that may be collected, warehoused, and shared about them. However, not all consumers feel the same way. Some consumers are willing to disclose personal information to marketers providing they receive something in return. This may include a targeted offer that meets the consumer's needs and wants, or informative updates on a certain topic of interest to them. In fact, it has been determined that a consumer's willingness to disclose personal data may actually depend on the type of information being disclosed.

Type of Information

The degree of control or the amount of restriction an individual wants to have over their personal information may depend upon the *type of information* being requested. We can divide personal information into four different categories: *general descriptive information, ownership information, product purchase information,* and *sensitive/confidential information.*[20] Let's discuss each of these types of information and look at some examples of each category.

General Descriptive Information

General descriptive information is the easiest to obtain. Often considered demographic or classification information, it includes race, height, age, gender, level of education, and occupation. Consumers are the *least restrictive* with this category of information and usually enable marketers easy access to this data.

Ownership Information

Ownership information contains data about the various products the consumer owns. Consumers consider some belongings to be status symbols, like a home, an expensive automobile, and/or an American Express Platinum travel and entertainment credit card. Consumers generally place *moderate restrictions* on the release of this data and it is believed that some may want to share this data to achieve greater self-esteem or status.

Product Purchase Information

The information contained in the product purchase information category includes a variety of purchase activity data, including magazine subscription information, credit record information, and lifestyle information obtained from such purchases as vitamins, cat food, hunting and fishing equipment, or certain medications. This category is similar to the "ownership information" category, however, these purchases are not necessarily considered to be status symbols. Consumers generally place *moderate restrictions* on this information category.

Sensitive/Confidential Information

The final category of information contains facts about an individual that are considered to be the most private: sensitive/confidential information, such as annual income, medical history, Social Security number, driving records (including any motor violations), and home value. Consumers are *most restrictive* with this category of information and usually exercise the strongest control over the release of these facts.

Consumer Privacy Segments

Not *all* consumers possess the same feelings and opinions about privacy issues, regardless of the type of information. Just as information can be grouped into categories, consumer opinions and behaviors toward information privacy can be categorized as well. In fact, research conducted by Professor Alan Westin of Columbia University and Lou Harris Organization/Equifax has concluded that consumers may be grouped into three possible segments (the privacy unconcerned, privacy fundamentalists, and privacy pragmatists) when it comes to their feelings about privacy.[21] Let's take a closer look at these segments.

Privacy Unconcerned

The **privacy unconcerned** group represents about 20 percent of the population and consists of those who literally do not care about the issue of privacy at all. They are aware of the benefits of giving information for marketing purposes and enjoy the information and opportunities they receive in exchange for it. These consumers say their lives are an open book. They feel they have nothing to hide. They welcome most contacts by businesses, nonprofits, and others and have little concern about information about them being transferred from one organization to another. This group is most likely to be receptive to the activities of direct marketers.

Privacy Fundamentalists

The **privacy fundamentalists** also consist of approximately 20 percent of the population. These individuals are likely to take the point of view that they own their name, as well as all the information about themselves, and that no one else may use it without their permission. This group includes activists who will write letters to their Congressional representatives or to the editor of a local newspaper about privacy. They will call companies and file complaints on this issue. Direct marketers should be certain to purge these consumers from their lists because they are the least receptive to direct marketing activities.

Privacy Pragmatists

The **privacy pragmatists** represent approximately 60 percent of U.S. consumers. They look at the contact, the offer, and the methods of data collection and mentally apply a cost/benefit analysis to make a determination about a marketer's use of information. They ask themselves

- What benefits can I get from this?
- Are there choices that I would not otherwise have?
- Is there an opportunity for me?
- Can I get a product or an offer that is valuable to me?
- What harm can come from this? For example:
  - Will I be inconvenienced in some way?
  - Will I be embarrassed or feel discomfort?
  - Will I be disadvantaged in some way?

They will allow their buying patterns to be tracked by supermarkets, if they get valuable coupons or other deals in return. They have no problem with a catalog company providing its list to another organization or company so long as they appreciate the subsequent offers they receive. They will receive telemarketing calls from an organization they patronize and respond to an offer they consider valuable. The privacy pragmatists represent the majority of consumers in the United States. Developing relationships with these customers is an important strategy for the direct marketer to take. So, what have companies done to respond to consumer's privacy concerns?

Corporate Response to Privacy

The **chief privacy officer (CPO)** is the newest arrival in corporate hierarchies, the new white knight of the 21st century. Like the CEO and the CIO, the CPO is overseeing something very important in the corporation: PRIVACY! The CPO is responsible for protecting the sensitive information the corporation collects, from credit card accounts to health records.

Privacy executives have an open-ended job. They must guard against hackers and articulate uses for sensitive personal, financial or medical information. They must not only set guidelines, but they must figure out how to communicate those guidelines to customers and employees. Figure 12-5 shows the privacy policy booklet the J. C. Penney Company, Inc., distributes to its customers.

At least 100 companies have named "chief privacy officers" and it is estimated that the number of these privacy executives will rapidly grow into the thousands by 2004.[22] Hiring chief privacy officers to oversee privacy matters may be the price of doing business in today's corporate world as consumers and government officials more aggressively sue companies over breach of privacy cases.

Many companies already have information privacy policies and actively communicate these to their customers. Take, for example, the following privacy notice provided to customers at Universal Bank:[23]

> Keeping customer information secure is a top priority for all of us at Universal Bank. We are sending you this privacy notice to help you understand how we handle the personal information about you that we collect and may disclose. This notice tells you how you can limit our disclosing personal information about you. The provisions of this notice will apply to former customers as well as current customers unless we state otherwise.

Universal Bank then goes on to provide their customers with a "Privacy Choices Form" which allows them to select one of the following four choices and return the form to the bank:[24]

1. Limit the personal information about me that you disclose to nonafflili-ated third parties.
2. Limit the personal information about me that you share with Citigroup affiliates.
3. Remove my name from your mailing lists used for promotional offers.
4. Remove my name from your telemarketing lists used for promotional offers.

Like Universal Bank, many direct marketers have become proactive in handling information privacy issues. Perhaps no organization is more proactive than the Direct Marketing Association. The DMA has initiated a "Privacy Promise" which provided public assurance that by July 1, 1999, all members of the DMA would be following certain specific practices to protect consumer privacy. The practices are designed to have a major impact on those consumers who wish to receive fewer advertising solicitations.

FIGURE 12-5   J. C. Penney Company, Inc., Privacy Policy

The DMA Privacy Promise

The "Privacy Promise" includes the following four components:[25]

1. Provide customers with notice of their ability to "opt-out" of information exchanges (see Figure 12-6 for examples of notice language).
2. Honor customer opt-out request not to have their contact information transferred to others for marketing purposes.

A. "We make our customer information available to other companies so they may contact you about products and services that may interest you. If you do not want your name passed on to other companies for the purpose of receiving marketing offers, just tell us by contacting us at _____, and we will be pleased to respect your wishes."

B. "We make portions of our customer list available to carefully screened companies that offer products and services we believe you may enjoy. If you do not want to receive those offers and/or information, please let us know by contacting us at _____."

FIGURE 12-6   Examples of Notice Language

Source: The DMA Privacy Promise Member Compliance Guide (New York: The Direct Marketing Association, Inc., 1999), p. 6. Reproduced with permission.

A. "If you decide you no longer wish to receive our catalog, send your mailing label with your request to _____."

B. "We would like to continue sending you information only on those subjects of interest to you. If you don't wish to continue to receive information on any of the following product lines, just let us know by _____."

C. "If you would like to receive our catalog less frequently, let us know by _____."

FIGURE 12-7   Examples of In-House Suppress Language

Source: The DMA Privacy Promise Member Compliance Guide (New York: The Direct Marketing Association, Inc., 1999), p. 9. Reproduced with permission.

3. Accept and maintain consumer requests to be on an in-house suppress file to stop receiving solicitations from your company (see Figure 12-7 for examples of in-house suppress language).

4. Use the DMA Preference Service suppression files which exist for mail, telephone, and e-mail lists.

In addition, the DMA has developed privacy principles and guidelines for those direct marketers operating on-line sites that we will discuss later in this chapter. Now that we have reviewed the main privacy issues affecting direct marketers and the various DMA and corporate responses to these issues, let's explore the regulatory authorities that are charged with enforcing these rules.

REGULATORY AUTHORITIES OF DIRECT MARKETING

By their very nature, direct marketing promotional activities, as they inform and persuade, often in very large numbers, are highly visible. The volume of direct mail grew rapidly over the past few decades. As it did, some of it was branded as "junk mail" by those people who received it and did not find it relevant; by those individuals who resented its intrusion; and even by those businesses that represented competing advertising media. This, coupled with the development and advances in telephone equipment, fiber optic cables, satellite transmissions, and the Internet, enabled direct marketers to transfer consumer data from internal or external databases to user databases quickly and easily and at low costs. During this period of proliferation of direct marketing, abuses by individual organizations ultimately resulted in intervention by regulatory authorities.

The Federal Communications Commission (FCC) and the Federal Trade Commission (FTC) have issued several very important trade regulation rules and guides that affect direct marketing as well as advisory opinions about unfair competition in the form of misleading or deceptive acts or advertising. State and local governments also intervene in advertising and selling practices as do the United States Postal Service, Better Business Bureau, trade associations the advertising media, and, ultimately, consumers themselves. Let's look more closely at each.

Federal Communication Commission

The Federal Communication Commission (FCC) is an independent U.S. government agency directly responsible to Congress. It was established by the Communication Act of 1934 and is charged with regulating interstate and international communications by radio, television, wire, satellite, and cable.[26] The FCC enforces the Telephone Consumer Protection Act (TCPA) and its new rules governing telephone marketing.

The TCPA prohibits both for-profit and nonprofit marketers from using an automatic telephone dialing system (including predictive dialers) to call any device when the called party is charged unless that called party has given prior, express consent. Therefore, marketers using automatic dialing systems should not call consumers or businesses' cellular phones, pagers, or toll-free numbers unless they have given you permission to do so. The FCC also has created strict rules concerning the use of fax machines for marketing purposes. We will discuss the TCPA in greater detail later in the case at the end this chapter.

Federal Trade Commission

The major federal legislation regulating the promotional activities of direct marketing is the Federal Trade Commission (FTC) Act together with its Wheeler-Lea Amendment. The FTC, created by the Act, is charged with regulating content of promotional messages used in interstate commerce. In Section 5(A), intended to prevent unfair competition, the Wheeler-Lea Amendment to the FTC Act strengthened this provision by making it a violation of the law whenever such competition injured the public regardless of its effect on a competitor. The amendment also prohibited false, misleading, or deceptive advertising by enumerating four types of products in which advertising abuses existed and in which the public health could be directly affected: foods, drugs, cosmetics, and therapeutic devices.[27]

In October of 1995, the FTC and the Direct Marketing Association produced a "check list" for direct marketers. It was written for mail, telephone, fax, and computer order merchandisers to give them an overview of rules or statutes that the FTC enforces. More information is available on these and other FTC rules and regulations at the organization's Web site at www.ftc.gov. Let's briefly examine each rule.

Advertisements: Product Offers and Claims

All products and/or services advertised, must be advertised truthfully. The FTC Act prohibits unfair or deceptive advertising. For example, under the rules and guides, you must

- Truthfully represent the experience or opinions of endorsers if your advertising uses them. Customer endorsements must reflect the typical experiences that

customers can expect from the product unless the advertising clearly and prominently says otherwise. Expert endorsements must be based on appropriate tests
or evaluations done by persons with expertise in the field.

- Not exaggerate environmental benefits of your products or packaging. If you
  advertise environmental benefits of products or packaging, the claims should be
  specific and must be substantiated.

Mail and Telephone Orders

In order to comply with the Mail or Telephone Order Merchandise Rule ("MTOR"),
you must have a reasonable basis for stating or implying that you can ship within a
certain time when you advertise mail or telephone order merchandise. If you make no
shipment statement, you must have a reasonable basis for believing that you can ship
within 30 days. If after the order has been place you find that you are unable to ship
within the time you stated, or within 30 days, you must inform the customer and seek
their consent to the delayed shipment.

Telemarketing

If your business uses either inbound or outbound interstate telephone calls to sell goods
or services, you must comply with the new Telemarketing Sales Rule (TSR). Before a
customer pays for goods or services you must disclose the following information:

- The total cost to purchase, receive, or use the offered goods or services;
- The quantity of goods and services;
- All material restrictions, limitations, or conditions to purchase, receive, or use
  the offered goods or services;
- Any policy of not making refunds, cancellations, exchanges, or repurchases, if
  there is one;
- All the material terms and conditions of your refund, cancellation, exchange, or
  repurchase policy, if it is mentioned in the advertising or sales presentation; and
- The odds of being able to win the promotion prize if one is offered (or, if the odds
  can't be calculated in advance, the factors used to calculate the odds), all of the
  material costs or conditions one must fulfill to receive or redeem the prize, and that
  no purchase or payment is necessary to win or participate in the prize promotion.

If you make outbound "cold" calls to consumers, you must make the following additional oral disclosures promptly:

- The identity of the seller;
- That the purpose of the call is to sell goods or services;
- The nature of the goods or services;
- That no purchase or payment is necessary to be able to win a prize or partici-
  pate in a prize promotion if one is offered (and if asked, you must describe the
  no purchase/nonpayment method of entry).

The FTC has recently provided amendments to the TSR. The amendments address
the following areas:[28]

1. ***Do not call list***—As discussed in Chapter 8, if enforced, direct marketers must
   fully comply with the pending federal DNC Registry. The penalty for

non-compliance is set at $11,000 for each violation.[29] To obtain current information regarding the Do Not Call Registry visit the Web site at https://telemarketing.donotcall.gov/.

2. *Transfer of pre-acquired account information*—The TSR will prohibit the trafficking only of unencrypted billing information.

3. *Predictive dialers*—Abandoned calls associated with predictive dialers are considered a violation of the TSR, but there is a safe harbor if the following four conditions are met:

   a. No more than 3 percent abandoned calls per day, per campaign;
   b. A consumer's phone must ring 15 seconds or 4 rings before the predictive dialer may disconnect the telephone;
   c. If no sales representative is available within 2 seconds of the consumer's greeting, a recorded message (that includes the name and number of the company and a statement that the call is for "telemarketing purposes") must be played; and
   d. The telemarketer retains records to illustrate compliance with the safe harbor. This safe harbor only applies to predictive dialers. If a live telerep hangs up on a consumer, it is a violation of the TSR.

4. *Caller identification*—The FTC requires telemarketers, where the telecommunications carrier's technology supports it, to transmit Caller ID that identifies the number and the name of the company whose product is being sold.

5. *Telemarketing of B2B Internet and Web services*—The telemarketing of Internet and Web services will not be excluded from the B2B exemption to the TSR.

6. *Novel payments*—Preauthorization is not required for the use of debit cards.

7. *E-mail and fax under the direct mail exemption*—Disclosures required for inbound calls that result for e-mail or faxes must appear in the text of the e-mail and fax communication.

8. *Charities/nonprofits*—Tax-exempt charities and nonprofit organizations and their for-profit solicitors are exempt from the national DCN Registry. For-profit solicitors must comply with company-specific do not call lists.

900 Numbers

All providers of 900 numbers must comply with the FTC 900-Number Rule requiring that they disclose the cost of the call. Additional advertising disclosures are required for services that

- Promote sweepstakes or games of chance;
- Provide information about a federal program (but are not sponsored by a federal agency; and
- Target individuals under 18 years of age.

Ads for 900-numbers cannot be targeted towards children under 12 years of age unless the service is a "bona fide education" service, as defined by the rule. The 900-Number Rule also requires the telemarketer to give an introductory message (a preamble) that provides both the name of your 900-number and an opportunity for the caller to hang up without being charged for the call.

Delayed Delivery Rule

Possibly the most important regulation affecting direct marketing firms was promulgated by the FTC on February 2, 1976, and popularly is referred to as the "30-Day Delayed Delivery Rule." The rule provides that, if the marketer believes that goods will not be shipped within 30 days of receiving a properly completed order, an advertisement must include a clear and conspicuous notice of the time in which delivery is expected to be made. If the direct marketer provides no such statement, shipment *must* be made within 30 days. The 30-day delayed delivery rule applies to all direct marketing media but specifically exempts photo-finishers, garden centers offering seeds and growing plants, and publication subscriptions *after* the first issue. Also exempt are COD orders, negative option plans (see the next section), and credit transactions in which the seller does not charge the buyer's account prior to shipment.

Negative Option Rule

This trade regulation rule, effective June 7, 1974, governs pre-notification negative option sales plans. Under negative option plans, sellers notify buyers of the periodic selection of merchandise to be shipped. Unless the buyer requests that the merchandise not be shipped, the seller ships and bills the buyer for the merchandise. Negative option plans are frequently used by direct marketers who offer book and CD or music clubs. The rules set forth the requirements for disclosure in the promotional material. They also provide that the seller cannot refuse, under certain conditions, to give the buyer full credit for a returned selection.

Guides Against Deceptive Guarantees

The FTC promulgated seven guides on April 26, 1960, for the purpose of self-regulatory adoption by marketers in their advertising of guarantees. These guides are intended to ensure that the buyer is fully apprised of the conditions governing any guarantee. The seven guides describe the general nature of guarantees, prorated adjustments, "satisfaction or your money back," lifetime guarantees, savings guarantees, nonperformance guarantees, and misrepresentations in guarantees.

Guides to Use of Endorsements and Testimonials

These FTC guides, which became effective May 21, 1975, relate to the use of expert and organizational endorsements and testimonials in advertising. Not only must endorsements reflect the experience of "actual consumers" but there must be disclosure of any material connections between the endorser and the seller that might affect the weight or credibility of the endorsement.

Advisory Opinion on Dry Testing

We saw in Chapter 11 that dry testing is a term used by marketers to describe the practice of promoting a product, such as a book or magazine, which has not yet been manufactured. Whether the product is actually made available will depend on the size of the response to the dry-test solicitation. An advisory opinion issued by the FTC on March 27, 1975, allows such dry testing under very strict guidelines to ensure that the potential customer is in no way misled about the terms of the offer.

Mailing of Unordered Merchandise

Coming under a category of fraud and deception, is the mailing of unordered merchandise, sent without the prior expressed request or consent of the recipient, an unfair method of competition, and an unfair trade practice in violation of the FTC Act. The recipient may treat any such merchandise as a gift without any obligation whatsoever to the sender. It is a separate violation for a shipper of unordered merchandise to mail to any recipient of such merchandise a bill or any dunning communication.

Guides Against Deceptive Pricing

Made effective January 8, 1964, these guides cover offers stating reductions from a "former," "regular," "comparable," "list price," or "manufacturer's suggested retail price." One guide is specifically concerned with bargain offers based on the purchase of other merchandise, such as "buy one—get one free" or "two-for-one sale."

Guides Against Bait and Switch Advertising

The four guides against bait and switch advertising that were issued by the FTC on December 4, 1959, define this type of advertising as that which is "alluring but insincere in offering to sell a product or service which the advertiser in truth does not intend or want to sell." Its purpose is to switch consumers from buying the advertised merchandise in order to sell something else, usually at a higher price or on a basis more advantageous to the advertiser. The mere presence of the advertised merchandise does not preclude the existence of a bait and switch scheme.

Guide Concerning Use of the Word "Free"

This guide issued by the FTC on December 16, 1971, is intended to prevent deceptive or misleading offers of "free" merchandise or services if, in fact, such is available only with the purchase of some other merchandise or service. If the purchaser is told that an article is "free" if another article is purchased, the word "free" indicates that the purchaser is paying nothing for that article and no more that the regular price for the other. The term "gift" is to be used so that the article described is actually a donation or a present, not dependent on the purchase of something else.

Advisory Opinion on the Use of the Word "New"

This advisory opinion, issued January 4, 1969, is concerned with merchandise that has been used by purchasers on a trial basis, returned to the seller, refurbished, and resold as new. The FTC has pointed out that the word "new" may be properly used only if the product so described is either entirely new or has been changed in a functionally significant and substantial respect.

Advisory Opinion on Disclosure of Foreign Origin Merchandise

Direct marketers, when advertising or promoting goods of foreign origin, must clearly inform prospective purchasers that such goods are not made in the United States if, in fact, the goods originate elsewhere. According to the FTC, "the underlying reason for the disclosure requirement is that mail-order purchasers do not have the opportunity to inspect the merchandise prior to the purchase thereof and be apprised of the material facts bearing upon this selection," such as would appear on a label or a sticker.

Warranties

The FTC is empowered by the Magnuson-Moss Warranty Act, effective July 4, 1975, with enforcement. Although no organization is required to give a written warranty and state a minimum duration for a warranty, the National Retail Merchants Association, in summarizing the act and the FTC rules relative to it, describes the following responsibility of direct marketers under the act:

> Catalog or mail order solicitations must disclose for each warranty product either the full text of the warranty or notice that it may be obtained free upon written request. This information must be located on the same page or the facing page as a description of the warranted product or in a clearly referenced information section of the catalog. In addition, the retailer must promptly fill the requests it receives for copies of written warranties.

On-line Direct Marketing

Due to the information explosion, on-line direct marketing activities have become one of the focal points of the FTC. In fact, the FTC has produced a four element "Privacy Policy" in an effort to assist companies in telling their customers what information they are collecting, how they will use it, what security is in place, and how consumers can opt out of providing information. The four elements in the FTC's "Privacy Policy" for on-line direct marketing are:[30]

1. **Notice:**   Web sites should provide consumers clear and conspicuous notice of their information practices, including what information they collect, how they collect it, how they use it, whether they disclose the information to other entities, and whether other entities are collecting information through the site.
2. **Choice:**   Consumers should be offered choices as to how their personal information will be used beyond completing a transaction.
3. **Access:**   Consumers should be offered reasonable access to the information that a Web site gathers about them, including the opportunity to review such data and correct and/or delete data.
4. **Security:**   Organizations that have Web sites should take reasonable steps to protect the security of information they gather from their consumers.

Those direct marketers using on-line mediums must be aware of and comply with the FTC regulations. The following is an example of how the FTC is regulating the marketing activities on this new medium.

On-line marketing activities are not alone in receiving FTC attention. As the case at the end of this chapter explains, direct marketing activities utilizing fax machines are being regulated as the FTC enforces the Telephone Consumer Protection Act (TCPA) of 1991. Although in some cases FTC actions have been controversial, the FTC has become much more aggressive in its enforcement, especially

During the 1999 Christmas shopping season, more than a million cybershoppers spent upward of $6 million at Web retailer Toysmart.com. Before entering their credit card numbers and addresses, many shoppers scanned the site's privacy policy, which promised never to disclose their personal information to a third party.

In June 2000: Toysmart, the Waltham, Massachusetts-based company, field for bankruptcy protection and put an ad in the *Wall Street Journal* offering to sell its customer database. In the face of insolvency, the retailer seemed to lose its commitment to customer privacy.

Alarmed, the Federal Trade Commission sued Toysmart to stop it from selling the names, addresses, and buying habits of its customers. Toysmart's case was a wake-up call for consumers, regulators, and all direct marketers using on-line mediums.

Source: Adapted from Janet Colwell, "Privacy and the Internet: Marketers' Boon, Consumers' Bane?" *Portland State University School of Business Annual Report* (Fall, 2000), 11–15.

when false or deceptive advertising is sent. All direct marketers should take note of the FTC rules and regulations prior to carrying out their marketing activities and utilizing various media.

United States Postal Service

Through its Inspection Service and in compliance with the Private Express Statutes, the United States Postal Service has established rules and regulations that bear impact on the promotional activities of direct marketers. The Inspection Service is constantly on the lookout for fraud and deception through the mail and the Private Express Statutes, by granting the United States Postal Service a form of delivery monopoly, determine classification and cost of promotional matter that can be circulated outside the postal monopoly.

State and Local Regulation

Certain organizations using direct marketing strategies, including insurance companies, small lending associations, banks, and pharmaceutical companies are closely regulated by state legislation, especially relative to promotion and pricing tactics. State legislators have become increasingly active in consumer issues and in privacy matters such as those that affect mailing lists and promotional use of the telephone. The matters of state sales and use taxes, as they relate to taxation of advertising and promotional services, are also of vital concern to direct marketers.

Some examples of state and local regulations that affect direct marketing activities are the Truth in Advertising legislation and the Green River Ordinance. Truth in Advertising was fashioned after a model statute first proposed in 1911. Most states have so-called truth in advertising legislation that govern the conduct of promotional activities in intrastate commerce. The Green River Ordinance was a type of local legislation designed to regulate personal selling. Such ordinances, which require prior licensing for any door-to-door selling, solicitation, or even marketing research interviews, have been named after the town of Green River, Wyoming, where it was first enacted. This ordinance has been challenged in court with mixed results.

An example of recent state legislation affecting direct marketers is an amended bill that has passed the California Senate on May 29, 2003. The original California bill (S.B. 27) would have required companies to keep records of all customer data that is shared with third parties off-line or on-line for direct marketing purposes. The bill would then require companies to provide a consumer with all the data that was shared and the names of the third-party data users within 30 days of a request by the consumer. However, a key amendment was added to the bill on September 5, 2003, that does *not* require direct marketers to provide consumers with details of what data has been shared and with whom providing the direct marketer has a privacy policy that gives consumers a choice not to have their personal information disclosed to third parties. In other words, direct marketers must notify the consumer of his or her ability to opt out for free. This bill will affect any company doing business in California and is scheduled to take effect January 1, 2005.[31]

Private Organizations

Better Business Bureaus, the history and influence of which go back more than half a century, are located in most major cities and are sponsored by private businesses and organizations to prevent promotional abuses though common sense regulation. Likewise, trade groups, as along with the Direct Marketing Association, have promulgated ethical guidelines for use by their members and others desiring to adhere to them.

THE FUTURE: SELF-REGULATION OR LEGISLATION

Self-Regulation

The preferred method to deal with the issues of the regulatory environment is through self-regulation by direct marketers. The DMA has attempted to assist member companies in complying with federal and state regulations, as well as industry self-regulatory responsibilities, attempting to lead the way for its members to meet their customer privacy expectations.

Years ago, Donn Rappaport, chairman of American List Counsel, presented an eight-step self-regulation plan for direct marketers to follow. Rappaport's plan included these suggestions:[32]

1. *Allow the consumer some measure of control over what lists or types of lists his or her name is on.* Include a notice in every marketing communication stating your list rental practices and offering to remove the name of anyone who prefers that his or her name not be released to other mailers.
2. *Ensure that we know who's renting our lists and what they are planning to do with them.* Direct marketers must pay close attention to list renters that plan to combine your file with other files, abstracts, or overlays.
3. *Review all third-party cooperative arrangements with regard to list rights.* From time to time, a credit card processor will lay claim to the names of people who charge mail-order purchases to their credit cards. Remember, they are your customers regardless of how they paid. Be wary of any arrangement that dilutes your rights of ownership.
4. *Make sure that information is used for the purpose for which it was gathered.* In other words, if you sell women's clothes and happen to sell a significant volume in large sizes, use that information to develop more large-size business. Don't rent your large-size customer names to a weight-loss program.

5. ***Stop scaring consumers unnecessarily over how much personal data on them is actually available.*** For example, Pacific Bell Telephone Company once began promoting its customer file with the announcement: "Now a business list from the company that has everyone's number." Is this kind of claim really worth the scare it may instill in the consumer?

6. ***Eliminate deceptive or misleading direct mail.*** Does direct mail that looks like an official document from the IRS really work in the long run? Even if it did, it's deceptive and it raises suspicion about the direct marketing industry.

7. ***Use personalization wisely.*** There is a fine line between familiarity with the consumer and an invasion of their personal privacy. Keep in mind that certain types of personal data should not be included in personalization.

8. ***Make sure that the consumer is not ripped off or compromised by the dissemination of personal data.*** Since consumers are serious about the issue of personal privacy, direct marketers must safeguard against privacy abuses.

Legislation and Permission Marketing

Permission marketing obtains the consent of a customer before a company sends out a marketing communication to that customer via the Internet. In other words, permission marketing gives the consumer control over what on-line communications come to them. It is a parallel to opt-out procedures, whereby the consumer must "opt in" to receive marketing messages from select organizations seeking to communicate with the consumer. Permission marketing must start with consumers' explicit and active consent to receive commercial messages and always give consumers the option to stop receiving messages at any time. According to research, many consumers are not able to differentiate between permission marketing and spam. This lack of differentiation may drive consumer attitudes toward opt-in e-mail down to the same negative level as spam.[33]

If direct marketers don't adhere to the privacy policies and procedures set forth by the DMA and others, additional legislation will become necessary that would limit direct marketers' access to public information. Bills have been proposed by members of the United States Senate and United States Representatives that would enable consumers to opt out of Department of Motor Vehicle lists that are available to direct marketers. Other legislation could include bills requiring direct marketers to obtain a consumer's consent before sending a marketing solicitation. Permission marketing is not limited to on-line marketing activities. It applies to telephone marketing as well. The proposed FCC/FTC Do Not Call rules specify that a person must grant written consent to receive a call if there is no established business relationship. Thus, the written permission is needed to override the DNC rule when that person has registered his or her name and number in the national DNC Registry.[34] The spread of permission marketing would certainly limit the ability to employ most marketing strategies with which we are familiar.

Summary

Upholding ethical guidelines in carrying out direct marketing activities is crucial to the present and future success of the direct marketing industry. The three primary areas of legislation include intellectual property rights, security, and privacy. Privacy is the area of greatest concern for direct marketers. Privacy issues encompass personal privacy, information privacy, and off-line and on-line privacy—including spam. The opt-in and opt-out mechanisms along with permission-based marketing are some of the ways consumer privacy issues are being addressed. Direct marketers must be mindful of the consumer's right to safety, be informed, selection, confidentiality, and privacy.

The regulatory environment is both dynamic and uncontrollable. Direct marketing regulatory authorities include the Federal Trade Commission, United States Postal Service, state and local entities, and private organizations. The FTC rules govern advertisements, mail and telephone orders, telemarketing, 900 numbers, delivery, negative option rule, guarantees, endorsements and testimonials, testing, merchandise mailing, pricing, bait and switch advertising, use of the words "free" and "new," disclosures of foreign origin merchandise, warranties, and on-line direct marketing. Direct marketers must maintain compliance with the many laws affecting direct marketing activities while not losing sight of the bottom-line objective: maximizing customer relationships and customer satisfaction while sustaining a profitable business.

Key Terms

- ethics, 289
- morals, 289
- code of ethics, 289
- right to safety, 292
- right to be informed, 292
- right to selection, 292

- right to confidentiality, 292
- right to privacy, 292
- intellectual property, 293
- Privacy Act of 1974, 295
- spam, 296
- annoyance, 298

- violation, 298
- privacy unconcerned, 300
- privacy fundamentalists, 300
- privacy pragmatists, 300
- chief privacy officer, (CPO) 301
- permission marketing, 312

Review Questions

1. What is the purpose of the Direct Marketing Association's (DMA) guidelines for ethical business practices?
2. List and briefly explain the five consumer rights.
3. What is a *chief privacy officer (CPO)?* What is her or his primary role in an organization?
4. What are the four components of the DMA's "Privacy Promise"?
5. Explain the "delayed delivery rule" and the "guides against deceptive pricing" set forth by the Federal Trade Commission (FTC).
6. What are the names and recommendations of some of the private organizations that provide ethical guidelines for direct marketing?

7. Explain the Privacy Act of 1974 and its impact on direct marketers.
8. What is *spam?* Why are there so many negative feelings toward spam? What is currently being done to eliminate spam?
9. What is the current status of the FCC/FTC Do Not Call Registry?
10. Using the on-line legal sources provided in the chapter, provide a legal update on permission marketing and spam as they affect direct marketing activities.

Exercise

Imagine you are the first chief privacy officer (CPO) for a major credit card company. Your organization, like all credit card companies, unfortunately has the typical reputation of selling your customers' information to various firms. You want to change the reputation your company has regarding this matter so that you may gain a competitive edge over your competition. What do you think are some of the regulations and ethical codes you are subject to follow set forth by legislation, private organizations, and organizations such as the FTC? Also explain steps that your company can take to regulate itself that aren't currently being taken by other companies.

CASE: THE TELEPHONE CONSUMER PROTECTION ACT (TCPA)

OVERVIEW

The Telephone Consumer Protection Act of 1991 provides a set of regulations for direct response advertising via the telephone and fax machine. Direct marketers must understand and comply with the TCPA in order to avoid costly lawsuits that can be filed against offenders of this law. This case explains the TCPA of 1991 and provides an example of what may take place when there is a violation of the law. (Please review Chapter 8: "Telemarketing for the Federal Trade Commission Rules.") The objective of this case is to provide details on the Telephone Consumer Protection Act (TCPA) that may be unclear to many direct marketers and marketing students. The TCPA of 1991 is still being enforced today and encompasses direct marketing activities via telephone and fax machines.

CASE

Most direct marketers who use telemarketing as a medium for promoting their products and services are well aware of the Federal Trade Commission's (FTC) Telemarketing Sales Rule. As discussed earlier in this chapter, this rule requires direct marketers to disclose certain kinds of information to the customer before the customer makes a purchase or places an order over the phone. However, what is less well known are the Federal Communication Commission's (FCC) rules implementing the Telephone Consumer Protection Act (TCPA) of 1991. Telemarketers must be aware of and comply with both sets of regulations. The FTC and FCC rules are similar in many ways; however, the TCPA and FCC rules govern issues that are not encompassed in the FTC regulations.

One of the most common areas of concern for direct marketers is how fax machines can be used for direct response advertising purposes. Since the fax machine is a common business tool, direct marketers must be crystal clear in their understanding of what is permitted and what is not permitted when using a fax machine for marketing purposes. But even rules for conduct may be interpreted with unexpected results by courts in various state and federal jurisdictions.

History
In 1991, Congress amended the Communications Act of 1934 with the enactment of the TCPA. The TCPA was enacted to "protect the privacy interests of residential telephone subscribers by placing restrictions on unsolicited, automated telephone calls to the home and to facilitate interstate commerce by restricting certain uses of fax machines and automatic dialers." The TCPA states: "It shall be unlawful for any telephone facsimile [fax] machine, computer, or other device to send an unsolicited advertisement to a telephone facsimile machine."[1] The FCC's rules apply not only to stand-alone fax machines, but also to computer fax boards or modems that can send a fax from a personal computer.

Effective August 25, 2003, there are some new FCC rules on sending faxes to both businesses and residents. However, the FCC recently announced that a portion of the new rules will not go into effect until January 1, 2005. This portion requires companies to receive signed written permission from anyone (including their own customers) before sending any commercial faxes. In addition, you cannot send a fax to prospects, consumers, (or even businesses) unless the prospect has contacted you. Prior to January 1, 2005, direct

[1]"Telephone Consumer Protection Act" The Direct Marketing Assoc. Telemarketing Resource Center, New York: NY Sept. 17, 2003.

marketers had a 3-month window to fax to an inquirer.[2] For more information you can visit the following FCC site: http://ftp.fcc.gov/cgb/consumerfacts/unwantedfaxes.html. The TCPA is a federal law, so violations of the act are heard in federal court. However, the TCPA allows jurisdiction on the various states to allow private citizens to sue in their own state courts if someone violates the TCPA. If the courts find the defendant liable, they could be subject to a $500 fine per fax or call as statutory damages. If the fax or call was a willful or intentional violation of the act, they could be fined $1,500 per fax or call which is "treble" damages.

In summary of the legal jargon, the TCPA, and in turn the FCC regulations, impose a general ban on the use of fax machines to send an "unsolicited advertisement." This includes any advertising material promoting the "commercial availability" of any goods, property, or services that is transmitted without the recipient's prior express invitation or permission. However, there is an exemption for "existing business relationships." The rule defines an "established business relationship" as: "a prior or existing relationship formed by a voluntary two-way communication between a person or entity and a residential subscriber with or without an exchange of consideration on the basis of an inquiry, application, purchase, or transaction by the residential subscriber regarding products or services offered by such person or entity, which relationship has not been previously terminated by either party." The FCC has stated that an existing business relationship with the recipient can be deemed to reflect the recipient's permission to send a fax with a commercial message. However, even if a prior or existing relationship exists, each fax must identify, on each page or on the first page, the date and time the fax is being sent and the sender's identity and telephone number of the fax machine sending the message. (This refers back to the regulations set forth by the FTC's Telemarketing Sales Rule.)

In summary, the basic premise behind these regulations is that sending unsolicited faxes to consumers is considered "junk faxing." Some consumers believe that junk faxers steal the resources of the recipients—fax paper, ink, and personnel costs—and tie up the equipment causing a busy signal to sound in place of receiving legitimate messages. In fact, some consumers felt so strongly about these issues that they developed a Web site (www.Junkfaxes.org) to disseminate information on various junk fax senders and assist the recipients in enforcing the above laws.

Examples of TCPA Violations

One recent enforcement of the TCPA in Georgia can be found in the case of *Nicholson et al. v. Hooters of Augusta, Inc.* In June 1995, Sam Nicholson filed a class action against Bambi Clark Value-Fax of Augusta and Hooters of Augusta, Inc., alleging that Hooters used Clark, an independent contractor, to send unsolicited advertisements to facsimile machines in violation of the TCPA. The trial court ruled in favor of Nicholson and found Hooters of Augusta, Inc., in violation of the TCPA. Hooters of Augusta, Inc., then appealed the ruling to the Court of Appeals in Georgia. However, the Court of Appeals in Georgia found that Georgia citizens had the right to seek the relief provided by the TCPA, even though Hooters of Augusta, Inc., claimed that Clark was an independent contractor. Even if the court found that Clark was an independent contractor, the TCPA states "the entity or *entities on whose behalf* facsimiles are transmitted are ultimately liable for compliance with the TCPA's rule banning unsolicited facsimile advertisements."

On April 25, 2001, a jury determined that Hooters of Augusta, Inc., willfully violated the TCPA by sending unsolicited advertising faxes and assessed full trebled damages of $1,500 per violation against Hooters. Hooters was ordered to pay each of the 1,321 class members who received six unsolicited faxed advertisements

---

[2]The Direct Marketing Association, "A Matter of Fax: What Direct Marketers Need to Know About Sending Faxes," August 25, 2003, <www.the-dma.org/guidelines/advertisingfaxes.shtml> (September 12, 2003).

a sum of $9,000 per party, for a total of $11,889,000.[3]

Other examples of recent offenders of the TCPA include the Dallas-based firm American Blast Fax. On March 14, 2001, 23 individual plaintiffs received judgments totaling $83,000 against American Blast Fax (ABF) and clients Cox Industrial Equipment Co., Inc., Advanced Digital Telemarketing, The Breve Company, Inc., and Richard Townsend d/b/a Financial Strategies Group. These companies had hired ABF to send fax advertisements on their behalf.[4]

In conclusion, the TCPA is an important law for direct marketers to be knowledgeable of and comply with when using the fax machine for direct response advertising and communications.

Source: Adapted from "Unsolicited Advertising Faxes are Illegal," September 24, 1998. The DMA Interactive Web site, <http://www.the-dma.org/library/guidelines/advertisingfaxes.shtml> (August 8, 2002). Reprinted with permission. ∎

Case Discussion Questions

1. How are the FTC's Telephone Sales Rule and the FCC's TCPA similar? How are they different?
2. Can direct marketers comply with the TCPA and still use distribute direct response advertising materials to consumers? If so, how?
3. Could Hooters of Augusta, Inc., have avoided the lawsuit that was waged upon them? Explain.
4. What is the position of your state in the interpretation of the TCPA?

Notes

1. Direct Marketing Association Telemarketing Resource Center, "Teleservices Fact Sheet," September 12, 2003, <www.the-dma.org/government/teleservicefactsheet.shtml> (September, 2003).
2. Adapted from Carl McDaniel, Jr., and Roger Gates *Contemporary Marketing Research,* 2nd ed. (New York: West Publishing Co., 1993).
3. Charles W. L. Hill, *Global Business Today,* (New York: McGraw-Hill/Inrwin, 2002), 50.
4. Elaine M. LaFlamme, "Know the liabilities of Data Collection," *New Jersey Law Journal* (March 14, 2003), <http://www.law.com>.
5. Ibid.
6. "Help Wanted: Steal This Database," *Wired News,* January 6, 2003; Elaine M. LaFlamme, "Know the liabilities of Data Collection," *New Jersey Law Journal,* (March 14, 2003), <www.law.com>.
7. Elaine M. LaFlamme, "Know the Liabilities of Data Collection," *New Jersey Law Journal* (March 14, 2003), <www.law.com>.
8. James Kindall, "Lists Help Build Dosier on You," *Kansas City Star,* September 5, 1978, p.1.
9. Adapted from The Privacy Protection Study Commission, *Report from the*

[3]Robert H. Braver, 2001, "Judge imposes maximum trebled damage of nearly $12 million against Hooters," <http://www.junkfaxes.org/news/ hooters-12.htm> (April 2001).

[4]Robert H. Braver, "American Blast Fax and Its Advertiser Clients Found Jointly Liable for Junk Faxes," "Blast Faxer and Clients Held Jointly Liable" access date 8/8/02. "Hooters Hit with $12 Million Damage Award" <http://www.junkfaxes.org/news/ abfmo.htm> March 14, 2001

Privacy Protection Study Commission (Washington, DC: GPO, July 1977), 147.

10. "Telephone Consumer Protection Act" The Direct Marketing Assoc. Telemarketing Resource Center, New York: NY Sept. 17, 2003.

11. "Crack Down on Spam," *New York Times,* April 29, 2003, sec. A, p. 28, col. 1.

12. Ibid.

13. Greene, Jenna, "The Slippery Fight Over E-Mail Spam," *Legal Times,* May 14, 2001, <www.law.com>.

14. Spam Laws, "United States Proposed Legislation," <http://www.spamlaws.com/federal/index.html> September 23, 2003.

15. Spam Laws, "United States 108th Congress Pending Lesgislation," <http://www.spamlaws.com/federal/summ108.html> September 23, 2003.

16. Emily T. Hackett, *Spam White Paper, Addendum,* August, 2003, Internet Alliance, Washington, DC. <http://www.internetalliance.org> (August 27, 2003).

17. Internet Alliance, *2003/2004 State Legislative Chart,* September 12, 2003, Internet Alliance, Washington, DC. <http://www.internetalliance.org> (August 27, 2003).

18. Saul Hansell, "Virginia Law Makes Spam, With Fraud, A Felony," *New York Times,* April 30, 2003, sec. C, p. 1, col. 5.

19. Ibid.

20. Karl Dentino, "Taking Privacy Into Our Own Hands," *Direct Marketing* (September 1994).

21. Richard A. Hamilton and Lisa D. Spiller, "Opinions about Privacy: Does the Type of Informatin Used for Marketing Purposes Make a Difference?" *International Journal of Voluntary Sector Marketing* 4, no. 3 (September 1999): 251–264.

22. Direct Marketing Association, "Privacy—What Is It?" *Privacy Action Now,* April, 2000.

23. Page Boinest Melton, "Business Trends To Watch", *Virginia Business* (February 2001), 78–81.

24. Universal Bank, *Important Information Regarding Your Privacy* (2001), 1.

25. Ibid., 5.

26. *The DMA Privacy Promise Member Compliance Guide* (New York: The Direct Marketing Association, Inc., September, 1998).

27. http://www.fcc.gov/

28. Federal Trade Commission Office of Public Information, 6th Street and Pennsylvania Avenue, N.W., Washington, DC, 20580.

29. Interpretation provided by the DMA Office of Ethics & Consumer Affairs, January, 2003.

30. Direct Marketing Association, "The FTC's New Telemarketing Sales Rule: Q & A's," <http:// www.the-dma.org> (September 12, 2003).

31. The Federal Trade Commission, *Privacy Online: Fair Information in The Electronic Marketplace* (Washington, DC: GPO, May 2000).

32. Kristen Bremner, "CA Assembly Passes Amended Privacy Bill," *Direct Marketing News,* September 17, 2003.

33. Donn Rappaport, "What We Should Say (and Do) About Privacy," *Direct Marketing News,* October 11, 1993.

34. T. Tezinde, B. Smith, and J. Murphy, "Getting Permission: Exploring Factors Affecting Permission Marketing," *Journal of Interactive Marketing* 37 (2002), 28–36.

35. The DMA Telemarketing Resource Center, "The DMA's FAQ Regarding the New National Do Not Call System and Regulations," <http://www.the-dma.org/government/teleresourcenter.shtml> (August 25, 2003).

BUSINESS-TO-BUSINESS (INDUSTRIAL) DIRECT MARKETING

B usiness-to-business **(B2B)** direct marketing is the process of providing goods and services to industrial market intermediaries, as opposed to ultimate consumers. Although the distinction is not always easy to make, we differentiate industrial goods from consumer goods based on their ultimate use. **Industrial goods** are generally used as raw materials or in the fabrication of other goods. Whereas iron ore is almost always an industrial good, a personal computer can be either an industrial or a consumer good, depending on its ultimate use.

John H. Patterson, who founded the National Cash Register Company (today's NCR), was the first to use direct mail to get qualified leads for follow-up by salespeople. The firm's lead generation, in the early 1900s, was oriented to specific industries. The salesperson assigned to call on each prospect expressing interest was provided with sales literature directed to firms using cash registers: groceries, druggists, movie houses, etc.—each identified by a Standard Industrial Classification (SIC) code. This literature was often stored in the trunk of the salesperson's car for reference and delivery to a qualified prospect. Today, this method of sales prospect qualification utilizing a variety of direct response media, not just direct mail, plays an important role in the total scheme of B2B direct marketing.

Direct marketing is employed throughout business-to-business distribution channels. This is not so much in the "direct" sense of bypassing middlemen (via a Web site or a catalog) as it is in the "directed" sense of targeting prospects, thus increasing the effectiveness and the efficiency of the salesperson. The salesperson is, in fact, an important adjunct to the direct marketing process, more than ever now used as an interactive medium, face to face or electronically.

Integrating direct marketing into an existing organization is not an easy task. It takes a great deal of top-down, long-range commitment. Direct marketing is not a "sometimes thing" but rather requires an ongoing belief coupled with adequate funding. Fortunately, use of the tools and techniques can be tested and fine-tuned before they are implemented. The wise traditional organization absorbs direct marketing slowly, testing as it goes, without throwing out what it already does well . . . thus creating havoc.

THE NATURE OF INDUSTRIAL MARKETS

The Direct Marketing Association, through its annual Economic Impact survey, estimates that business-to-business sales generated through direct marketing exceeds $1.129 trillion, about 6.45 percent of total industrial sales. This compares to consumer sales generated through direct marketing, estimated to be $1.207 trillion, which is about 15.1 percent of total consumer sales. In recent years, according to the Economic Impact survey, the utilization of direct marketing tools and techniques by B2B organizations has grown at a rate of 10.3 percent, nearly double that of total industrial sales.[1]

As much as 50 percent of manufactured output is sold to the industrial market and as much as 80 percent of farm produce is considered industrial. Wheat, for example, is an industrial good when it is sold for the production of flour; flour is an industrial good when it is sold for the baking of bread; and bread is an industrial good when sold to a restaurant. But bread is a consumer good when sold to a household.

Types of Industrial Goods

In the case of consumer goods, the buyer usually visits the seller. The opposite is true of industrial goods: usually, the seller comes to the buyer. Direct marketing techniques are often used in lead-generation among potential buyers of industrial goods. An IBM system, for example, is usually not shopped for in a retail store, but a well-designed direct-mail letter can often entice an industrial prospect to invite an IBM representative to make a presentation. A further characteristic of industrial goods is that their purchase usually involves group decision making, and, because a particular component represents only a part of the whole.

Like consumer goods that we classify into three categories—*convenience, shopping,* and *specialty* goods—industrial products fit into several types as follows:

Raw materials: **Raw materials** such as wheat and silicon are products destined to become part of another product, subject to further processing.

Fabricated materials and parts: In contrast to raw materials, **fabricated materials** have already been processed; that is, flour (from wheat) or iron (from ore).

Installations: Major equipment with long lives such as buildings, generators, and aircraft are **installations.**

Accessory equipment: **Accessory equipment** aids and implements production and includes office machines as well as machine tools.

Operating supplies: We might think of **operating supplies** as analogous to convenience goods in that they are consumable. Examples include lubricating oil, ball-point pens, and floor wax.

Characteristics of Industrial Demand

Industrial demand differs from consumer demand by these four characteristics, worth noting and understanding:

Derived demand: Demand for industrial goods is derived ultimately from consumer demand. The industrial demand for automobile tires, steel, or glass, for example, depends in part on the consumer demand for automobiles.

Inelastic demand: Because a variety of industrial goods go into the manufacture of a single product, and thus each represents only a fraction of the product's total cost, there is not as much price sensitivity in industrial goods. The cost of tires for an automobile, for example, might double, but this increase would represent a relatively small part of the total cost of the car.

Widely fluctuating demand: The demand for industrial goods is subject to wide fluctuation, ultimately dependent on consumer demand but also dependent on rises and falls in inventories as well as in the optimism of entrepreneurs.

Knowledgeable demand: Industrial buyers are usually much better informed about their purchases than consumers are about theirs, have more specialized interests, and benefit from the process of joint decision making.

Although the number of industrial organizations is but a fraction of the number of consumers, the volume of purchasing is as great in the industrial market as it is in the consumer market. Buying power of industrial organizations is highly concentrated, however, within certain industries (i.e., manufacturing), and there are also heavy concentrations regionally and geographically. This buying power is often measured by various forms of activity such as manufacturing, wholesaling, retailing, mining, agriculture, and construction.

In comparing business-to-business transactions with business-to-consumer transactions, we should note (again) that consumer purchases are normally consummated at the seller's location (i.e., clothing bought at a retail store). Whereas, in industrial buying, the seller normally comes to the buyer's location (i.e., a computer installation sold to a chain of retail stores). A major factor contributing to the increasing use of direct marketing by business and industry is the rising cost of these personal sales calls made to a buyer's location. According to ongoing McGraw-Hill research, the cost of the average B2B sales call, which was about $50 in 1969, has now risen to more than $300, a sixfold increase. Please note that this cost is per *call,* not per *sale* . . . it takes an average of three calls to make one sale.

In contrasting business buyers with consumer buyers, apparent differences between these are sometimes exaggerated. Individual buyers within business organizations are obviously also consumers in their own rights. And, conversely, many consumers also wear different hats when they are at work as industrial buyers. Some B2B organizations, recognizing this comparison, have gone so far as to look at the demographics of buyers within organizations at the same time as they look at the demographics of organizations themselves. A comparison of database demographics, contrasting consumer and industrial markets, is shown in Figure 13-1. These characteristics are not all-inclusive, of course, but they do indicate some interesting differences and, at the same time, similarities.

All buyers—consumers as well as industrial organizations—have a name and address. Beyond that identification, a consumer's age can be important in product differentiation as can the years a company has been in business. The gender of an industrial buyer may very well have the same influence as it does on that buyer making a purchase as a consumer. A consumer's income can be looked at in the same light as an

CONSUMER	INDUSTRIAL
Name/Address	Name/Address
Source code	Source code
Age	Year started
Gender	Gender of decision maker
Income	Revenue
Wealth	Net worth
Family size	Number of employees
Children	Parent firm or subsidiary
Occupation	Line of business
Credit evaluation	Credit evaluation
Education	Education of decision makers
Urban/rural resident	Headquarters/branch
Own or rent home	Private or public ownership
Ethnic group	Minority ownership
Gender	Gender of decision makers
Interests	Interests of decision makers
Life-style of ZIP area	Socio-economics of location
Mail respondent	Mail respondent
Transactions & R/F/M	Transactions & R/F/M

FIGURE 13-1 Comparison of Demographic Items in Consumer and Industrial Direct Marketing

organization's revenue, . . . just as a consumer's wealth can be looked at in the same light as an organization's net worth. While many marketers see lists of business buyers being different from lists of consumers, we argue that there is as much sameness as there is difference!

USES AND USERS OF BUSINESS-TO-BUSINESS DIRECT MARKETING

Mail order and lead generation for follow-up by salespersons, utilizing the tools and techniques of direct marketing, are major contributors to the rapid growth of business-to-business direct marketing. A major stimulus, too, has been the Internet and its commerce partner, the World Wide Web. Even though the number of consumer households in the United States is at least 10-fold and the number of individual consumers is at least 25-fold that of the number of businesses, total B2B sales volume is at least double that of business-to-consumer sales.[2] And, since the average revenue per industrial response is typically larger, it follows that response rates from B2B direct response advertising can be lower than from that which is consumer directed and still be profitable for the direct marketer.

The tools and techniques of direct marketing which are utilized by businesses are basically the same as those for consumer direct marketing, as presented throughout this textbook. These tools and techniques are used in industrial markets to

- Generate qualified "leads" for salesperson follow-up.
- Achieve direct sales remotely (i.e., via catalogs and Web sites).
- Reinforce all sales efforts.
- Introduce new products.
- Develop new markets and applications.
- Build industrial customer goodwill.
- Conduct industrial market research.

Notable users of the tools and techniques of direct marketing have been makers of office products, industrial plant supplies, computers and their peripherals, building equipment, and even aircraft and the complex array of aircraft parts. Much has changed since John H. Patterson founded the National Cash Register Company and first used direct mail to get qualified leads for follow-up by salespeople. Today, the direct mail and Web site methods of sales prospect qualification as well as direct selling, when augmented by direct response advertising in a variety of print and broadcast media and the telephone all play an important role in the total scheme of business-to-business marketing.

As noted earlier in this chapter, an important feature of business-to-business distribution that makes it especially susceptible to the tools and techniques of direct marketing is this: producers and their middlemen are more likely to make sales calls on buyers of industrial goods, whereas buyers of consumer goods are more likely to make purchases at the locations of producers and middlemen. Direct marketing has been used effectively throughout industrial distribution channels—producer to agent to distributor to industrial user—to augment personal selling.

Business-to-business marketers, like business-to-consumer marketers, combine relational databases to obtain information about their customers *as well as their customers' customers.* They perform statistical analyses to identify their own best customers and then they seek prospects that look like these. An example of such analysis is presented later in this chapter.

Just how does a manufacturer of earthmoving equipment or heavy industrial cranes use direct marketing to find prospects? The principles for creating and cultivating industrial customers are the same ones applied in consumer markets.

The manufacturer of a highly specialized form system for heavy-duty concrete construction estimated that there were no more than a few hundred prospects for its product *worldwide*. Demonstration was a powerful sales tool but it required a lot of travel and time. So, this specialized manufacturer produced a demonstration video of several installations and successfully offered it, via direct mail, to a carefully compiled database of prospects. Those expressing interest were then called on by salespeople, who consummated the sale.

The manufacturer of the type of crane, large and cumbersome, around which tall buildings are built, had a similar experience. "How do you find and maintain contact with prospects?" this manufacturer was asked. The reply: "We regularly compile prospect lists from news and trade press reports. We write letters. We telephone. We refer prospects to our Web site for more detailed information. After qualification, there is appropriate personal follow-up."

Boeing Company, reporting in a *Wall Street Journal* article that it had saved hundreds of millions of dollars in so doing, offers its complex array of aircraft parts to its airline customers with millions of pages of technical manuals accessible and orderable on the World Wide Web.

A Special Case: Industrial Computer Installations

Computer mainframes, peripherals, and personal computer networks, largely industrial installations, have all been offered by salespersons of manufacturers calling at the buyer's location. While companies generate leads through direct response advertising in a variety of media, the "marketing representative" has been—and remains—a key player. But, personal computers have paved the way for many innovative direct marketing applications.

Buyers of software for personal computers often register their purchases with the producers of operating systems as well as applications, usually in order to receive technical assistance and information about modifications or upgrades.

Thanks to this action, software producers such as Microsoft, Intuit, and McAfee have built extensive databases and Web sites to direct delivery of their products. Through trade magazines, newsletters, direct-mail solicitations, and their Web sites, they are able to maintain ongoing relationships with their customers . . . seizing many opportunities for continuity selling as well as cross-selling.

Their most frequent offers are for system upgrades and new applications. And because these firms often make their customer databases available for noncompetitive offers—by mail, telephone, Web site links, or even through resellers—customers can also purchase technical publications, continuous forms, and stationery, entertainment, or utility software.

Hardware—the PCs themselves as well as their peripherals and accompanying software—had been largely distributed through dealer networks of retail stores. Then, one manufacturer, Dell, became a worldwide leader in both mail-order sales and computer manufacturing. Now, Dell, Gateway, Hewlitt-Packard, and a host of mail-order price discounters have made an impact on the retail stores, taking sales but not necessarily service from them. While IBM only experimented with "direct" as these business-to-business distribution innovators emerged, it, too, is now committed to it. So, too, is Apple—often via the World Wide Web.

Another Special Case: Industrial Vending Machine Installations

Soft-drink bottlers have made their products conveniently available through vending machines located in high-traffic locations such as industrial plants, offices, hospitals, hotels, airports, bus terminals, and educational institutions.

Typically, salespeople representing these bottlers have selected prospects from lists coded by standard industrial classification and then have visited them personally. A group of bottlers in New England, however, some years ago discovered that it was closing only one sale out of ten calls by using this procedure. Since ongoing research by McGraw-Hill tells us that it costs a business-to-business marketer upwards of $300 per sales contact, and an average of three contacts to close a sale, that comes to $900, on average, to make one sale! Striving for efficiency, the New England bottlers turned to the tools and techniques of direct marketing. Using the same SIC-prospect list, they now sought to generate more highly qualified expressions of interest via direct mail.

But they went beyond simply name and address of the prospect. How many employees were there in each plant or office? How many rooms in the hotel? How many students at the university? How many beds in the hospital? How many passengers passed through the airport or bus terminal? Further, how strong was competition in each locale? What soft-drink brands were preferred in each market? How unbearable were the local heat and humidity?

All of these factors had a bearing on how many vending machines were needed at a location and the resulting size of the installation (i.e., the sale). Not only could the direct-mail copy address the benefits to be derived for a particular type of location, but the salesperson could advise intelligently during a follow-up visit.

After testing it, the New England soft-drink bottlers reported that the program generated one sale for every 3.7 contacts, at a cost-per-sale of $89. Better yet, 6.3 fruitless sales contacts were avoided, saving $300 each! As this case demonstrates, the only way an entrepreneur will ever know whether direct marketing "pays" is to measure results versus costs. Business-to-business distribution (mail order, as well as lead-generation programs to aid sales people) now appears to be the fastest-growing segment of direct marketing.

FedEx Is a Model B2B Direct Marketer

FedEx offers and prices its delivery services in a variety of categories including, several years ago, a category called Priority 1. To expand its market, increase its penetration, and hold its present customers for this premium service, FedEx conceived a business-to-business direct-mail campaign to announce a new discount schedule. Based strictly on its potential value in the immediate future, the direct-mail program was divided into three segments:

1. Frequent users of Priority 1: 19,126 individual customers
2. Infrequent users of Priority 1: 121,705 individual customers
3. Other FedEx customers who had never used Priority 1: 63,431 individual customers

The symbol to be used for dramatizing the Priority 1 service was the same for all three market segments: a 5-pound reproduction of a 1913 exercise weight. Frequent users of Priority 1 received the exercise weight immediately as a goodwill gift; infrequent users had to request it; nonusers received it as a premium with the purchase of Priority 1 service for the first time. Frequent users were also asked to identify other prospects and decision makers within their own organizations. A total of 7,044 (24.1 percent) of the 29,126 frequent user recipients of the promotion did just that.

Of the 121,705 infrequent users contacted, a total of 25,985 (24.0 percent) responded by requesting the gift, and, in the process, they also supplied 14,723 names of new prospects within their own organizations.

Of the 63,431 nonusers of Priority 1 among FedEx customers, a total of 9,300 (15 percent) actually purchased the service and submitted a copy of the FedEx air bill as proof of purchase to receive the exercise weight.

In summary, the following total results were tabulated:

21,767 new prospects
40,000 responses from *old* customers
25,985 "market research" forms returned
9,300 proven direct sales to *new* customers
$500,000 in immediate traceable sales to these new customers alone

Since each user of Priority 1 service was known to average $4,000 in sales per year for an undetermined number of future years, the potential value of these new customers is impressive.

CHALLENGES OF B2B DIRECT MARKETING

Changes in today's global economy are forcing business-to-business marketers to adapt to many challenges. To be successful, these marketers must be able to account for each nuance of change in their customers' organizations, as well as in their own organizations and in the overall economy. In addition, they must find new ways to cultivate their current customer database, locate qualified prospects, and reduce marketing costs.

The challenges facing industrial marketers include

- Marketing costs that are increasing while the audience reached is decreasing. It costs more to generate awareness than ever before.
- Face-to-face selling, down in efficiency, is up in cost. Travel expense is up and the cost of a salesperson's call on a prospect/customer is a larger part of revenue than before.
- Communication clutter brings individuals up to 10,000 messages per day and many have tuned out nonrelevant marketing messages.
- Customer relationship managers often do not integrate an analytical approach to combining operations with marketing programs and campaigns. There is generally not nearly enough analysis of customer data.
- Industry classification of customers/prospects, most commonly used in the past, is not adequately predictive in the current business environment. Such market

segmentation assumes businesses within the same industry type are similar; however, a business in a rural area can be dramatically different from an inner-city business with the same industry classification.

HOW TO IDENTIFY B2B MARKET SEGMENTS

Industrial markets are much smaller in number than consumer markets, but are certainly not smaller in sales volume. Like consumer markets, industrial markets break down into smaller, more homogeneous segments of the heterogeneous total industrial market. Market segmentation may be even more important in industrial applications than in consumer, because of the diversity of activities in each segment.

Business-to-business market segments can be identified by industry, by financial strength or size, by number of employees, and/or by sales volume. Geographic selectivity includes urban/rural orientation, city size, and location. There can also be selection by form of ownership, by branch/headquarters, . . . or even by extent of telephone directory advertising.

Within organizations, industrial markets also can be segmented by job functions. Demand within firms is not generated by purchasing agents alone but by engineers, chemists, architects, and a good many other specialists. Direct marketers must appeal not only to firms as such, but to many relevant individuals within them.

Maintaining customer/prospect databases is a real challenge to business-to-business direct marketers. The most important database, of course, is that of its customers. Such a compilation should include, in addition to names/addresses, prior purchase behavior, as well as the organization's—and, possibly, even the individual buyer's—demographic profile.

Standard Industrial Classification (SIC)

The **Standard Industrial Classification (SIC)** coding system is a means of industrial market segmentation developed by the federal government a good many years ago. SIC codes, which identify businesses by industry and by segment of industry and serve as a basis for statistical data about industries, are in broad use by government, trade associations, and business enterprises. Within the broad SIC classification system, these are the terms in frequent use:

> *Industry:*   A grouping of establishments engaged in a common economic activity is identified by the four-digit primary SIC code. Approximately 950 industries make up the U.S. economy. These produce approximately 75,000 products and services that are further divided by five- and seven-digit SIC codes.
>
> *Establishment:*   Within four-digit SIC codes describing their primary lines of business, these are economic units producing at a single physical location, such as a manufacturing plant, a farm warehouse, or a retail store.
>
> *Company:*   An entity that owns one or more establishments. SIC codes are assigned to establishments (economic units) rather than to companies (legal entities). These, in turn, may be further designated as *headquarters* or *branch offices*. The SIC codes also identify their *form of ownership:* individual, partnership, or corporation.

Within SIC codes, which designate the primary and secondary lines of business, establishments can also be segmented on other bases: sales volume, credit rating, age of business, number of employees, net financial worth, subsidiary, and location.

The first two digits of the four-digit code indicate a major classification of industry, of which there are ten:

- 01–09 Agriculture, forestry, and fisheries
- 10–14 Mining
- 15–17 Construction
- 20–39 Manufacturing
- 40–49 Transportation, communications, public utilities
- 50–51 Wholesale trade
- 52–59 Retail trade
- 60–67 Finance, insurance, real estate
- 70–89 Services (medical, legal, schools, churches, etc.)
- 91–97 Public administration
- 99   Nonclassifiable establishments

The final two digits of the four-digit SIC code classify individual organizations by subgroup within industry. For example, SIC #2300 identifies manufacturers of wearing apparel. Within this classification, SIC #2311 identifies men's suit and coat manufacturers. An example of the primary four-digit coding system applied to manufacturers of apparel and other textile products is shown in Figure 13-2. This example breaks down

FIGURE 13-2 Standard Industrial Classification (SIC) System

SIC #	DESCRIPTION
2300	Apparel and other finished product mfgrs.
2310/2320	Men's, youth's, and boy's clothing
2311	Suits and coats
2321	Shirts except work shirts
2322	Underwear and night wear
2323	Neckwear
2325	Separate trousers and slacks
2326	Work clothing
2329	Clothing not elsewhere classified
2330	Women's, misses, and junior's outerwear
2331	Blouses and shirts
2335	Dresses
2337	Suits, skirts, and coats
2339	Outerwear
2340	Women's, misses, and junior's undergarments
2341	Underwear and night wear
2342	Brassieres, girdles, and allied garments
2350	Hats, caps, and millinery
2353	Hats, caps and millinery
2360	Girl's, children's, and infant's outerwear
2361	Dresses, blouses, and shirts
2369	Outerwear, not elsewhere classified

the 2300-series SIC codes, assigned to such manufacturers, into subgroups, such as men's and women's categories, and further divides these categories into specific types of apparel manufacturing concerns.

North American Industrial Classification System (NAICS)

SIC codes have for some time done a good job of detailing the manufacturing industry but many feel it fails to recognize the existence of today's information technology. With rapid growth of the service industry, high technology, and international trade, a new system has arisen, in response to the North American Free Trade Agreement (NAFTA) of 1994, to compare U.S. statistical information with that of Canada and Mexico and to ensure future compatibility with an International Standard Industrial Classification System being developed by the United Nations.

All three countries have agreed on a system now called the **North American Industrial Classification System (NAICS).** This system has formulated a six-digit code, with the first five digits denoting the NAICS levels used by all three countries to produce compatible data. NAICS is an entirely different classification system than SIC, because it focuses on production activities rather than on those that the industries serve. A more detailed explanation of NAICS appears in Chapter 2.

Different agencies within governments are now converting to NAICS coding, but business has done relatively little to adopt the new coding system in marketing applications.

Input-Output Analysis of Industrial Markets

Input-output analysis, derived basically from Census Bureau data, traces the distribution of goods from their origins to their destinations. In matrix form, each industry (SIC) appears as both seller and buyer in row and column headings. At the point at which the rows and columns of any two industries intersect, the matrix records the transaction between them. Such analysis is the means by which our country's gross national product is calculated.

Input-output analysis determines the impact that specific industries have on the total economy, not just in terms of what they sell but also in terms of what they buy. A decrease in sales of new automobiles, for example, would result in reduced purchases from the steel industry. This, in turn, would result in reduced sales by the steel industry and would ultimately reduce the steel industry's purchases from the mining industry. Input-output matrices can be particularly useful to business-to-business marketers wanting to reach organizations producing industrial goods for further processing by other organizations. Such a table can systematically record how much of the organization's product is consumed by every other industry in the economy and describe market segments utilizing that product.

An example (see Figure 13-3) relates to the demand for corrugated boxes (SIC #2653), which are used by at least 75 percent of all SIC manufacturing industries. A box manufacturer seeking a description of the national market for corrugated boxes can compile consumption data for each plant in each county (or ZIP code area) in each state in the nation. The seller would determine the total number of plants in the compilation by the number of consuming industries for the product (corrugated boxes) as well as, in each industry, the number of plants using corrugated boxes.

STATE AND COUNTY NAME	SIC #	# OF PLANTS	ANNUAL PURCHASE OF CORRUGATED BOXES
ALABAMA			
Autauga County			
Botany Inds., Inc.	2256	1	$10.9M
Nappies, Inc.	2631	1	25.8M
Continental Gin Co.	3559	1	15.0M
County Total		3	$51.7M
Baldwin County			
Woodhaven Dairy	2024	1	$22.4M
Hale Mfg. Co.	2221	1	8.0M
Bay Slacks, Inc.	2253	1	20.4M
Std. Furn., Mfg. Co.	2511	1	82.0M
Kaiser Alumn. Co.	3643	1	31.9M
County Total		5	$164.7M
Barbour County			
Cowikee Mills	2211	1	$13.3M
Dixie Shoe Corp.	3141	1	9.2M
County Total		2	$22.5M

FIGURE 13-3   A Prospect List of Users of Corrugated Boxes (SIC #2653) Derived from Input-Output Analysis and Showing User's Name and SIC Arranged Within County (or ZIP Code) Within State

The Census Bureau's TIGER System

The **Global Positioning System (GPS)** and the Census Bureau's **Topologically Integrated Geographic Encoding Referencing (TIGER)** system both associate latitude and longitude coordinates with street addresses. Used to pinpoint geographic locations, they can establish business sites, locate competition, measure distance, and generate data about the demographics of a business location.

With mapping capabilities and information in its database, a business-to-business direct marketer can visualize reach and penetration of the geographic territories of its resellers.

Figure 13-4 illustrates how the Hewlett-Packard Web site, from visitor-provided registration data and utilizing the global positioning system, determines location and directs the visitor to resellers, at the same time linking to its own on-line store.

Business Clusters

Industrial markets can be clustered and defined by ZIP code area just as are consumer markets.[3] Data by SIC classifications have been associated with ZIP code area data. Ruf Corporation, Olathe, Kansas, has identified ZIP code areas in terms of economic activity (number of businesses, commerce input-output, bank savings, retail sales, etc.) as well as in terms of consumer demographics and lifestyles (number of households, home value, income, autos owned, etc.) Ruf's **business clusters** reveal the impact these variables have on the buying behavior of businesses located in these areas.

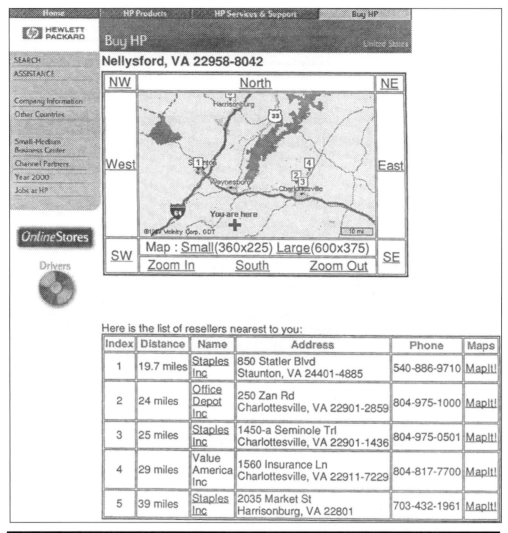

FIGURE 13-4   Utilizing Registration Information, a Web Site Directs a Visitor to a Reseller

Marketing professionals know that customers are not equal in value. In fact, it is quite simple to distinguish between the repeat customer and the customer who has made a single, inexpensive purchase some time ago. Such cluster analysis is more descriptive than traditional segmentation methods because it can reveal hidden relationships. For example, cluster analysis may reveal that past purchasing patterns, economic growth, and interdependency factors are far better predictors of future purchases than size of the firm, its revenues, or industry classification.

Customers can be segmented into clusters, which, when combined, become the overall customer profile. Companies can then target each group effectively through individualized marketing messages. Customer profiles are the key to effective prospecting; businesses should target prospects that look like their best customers.

By using underlying variables, clusters can essentially differentiate between two similar businesses in the same approximate location by comparing differences to an average of the universe of all businesses.

By analyzing data from many firms across the spectrum of industries, a marketer can derive "business lifestyles." Using input-output matrices, the marketer can use statistical models to describe the *consumption and digestion* of products and services a company uses to produce its final products and services. Once indexes are attached to a business file, hidden relationships of the business environment are revealed. Clusters thus provide detailed understanding of businesses by summarizing their "lifestyles."

Business cluster analysis can also incorporate consumer factors to provide an additional dimension to the picture. A correlation exists between the location of a business and the consumer behavior in the same location. The final demand of consumers can define the commerce area's footprint.

By incorporating the consumer component, business clusters can reveal the hidden relationships of the surrounding economy. Additional matches allow business owners and their employees who purchase to be linked to their home addresses. This results in a descriptive profile giving expanded information on consumption, media usage, and credit behavior.

Business clusters provide meaning to the thousands of variables and hidden relationships in the business ecosystem. They allow the zeroing-in of target markets necessary to survive and thrive. Business-to-business marketers can identify their best customers, increase market penetration, and boost advertising effectiveness. They can optimize location of markets (identified by ZIP code areas), target new customers more precisely, and more clearly visualize their markets for better strategic decision making.

Other Industrial Market Segmentation Criteria

We can also categorize industrial organizations by financial strength or size as well as in terms of number of employees and/or sales volume. Geographic data also is often used, including city size and location.

Other criteria differentiate form of ownership and whether the enterprise is a headquarters or branch office, a parent or a subsidiary. A proven predictor for many business-to-business direct marketers, too, is the extent of telephone directory Yellow Pages advertising.

Direct marketers must appeal not only to organizations but to individuals within organizations. Purchasing agents alone do not generate demand. More likely, engineers, chemists, architects, production managers, and a host of other specialists make joint decisions. Personalities and demographics of these decision makers and influencers are now also becoming a basis for market segmentation. With data on contacts within the business, further market segmentation based on titles and utility of the function can enhance response rates. Experimentation by IBM has justified the acquisition of such data and direct response copy has been versioned to appeal to, as examples, "scientists" or "creatives" or "egocentrics."

When all is said and done, certainly the most important basis for business-to-business market segmentation is an industrial organization's own customer list including prior purchase behavior, recency/frequency/monetary scoring, and each customer's own demographic profile.

USING A DATABASE TO IDENTIFY B2B MARKETS

In this section, we present a hypothetical example to illustrate the process of analyzing customer data in order to segment an industrial market. It is an amalgamation of many experiences. Don't try to identify the organization. It exists nowhere but in our imagination! The name of the hypothetical organization is Computer Software and Hardware (CSH). It is a provider as well as a producer of products described in the company's name. Many business-to-business firms operate like this one, through resellers as well as direct.

CSH produces and/or provides a variety of product lines: personal, mid-range, and mainframe computers; storage devices; networking; and operating and applications software. It has learned that market segmentation varies by product line and that sequencing as well as recency/frequency/monetary (RFM) attributes of purchase transactions can be predictors of future sales. Distribution of CSH products is multichannel. Its primary channel is through intermediaries including computer dealers, discount retailers, and full-service department stores. It sells and services these middlemen through its own sales force, which also calls on selected organizations who purchase direct from CSH. Direct response advertising is used to create retail traffic for its intermediaries as well as to generate leads for its own sales force. For small businesses, a mail-order catalog, CSH Direct, is employed, along with a Web site.

CSH sells in both consumer *and* industrial markets, so its direct marketing embraces both business-to-business and business-to-consumer activities. Its database includes those who buy direct from it as well as those who buy from resellers. These buyers return warranty and registration information direct to CSH. Salespersons provide information, too. Transactions are recorded. Enhancements to the database, such as industry classification, are provided from outside sources.

As one step in profiling its present customers in the industrial market, CSH looks at the characteristics of these firms. Some of these variables, which are illustrative only and are not all-inclusive, are shown in Figure 13-5. Each organization needs to determine that data which is useful for market segmentation and predicting future response. Certain data, such as credit evaluation, are enhancements garnered from other databases.

Data is presented in the form of frequency distributions. The frequency of occurrence of a characteristic, such as years in business, is shown in a banded table as a percentage of all customers. Analysis of demographics has been quite valuable to CSH for identifying prospective customers who have similar characteristics. Keep in mind, however, that this is a snapshot of present customers, and is not always indicative of response to an offer.

There are many ways to segment an industrial market, such as according to SIC code or size of firm. However, if one is selling computer products to businesses, not all are prospects. So, CSH looks for *other* qualifiers. Prior actions taken can be one such qualifier. The demographics of consumers in the area of a firm's location, as described in Ruf's business clusters, are others.

Figure 13-6 visualizes certain ways in which CSH has been able to perform market segmentation through identifying groups according to their transaction history with the organization, as derived from the CSH customer database. These are representative of a larger variety of possibilities which they have considered.

FIGURE 13-5 Industrial Market Frequency Distribution of Selected Variables

SIC Code	Description	#	%
1521	Genl Bldg Cntrctrs	1,082	4.86%
3900	Manufacturers-Misc	1,233	5.54%
4000	Trnsp/Comm/PbUtl	911	4.09%
5081	Whlsl-Cml ch&Eqp	1,169	5.25%
5311	Department Stores	1,130	5.07%
5961	Mail Order Houses	195	0.88%
5943	OfficeSupplyStores	256	1.15%
5999	Computer Stores	577	2.59%
6000	Finance/Ins/RlEst	1,308	5.87%
7011	Hotels & Motels	749	3.36%
7311	Advert'g Agencies	894	4.01%
7321	Credit Report & Coll	804	3.61%
7331`	Direct Mail Advert'g	1,480	6.64%
7372	ComputerSftwrSvcs	1,757	7.89%
7374	Data Proces'g Svcs	1,734	7.78%
7379	Computer Rltd Svcs	1,779	7.99%
7399	Business Services	1,707	7.66%
8911	Eng'g&Archit Svcs	1,732	7.78%
8931	Acct'gAudit&Bkp'g	1,777	7.98%
		22,274	100.00%

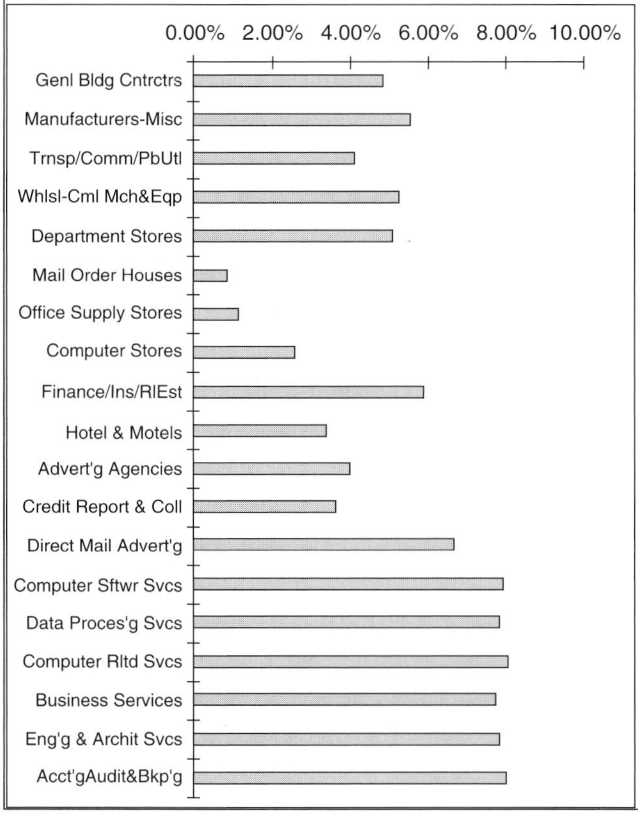

YrsInBiz:	#	%
Under 1	2,589	11.62%
1 to 5	8,770	39.37%
6 to 10	7,768	34.87%
Over 10	3,147	14.13%
	22,274	100.00%

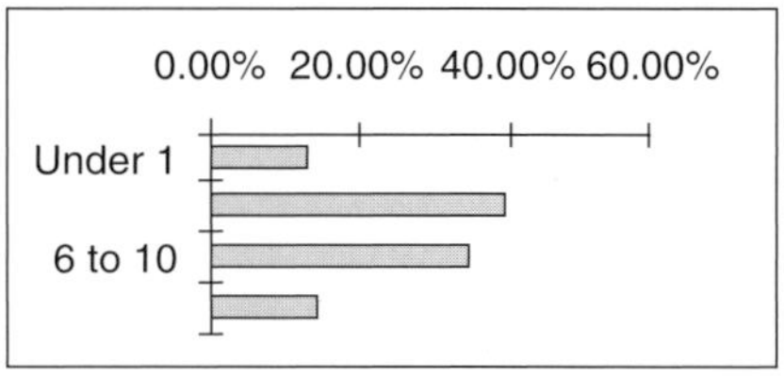

Employs	#	%
1 to 10	8,660	38.88%
11 to 25	5,324	23.90%
26 to 100	4,743	21.29%
101 to 500	2,526	11.34%
501 plus	1,021	4.58%
	22,274	100.00%

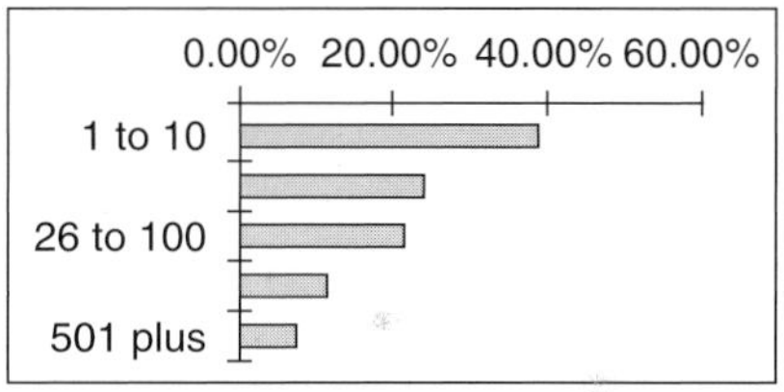

CredtEvl	#	%
Not Eval	8,938	40.13%
Good	8,748	39.27%
Reasnabl	2,410	10.82%
Pot'l Risk	877	3.94%
Prob Risk	617	2.77%
SignifRisk	572	2.57%
Seri's Risk	112	0.50%

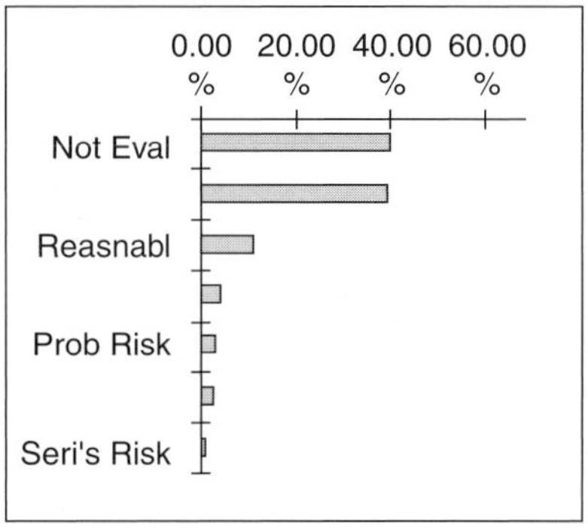

FIGURE 13-6 Industrial Market Segmentation by Product, Sequence, and Source of Purchase

Product Lines and Sequencing	All Product Lines Combined		First Purchase from CHS		Second Purchase (First:Hardware)		Of Those Who Did	Second Purchase (First:Software)		Of Those Who Did
	#	%	#	%	#	%	%	#	%	%
Product Line:										
Personal Comp's	386,681	32.82%	197,973	38.09%	37,349	14.19%	18.73%	85,243	33.23%	41.13%
Mid-rangeComp's	171,058	14.52%	27,558	5.30%	19,866	7.55%	9.96%	14,341	5.59%	6.92%
MainframeComp's	25,712	2.18%	7,718	1.48%	1,034	0.39%	0.52%	109	0.04%	0.05%
Storage Devices	37,949	3.22%	10,491	2.02%	4,453	1.69%	2.23%	2,034	0.79%	0.98%
Networks	32,681	2.77%	19,509	3.75%	9,362	3.56%	4.69%	9,093	3.55%	4.39%
Operat'g Software	271,058	23.01%	118,213	22.74%	30,809	11.70%	15.45%	19,138	7.46%	9.23%
Applic'n Software	252,949	21.47%	138,278	26.61%	96,536	36.67%	48.41%	77,315	30.14%	37.30%
No Second Purch	na	na	na	na	63,840	24.25%	na	49,218	19.19%	na
	1,178,088	100.00%	519,740	100.00%	263,249	100.00%	100.00%	256,491	100.00%	100.00%
Source:										
DM Lead	829,054	70.37%	417,874	80.40%	156,377	59.40%	na	169,223	65.98%	na
Mail order	66,176	5.62%	41,630	8.01%	13,994	5.32%	na	11,348	4.42%	na
Salesperson	282,858	24.01%	60,236	11.59%	92,878	35.28%	na	75,920	29.60%	na
	1,178,088	100.00%	519,740	100.00%	263,249	100.00%	na	256,491	100.00%	na

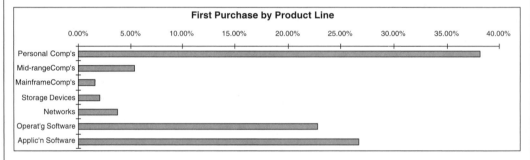

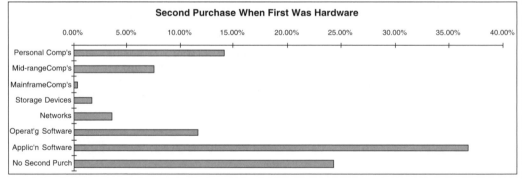

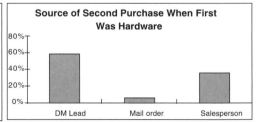

Illustrated in Figure 13-6 is a distribution of first purchases from CSH by new customers according to its seven product lines, with personal computers accounting for 38.09 percent of these. CSH also learned the importance of sequencing in cross-selling to active customers, noting that 18.73 percent of second purchases were of personal computers among those who had initially purchased hardware. Among customers first purchasing software, however, 41.13 percent of second purchases were for personal computers.

From analysis of Figure 13-6, CSH learned to direct its ongoing promotion, whether it was lead-generation direct mail or calls by salespersons, only to customers most likely to be interested in what is being offered. Since those customers whose first purchase was of hardware products had shown a propensity for their second purchase to most likely be applications software, promotion to follow-up first purchases featured such software.

The source of ongoing purchases—direct-mail leads, mail order, Web site visits, salesperson calls—was found by CSH to be an important consideration, too. Personal follow-ups by the CSH sales force were more productive in generating second purchases. Direct-mail leads were more productive for qualifying first-time buyers.

CSH knows that a major objective of direct marketing, first, is acquisition of new customers, and then development of continuing relationships with these customers. They also are adept at continuity selling, the renewal of initial sales. They also are adept at cross-selling, the sale of additional and related products. Further analysis of the CSH customer database provides the information shown in Figure 13-7. This will become input for later calculation of the lifetime value of their customers (LTV), as described in Chapter 3.

The good news for them, as derived from Figure 13-7, is three-fold: (1) customer attrition declines over time; (2) frequency of purchases increases over time; (3) average revenue per purchase increases as customers remain active.

FIGURE 13-7 CSH Customer Continuity, Purchase Frequency, and Average Revenue

CSH Customer Continuity	1st Purchase	2nd Purchase	3rd Purchase	4th Purchase	5th Purchase	Total 2++
# Customer Purchases	519,740	406,682	335,279	298,151	279,886	1,319,998
% of First Purchase	100.00%	78.25%	64.51%	57.37%	53.85%	253.97%
% of Prior Purchase	100.00%	78.25%	82.44%	88.93%	93.87%	na
Avg Time Lapse (Months)	na	14.54	13.77	12.88	12.12	53.31
Avg Rev/Purchase	$2,637	$2,746	$2,847	$2,938	$3,033	$11,564

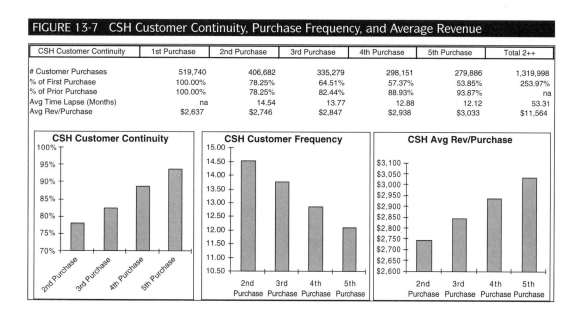

Summary

Business-to-business (B2B) direct marketing is the process of providing goods and services to industrial market intermediaries, as opposed to ultimate consumers. According to the Direct Marketing Association's ongoing Economic Impact survey, the utilization of the tools and techniques of direct marketing by B2B organizations is growing at a rate of more than 10 percent a year, nearly double the growth rate of total industrial sales.

Direct marketing plays an important role in B2B distribution. This is not so much in the "direct" sense of bypassing the middleman as in the "directed" sense of targeting prospects. The salesperson is, in fact, an important adjunct in the direct marketing process.

We differentiate industrial goods from consumer goods based on their ultimate use. In the case of consumer goods, the buyer usually visits the seller, for example, a clothing store. The opposite is true of industrial goods; the seller usually comes to the buyer. Although the number of industrial buying organizations is but a fraction of the number of consumers and households, the volume of B2B revenue is much greater

In much the same way that consumer markets are described in terms of geographics, demographics, psychographics, and actions taken, B2B direct marketers segment markets through industry classification systems, input-output analysis, the global positioning system, business clusters, and other criteria such as financial strength, size, number of employees, sales volume, and geographic location. Other criteria differentiate whether the enterprise is a headquarters or branch office, a parent or a subsidiaries as well as form of -ownership,

Personalities and demographics of decision makers and influencers are now also becoming a basis for market segmentation. With data available on contacts within the business, further segmentation on titles and utility of the function can enhance response rates. The most important basis for business-to-business market segmentation is a firm's own customer profile including prior purchases.

Business-to-business direct marketers have become quite adept at utilizing databases to generate leads for personal sales follow-up, to encourage browsing of their informative Web sites, and to consummate direct sales.

Key Terms

- business-to-business (B2B) direct marketing, 318
- industrial goods, 318
- raw materials, 320
- fabricated materials, 320
- installations, 320
- accessory equipment, 320

- operating supplies, 320
- Standard Industrial Classification (SIC), 326
- North American Industrial Classification System (NAICS), 328
- input-output analysis, 328

- Global Positioning System (GPS), 329
- Topologically Integrated Geographic Encoding Referencing (TIGER), 329
- business clusters, 329

Review Questions

1. Distinguish between consumer and industrial markets.
2. Name and define the different types of industrial goods.
3. What distinguishes industrial demand from consumer demand?
4. What are major factors contributing to the increasing use of the tools and techniques of

direct marketing in business-to-business distribution?

5. List similarities between consumer and industrial market definition (i.e., age of consumer versus age of business).
6. What does the term *lead generation* mean?
7. How does the Internet fit into business-to-business direct marketing?
8. Name some challenges facing business-to-business marketers.
9. Describe the U.S. Commerce Department's long-time system of Standard Industrial Classification (SIC). What is its key feature relative to the emerging North American Industrial Classification System (NAICS)?
10. Describe input-output matrices and show how these can be effectively utilized by direct marketers.
11. What is the Census Bureau's TIGER system? What does acronym TIGER stand for?

Exercise

Because of your knowledge of direct marketing, you've just been promoted to a sales representative position with a large pharmaceutical company. They want you to recommend different ways they can implement direct marketing techniques when marketing their prescription drugs to physicians. Outline the various uses of direct marketing you would recommend to the company and explain what each activity will produce.

CASE: A BUSINESS-TO-BUSINESS DATABASE-DRIVEN SALES PROGRAM

OVERVIEW

The purpose of this case study is to apply certain of the concepts described in this chapter to actual practice. It demonstrates how the tools and techniques of direct marketing have been applied in a real-world business-to-business situation.

Direct marketing, emerging as it has from mail-order selling, has been mainly applied to consumer markets. Recently—and especially since introduction of the Internet and its World Wide Web—industrial organizations have seen its relevance in their business-to-business marketing. This case is a presentation of a true experience—even though the actual manufacturer of corporate aircraft prefers anonymity—showing that the principles of large-purchase prospect qualification are not unlike mail-order customer generation and cultivation.

CASE

A manufacturer of corporate aircraft developed a state-of-the-art database of key prospects for its high-cost, limited-demand products. It used this database to generate qualified leads for follow-up by its dealers, who were involved in this direct marketing process every step of the way.

The database was a composite derived and enhanced from many independent sources. It identified key characteristics of each prospect organization: industry, size, length of time in business, number of employees, sales revenues, and other relevant factors. It also identified key decision makers by name and title along with their addresses and telephone numbers.

Matching this file to other sources provided key data about aircraft ownership, prior or current, such as the manufacturer of and the type of aircraft, as well as its age.

The manufacturer's own database was scanned, and mail/telephone surveys authenticated and augmented this information. Dealers were called in to verify facts of the compilation. Each dealer then ended up with a comprehensive notebook containing a full page of information to qualify each prospect.

The direct mail sent to generate meaningful leads on behalf of the dealers was itself a textbook model. Benefit-oriented direct response copy addressed the interests of the individual recipient, be that the chief executive officer, the chief pilot, or the chief financial officer. Relevant in copy, too, was whether the organization now owned the manufacturer's or a competitor's aircraft or does not own aircraft now or used to, but not at this time. The first two paragraphs of a personalized lead-generation letter sent to a Chief Executive Officer, for example, read

Would you be interested in a business tool that would give you greater control of your own time and offer you as much as a month of additional productive time each year? If so, let me send you, at no obligation, a new booklet titled *Choosing a Business Aircraft*.

With this complimentary guide, you can define your firm's travel needs and see what type of airplane can help you meet those needs. You can determine what type of aircraft is ideally suited to your business, offering the best balance of comfort and performance.

The Direct Response Program's Objectives
The aircraft manufacturer first sought to define its objectives, which were to

- Provide an organized and planned system of contacts.
- Produce qualified leads for dealers from both aircraft-user and nonuser segments.

- Maintain "grassroots" presence in local market areas where business happens.
- Create a positive image from which to build a long-term customer affinity.
- Build a database providing ability to segment prospects, differentiate marketing approaches by segment, and create predictive models for scoring prospective buyers.
- Measure both costs and results.
- Expand the program with confidence.

Steps Involved in Building a Successful Sales-Support Program

The firm next developed a "road map" for achieving its objectives, seeking to

> ***Step 1.*** Involve sales managers in preplanning.
>
> ***Step 2.*** Define short-term and long-term marketing objectives.
>
> ***Step 3.*** Set interim goals to measure the program's effectiveness.
>
> ***Step 4.*** Profile current customers; develop prospect assumptions.
>
> ***Step 5.*** Lay the foundation for a relational database.
>
> ***Step 6.*** Validate prospect assumptions with a survey mailing.
>
> ***Step 7.*** Develop offer strategy.
>
> ***Step 8.*** Test lead-generation mailings in selected marketing areas.
>
> ***Step 9.*** Measure and analyze test results using a scoring model.
>
> ***Step 10.*** Roll out with mailings that meet or exceed break even.
>
> ***Step 11.*** Augment with direct response ads in selected publications.
>
> ***Step 12.*** Invite high-scoring prospects to special events.

Determination of Criteria to be Used for Evaluating Sales Leads

Insistent on its need for measurement and accountability, the firm set forth these criteria for evaluating its program to generate sales leads:

- Why does the prospect need a corporate aircraft?
- What alternatives are being considered?
- What is the prospect's financial status?
- Where is the prospect in the decision-making process?
- Who are the decision makers and who are the influencers?
- What makes/models, new/used, aircraft are being considered?
- When does the prospect plan on reaching a decision?

Dealers' Perceptions of Prospective Customers

It was important to involve dealers in the process, so they were asked in advance their feelings about the database of prospects being developed, which included

- Companies in growth industries; annual sales of $30+ million.
- Companies in service industries (e.g., advertising agencies, attorneys, developers, architects, engineers, etc.) with sales of $20+ million per year.
- High-volume, low-margin retailers with sales of $100+ million per year.

Dealers' Perceptions of Decision-Making Roles

Dealers were also asked to authenticate these perceived decision makers:

- ***Board of directors:*** Ultimate decision makers.
- ***Chief executive officer/president:*** Must sell this person first. In turn, he or she will sell to Board of Directors if given sufficient justification. This person regards an airplane as a "time servant" that will allow him or her to do more by being more efficient and expects the airplane to pay for itself. He or she intends to use an airplane to transport key personnel; mid-management people will continue using commercial carriers.
- ***Chief financial officer:*** Must sell this person second. The CFO is concerned about costs, risks, and asset value.

Marketing Database: Secondary Sources
It was determined that compilation of the proposed prospect database would merge data from a variety of sources, including

- **Dun's Marketing Services:** All U.S. corporations with annual sales volume of $30+ million (including state governments, hospitals, universities, public utilities, and corporate branches with 1,000 or more employees), financial institutions, service businesses, developers, and computer facilities with annual sales of $20+ million.
- **FGL Associates:** U.S. corporations that operated jets, turbo props, and turbine helicopters.
- **AvData:** U.S. corporations that own and/or operate Class 5, 6, and 7 piston aircraft that are less than 11 years old (excluding aircraft registered to individuals).
- **Aircraft Bluebook Corp.:** Aircraft serial numbers by year for all manufacturers.
- **Time, Inc.:** Fortune 500 current listing of the largest industrial corporations.
- **Goldhirsh Group:** INC 500 current listing of the 500 leading growth companies.
- **Value Line:** Current listing of the top 50 growth industries.

Marketing Database: Primary Sources
Mindful of the important role that dealers would play at the point of sale, they were asked to review, in their own territories, the secondary sources listed and augment them:

- Dealers' validation of secondary sources of prospect data.
- Survey mailings to both owner and non-owner companies
- Direct mail questionnaire information.
- Outbound telemarketing follow-up calls to mail recipients
- Dealers' sales call reports.
- Lead-generation direct-mail responses.

Direct Response Promotion Mailings to the Marketing Database
The database stage was set and now the firm created its direct-mail promotion:

- Mailings consisted of an outside envelope, letter, and postage-paid business reply card.
- Letters were versioned to the needs of and the benefits to be derived by chief executive officers, chief financial officers, chief pilots, and chief maintenance officers.
- Letters were versioned between current, former, and nonowners of aircraft; they were also versioned between owners of the manufacturer's product and competitive products.
- Letters could also be versioned according to the current maintenance scheduled of owned aircraft.

Direct Response Promotion Mailings Roll-Out Results
When all was said and done, these were actual results of a highly successful program:

- From about 42,000 mailings to the meticulously compiled and qualified database, there were 3,560 respondents . . . a response rate of 8.5 percent.
- Sixty-one percent of the respondents were chief executive officers.
- Sixty-one percent of these chief executive officers were nonowners.

Source: This model program was conceived and developed by Hogan & Associates, Inc., Direct Marketing Services, 5536 Tahoe Lane, Fairway, KS 66205–3308. It is presented with permission. While the program was eminently successful, it was dropped when the manufacturer's traditional advertising agency convinced it that budget could be more productively applied to brand/image advertising. The manufacturer, now in the process of reinstating the program, is unnamed but the facts of this case are real. ∎

Case Discussion Questions

After studying this case, you should be prepared to verbalize just how the tools and techniques of direct marketing utilized in consumer markets can be applied to industrial markets by business-to-business direct marketers. Discuss the specific concepts and principles.

Notes

1. *The Statistical Fact Book 2000* (New York: Direct Marketing Association, Inc., 2000), 254.
2. Ibid.
3. Martin Baier, Kurtis M. Ruf, and Goutam Chakraborty, *Contemporary Database Marketing: Concepts and Applications* (Homewood, IL: Racom Communications, 2002), 192–194.

"Don't throw it away . . . raise funds today!!!" was the message on the flyer the elementary school boy brought home to his parents. It continued . . . "Did you know that over 250 million pounds of empty cartridges are thrown into our landfills annually? . . . Reports predict that by 2005 as many as 500 million cell phones will be headed for our landfills!" The flyer contained an email address, toll-free number, and Web site address (www.cfktoday.com) of an organization called Cartridges for Kids® (CFK) who offers educational and environmentally friendly recycling fundraising programs to schools and organizations. CFK is employing several direct marketing techniques to create awareness of its programs, secure business sponsors, enroll schools and organizations in its fundraising program, and educate children and adults about the value of recycling. That's one example of how direct marketing can work for nonprofit causes and that is the topic of this chapter.

Whether an organization is for profit or not for profit, direct marketing strategies still apply. In fact, direct marketing is ideal for nonprofit organizations since it is measurable, accountable, targeted, cost-effective, and requires a direct response—qualities that are all of particular importance to organizations that exist to support and advance a cause. Nonprofit organizations serve as a forum for the creation and distribution of new ideas. These organizations, like hospitals and universities, may deliver services. The American Cancer Society and the March of Dimes are actively supporting advancing medical research in an attempt to find a cure for diseases. Mothers Against Drunk Driving (MADD) is focusing on safety issues. What they all have in common is that they want people to know about their cause and respond to their plea for support. This response could be in the form of a donation to a charitable organization, a vote for a political candidate, or help to achieve any number of an organization's communication objectives. Any nonprofit or governmental organization can effectively use direct marketing to achieve its communication objectives. This chapter is designed to present direct marketing strategies for nonprofit organizations. It will address the important area of fundraising and will also provide numerous examples of successful direct marketing campaigns that have worked for a variety of nonprofit organizations.

DIRECT MARKETING FOR NONPROFIT ORGANIZATIONS

According to a Direct Marketing Association (DMA) study conducted by the WEFA Group, nonprofit organizations rank second in consumer direct marketing sales and ninth in business-to-business direct marketing sales.[1] Just think about that fact the next time a local girl scout asks you to buy a box of cookies or when a local boy scout asks you to purchase a box or jar of popcorn. Nonprofit organizations employ about 80 million people in the United States—therefore, they could be considered the country's largest employer. There were close to 463,640 people employed in direct marketing educational services in 2001, mostly in the telephone sector (195,556). More than 660,569 people worked in direct marketing social services and more than 41,995 in the direct marketing of museums and galleries in 2001.[2] Did you know that 44 percent of all adults volunteer? That represents 83.9 billion American adults.[3] On average, each person volunteers about 3.6 hours a week for an organization for a total of 15.5 billion hours of volunteered time in 2000.[4]

The goal of most nonprofits is to maximize their relationships with their many constituents, including clients, donors, volunteers, and customers. Nonprofit organizations recognize the efficiency of direct marketing as a means of raising funds, driving memberships, and creating greater awareness for their cause. The Direct Marketing Association shows that the nonprofit sector in the United States generated nearly $102.5 billion in funds, memberships, sales, and other revenue using direct and interactive marketing methods.[5] The next section will discuss the different kinds of nonprofit organizations using direct marketing.

Direct Marketing Applications

What nonprofit organizations are employing direct marketing strategies to achieve their goals and objectives? The answer is probably every organization. Most health-concerned organizations, such as the American Cancer Society, the American Heart Association, the American Diabetes Association, and the American Lung Association, are avidly practicing direct marketing to obtain donations to support research for their worthy causes. Organizations concerned with protecting the environment, such as the World Wildlife Fund, Nature Conservancy, and Rails-to-Trails, are using direct marketing. Educational institutions have long relied on direct marketing to obtain student enrollments, offer continuing education courses, raise funds, garner political support, and communicate with alumni and the larger community. Other nonprofit organizations include those concerned with helping our youth, such as Big Brothers Big Sisters of America, Boys Club, and Rappahannock River Rats Youth Hockey Association. Nonprofit organizations also exist to protect women, such as the Miles Foundation and Battered Women Organization, while others exist to provide support to minorities, such as An Achievable Dream.

Most political organizations rely on direct marketing, too. Just take a look at the Direct Marketing Association membership roster and you'll see many political organizations listed from every part of the political spectrum. The National Women's Political Caucus, People for the American Way, Citizens for Free Enterprise, and the Physician's Committee for Quality Medical Care have been shaping public opinion with their direct marketing efforts. So, if you want to be elected to city council, or become mayor of your town, governor of your state, or president of the United States, try direct marketing!

The government has also relied on direct marketing for many of its public interactions. For many years tax refund checks issued by the Internal Revenue Service (IRS) have been accompanied by mail-order forms for U.S. Liberty Coins from the U.S. Mint. In fact, one of the busiest days for the United States Postal Service is April 15th—the day tax returns are due. Just think about the response rate the Internal Revenue Service receives on its annual mailings.

Customer Relationship Building

Regardless of the direct marketing application, most nonprofit organizations look to individual volunteers and private organizations for support. Clients, patrons, donors, members, board members, students, volunteers, the public—they are all *customers;* even if most nonprofit organizations would not refer to them that way, we will throughout this

- Newsletters--informal
- Telephone calls--nonsoliciting
- Video tapes demonstrating the organizations recent work
- On-line computer bulletin board service
- Audio tapes of Executive Board meetings
- Financial reports and strategic plan--copies mailed

FIGURE 14-1 Forms of Direct Marketing Response Communications with Donors

chapter. And while initiating customer relationships is challenging for many nonprofit organizations, maintaining them is the key to success. Building lifetime customer relationships is critical to successful nonprofit direct marketing. For the nonprofit organization, **customer relationship management (CRM)** simply means developing a relationship with donors, thus ensuring their future support.[6] Nonprofit organizations must cultivate relationships with donors by communicating regularly with them and making them feel valued. Figure 14-1 provides some forms of direct response communication that can be used by nonprofit organizations to keep in touch with their customers or donors.

Nonprofit organizations, especially charitable organizations must understand *each* donor, understand what motivates them to contribute their time, talents, and money to the organization's cause. Most people purchase or donate to support a cause and see it advance. People are normally driven in their donation choices by their personal/core values and donating to specific causes helps them to act in accordance with these personal values. Thus, people do not normally give just to help an organization improve its revenue stream. To ensure a customer's long-term support, the nonprofit organization must focus on meeting its customer's needs—instead of its own. Figure 14-2 presents

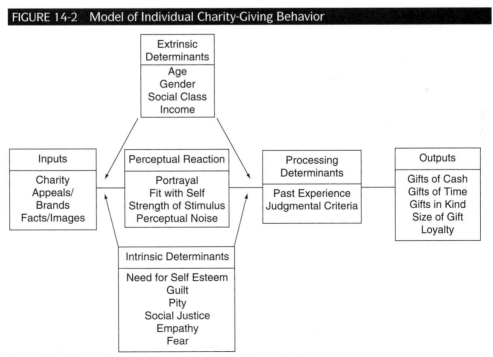

FIGURE 14-2 Model of Individual Charity-Giving Behavior

Source: Model created by Adrian Sargeant. Used with permission.

a model of donor behavior which shows how donors process and act on the appeals made by nonprofit organizations.

The components of this model of a donor's giving behavior includes inputs, perceptual reaction, extrinsic determinants, intrinsic determinants, processing determinants, and outputs.[7]

Inputs

Nonprofit organizations use a variety of fundraising techniques, each an input to the decision-making process, such as rational and emotional appeals, and a variety of direct response media including direct mail, telemarketing, personal selling, radio advertising, and direct response television to influence a donor and encourage a specific action.

Perceptual Reaction

The key variables affecting the way the donor perceives the organization include the portrayal of the individual(s) in need, the fit of the charity with a given donor's self-image, the strength of the stimulus, and the degree to which perceptual noise (any distraction) is present.

Extrinsic Determinants

The demographic profile of the donor/prospect appears to be directly related to both his or her propensity to engage in charitable giving and the level of giving. For example, 60 percent of charitable gifts in the United States of America come from people aged 60 to 76 years old.[8]

Intrinsic Determinants

The intrinsic determinants address the underlying individual motives for electing to support a charity at a given level. These determinants assist donors in filtering out those appeals that are least relevant and helps them decide how much to give. One of the key intrinsic variables is the extent to which the donor feels empathy with the nonprofit organization.

Processing Determinants

The past experience and the evaluation criteria used by the donor will certainly affect the way he or she views the organization and subsequent decisions he or she makes about it. These influences are complex and interrelated—but the direct marketer must explore them in order to understand the donor's decision-making process.

Outputs

Donor outputs can support nonprofit organizations in a number of different ways. Gifts may be monetary donations, gifts of time as a volunteer, or gifts in kind (goods or services given to the nonprofit organization). Other output variables include the level or amount of the gift and the degree of donor loyalty. Donor loyalty is of extreme importance to nonprofit organizations. Research has shown that uncommitted givers (individuals giving a series of single donations) tend to remain loyal to an organization for a period of no more than five years, with a 50-percent attrition rate between the first and second donation. Committed donors tend to remain loyal for somewhat longer, but even then the duration of the relationship extends no further than 6 to 7 years.[9] Therefore, maintaining loyalty is of paramount importance in maximizing the strength and duration of the donor's output.

Next, we'll discuss strategies for maintaining customer relationships once they have been established.

Customer Relationship Maintenance

Nonprofit organizations can effectively maintain and strengthen relationships with their customers by adding a feedback element to each communication form they utilize. Today's customers want to tell you their opinions and develop their own visions for your organization. Let them. The single most important way to enhance customer relationships is to *listen* to these customers and, while maintaining focus on the organization's mission, incorporate the ideas and suggestions they offer. Provide networking opportunities for them so that they feel a part of your organization. Keep them up to date on your activities. According to a recent survey, donors agreed that it was very important to be kept up to date on a nonprofit's activities. The following methods for providing this update were rated most desirable:[10]

- Videos sent every three or four months, showing some of the organization's recent work;
- On-line computer bulletin board services to give donors information and let them ask questions and receive answers electronically;
- Tapes of the organization's board meetings;
- Periodic phone calls, not asking for money but letting donors know what the organization is doing;
- Copies of the organization's internal documents, such as financial reports and strategic plans; and
- Newsletters sent regularly to notify donors about the work, needs, and impact of the organization.

While it may seem complicated, direct marketing in the service of customer relationship management is the most effective way to satisfy the needs of a nonprofit organization's current customers.

As we saw in Chapter 3, focusing on customer retention is far less costly and much more productive than trying to obtain new customers. CRM is well suited for nonprofit organizations with limited budgets. It can initiate and cultivate relationships, encourage charitable giving, and foster partnerships with businesses in the local community to join in the support of the nonprofit organization's cause. Beyond customer retention, cultivating partnerships with businesses is another way to support a nonprofit organization's cause. The next section will investigate that avenue.

Corporate Partnerships

For nonprofit organizations, CRM hasn't always meant customer relationship management. In fact, for years it meant "cause-related marketing." **Cause-related marketing** is defined as a commercial activity by which businesses and charities or causes form a partnership with each other to market an image, product, or service for mutual benefit.[11] These cause-related marketing partnerships may include more than one partner.

For decades, corporations and nonprofit organizations have been forming partnerships to create innovative cause marketing campaigns. However, in the past, many nonprofit organizations found themselves in uncharted waters, with considerable demands for information, strategic plans, and program details made on them in return for this private-sector funding. Thus, corporate partnerships required too much effort to attempt. Today these nonprofit organizations have become more savvy marketers and understand the workings of the corporate community. Therefore, cause-related marketing is again on the rise. In fact, corporate executives are commonly knocking on the doors of nonprofit organizations to initiate business relationships.

Linking with a charity or cause can bring significant benefits for both the business and nonprofit organization. Greater awareness and support for both is one of the likely benefits. Examples of cause-related marketing are all around us. There are many companies sponsoring local marathons, 5K and 10K races, walkathons, and other events in support of national organizations such as the American Cancer Society, March of Dimes, or the Cystic Fibrosis Foundation. There are also many companies that sponsor special events to support local organizations, such as a local rehabilitation center, youth group, or a local religious organization. In addition, many manufacturers exercise cause-related marketing by donating a set amount to select charitable organizations for each product or service sold. For example, when consumers purchase Purina cat food, the company makes a donation to the American Association of Zoological Parks and Aquariums. When consumers rent automobiles from Dollar-Rent A-Car, they may also be supporting Mothers Against Drunk Driving. Even local grocery stores and discount stores support local schools. These programs are normally linked to customer loyalty card programs through which the retailer allows a percentage of the customer's store purchases to be donated to the school of the customer's choice. Figure 14-3 provides some specific examples of business–nonprofit alliances.

Nonprofit organizations have long used direct marketing activities in building donor relationships, maintaining and strengthening these relationships, and establishing corporate partnerships to advance their respective causes. Nonprofits have effectively used direct marketing methods in their fundraising efforts as well. Let's now look at direct marketing fundraising strategies used by nonprofit organizations.

FUNDRAISING

The basic foundation of all good fundraising is marketing, and all fundraisers are involved in marketing campaigns. It has been said that "fundraisers are in the vanguard of direct marketing because their's is one of the most competitive situations."[12] With so much competition out there, how does a person or an organization determine whom to support? What are the primary causes the public supports? According to the Direct Marketing Association, charities reported receiving $212 billion in 2001.[13] This marks an increase of more than $8 billion from the $203.45 billion that charities reported receiving in 1999.[14] Reasons for the increased generosity of Americans may be attributed in part to the terrorist attacks of September 11, 2001. According to survey research, 70 percent of Americans reported some form of charitable involvement in response to September 11th and 73 percent of September 11th givers say they will continue to give as much or more than they usually give to other charities.[15] Figure 14-4 provides a breakdown of the contributions received by type of recipient organization. Religious organizations received the overwhelming majority of donations, with educational institutions coming in a distant second place.

BUSINESS PARTNER	NONPROFIT PARTNER	DESCRIPTION
Walt Disney Co.	Habitat for Humanity	Walt Disney donated $70,000 for construction of a townhouse in Burbank, California.
Florida Department of Citrus	American Cancer Society	American Cancer Society's logo has been used to promote the role of orange products in preventing cancer.
Nabisco	American Zoo Aquarium Association	In 1995, Nabisco produced a special edition of its Barnum's Animal Crackers. Five cents from the sale of each box up to $100,000 was donated.
SC Johnson Wax	15th Annual Night Out Against Crime	In 1998, SC Johnson Wax agreed to pledge up to $200,000 based on consumers coupon redemption for various products (Glade, Ziplock, Shout).
Borders Bookstores	National Literacy Nonprofit Organization, Reading Is Fundamental (RIF) and local libraries	At the checkout, Borders asks each customer to donate $1. On a quarterly basis, Borders Bookstores matches customer donations and gives money to targeted nonprofit organizations.

FIGURE 14-3 Examples of Business–Nonprofit Alliances

Research shows that 89 percent of American households donate to nonprofit organizations and the average annual contribution for contributors is $1,620.[16] With that much money at stake, nonprofit organizations cannot afford not to practice savvy direct marketing fundraising techniques in an attempt to garner support for its worthy cause.

Basic Fundraising Principles

Bob Stone, direct marketing guru and member of the Direct Marketing Hall of Fame, presented the classic way to raise funds for a worthy cause. His advice was to take the following three-step approach:[17]

> *Step 1:* Form a committee of influentials to make contacts with potential contributors, establishing a targeted contribution amount for each potential donor.
>
> *Step 2:* Mount a direct response campaign to a list of identified prospective contributors.
>
> *Step 3:* Organize a follow-up campaign to support the initial direct response campaign and/or to reach those who have not responded to the direct-mail campaign.

ORGANIZATION	AMOUNT ($ IN BILLIONS)	% OF TOTAL
Religious	$80.96	38.2
Education	31.84	15.0
Human Services	20.71	9.8
Health	18.43	8.7
Arts, Culture & Humanities	12.14	5.7
Public/Society Benefit	11.82	5.6
Environment/Wildlife	6.41	3.0
International Affairs	4.14	2.0
Other	25.55	12.0
TOTAL	$212.00	100.00%

FIGURE 14-4   Contributions Received by Type of Recipient Organization

Source: "AAFRC Trust for Philanthropy/Giving USA 2002," *The Statistical Fact Book 2002*, 24th ed. (New York: The Direct Marketing Association, Inc., 2002), 232.

This three-step approach is still applicable today, as is the following eight-step fundraising plan for nonprofit organizations:[18]

Step 1: Listen to your donors.   It is vital that your donors feel that you listen to them and that their input makes a difference in the operation of the nonprofit organization. Involving them as partners in solving your organization's problems often leads them to become long-time supporters, rather than one-time funders.

Step 2: Keep your mission in mind.   Each nonprofit organization must communicate its mission clearly and implement its goals and objectives effectively. In addition, it must remember that the organizational mission will assist it in building long-term relationships with donors.

Step 3: Tell your story vividly.   The best people to tell the story of a nonprofit organization are volunteers and clients. Include them. Their personal, heartfelt experiences make a unique impact on potential donors. Put these stories in brochures and videos and on Web pages. Making these stories both memorable and credible will yield more dollars from donors.

Step 4: Go high-tech, but stay people focused.   Using the Internet to communicate with a vast number of donors and volunteers is both fast and efficient. If the organization doesn't have a Web site, it should create one. A homepage is a good way to stay in touch with donors and volunteers and strengthen relationships with them.

Step 5: Let donors fund projects.   It is well known that when donors know exactly what their donations are being used for, they are much more generous.

People like to feel they are helping to accomplish something good with the money they donate . . . it goes back to *why* they give in the first place. To that end, the nonprofit organization should keep its "wish list" updated, in case a donor inquires about the organization's current needs. See Figure 14-5 for some examples of wish lists that have been included in past newsletters mailed to the

FIGURE 14-5   Rescue Mission Wish Lists

MISSION NEEDS

Pine-Sol
Bleach
Toilet Paper

Please consider clipping this out for your next trip to the grocery store.

MISSION NEEDS

Cold & Flu Medicines
Stocking caps & Gloves
Paper towels & Toilet Paper

Please consider clipping this out for your next trip to the grocery store.

MISSION NEEDS

Pork & Beans
Canned tomatoes
Canned spaghetti sauce
Sugar
Paper towels
Toilet Paper

Please consider clipping this out for your next trip to the grocery store.

regular donors of the Peninsula Rescue Mission in Virginia. Note that the items on each wish list vary and that the Peninsula Rescue Mission only asks for a few items at any given time.

Step 6: Target your audience. Using technology and databases to target the best possible list of customers is the most efficient method of selecting who will receive a fundraising request. In fact, when database technology is used properly, the nonprofit organization can send out several different fundraising letters requesting different amounts from targeted donors—all at the same time.

Step 7: Involve the CEO and Board of Directors. Fundraising is part of the job description of the CEO as leader, facilitator, and communicator. In fact, many potential donors will not give unless the CEO makes the solicitation. Likewise, fundraising should be a part of every board member's job, and board members should be the first to make donations to the organization.

Step 8: Launch a fundraising campaign. A good fundraising campaign should go beyond raising money and focus on building the reputation of the nonprofit organization. Creating brochures and newsletters, hosting special events, and distributing press releases are some of the ways to reinforce the reputation of the organization and communicate with the organization's many different constituents as well as the general public.

Stone noted some additional fundraising facts to keep in mind as nonprofit organizations develop their fundraising campaigns:[19]

- The highest percentage of response in a fundraising effort comes from previous contributors.
- Favorable response to telephone solicitations usually can be enhanced when calls are made by people of stature in a community or in an industry.
- People respond best to emotional appeals when they are backed by a rationale for giving. See Figure 14-6 for some examples of emotional appeals.
- People tend to respond more readily to appeals for specific projects rather than to appeals for general needs. For example, an elementary school's request for funds to help build a new playground for the children is a more effective appeal than a request to help reduce the school's debt.
- When pledges are made by telephone, 75 to 80 percent of the pledges will be collected, if they are properly followed up.
- The total amount pledged tends to be greater when a multipayment plan is offered.
- The average contribution tends to increase when specific contribution amounts are suggested. Example: "You contributed $15 last year. May we suggest you contribute $20 this year to help cover our expanded needs."

FIGURE 14-6   Examples of Emotional Fundraising Appeals

"Every minute of every day there are 14 incidents of child abuse or domestic violence happening somewhere in this country."

"In the few seconds it took you to open and read this letter, four children died from the effects of malnutrition or disease somewhere in the world."

- Setting a specific date for meeting a fundraising goal tends to increase response and total contributions.

The Fundraising Appeal

While these fundraising basics might help the nonprofit organization get started in its fundraising efforts, most fundraising experts agree that crafting the *right* appeal is the first priority in fundraising and is of utmost importance to the success of a fundraising campaign. According to fundraising expert Kay Partney Lautman, there are five important elements in any fundraising appeal. They are[20]

1. *Audience/lists/segmentation.* The single most important element of any fundraising appeal is choosing the audience through careful selection of lists of people who believe as you do and who have donated or spent money toward a given cause as evidence of their interest.
2. *Basic membership offer/suggested gift.* Determine the appropriate gift amount to request from your donors or members. To arrive at this magic number, most experts recommend testing various dollar amounts to determine which level(s) yield the highest response rate.
3. *Copy.* Writing effective copy for any fundraising appeal is more of an art than a science. What works for one cause, may not work for another. Therefore, once again, savvy nonprofit organizations will conduct tests or experiments to determine which copy is the most effective for the cause. Once you have effective copy, you can use it again and again to establish consistency and credibility with the message. Figure 14-7 presents several copywriting tips for organizations to follow when writing copy to solicit funds. You can think of these as "the etiquette of asking for donations."
4. *Format/presentation.* The format of the fundraising, especially if it is a direct-mail package, determines whether or not the target donor will open and read the appeal. The most important thing to remember when creating the format is to "keep it simple." The response device in particular should be designed so that it is easy to understand and fill out.
5. *Premiums/benefits.* Selecting affordable premiums is crucial to the appeal. As we discussed earlier in Chapter 6, a premium can enhance the appeal of the offer and entice the recipient to take the action requested. Use the premiums other nonprofit organizations offer as no more than a starting point for generating ideas. Careful testing is recommended. The following award-winning campaign illustrates the importance of testing premiums.

Despite what many people think, nonprofit organizations are not always seeking money. Sometimes they want what is even harder to come by: a commitment. Nonprofit organizations realize the great value of long-term commitments from donors. It is one thing to obtain a single monetary donation, but to secure a long-term commitment to help move a particular cause forward in the future is another thing. Additionally, nonprofit organizations recognize the great value of dedicated volunteers. The dollar value of a volunteer hour to an organization was $15.40 in 2000, while the total assigned dollar value of volunteer time, excluding informal volunteering was $239.2 billion in 2000.[21]

NEVER, NEVER, NEVER ...

- Send a request to "Dear Friend"
- Ask the right donor for the wrong thing
- Ask the right donor at the wrong time
- Assume you're the only one asking
- Disregard donor's guidelines for giving
- Bypass the decision maker
- Be a pest
- Whine at those who turn you down
- Be too confident to thank donors
- Contact the donor only for money

ALWAYS, ALWAYS, ALWAYS ...

- Look for ways to collaborate
- Do a quality control check
- Send a request to the right person
- Give plenty of lead time
- Follow up on requests
- Ask donors how you can show your appreciation
- Strengthen relationships even if you're turned down
- Seize an opportunity to involve donors
- Follow the *Golden Rule ... Do unto others!*

FIGURE 14-7 The Etiquette of Asking for Donations: Nonprofit Direct Marketing

Source: Adapted from Jean Block, "Don't Let the Gotchas Getcha When Asking for Money or, the Etiquette of Asking," *Nonprofit World* 16, no. 5 (1998): 16–19.

During one holiday season, the Paralyzed Veterans of America (PVA), tested a Christmas music cassette against its usual premium—a Christmas booklet. The challenge was to find a premium that would out-pull the less expensive Christmas booklet with a high-perceived value but not a prohibitively high price. PVA targeted its own house file of active donors in the past 12 months who had given $5 or more. PVA mailed fifty thousand direct-mail packages with the cassette to a random sample of their active donors in November along with an identical number of direct-mail packages containing the booklet to their other active donors.

The results illustrate the testability and trackability of direct mail fundraising. The cassette package, which costs $100,787, generated a 23.3-percent response, brining in $144,541 net income, an average contribution of $24.08 and a low $8.62 cost per response. The control package containing the usual premium (the Christmas booklet) cost $21,890 and pulled a 13.2-percent response with an average gift of $10.45. In conclusion, both premiums were successful in generating funds, although the cassette—as determined by the test results—was a more effective premium to be used for future fundraising campaigns.

Source: Adapted from Greg Gattuso, Elaine Santoro, and George R. Reis, "Holiday Sounds Bring Fund-Raising Cheer," *Fund Raising Management* 27, no. 10 (1996): 13–14.

Thousands of nonprofit organizations are using direct marketing methods to secure volunteers to assist in carrying out their mission. Just check out the Web site of the Make-A-Wish Foundation (www.wish.org) and you will see that volunteers serve as wish granters, fundraisers, special events assistants, and in numerous other capacities in order to help the organization grant the wishes of children with life-threatening medical conditions. Or visit the Web site of Operation Smile (www.operationsmile.org) and you will learn how that organization relies on physicians and other medical professionals who serve as volunteers to provide reconstructive surgery and related health care to indigent children worldwide. There is a nonprofit organization for almost every cause—regardless of whether the cause is medical, environmental, social, educational, or political.

Regardless of what the nonprofit organization is seeking, the right appeal is of great importance for the organization when communicating with potential donors. The appeal must come from an individual (not the organization as a whole) and it should request action for a specific activity. The direct response fundraising message must accomplish the following three things:[22]

1. ***Strike fast.***   Gain the attention of the potential donor in a world where there are so many other organizations clamoring for attention is a challenge. A rule of thumb for attracting attention is to segment your message to your target audience. A couple strategies to attract attention include telling stories and explaining how each person can "make a difference" in a campaign.

2. ***Personally grab and shake.***   The appeal must hit the donor or customer on a personal level. It must motivate them to take action. For example, a person who is an outdoor enthusiast is naturally more prone to make purchases of outdoor equipment and to support organizations that protect the outdoors. H. G. Lewis offers some tips for grabbing and shaking. He points out that examples are more personal and usually generate a greater response than do mere statistics; single causes have more personal impact than do multiple ones; and it is more effective to relate to the donor on the local and personal level, than on the national level.

3. ***Make action easy.***   The goal of any fundraising message or appeal is to inspire action from the target audience. A smart nonprofit organization will make responding to its request for support as easy as possible. Some tips for doing so include: supplying a reply card with any direct-mail package; presenting a toll-free number and Web address often and in prominent places; specifying certain amounts or categories of donations; and suggesting realistic figures based on the purpose of the request.

An Example of an Effective Fundraising Campaign

Figure 14-8 presents a fundraising campaign that was used by the Peninsula Rescue Mission in Virginia to raise both awareness and funds for feeding homeless people at Thanksgiving. It was sent to select ZIP code areas as a newspaper insert and delivered to 25,000 residences throughout the Virginia Peninsula, a section of the greater Hampton Roads region located in Southeastern Virginia.

The campaign was effective in generating $8,000 in funding and eliciting a response from 529 new donors. Its success came about because the campaign followed the fundraising principles we've discussed. Let's take a look at some of the details of the campaign and the fundraising appeal:

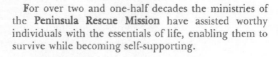

FIGURE 14-8   Peninsula Rescue Mission Operation Drumstick Flyer

Helping people help themselves... that's us!

For over two and one-half decades the ministries of the **Peninsula Rescue Mission** have assisted worthy individuals with the essentials of life, enabling them to survive while becoming self-supporting.

Without any tax money, we ministered last year to thousands of people, providing shelter, meals, groceries, clothing, furniture, and other necessities - all **at no charge!** We were able to do this with the prayers and financial help of many kind friends.

It is no small miracle that we could share nearly **44,000 meals** with the hungry, provide over **14,650 nights lodging** for the homeless; we took **120 needy children** to a free week of summer camp - an experience which changed some of them for life.

As we approach our 26th Thanksgiving, *Operation Drumstick* gives you an opportunity to share with some needy person or family with a Thanksgiving Day meal or other food help.

We look forward to hearing from you in this matter. Our success in Operation Drumstick depends entirely on the generous support that we receive from concerned and caring community members like yourself. **Help someone else to help themselves. Your kind gift can give someone a new chance in life. Will you help?**

Please support generously

OPERATION DRUMSTICK

and

Peninsula Rescue Mission Ministries

Rev. Lindsay Poteat, Executive Superintendent

"I command you to be openhanded toward your brothers and toward the poor & needy in your land."
Deuteronomy 15:11

Please fold here and place this card at your Thanksgiving table as a reminder of your generosity.

May God bless you
for remembering us
on
Thanksgiving Day

Yes, I want to be a part of OPERATION DRUMSTICK. Please accept my gift so that I may sponsor the following number of meals for the hungry. *(Please check one)*

☐ $12.16 *will provide 8 meals in our shelter dining room.*

☐ $23.85 *will provide boxed goods for 5 Thanksgiving baskets.*

☐ $53.28 *will provide turkeys for 6 Thanksgiving baskets.*

☐ $76.00 *will provide 50 meals in our shelter dining room.*

☐ $98.80 *will provide 65 meals in our shelter dining room.*

☐ _____ *Other*

OPERATION DRUMSTICK

Name _____

Address _____

City _____ State _____

FIGURE 14-8   Continued

- The fundraising campaign targeted the local community to benefit a local cause—providing meals for the homeless.
- The message attracted attention because it played off the "Desert Storm" operation in which the U.S. military was involved at the time.
- It injected guilt. The appeal was asking for funds to help feed those people less fortunate at a time when people were to be giving "thanks" for their plentiful bounty. How could anyone be planning his or her own annual Thanksgiving celebration and not have feelings for those who could not afford a meal?
- It provided premiums that were designed to make the donor feel good about his or her decision to support the Mission. One of these that worked particularly

well was a table tent (which is a small tent-shaped sign designed to be placed on a table) that could be displayed on the donor's dinner table as a reminder of his or her generosity in helping the less fortunate and a reminder to give "thanks" at Thanksgiving.

- The funding request provided realistic figures (e.g., "$12.16 will provide 8 Thanksgiving meals; $23.85 will provide boxed goods for 5 Thanksgiving baskets; $53.28 will provide turkeys for 6 Thanksgiving baskets, etc.). By design, the Peninsula Rescue Mission did not round off the numbers. The Peninsula Rescue Mission could have stated "$12.00 will provide 8 Thanksgiving Dinners." These figures certainly would have made the accounting tasks of the organization much easier, however, the figures would not appear as realistic to the potential donor as the exact (dollar and cent) amounts.
- The campaign made it easy to take action. A reply envelope was included, as was a reply card where the donor only needed to check a box indicating how many Thanksgiving meals they wanted to provide.

Any fundraising campaign can succeed when it follows the basic principles and strategies of direct marketing and, especially, direct response fundraising. We can learn a great deal from examining other successful direct marketing fundraising campaigns, although what worked for one organization at one time, may not work (a) at a different time and (b) for a different organization. Nonetheless, we can mine examples to generate ideas for future fundraising campaigns and to find models that allow us to analyze and evaluate the components of a good campaign.

MEDIA STRATEGIES AND AWARD-WINNING CAMPAIGNS

Like any other organization, nonprofit organizations can effectively use a variety of media in conducting direct marketing activities. In fact, many nonprofit organizations find great success in mixing the media and launching campaigns supported by several different media strategies. Understanding a donor's media habits and news consumption habits is very important when attempting to secure loyalty, enhance relationships, and cultivate new support. According to recent research, the number one method in which contributors get information about charities to which they donate is direct mail (49 percent) followed by church (43 percent) and friends and relatives (37 percent). That research also showed charity/fundraising direct mail was the type of direct mail that is most often read (55 percent) followed by entertainment (50 percent) and subscriptions (42 percent).[23]

In this section we'll look at some statistics providing insight into how effective each type of media is for nonprofit organizations. We'll also look at some examples of nonprofit organizations that have used different media in executing their direct marketing campaigns, including some ECHO award-winning campaigns. The ECHO award is the premier professional award that is presented on an annual basis by the DMA to direct marketers who have created the best direct and interactive marketing campaigns.

Direct Mail
Direct mail is the stellar medium for nonprofit organizations. According to the United States Postal Service, charities send more than 12 billion pieces of mail annually. And the number of charities and political candidates asking for money in support of their specific

causes continues to rise.[24] Many of these charities and political candidates are experiencing great success with direct mail. In fact, survey research shows that 55 percent of all respondents said that mail from charities is the most popular type read.[25] Nonprofit organizations are using direct mail to maintain contact with their membership. Larger, more personalized formats have been one way to build and sustain donor/member relationships. In fact, research has shown that nonprofit newspapers/magazines (48.1 percent) were most likely to inspire a response to a request from a nonprofit organization in 2000, followed by flyers (44.7 percent) and postcards (36.9 percent).[26] Nonprofit organizations use direct mail to solicit funds from membership, as well as to keep members informed and engaged in supporting an organization's cause. Research has shown that donors recruited by mail tend on average to support the organization for the longest period of time.[27]

In 1998, a DMA research study found 63.2 percent of surveyed consumers reported they immediately read nonprofit mail from their church, while 57.6 percent read mail from veterans groups right away. However, in 2000 research revealed the proportion of respondents immediately reading nonprofit direct mail fell almost equally in all categories (medical, union/professional, church, veterans, educational, charities, and political).[28] In addition, the DMA reports that the largest category of advertising mail requesting a donation comes from charities (79 percent), followed by veterans groups (65.2 percent).[29] Let's take a look at an effective direct-mail campaign for a nonprofit organization. This direct-mail campaign, entitled "August Notebook Bounceback" was created for World Vision and received a Gold ECHO Award in the Flat Mail category several years ago.

World Vision needed to raise at least $800,000 to continue caring for unsponsored children in developing countries. The charity decided to target current sponsors to see if they would be willing to expand their gifts to sponsor additional children. The direct-mail package included a letter from World Vision President, a sticker with the sponsored child's name on it and a small notebook. World Vision explained in the letter that paper for schoolchildren is extremely scarce. It asked the potential donor to affix the sticker to the cover of the notebook, sign the inside cover, and mail the book back in an enclosed, postage-paid envelope. The organization would then deliver the notebook to the sponsored child, along with another rarity—a pencil. The letter was highly personal, mentioning both the sponsor and the sponsored child by name and made a compelling case for sending money to aid additional children. World Vision enclosed a tear-off coupon requesting a gift of $20, $50, or "other."

The results were tremendous. With a total budget of $117,796, World Vision mailed 240,893 direct-mail packages and received a response rate of 46.1 percent, beating their previous campaign by almost 26 percent. The cost per response was a low $1.06 and the total income generated exceeded their goal by $197,000 (23 percent). In addition, more than 80 percent of sponsors returned their notebooks for their children, thus bonding their relationship even further.

Source: Adapted from Greg Gattuso, Elaine Santoro, George R. Reis, "Notebook Open Hearts of Sponsors," *Fundraising Management* 27, no. 10 (1996): 10–11.

Telephone

Technological advances and increased list penetration can help phone-a-thons attain a first-time pledge rate of nearly 25 percent.[30] The new technology allows an organization to reduce staff while increasing the amount of time callers spend actually talking to potential donors. Let's examine an example of a successful telephone fundraising campaign conducted by the Ohio Special Olympics a few years ago.

The objective of the Ohio Special Olympics campaign was to add the element of the telephone to its direct-mail campaign in an effort to reactivate as many donors as possible to support their Summer Special Olympics games. An additional objective was to thank donors for their support, building goodwill and cultivating a closer relationship. Because many of the donors had family or friends participating in the Ohio Special Olympic Games, it was important to train the telephone operators to answer questions about the Summer Games and specific events. The organization employed two strategies to enhance the response rate. First, a focus was placed on an athlete in each of the 13 local regions of Ohio. The organization programmed each computer so that the athlete's name and area would appear on the computer screen for reference in the telephone script. This enabled a more personal interaction, since many of the donors recognized the athlete's name in their area. Second, the organization timed the campaign so that the operators placed calls just prior to the time of the games—which reinforced the urgency of the campaign.

The program was a success. It yielded an average contribution of almost $28 and the program's net income totaled over $28,000.

Source: Adapted from Greg Gattuso, Elaine Santoro, George R. Reis, "Summer Games Soar for Goodwill," *Fund Raising Management* 27, no. 10 (1996): 18–19.

Television

Television has earned its fame as a fundraising medium courtesy of the annual Jerry Lewis Labor Day Telethon for Muscular Dystrophy in the United States. Legendary actor Jerry Lewis is the National Chairman of the Muscular Dystrophy Association. He has been hosting this 24-hour telethon every Labor Day weekend for more than 38 years. For more information about the telethon, check out the Web site of the Muscular Dystrophy Association (www.mdausa.org/telethon/).

Research shows that direct response television (DRTV) donors tend to give somewhat higher sums on average than any other category of donor.[31] Most fundraising appeals on television are in the form of infomercials. The typical 30-minute nonprofit infomercial has a life span of about 9 to 18 months, according to Gene Silverman, president of Fairfield, Iowa-based Hawthorne Communications.[32] Silverman notes that to be successful on television, the nonprofit organization must know what it wants to accomplish, know what it wants the viewer to take away, and clearly present the benefits of donating. The goal of most infomercials is still to get the viewer to the telephone.

Other nonprofit organizations have effectively used direct response television advertisements and public service announcements (PSAs) to generate awareness of their organization and its worthy cause. The United States Golf Association (USGA) television campaign is a prime example. Here's an overview of this television campaign, which received a Silver Echo Award from the DMA a few years ago:

The USGA aired television spots during the week of the U.S. Golf Open that were intended to drive in new memberships. Membership in the USGA is a contribution to the game of golf and a show of support for the projects for which the USGA provides funding. Because USGA is a nonprofit organization that hosts the U.S. Open, its network contract specifies that 80 percent of its broadcast communication must be run in the form of public service announcements. That meant that fewer than one out of four television spots could include membership drive messages. The solution was to use television PSAs as a "pure image" foundation on which to build a direct response television campaign.

To communicate the century-old mission of the USGA, the television spots used archival footage and still photography of golf heroes past and present. The USGA was able to connect on a nostalgic note with older golfers, and establish themselves as the credible steward of the game among younger golfers. After the PSAs ran, a direct response television (DRTV) ad provided a telephone number for golfers to call. The TV spots, combined with a traditional direct mail campaign, appealed to over 2 million golfers.

The results proved the effectiveness of both the television campaign and the media mixing. The budget for the television campaign totaled $300,000, with an additional $30,000 spent on direct mail. The TV ads generated 21,503 calls, 67 percent of which were converted into memberships. Officials said results of the campaign far exceeded objectives, and membership in the USGA soared 60 percent over the previous year figures.

Source: Adapted from Greg Gattuso, Elaine Santoro, George Reis, "For the Sake of the Sport," *Fund Raising Management* 27, no. 10 (1996): 11.

The Internet

It was inevitable that as more companies enter the information highway, nonprofit organizations would head in that direction as well. Given the increases in postal rates and cost of paper along with increasing legislative restrictions on the telephone marketing, the Internet may become an important media for nonprofit organizations. The first step nonprofit organizations should take before investing funds in support of the Internet is to determine what their customers/donors preferences are for receiving information. How often do they want to receive information about the organization? How accessible is the Internet for them?

Nonprofit organizations are effectively using the Internet to solicit potential volunteers, communicate with regular volunteers, and cultivate stronger relationships with current donors/member. The Internet has not been overly successful as a fundraising medium for most nonprofit organizations. People do not normally use a search engine to find places where they can donate their hard-earned dollars. However, since the terrorist attacks of September 11, 2001, "donate here" buttons on charity Web sites are no longer idle. Experts claim that the Internet has accounted for as much as $150 million or 10 percent of an estimated $1.5 billion in individual relief donations during the six-month period after the attacks. Prior to the September 11th attacks, on-line donations accounted for less than 1 percent of U.S. charitable giving.[33]

Nonprofit organizations also have new opportunities to raise funds on the Internet thanks to numerous on-line marketing initiatives. To learn more about these opportunities check out the Internet Nonprofit Center (www.nonprofits.org/fundraising.html) for an alphabetic listing of resources for on-line fundraising. Let's explore a couple of these avenues. One opportunity is sponsored by BarnesandNoble.com, a subsidiary of Barnes & Noble, Inc., headquartered in New York City. Nonprofit organizations joining the affiliate program may create links to BarnesandNoble.com bookstores (www.bn.com) on their Web sites. Whenever someone uses the link, the sender receives 5 percent—which they can donate to a charity or keep for themselves. In addition, 1 percent of such sales are donated to First Book, a group in Washington, DC, that gives books to poor children.[34] Another opportunity is Donor Trust. This is a full-service e-donations solution created by Merkel Direct Marketing, Inc., to benefit nonprofit organizations seeking to offer potential donors a quick, secure, and cost-effective way for donating on-line via the Internet. Donor Trust attaches a "Donate Now" link to a Web site to provide donors with an instant connection to the donation process.[35] This new service provides nonprofit organizations a way make their Web site secure for credit card donations without having to invest their own time and money in the technology associated with building and maintaining a secure e-commerce Web site. Moreover, donors can sign in and make an on-line donation with a major credit card; and upon completion of the transaction, the Donor Trust system will automatically generate a customized e-mail confirmation and thank you acknowledgment.

The Internet was also a critical tool the Republican National Political Party used effectively to raise funds in support of George W. Bush's 2000 presidential campaign. Let's now take a closer look at political campaign marketing.

POLITICAL CAMPAIGN DIRECT MARKETING

During an election year, most people receive at least one direct response ad or direct-mail package promoting a political candidate. But political fundraising marketing takes place in nonelection years as well. The National Republican Congressional Committee (NRCC) currently has a house list of over 10 million names and has been very successful in raising funds via direct mail. Some of the direct-mail pieces sent out by the NRCC to donors/prospects are shown in Figure 14-9. Notice the small gifts (photograph, book) that are used to generate a favorable response from the donor/prospect.

According to Hal Malchow, direct marketing consultant to the Democratic National Committee, "prior to 1995, the most prospect mail the Democratic Party had ever mailed was 8 million pieces—and this number was mailed in the 1992 Presidential election year when the returns were the highest. However, in 1995, a nonelection year, the Democratic Party mailed almost 30 million pieces."[36]

The Internet was a valuable tool used by both Republican and Democratic parties to raise funds to support their 2000 campaign candidates. Each of the two parties collected over 250,000 e-mail addresses for this campaign.[37] The Internet also allowed

Dr. Spiller,
Thank you very much for your support of our Republican Candidates.

FIGURE 14-9   Direct Mail From the National Republican Congressional Committee

the parties to send customized messages to specific groups and individuals and to use on-line discussions and instant messaging in support of their candidates. In particular, President George W. Bush disclosed a list of campaign contributors on his Web site.[38]

Political direct marketing activities are not always aimed at raising money. Oftentimes these political parties are interested in gaining support for their cause and securing new members. With restrictions being placed on ad spending, political parties are trying to secure support via other means. Direct marketing offers several alternatives to mass advertising—like distributing a newsletter to current and prospective members. The ultimate question is "*just how successful are political direct marketing efforts?*" Unlike most nonprofit organizations, political parties don't measure their success by response rates or dollars. They measure it by votes.

Summary

Nonprofit organizations have embraced direct marketing methods because of their unique cost-effective and personalized format. Direct marketing is highly effective in enabling nonprofit organizations to establish stronger relationships with their donors. This, in turn, means greater support for the nonprofit cause. However, to be effective, the nonprofit organization must understand their donor's giving behavior. This requires an understanding of the donor's media preferences and knowledge of basic fundraising principles. Nonprofit organizations should develop a committee of influential people to spearhead their fundraising campaign, launch a targeted direct response campaign, and follow up the campaign to maximize the response rate. Direct response fundraising appeals must be specific and follow certain guidelines as presented in this chapter. The fundraising appeal should be targeted, provide suggested donation amounts, carefully create and test the copy of the message, keep the format or presentation simple, and select the premium or free gift cautiously based on the results of tests.

Additionally, the nonprofit organization must understand how to effectively communicate with their donors. Each medium (direct mail, telephone, television, and the Internet) can be used to support a nonprofit organization's cause. While direct mail has been the primary medium used by nonprofit organizations, the Internet is providing new opportunities. Finally, understanding the dynamics of voter behavior prior and during elections is critical for political associations employing direct marketing methods.

Key Terms

- customer relationship management (CRM), 345
- cause-related marketing, 347

Review Questions

1. How does direct marketing help nonprofit organizations reach their goals?
2. How can nonprofit organizations maximize their relationship with their customers?
3. Fundraising is extremely competitive. How can nonprofit organizations convince donors that they should donate to their organization?
4. What three things must the direct response fundraising message do?
5. Is an understanding of donors' media habits and news consumption habits important for nonprofit organizations? Why or why not?
6. Discuss using direct mail, telephone, and television as a means of media for nonprofit organizations. What do statistics reveal about the effectiveness of each medium?
7. Most nonprofit organizations will include the Internet in their media mix. What are some reasons for this?
8. What should nonprofit organizations consider about their donors before deciding to use the Internet?
9. Why has direct marketing recently become more important to political parties? What are the objectives of political direct marketing methods?
10. What is cause-related marketing? Provide some examples of how direct marketers use cause-related marketing and why.

Exercise

You are working for an animal shelter in your city. The animal shelter is of course nonprofit and funds are needed—fundraising is necessary. Identify who you think your customer will be and whom you believe the organization should ask for donations. How can you maximize your relationship with these donors? Review the fundraising principles presented in this chapter and relate each step to your animal shelter. Finally, explain what media outlet(s) you will be using to reach donors. Do you think the Internet would be beneficial in reaching donors for your shelter? Be sure to support your position.

CASE: THE NATIONAL TRUST FOR HISTORIC PRESERVATION

LEARNING OBJECTIVE

The purpose of this case study is to help understand how segmentation of members' names increases response rates and average gift levels in a nonprofit fundraising drive. It shows how a database of contributors can be effectively segmented and how different marketing tracks for these segments increase overall response levels.

OVERVIEW

Direct marketing traditionally utilizes a segmented "rifle-shot" approach to achieve response in specialized markets. For-profit as well as not-for-profit organizations are finding that segmentation of their member (customer) list improves response rates as well as average gift amounts. This case illustrates how one nonprofit organization, the National Trust for Historic Preservation, analyzed its donor list and then developed marketing approaches and varying offers to appeal to these segments within its database.

CASE

The National Trust for Historic Preservation is a nonprofit organization chartered by Congress to work for the preservation of America's historic places. It serves its members in a variety of ways including providing seminars and publishing a number of specialized booklets, magazines, and other services relating to historic preservation. The National Trust has a membership file of 200,000 citizens acquired primarily through direct-mail solicitations. Membership levels range from $35 to $1,000 a year. To support its work the National Trust solicits renewals, including upgrades to higher levels, as well as additional special gifts by using such media as direct mail and telemarketing.

At its beginning, the National Trust had a limited membership, primarily of wealthy citizens who lived in substantial homes. Beginning in the late 1970s, however, the National Trust instituted an extensive direct-mail campaign to increase its membership and attract a broader, more diversified base of membership. These efforts were successful and today the membership rolls have swelled to over 200,000 citizens with an interest in historic preservation. In order to advance its cause, the National Trust actively promotes "upgrade giving" through participation in higher membership categories or the giving of special one-time, tax-deductible gifts. Direct mail, telemarketing, and the Internet are the media that the National Trust currently uses for gift solicitation.

With the increase in membership the National Trust realized that their members were not all of one stripe. This was discerned in telemarketing calls to members. The telephone representatives found that the interests of members were quite varied. While all had a measure of interest in historic preservation, the lifestyles and income levels of members were radically different. To assess the extent of these differences, the National Trust applied to its membership database, at the ZIP code level, an overlay of demographic and psychographic information. The first result from this research was that mailing to neighborhoods where a higher percentage of members lived produced good results. Initially, the National Trust used these "best" categories by selecting only names in these "good" clusters in their direct mail. Initial direct-mail results looked promising but not conclusive. They needed to go a step further. Through cluster analysis, the National Trust segmented its members into these three groupings:

1. ***Champagne and Caviar:*** These members generally lived in expensive homes, went

to charity events, and liked recognition for their social causes.

2. *First Class and Phone:* While wealthy, these members didn't especially crave recognition; would respond to first-class direct mailings and high-quality telephone solicitations.

3. *Paint Brushes and Plaster:* These members were do-it-yourselfers already living in historic homes. They liked the old architecture and actively worked to restore their houses.

After getting the names grouped into these three separate and distinct categories the National Trust instituted a telemarketing campaign. Telemarketers were salaried people who were highly trained to listen and to take notes on the interests of the members called. Specific information acquired this way was appended to the database record. This targeted, low-key effort allowed the callers to utilize the telemarketing medium to its fullest potential. The members were respected and listened to. Their suggestions were taken to heart and resulted in some interesting changes.

Now, the National Trust—armed with its improved research and specific details on what members were concerned about and interested in—was able to do some powerful new things. First, they were able to sincerely talk with members and remember what the *member's* interests were. Second, they were able to craft different offers for different types of members. For example, they found out that members in the Paint Brush and Plaster cluster had a strong interest in the content of a magazine called *Old-House Journal*. So they began offering a gift subscription to this magazine for members who contributed $100. Through their "listening" to members they also found out that the directory of suppliers put out by *Old-House Journal* was also of interest to members. They offered this to members who contributed $250.

The Direct Response Program's Objectives

- Conduct a demographic/psychographic study of members through an analysis of

their ZIP codes, grouping members into basic cluster groups with varying characteristics.
- Validate these results by coding renewal direct-mail efforts.
- Interview members by trained telemarketers to develop additional data on individual members. Append significant data acquired to the membership records.
- Keep track of telemarketing results based on the newly acquired data on members.

Steps Involved in Building a Successful Direct Response Fundraising Program

- Carry out member profiling through a ZIP code cluster analysis.
- Analyze results from current fundraising efforts to members.
- Conduct test-mail campaigns with special codes for test groups that identify the cluster groups.
- Train telemarketers to do in-depth interviews with members.
- Append additional information acquired to membership records.
- Determine what benefits would motivate the members to give additional gifts.
- Prepare talking points for telemarketers based on interviews with members.
- Call members in pre-determined cluster groups.
- Measure responses from cluster group calls and compare these to a control group.
- Create a special Web site for members to exchange information with each other.

Determination of Criteria for Successful Fundraising to the Membership Base

- What are the prime motivating factors for making additional gifts to the nonprofit?
- What type of benefits would make for a stronger incentive to make a contribution?
- Where is the nonprofit failing the expectations of its members?
- Who in the household makes the decision to give an additional contribution?

Techniques to Be Followed in Conducting Direct Response Fundraising

- Develop test-group samples and compare results with a control group of members.
- Prepare direct-mail letters and marketing scripts based on member research.
- Analyze results, both initial test results and the long-term value of members.

The Results of the National Trust's Direct Response Fundraising Program **Did this nonprofit organization's utilization of the tools and techniques** work? The National Trust reports that pledges are up by 12 percent, average pledge is up 17 percent, dollar per contact is up 31 percent and the net per contact is up an incredible 53 percent. According to the National Trust, the real payoff has been listening to what their members say—hearing a wish list from their members and having one-on-one conversations with them about their own personal homes. In summary, the results of this program make a compelling case for the importance of using direct marketing and market segmentation techniques for nonprofit organizations.

FIGURE 14-10 Each year, the National Trust for Historic Preservation publishes an 11 Most Endangered Places list, which has become one of the most effective tools in the fight to save America's irreplaceable heritage. The prairie churches of North Dakota were recently featured on the list.

FIGURE 14-11   The Cleveland Arcade in Ohio recently won a National Trust Honor Award for the revitalization of this historic landmark into a hotel and shopping complex after years of decline.

Case Discussion Questions

1. Explain the desired results of using market segmentation techniques for the National Trust for Historic Preservation.

2. To what other uses might the National Trust put the knowledge acquired through its cluster analysis?

Notes

1. *DMA WEFA Study* (New York: The Direct Marketing Association, Inc., 2000).

2. *Economic Impact – U.S. Direct Marketing Today* (Non-Profit Sector Report) (New York: The Direct Marketing Association,

Inc., 2002); *The Statistical Fact Book 2002,* 24th ed. (New York: The Direct Marketing Association, 2002), 233–235.

3. Independent Sector, "Giving and Volunteering in the United States," 2001,

<http://www.independentsector.org/
programs/research/GV01main.html>
September 5, 2003.

4. Independent Sector, "Value of
Volunteer Time," 2002,
<http://www.independentsector.org/
programs/research/volunteer_time.html>
September 5, 2003.

5. "The DMA Acquires Federation of
Nonprofits," *Direct Marketing* 63, no. 5
(September 2000): 11.

6. Dirk Remley, "Relationship Marketing:
Guaranteeing the Future," *Nonprofit World*
14, no. 5 (September/October 1996): 15–16.

7. Adrian Sargeant, "Charitable Giving:
Towards a Model of Donor Behavior,"
Journal of Marketing Management 15
(1999), 215–238.

8. M. Royer, "Please Give Generously, Okay?"
NSFRE Journal (Summer 1989), 17–20.

9. A. Sargeant and J. McKenzie, "A Lifetime
of Giving: An Analysis of Donor
Lifetime Value," *West Malling, Charities
Aid Foundation* (1998).

10. Adapted from Dirk Remley, "Relationship
Marketing: Guaranteeing the Future,"
Nonprofit World 14, no. 5
(September/October 1996): 13–16.

11. <http://www.bitc.org.uk/marketing.html>
August, 2000.

12. Hershell Gordon Lewis, "Direct Mail Fund
Raising Tactics," *Fund Raising Management*
28, no. 5 (July 1997): 17.

13. "AAFRC Trust for Philanthropy Giving
USA 2002," *The Statistical Fact Book 2002*,
24th ed. (New York: The Direct Marketing
Association, 2002), 232.

14. "AAFRC Trust for Philanthropy Giving
USA 2000," *The Statistical Fact Book 2000*,
24th ed. (New York: The Direct Marketing
Association, Inc., 2000), 252.

15. Independent Sector, "Charitable Giving:
September 11th and Beyond," 2003,
<http://www.independentsector.org/sept11/
survey.html> September 7, 2003.

16. Independent Sector, "Giving and
Volunteering in the United States," 2001,

<http://www.independentsector.org/
programs/research/GV01main.html>
September 5, 2003.

17. Adapted from Bob Stone, *Successful Direct
Marketing Methods*, 5th ed. (Lincolnwood,
IL: NTC Publishing Group, 1994), 168.

18. Adapted from Rajan Selladurai, "8 Steps to
Fundraising Success," *Nonprofit World* 16,
no. 4 (1998): 17–19.

19. Ibid., 169.

20. Adapted from Kay Partney Lautman, *Direct
Marketing for Nonprofits: Essential
Techniques for the New Era* (Gaithersburg,
Maryland: Aspen Publishers, Inc., YEAR),
1–2.

21. Independent Sector, "Value of
Volunteer Time," 2002,
<http://www.independentsector.org/
programs/research/volunteer_time.html>
September 5, 2003.

22. Adapted from Hershell Gordon Lewis,
"Direct Mail Fund Raising Tactics," *Fund
Raising Management* 28, no. 5 (July 1997):
17.

23. "Customer Focus 2001 Direct Marketing
Survey, Webcraft L.L.C., the Direct
Marketing Service of Vertis," *The Statistical
Fact Book 2002*, 24th ed. (New York: The
Direct Marketing Association, Inc., 2002),
231.

24. Rob Yoegel, "New Ways to Raise Money,"
Target Marketing 19, no. 6 (1996): 48.

25. "Vertis Customer Focus 2001: Direct
Marketing Survey," *The Statistical Fact
Book 2002*, 24th ed. (New York: The Direct
Marketing Association, Inc., 2002), p. 33.

26. "USPS Household Diary Study, 2001," *The
Statistical Fact Book 2002*, 24th ed. (New
York: The Direct Marketing Association, Inc.,
2002), 224.

27. A. Sargeant and J. McKenzie, "A Lifetime of
Giving: An Analysis of Donor Lifetime
Value," *West Malling, Charities Aid
Foundation* (1998).

28. *The Statistical Fact Book 2002*, 24th ed. (New
York: The Direct Marketing Association,
Inc., 2002), 222.

29. *The Statistical Fact Book 2002,* 24th ed. (New York: The Direct Marketing Association, Inc., 2002), 223.

30. Adapted from Rob Yoegel, "New Ways to Raise Money," *Target Marketing* 19, no. 6 (1996): 48–54.

31. A. Sargeant and J. McKenzie, "A Lifetime of Giving: An Analysis of Donor Lifetime Value," *West Malling, Charities Aid Foundation* (1998).

32. Adapted from Rob Yoegel, "New Ways to Raise Money," *Target Marketing* 19, no. 6 (1996): 48–54.

33. "Charities Hope 9/11 Inspires 'E-Philanthropy'–Nation Contributes with a Quick Click," *USA Today Online,* March 19, 2002, p. 4d., <http://www.usatoday.com/usatonline/20020319/ 3950825s.htm> accessed on September 5, 2003.

34. Internet Nonprofit Center, <http://www.nonprofits.org/fundraising.html> September 7, 2003.

35. "E-Donation Service Facilitates New Revenue Paths for Non-Profits," *Fund Raising Management* 31, no. 1 (2000): 10.

36. Adapted from Rob Yoegel, "New Ways to Raise Money," *Target Marketing* 19, no. 6 (1996): 48–54.

37. U.S. NET, "Mobiizing Virtual Volunteers Online", <http://www.us.net/indc/column2.htm> accessed in August, 2000.

38. Ibid.

15 INTERNATIONAL DIRECT MARKETING

The world is getting smaller. Facing saturated U.S. markets, many companies are looking overseas to achieve increased sales volume and greater profits. While those are the two reasons frequently named by businesses seeking international business, other reasons include the hope of expanding into new markets, diversification, achieving economies of scale, and business survival. The United States exports nearly $850 billion in products to foreign countries each year and almost one-third of U.S. corporate profits is derived from international trade and foreign investment.[1] It is predicted that by 2005, North American global advertising expenditures will reach $16.9 million, while Europe and Asia are expected to spend approximately $5.2 million and $3.3 million respectively.[2]

Revenue generated by international direct marketing activities has continued to increase over the years. Approximately 31 percent of U.S. company sales were generated from international direct mail (including catalogs).[3] However, recent survey research shows that companies in both the United States and abroad say they are substituting e-mail (36 percent) and on-line advertising (27.2 percent) for international mail promotions.[4] International e-mailing volume has increased from 2001 to 2002. DMA research reports almost 45 percent of U.S. direct marketers have increased international e-mail volume.[5] In 2002, U.S. companies spent $5.6 million on on-line ads.[6] Approximately 20 percent of the DMA's hard goods membership is doing e-commerce internationally.[7]

The Internet is one of the reasons why many companies have entered international markets via direct exporting. As discussed in Chapter 9, marketing on the Internet and creating a Web site are the same thing today as opening a global business with a worldwide audience. Unlike traditional exporting, which began with brokers and other intermediaries who assisted companies in generating international sales from pre-selected foreign countries, a Web site is immediate and inexpensive. It does not, however, permit much selectivity in choosing markets. Research has shown that more than 37 percent of Internet users are based in countries other than the United States and Canada.[8] This may often lead to fulfillment problems for direct marketers, who don't have the distribution network or capability of fulfilling international orders in some countries.

Figure 15-1 shows the top international markets in which U.S. catalog companies are doing business. Canada continues to be the top market, followed by Japan.

There are four compelling reasons for direct marketers to decide to go international in their marketing efforts. These are limited growth share in the domestic market, shared global values, the high cost of new product development, and competitive forces.[9] The market potential of many international markets is extremely attractive for direct marketers and has been for a number of years. International direct marketing is not new. Let's take a short look at the use of direct marketing around the world.

DIRECT MARKETING AROUND THE WORLD

According to the Direct Marketing Association (DMA) *Fact Book,* the oldest known catalog was produced by Aldus Manutius of Venice in 1498, and listed the titles of 15 texts Manutius had published.[10] Next came seed and nursery catalogs, the earliest known

INTERNATIONAL MARKET	% CONDUCTED BUSINESS IN YEAR 2000
Canada	75%
Japan	67%
Australia/New Zealand	54%
England	54%
Germany	54%
Mexico	50%
Other European	42%
South America	42%
Other Asian	38%
France	38%
Other	25%

FIGURE 15-1 Top International Markets of U.S. Direct Marketers

Source: "The DMA State of the Catalog/Interactive Industry Report, 2001," The *Statistical Fact Book 2002,* 24th ed. (New York: The Direct Marketing Association, Inc., 2002), 81.

mercantile gardening catalog being a printed price list issued by William Lucas, an English gardener. But it was in Germany that direct marketing truly has its roots. Germany had a parcel post system by 1874, and a collect on delivery (COD) system by 1878. The first known European consumer catalog was distributed in 1883, about the same time that Richard Sears was creating his first catalog in the United States.[11]

By 1912, a German businessman, August Stuchenbrok, produced a 238-page catalog—which was five years before Leon Bean (of L.L. Bean) sold his first pair of boots.[12] The largest catalog house in the world today is also owned by a German company, Otto Versand, who owns Spiegel, Eddie Bauer, and Newport News, Inc., among others.

Today, the United States remains the world leader in mail-order markets earning more than $90 billion annually. Germany ranks second with $30 billion, Japan is third with $22 billion, France ranks fourth with $11 billion, followed by Great Britain with $7 billion, and, finally, Switzerland and Austria at $2 billion combined.[13]

DIFFERENCES BETWEEN DOMESTIC AND INTERNATIONAL DIRECT MARKETING

What makes international direct marketing different from domestic direct marketing? Market uncertainty is one of the biggest differences. The uncertainty of different foreign business environments is due to differences in infrastructure, technology, competitive dynamics, legal and governmental restrictions, customer preferences, culture, and many additional uncontrollable variables. These factors make many direct marketers hesitate to leap into international markets, regardless of their potential. For example, Tang, the orange-flavored powdered drink, was marketed successfully in the United States as an orange juice substitute. However, in France, Tang had to be marketed as a refreshment since the French do not normally drink orange juice at breakfast. Thus, customer preferences dictated the marketing strategy.[14]

Different country laws can also dictate marketing strategies. For example, in Europe there are many restrictions on advertisements for cigarette and tobacco products, alcoholic beverages, and pharmaceutical products. Ads for other products may also be regulated. Advertisements in the United Kingdom cannot show a person applying an underarm deodorant. Therefore, ads are modified to show an animated person applying the product.[15] There may be tremendous opportunities in foreign markets, but direct marketers must do careful, calculated research before they venture abroad.

MAKING THE DECISION TO GO INTERNATIONAL

Various researchers have offered tips or processes to follow when deciding to begin international direct marketing activities. The following five-step approach is a synthesis of the many processes suggested for screening, selecting, and marketing to an international country:[16]

Step 1: Assess Your International Potential
Direct marketers must analyze their domestic position in their industry to provide an indication of the strength of their foundation and resource base from which they can expand. A part of this assessment is determining whether or not there are adequate external resources to assist them in penetrating international markets. Some of these external resources may include *expert advice and counseling*. Many organizations exist in the private and public sector to assist firms in beginning an international marketing program. Figure 15-2 provides a listing of some of these resources. In addition, many industry trade

---

FIGURE 15-2   International Marketing Resources

U.S. Department of Commerce (Foreign Trade Highlights) www.doc.gov

U.S. Trade Information Center (1-800-USATRADE)

U.S. Small Business Administration (www.sba.gov)

Bureau of the Census (www.census.gov)

DMA/International Council (www.the-dma.org)

FEDMA and/or in-country DMA (www.eurocallcentre.com/index.htm)

U.S. Chambers of Commerce – AMCHAMS (www.uschamber.org/intl/amcham.la.htm)

U.S. Department of State (www.state.gov)

CIA (Country Fact Sheets) (www.cia.gov)

Source: Rainer Hengst, "Plotting Your Global Strategy," *Direct Marketing* 63, no. 4 (2000): 55.

associations and graduate business programs at universities provide assistance to companies beginning international marketing activities.

Step 2: Conduct Marketing Research

Conducting market research is critical to understanding the cultural differences and country market nuances that may exist. Identifying potential overseas markets involves a great deal of time, effort, and research. However, given the vast amount of data available about each foreign market, researching a single market is likely to provide information overload. Savvy direct marketers sort through all the data and determine the pertinent information they need to analyze the potential of a foreign market.

Direct marketers must determine whether consumers have a basic need for their products/services and whether the resources necessary for them to carry out local business activities are available. International direct marketers must understand the "local color" of the destination country, including such information as what consumers buy, why they buy, how they pay for it, and what motivates them to make a purchase. At a minimum, direct marketers must understand local buying behavior, typical payment methods, advertising practices, and privacy laws. The customers in other countries are not Americans who simply live abroad. They have different cultures, different tastes, different needs and wants, and must be segmented accordingly. For example, the population of Europe is fairly well dispersed with Germany making up 22 percent of the population, France, United Kingdom, and Italy each possessing 16 percent, Spain with 11 percent, and the remainder of the continent comprising 19 percent. Europe is highly diverse in terms of geography, language, economic development, spending habits, disposable income, etc. Therefore, direct marketers aiming at one unified European Union will likely fail.

Direct marketers must also research the national business environment of the target country including its cultural, political, legal, and economic situation. Determine whether the language, attitudes, religious beliefs, traditions, work ethic, government regulation, government bureaucracy, political stability, fiscal and monetary policies, currency issues, cost of transporting goods, and the country image are clear and acceptable.

The state of a country's infrastructure must be factored into the potential for success in that country's market. Infrastructure is normally a leading indicator of economic development and must be in place to support the direct marketer. A country's **infrastructure** represents those capital goods and services that serve the activities of many industries. At a minimum, the infrastructure analysis should include the following essential services: transportation, communications, utilities, and banking. There are really three infrastructure pillars that support the international direct marketing industry—the publishing industry, the transportation industry, and advances in high technology.[17] Because of its importance, we will discuss infrastructure in greater detail later in this chapter. Marketing research should also investigate the potential market or site to determine the suitability of the market for the particular product or service. Would the product succeed in this market? Certain locations may not be acceptable due to the lack of resources available for marketing a specific product or service. Therefore, direct marketers must conduct a detailed country-by-country analysis to properly select which markets to penetrate. Market research for each country under consideration can be boiled down to the following primary international market indicators. These include population, political stability, GDP/inflations, distribution of wealth, age distribution, currency, tariffs and taxes, and computer ownership. Let's look briefly at each.

Population

Direct marketers should consider the size of the population segments that fit your targeted prospect profile. Direct marketers should take into consideration a country's population along with its overall wealth. For example, direct marketers should be cautious in entering a country with a large population but little monetary wealth. Direct marketers may prefer entering a market with a small population that has a high per capita Gross Domestic Product (GDP), such as Singapore.

Political Stability

The political stability of a country becomes extremely important for those direct marketers planning to establish a physical presence within that country. In addition, political shifts in power and leadership may affect foreign exchange rates and tariffs.

GDP/Inflation

The rate of inflation of a country affects the purchasing power of consumers within a country and is closely related to the country's GDP. GDP stands for **gross domestic product,** which is the total market value of all final goods and services produced within a nation's borders in a given year. When assessing a country's GDP and inflation rates, most direct marketers look for annual trends going back as far as five years.

Distribution of Wealth

Direct marketers must assess the distribution of wealth in a country to determine whether there are a substantial number of consumers who are able to afford the product or service. As in the United States, some international countries, such as Mexico, have the situation where the top 10 percent of the population possesses more than 50 percent of the wealth. Thus, the size and viability of a market in any country depends on the target market customer's disposable income.

Age Distribution

A look at age distribution assesses both the average longevity of the citizens as well as the age breakdown of the population. For example, a population comprised primarily of young adults is great if you are marketing soft drinks, however, if you are marketing automobiles, the likelihood of these young people having the income to purchase the product is considerably lessened.

Currency

An assessment of the currency of a foreign country includes an evaluation of the convertibility and ease of exchange of currency, inflation rates, and credit card penetration.

Tariffs and Taxes

How difficult and expensive is it to bring goods across a country's international border? Do local regulations such as tariffs and taxes favor locally produced goods and services over imported ones? These are the types of questions with which direct marketers must be concerned when deciding to go international.

Computer Ownership

How widely are computers used, and how many computer users have Internet access? In many countries, the majority of consumers do not have easy Internet access. This poses a problem for direct markers who seek to create a virtual business.

Postal/Delivery Services

This category includes the postal system as well as private delivery alternatives. Some areas to address include the following:

a. Adequacy of the change-of-address system available;
b. The existence of parcel collect-on-delivery (COD) system;
c. The existence of a track-and-trace system for parcels; and
d. The level of sophistication and format of the postcode system.

If any of these researched items do not satisfy a business's requirements or justify the modifications necessary to carry out necessary marketing activities in that country, then perhaps that country should be eliminated from further business consideration.

Step 3: Select Your Countries

Based on the research collected and analyzed in step two, careful analysis should provide an indication as to which markets would be receptive to the particular product and/or service. Direct marketers should select the market or site that holds the greatest potential for successful international marketing. Although many companies are anxious to get an international direct marketing campaign started, it can be extremely taxing on a company. Most experts suggest targeting only one country at a time. Multi-country rollouts are very difficult to successfully execute.

This is the step of the process that may require traveling to those countries or markets that have been selected. During these field trips, direct marketers should investigate the nuances of the market and perform a competitor analysis.

Step 4: Develop an International Direct Marketing Plan

Direct marketers should create a detailed marketing plan itemizing their long-term goals along with the competitive niche the firm is attempting to fill. They should prepare the marketing plan to cover a two-to-five-year period, along with a competitor analysis. This plan should detail communication and distribution strategies. For example, direct marketers must determine the media mix for communicating the promotional message. Keep in mind that internationally, postal reliability and postal rates may limit mail-order offerings, including many catalogs.

Regarding distribution strategies, direct marketers must determine whether or not they will have a physical presence in the country. Although, many international consumers look for U.S. products on the basis of reputation and prestige, they also want the feel of a "local presence." This translates into the need to have a local in-country return address along with customer addresses without country codes, response call centers handled in the native language, country- and language-specific Web sites, prices quoted in local currencies, etc. However, given today's technological advances, it is possible for U.S. direct marketers to create a "virtual" local presence if the firm cannot attain a physical presence.

Step 5: Begin International Direct Marketing Activities

Implementing a direct marketing plan is expensive and time consuming. However, for many direct marketers, it is very well worth it. As direct marketers begin to implement their strategies, revisions may be necessary. The international business environment is extremely unpredictable. It is a dynamic environment that must be constantly monitored. Therefore, as direct marketers begin international direct marketing activities, they will need to continue researching and analyzing the changing business environment.

With all the necessary research and preparation, of course, direct marketers entering foreign markets still do so with greater risk than they face when entering the domestic marketplace. Thus they should slowly, not hastily, penetrate one country's market at a time. International direct marketing is all about differences. It should be no surprise then that different foreign-market entry strategies exist. Let's now turn to market entry modes.

MODES OF MARKET ENTRY

There are six basic modes of market entry for penetrating an international market: exporting, licensing, joint venture, contract manufacturing, direct investment, and management contracting.

Exporting

An **exporting** company sells its products from its home base without maintaining any of its own personnel overseas. IBM used direct exporting to expand its global distribution of products like the OS/w Warp operating system to businesses and consumers in Japan.[18] Many successful, well-known direct marketers, such as L.L. Bean, conduct their international marketing via direct exporting from their respective home bases. L.L. Bean is located in Freeport, Maine, yet fulfills orders from customers all over the world. However, sometimes the company must have a local mailing address because some customers are reluctant in placing orders and sending money overseas. For example, in Japan, L.L. Bean works with McCann Direct, the specialized direct-marketing division of McCann-Erickson Hakuhodo Inc., Japan's largest foreign advertising agency. When L.L. Bean places ads for its catalogs in Japanese media, those catalog orders are sent locally to McCann Direct. McCann Direct then forwards the orders to L.L. Bean's headquarters in Maine, where all the orders for catalogs or products are fulfilled.[19] L.L. Bean also has a distribution arrangement with FedEx for parcel fulfillment, enabling it to cut delivery time to Japan from two weeks (using air parcel) to three or four days, averaging deliveries of 9,000 parcels a day to Japanese customers.[20]

Licensing

Licensing occurs when a **licensor**, a company located in the host country, allows a foreign firm to manufacture or service a product or service for sale in the **licensee's** country. Licensing is similar to franchising in that a local business in an international country becomes authorized to manufacture or sell specific brand products for another company. The right to use a patent or trademark must be granted to a foreign company under the license agreement contract. The most common licensing agreements occur when a direct marketer allows a firm in a local country market to reproduce a direct marketing catalog in the local language. The well-known Sharper Image catalog, for instance, is published under licensing agreements in Germany, Japan, and Switzerland. In these countries, local firms produce and mail out Sharper Image catalogs using the native language of the international country. Another example of a direct marketer using licensing agreements to market internationally is that of the Orvis Company. It markets its outdoor clothing, accessories, and fishing equipment by mailing 50 million catalogs a year through six different titles, and offers a complete line of merchandise in 28 company-owned retail stores and 700 independent dealers worldwide. It also partners with select licensees.[21] In fact, if you go to its Web site, www.orvis.com, you can obtain a listing of its worldwide dealer network along with a listing of international market opportunities Orvis wants to pursue in the future.

Joint Venture

A **joint venture** is created when two or more investors join forces to conduct a business by sharing ownership and control. It is similar to a partnership. Companies understand that marketing alliances with a foreign company can provide a number of benefits. These benefits include easy access to a foreign market, elimination of tariffs and quotas, faster growth and market coverage, and ability to penetrate markets that normally would have been closed to wholly owned enterprises. Joint ventures are normally a "win-win" situation for each of the partners. For example, Recreational Equipment Inc. (REI) and Austad's, a golf supply cataloger, worked out a cooperative venture with one another and mailed their catalogs together to names on both of their Japanese lists.[22] Another example of a joint venture is that of E*TRADE. E*TRADE, a U.S. Internet-based stockbroker, recently entered into a joint venture with Softbank Corporation of Japan to offer on-line investing services in Asia. E*TRADE also entered into a second joint venture with Electronic Share Information in Great Britain.[23]

Contract Manufacturing

Many times, a company will contract a local manufacturer to produce goods for the company. This strategy, known as **contract manufacturing,** enables companies to take advantage of lower labor costs and faster market entry, while avoiding local ownership problems, and satisfying legal requirements that the product must be manufactured locally in order for it to be sold in that country. For example, visit the Web site of Texas Instruments at www.ti.com and click on TI Worldwide and you will learn that TI Global has manufacturing sites and sales and support offices located in Europe, Asia, Japan, and the Americas.[24] While you're there, take note of the selection of TI Web sites featuring different languages designed to serve its international customers.

Direct Investment

In a **direct investment** a company acquires an existing foreign company or forms a completely new company in the foreign country. The German company Otto Versand, for example, became the largest mail-order company in the world by buying existing companies or building new ones. Otto Versand owns mail-order companies or is part-owner of direct marketing firms in Belgium, France, Italy, Japan, Spain, and the United States.

Management Contracting

In **management contracting** local businesspeople or their government signs a contract to manage the foreign business in their country's market. An example of management contracting is Day-Timers, a U.S. firm located in East Texas, Pennsylvania. Day-Timers uses direct mail to market to millions of business people in the United States. However, it opened offices in Australia, Canada, and the United Kingdom and hired local employees to manage its foreign business locations because it needed to have people who were familiar with the culture and could handle incoming telephone calls.[25]

Each direct marketer must carefully weigh the advantages and disadvantages of each method and determine which is best for his or her company. The choice mode of market entry depends in the end on many factors, one of which we address next.

INTERNATIONAL DIRECT MARKETING INFRASTRUCTURE

Direct marketers must assess the degree of sophistication of each country's direct marketing infrastructure with the goal of determining how well they can use it to implement direct marketing activities. Some questions and issues direct marketers might investigate include

- Does the country have an active Direct Marketing Association?
- What is the degree to which the support services (printing and publishing services, transportation or package delivery services, postal services, and technological services) are present?
- How sophisticated is the credit card and banking system in the country?
- Is there an established pattern of purchasing via direct channels?
- What legislative issues will affect direct marketing activities?

Figure 15-3 provides an itemized list of the direct marketing infrastructure needed to support international direct marketing activities. Let's briefly look at some of the infrastructure supporting international direct marketing activities.

Lists and Databases

Lists of both consumer and business customers are normally available for most countries, although different kinds of lists are available in different countries. For example, in Europe, there are multinational lists and local lists. In China, lists of factories, ministries, professional societies, research institutes, and universities are available, though quite expensive.[26] Although a number of vendors in the United States offer international lists, the quality will vary. It is good practice to test a small representative sample of any list

List Availability
Quality of Postal Service
Average Postage Costs
Percentage of Mail Friendly Households
Internal or External Database
Average Direct-Mail Cost per Piece
Availability of In-Line Personalization
Standardized Addresses
Postal Codes
Inbound Telemarketing Availability
Outbound Telemarketing Availability
Availability of Credit Cards
Response Channel Opportunities

FIGURE 15-3 Direct Marketing Infrastructure

before renting it. Because mailing lists in Russia are so unreliable, Hearst publishing bypassed direct mail and opted for newsstand sales to distribute the first issues of *Cosmopolitan* to the consumer market.[27] However, Magnavox CATV, which markets cable television equipment, has increased its international mailings to support its many trade shows in developing regions.[28]

Also be aware that a number of laws pertain to information privacy—which normally affects direct marketing list and database activities. Canada's Personal Information Privacy and Electronic Documents Act has had significant impact for direct marketers on both sides of the border.[29] Lists and databases are certainly key areas of importance to international direct marketers.

Fulfillment

Distributing products to the customer is one of the prime difficulties associated with international direct marketing. Direct marketers have two main distribution options available to them—ship products from the home location or establish a bulk distribution operation overseas. Those direct marketers using their home location have three basic options for distributing products—(1) the United States Postal Service (USPS) international mail; (2) non-USPS postal delivery via a foreign postal administration such as the Royal Mail; or (3) consolidators within the United States (such as Worldpak, Global Mail, FedEx, and DHL)—that act as a service agent for the international direct mailer.

Besides distribution issues, fulfillment concerns also include the determination of payment options. In the United States, most direct marketers offer consumers the option to pay by credit card, check, or money order. These are not necessarily the standards in foreign markets. Credit card penetration is considerably lower in other countries than it is throughout the United States. In addition and unlike the United States, many consumers in foreign countries primarily use their credit cards for vacation purposes only. Checks, direct debit, bank transfers (wire services), and invoicing are other payment options to be considered.

Another important fulfillment issue is customer service. Direct marketers must make their return policies simple and easy to understand, as well as have toll-free numbers available for consumers to place inquiries and/or complaints. Local fulfillment centers should be established to handle orders for foreign countries with language barriers. For example, U.S. inventory for Lands' End's U.K., German, and Japanese catalogs is shipped in bulk to local operations in the United Kingdom and Japan. The U.K. fulfillment center handles orders originating from its U.K. catalog and German-language catalog, while the Japanese fulfillment center handles orders for its Japanese-language catalog.[30]

Determining the locations for fulfillment centers and deciding whether to centralize fulfillment operations are among the other decisions international direct marketers must make. Garnet Hill and Paper Direct have centralized fulfillment. Garnet Hill is a consumer apparel cataloger that fulfills orders to customers in about 20 different countries from its centralized facility in Franconia, New Hampshire. Paper Direct is a leading direct marketer of preprinted papers and supplies for the laser and desktop publishing industry and offers more than 3,000 items through two separate catalogs to customers in 35 countries, fulfilling all orders from three distribution centers located in Lyndhurst, New Jersey, Hinckley, England, and Northmead, Australia.[31] Visit the Web site of Paper Direct (www.paperdirect.com) and you will learn that Vista Papers, based in Leicestershire in the United Kingdom, is the exclusive European supplier of Paper Direct products (www.paperdirect.cooom.uk).[32]

Media

Direct marketers must determine the most effective media mix based on consumer preferences in each foreign market. Media decisions are based on a number of market specific factors, such as media availability, legal restrictions, literacy rates, and cultural factors. A country's level of economic development may also enter into the media mix decision. For example, literacy rates, television ownership, and computer ownership and technology tend to be lower in less-developed countries. Shipping products overnight and using telemarketing may also be difficult in less-developed countries. In these countries, the establishment and maintenance of databases may prove difficult.

In some countries the price of postage is very low; in others, it is quite expensive. You might be wondering whether the recent increases in U.S. postal rates have affected international direct marketing. The answer is . . . not really. According to the DMA, 34 percent of direct marketers have increased international mail volume from 2001–2002, while 34 percent remained the same.[33] The U.S. Postal Service is aware that it is competing with many foreign postal services. Savvy direct marketers investigate postal rates with six or seven competing postal administrations and then they negotiate the best price.[34]

In many developing countries the mail system is slow and not secure. For example, in Mexico, there is a dearth of mailboxes and the mail system is very slow, although improving. However, despite these poor conditions, Neiman-Marcus Direct sent Mexico 100,000 copies of a Spanish version of its American catalog. Prices were listed in pesos and included all tariffs and duties. All orders were sent to a bilingual telemarketing center in Dallas. Because the response generated was positive, Neiman-Marcus Direct now mails catalogs four to six times a year.[35]

E-mail marketing can offer direct marketers lower development costs and excellent targeting. E-mail is an efficient and cost-effective alternative to direct mail. For example, a two-color direct-mail campaign would cost approximately $600 per thousand, whereas an e-mail campaign would cost around $250 per thousand.[36] In addition, e-mail marketing can provide a faster response—compare a direct-mail campaign that takes four months to roll out to an e-mail campaign that takes as little as four weeks to execute with click-through rates ranging from 3 percent to 12 percent.[37] E-mail newsletters are a recommended first step into international e-mail marketing, since their circulation tends to be greater than that for solo campaigns. However, to successfully implement e-mail marketing, direct marketers must be aware of each country's local privacy laws.

International acceptance for direct response television (DRTV) has grown. Latin America has become one of the first regions outside the United States to be explored. In order to successfully use DRTV, direct marketers must be keenly aware of the media landscape, including the key television stations, cable, and satellite opportunities; the role of third-party negotiators (representatives); federal regulations concerning advertising and infomercials; audience trends; media penetration; and viewing share.[38] Direct marketers normally have two options when launching a DRTV campaign—(a) set up local operations on their own; or (b) use an established DRTV international company.

General Motors recently used a DRTV campaign in Argentina supported with a series of follow-ups via direct mail, telephone, and fax. The campaign, designed to increase test drives and sales of its Astra, offered consumers a free Astra video by calling a toll-free number. The results were phenomenal. Astra's market share in Argentina increased from 5 percent to 11 percent.[39]

Telemarketing is another medium for direct marketing overseas, however, it is more limited than in the United States and varies greatly from country to country. In many countries, such as Japan, telemarketing is perceived to be too aggressive. As is the case with other types of media, the successful use of telemarketing depends upon the level of sophistication of the telecommunications infrastructure.

Creative

In the process of developing the creative materials for any international direct marketing campaign, the four words of wisdom seem to be: research, test, translate, and adapt. Visit the Web site of Nestlé in Peru (www.nestle.com.pe) and you will see how Nestlé effectively translated its Web site for Peruvians. It is critical to present your promotional message in words and images to which your audience can relate. That is why direct marketers must properly research their audience, testing the offer and the copy, carefully translating the message into the proper language, and adapting to the local nuances of different cultures. Words that are entirely appropriate in one country's language are inappropriate and insulting in another. Certain colors, symbols, and designs may also be inappropriate to use in a marketing campaign.

One well-known example of a company adapting to local cultural differences is that of the Coca-Cola Company. In Japan, the word "diet" has a negative impression, since Japanese women do not like to admit they are drinking a product for weight loss. Therefore, the Coca-Cola Company revised the brand name of Diet Coke to "Coca-Cola Light" and successfully introduced and positioned the product in Japan as a soft drink for figure maintenance opposed to weight loss.[40] Another example of the need to adapt to different cultures and consumer lifestyles is that of N.W. Ayer's Bahamas tourism campaigns designed for the European market. While the overall campaign focused on clean water, beaches, and air, it incorporated different appeals for select European markets. It emphasized sports activities to the German market, while it utilized humorous ads in the United Kingdom.[41]

To get maximum results, direct marketing campaigns must use promotional appeals that motivate prospects. However, consumer motives vary country by country and what works in one market may not work in another. Direct marketers using the Web as a marketing medium must also be aware of the legal regulations that vary by country. For example, a few years ago, Germany sued Benetton (www.benetton.com) for "exploiting feelings of pity" with one of its on-line campaigns.[42] Again, careful market research and cultural adaptation is the key to developing successful creative materials. For example, U.S. consumers are more receptive to advertisements that affect the emotional or even sensual aspects of their decision-making process, whereas the Japanese are more comfortable with logical and rational appeals. Then again, U.S. consumers are said to be far more conservative than are Canadians and Europeans. Regardless of whether the message appeal is emotional, rational, conservative, or liberal, it must be produced to maximize the response from the targeted customer. Cultural adaptation is crucial to the success of the direct marketing campaign when developing the creative appeal.

One of the first measures a direct marketer can take to ensure cultural adaptation is to determine the country's receptiveness to direct marketing activities. Let's look briefly at the indicators used in this assessment.

COUNTRY MARKET ANALYSIS

Canada

Most Canadians are very familiar with products and services from the United States because the majority of Canadians reside within 100 miles of the U.S. border. In fact, Canada and the United States have many things in common—they even share a professional ice-hockey league. However, there are some distinct differences that direct marketers should bear in mind when marketing to Canadians. For example, Canada is officially bilingual in English and French. However, in Quebec, local language laws require all advertising materials to be printed in French.

Taxes and duties assessed in Canada are another area of difference. Three taxes may come into effect when a U.S. company ships products to Canada. These are[43]

1. *The Goods and Services Tax (GST)*—A seven-percent tax on the total value of the parcel. This tax is applied to all goods imported into Canada with the exception of prescribed property such as magazines, books, or similar printed publications.
2. *The Harmonized Sales Tax (HST)*—A 15-percent tax on the parcel's total value, applicable to all imported goods destined for Nova Scotia, New Brunswick, and Newfoundland, with the exception of prescribed property.
3. *The Provincial Sales Tax (PST)*—An eight-percent tax on the parcel's total value applied to all noncommercial goods imported to Ontario.

Duties, or charges imposed on shipments based on a country of origin and commodity, are also imposed by Canada. Under the North American Free Trade Agreement (NAFTA), products manufactured outside the United States or Mexico are subject to duty charges when shipped to Canada. Shipments of noncommercial goods at $20 (Canadian) or less are exempt from duties because they fall into an international category of Low Value Shipment (LVS).

According to the Canadian Marketing Association (CMA), Canadians receive half the mail that Americans do, but tend to spend twice as much via direct mail.[44] Canada's direct marketing industry is rapidly growing with more than $11 billion worth of products sold through direct channels.[45] Canadians are experiencing the same societal pressures as their neighbors in the United States (single-parent families, two parents working outside the home, constant time pressures) that make the ability to shop from home appealing. Privacy issues are also on the rise. However, unlike the U.S. Direct Marketing Association (DMA) who has been a proponent of industry self-regulation with regard to privacy, the CMA has been active in calling for federal privacy legislation.

Other differences between the United States and Canada include cultural ones. For example, Canadian direct marketing appeals don't normally include appeals to patriotism and vanity as U.S. appeals often do.

Europe

The European Union represents 350 million consumers and 10 million businesses at the time this text is being written. However, it is expected that several more countries will be joining in the next year or so. The European Union is made up of many different countries with different languages (eleven of them), cultures, and legal systems. For example, in Switzerland, 66 percent of the population speaks German, 17 percent French, 7 percent Italian, and a very small minority speak Romansch—the closest language to Latin.[46] Direct marketers are advised to conduct an in-depth study of each country market prior to conducting business in that country. The European Mail Order Trade Association (EMOTA) data indicate that mail-order operators generated over 52.4 billion euro in 2001. Mail order turnover per capital in the European Union equaled 132 euro in 2001.[47]

Differences between U.S. and European markets also exist. For example, European stores are not open 7 days a week as many are in the United States. In fact, many European stores maintain hours and service levels that most U.S. consumers would find unacceptable. Is Europe still an attractive avenue for direct marketing? The answer is you bet! There are many successful U.S. direct marketers in Europe including Lands' End, Viking, and Allstate Insurance. In U.S. dollars, Germans spend some $300 per year on mail order, followed by the United States at $200, Switzerland at $160, Austria at $145, and Great Britain at $140.[48] Despite the high level of spending on mail-order products, most Europeans are not bombarded with direct mail as are U.S. consumers. On an annual basis, the Swiss receive 120 direct-mail solicitations, Belgians receive 95, and Germans receive only 80 compared to the 350 direct-mail pieces received by the average U.S. consumer.[49]

Some factors affecting direct marketing activities in Europe are

- Postal requirements—formats, location of the window, teaser copy on the outer envelope—must comply with local postal authorities which differ by European country.
- Data protection is far more stringent in Europe than it is in the United States. Throughout Europe, an "opt-out" provision is mandatory at the point where you collect data. Until recently, individual countries had their own privacy legislation—which varied from country to country. However, now a European-wide privacy directive is in place and must be adopted by every European Union country.[50] The Safe Harbor Provision, as previously discussed in Chapter 12, requires direct marketers to know the laws and liabilities associated with data collection and information privacy.
- Mailing restrictions and policies may differ by European country. For example, in the United Kingdom, each direct-mail package must be approved by the Advertising Standards Authority (ASA).
- The list industry is strong in Europe. Multinational lists include names and data about individuals who are usually responsive to direct-mail offers, speak English, and are internationally minded. The list selections available, output formats, and guarantees equal U.S. standards. Multinational lists allow the direct marketer to test many countries at the same time without incurring additional fees. Local lists tend to be more numerous and offer greater selections.

- The Benelux—which includes the countries of Belgium, Netherlands, and Luxembourg, is ideal for direct marketing because of its well-developed direct marketing infrastructure. Lists, payment options, and call centers are all quite advanced in this region of Europe.[51]

Latin America

The population of Latin America is 650 million—which is twice the size of the European Union. Different dialects of Spanish are spoken across Latin America, while Portuguese is spoken in Brazil. Overall, the direct marketing industry—commercial and business to business—is growing at a rate of about 40 to 50 percent per year in most of Latin America.[52] Latin America is a continent of countries made up of very different direct marketing infrastructures. It cannot be treated as a single market except on paper.

For direct marketers, Brazil is the most sophisticated market in Latin America. The lists and databases available there are of fairly high quality. However, fewer public sources of data are available in Latin America than in the United States. With the exception of Brazil, direct marketing is largely underdeveloped in terms of the number of agencies and telemarketing companies in Latin America. However, Latin America is not expected to follow the path the United States did in developing sophisticated direct marketing machinery. The Internet will likely enable Latin America to make revolutionary strides in direct marketing development.

Although the direct marketing industry is trailing behind in Latin America, the outlook is promising. One reason for this is that the amount of communication one Latin American consumer receives is much lower than that received by U.S. or European consumers. For example, the average household in Mexico receives only six or seven pieces of mail per month.[53] Therefore, the amount of communication clutter is significantly reduced. However, keep in mind that mail services in Mexico are considerably slower than in the United States.

Latin American consumers are very receptive to products made in the United States and have recently shown acceptance of direct response television (DRTV) media as well. Some successful DRTV marketing campaigns in Latin America include the following:[54]

- AB Flex, one of the fitness industry's top-performing products, generated more than $10 million of sales in a nine-month period.
- Murad International Skin care generated more than $7 million in sales in Mexico alone. The brand awareness generated created an extremely successful continuity program and catalog.

A large part of Mexico's close to 100 million population subsists below the poverty line. It's the top ten percent, which commands 41.2 percent of the nation's wealth, as well as the next 10 percent, with 14 percent of the wealth. This may be of concern to direct marketers. With 39 percent of the Mexican market under the age of 15, the prospect for future success in direct marketing is great. Thus, Mexico is a very concentrated market—ideal for direct marketers.[55]

Building relationships may be important in direct marketing, but it is especially so in Latin America where consumers crave personal contact and confianza (trust). Most business deals will not develop until a friendship has been established. Unlike the case in the United States, time is not money in Latin America.

Asia

Asia has a population of over 500 million consumers and millions of businesses. Catalog marketers have struggled with the Asian market for over a decade. The major challenges include the lack of reliable mailing lists, a scarcity of local talent, inadequate telephone systems, and the inability to fulfill orders through traditional retailers. In fact, some 60 U.S. catalogs have been tested in Japan over the past five years, and only 15 of them remain today. Those that have survived (L.L. Bean, Sharper Image, Lands' End among others) are very successful.[56] Among the lessons many direct marketers have learned in Asia is that you must treat each country separately and understand the local laws and policies. All Asian markets are not equally attractive. Recent research shows that the more accessible Asian countries for direct marketers include South Korea, Taiwan, Hong Kong (China), and Japan.[57] Let's take a closer look at each of these markets.

South Korea

Direct buying in South Korea is growing at 30 percent per year, and South Koreans import $25 billion in U.S. goods annually. Furthermore, U.S. products are desirable to South Koreans because most of the population is concentrated in cities, especially near Seoul, which accounts for about 20 percent of the entire population.[58] These urban consumers tend to possess a stronger desire to keep up with the latest innovations in technology and trends in fashion.

Taiwan

The direct marketing infrastructure in Taiwan is not fully developed. List availability is very poor and telemarketing is available, but not yet popular. Although the postal service is of very good quality, there is no bulk discount rate for mailings. Direct marketing in Taiwan should expand as its infrastructure improves.

China

Direct marketing in China is relatively new, but growing. With 1.3 billion people, China has great potential for direct marketers with heavy concentrations of wealth in mostly coastal cities.[59] However, like Taiwan's, its direct marketing infrastructure is lacking. Although the middle class is growing, the vast majority of the Chinese population has little money, no credit cards, no telephones, and no direct way to receive merchandise.[60] Surprisingly, information privacy is very strict in China and there are privacy code laws in place. Anyone caught breaking the privacy code laws may be subject to a prison term.

Japan

Japan is one of the most advanced countries in the Pacific Rim. Its direct marketing infrastructure is superior to that of its Asian counterparts. Direct mail, telemarketing, home-shopping programs, and even infomercials have grown in popularity in Japan.[61] Japan leads all non-U.S. countries in direct marketing advertising expenditures. In 2002, Japan spent $71.7 million on international direct marketing ad spending, and this figure is expected to rise to $97.2 million by 2007.[62] Japan also ranked first in direct marketing sales among non-U.S. countries in 2002, generating $586.1 million dollars in sales revenue.[63] Catalog shopping was the most popular direct marketing media in Japan in 2001. Japanese consumers used the telephone (61.1 percent) and mail (53.9 percent) when ordering products in 2001.[64]

However, Japan, like the other Asian countries, has experienced economic set-backs, and some U.S. direct marketers are cutting back or abandoning Japanese mailings. Direct marketers must be sensitive to cultural differences when marketing to Japanese consumers.

Summary

International direct marketing is on the rise. Many U.S. businesses are seeking to expand by penetrating international markets. In doing so, direct marketers must keep in mind the many unique differences between domestic and foreign markets. Many researchers offer suggestions for how to enter a foreign market. These steps include assessing your international potential, conducting marketing research, selecting your country markets, developing an international marketing plan, and implementing your international marketing strategies. Careful market research, including an assessment of consumer needs, direct marketing infrastructure, and political, economic, and business environments, is necessary prior to commencing international direct marketing activities.

Direct marketers must make decisions involving the mode of market entry—direct exporting, licensing, joint venture, contract manufacturing, or direct investment that they will employ. Direct marketers must make a careful examination of the unique infrastructure needed to support direct marketing operations including an analysis of lists and databases, fulfillment operations, media, and creative. The direct marketing infrastructure varies by country market and each market must be thoroughly researched and analyzed. This chapter briefly examined four markets—Canada, Europe, Latin America, and Asia.

Key Terms

- infrastructure, 375
- gross domestic product (GDP), 376
- exporting, 378

- licensing, 378
- licensor, 378
- licensee, 378
- joint venture, 379

- contract manufacturing, 379
- direct investment, 379
- management contracting, 379
- duties, 384

Review Questions

1. What makes international direct marketing different from domestic direct marketing?
2. Why are companies looking outside the United States to do business?
3. Describe the different modes of market entry that can be used to enter a foreign market.
4. Discuss the primary infrastructure necessary for international direct marketing activities to be carried out with success.
5. Name some of the ways direct marketers have adapted to cultural differences when marketing internationally.
6. Identify and explain the five step approach direct marketers should follow when marketing to an international country.

7. How do the media preferences vary by country markets? Which country is attractive for DRTV?
8. Compare and contrast direct mail and e-mail as international direct marketing mediums. Which one would be most appropriate to use when marketing in Canada? Europe? Latin America? Asia?
9. Discuss fulfillment operations. What advantages do both centralized and decentralized fulfillment operations offer international direct marketers?
10. Overview the history of direct marketing around the world. Be sure to explain when and where it began and how it grew.

Exercise

The U.S.-based motorcycle company that you are now employed with wants to expand its business overseas. Using the marketing research issues described in this chapter, describe how the company should go about doing this. Based on your analysis, which countries might be considered likely candidates for international expansion. Provide an explanation to support your selections.

CASE:　GLOBALIZING AN AMERICAN CATALOG

OVERVIEW

Mail order's historical roots were in Europe, where catalogs first appeared in the mid-fifteenth century, soon after the invention of movable type and the advent of printing. Its popularity, however, emerged in the United States after the Civil War via the efforts of Aaron Montgomery Ward and Richard Sears. Its burgeoning growth occurred after World War II, spearheaded by a diverse proliferation of catalogs and, most recently, the World Wide Web coupled with electronic ordering. This case is a presentation of a niche catalog, one most likely to succeed in the direct marketing environment of segmented markets, benefit-oriented promotions, and scientific decision making. The purpose of this case study is to demonstrate the application of certain considerations in the globalization of direct marketing, as presented in this chapter, to actual practice. It illustrates how the tools and techniques of direct marketing, utilized by a successful American catalog, the Peruvian Connection, were applied as the catalog entered, first, Japan, and then the United Kingdom and Germany.

CASE

The Peruvian Connection began when Annie Hurlbut, age 19, packed a duffel bag and headed for South America. It was the summer of her sophomore year at Yale and, drawn by an interest in archaeology, she volunteered to help an American archaeologist working at the pre-Inca site of Pachacamac outside Lima. She arrived in Peru knowing not a word of Spanish, and unsure if anyone would understand her. Asked how she survived those 3 months in South America, Annie grinned and said, "Blind luck, I guess." But what started as a whimsy evolved into a fascinating business.

Midway through graduate school in anthropology, much of which was spent doing research on women who sell in markets in the Andes, Annie learned about the extraordinary properties of alpaca wool. It is light enough for year-round wear, but warm due to unusually high lanolin content, and few fibers in the world equal its softness. Annie began to export alpaca wool sweaters, and within a few months the new company was christened the Peruvian Connection. Her mother, Biddy, a partner in the business, received the first orders while Annie was doing fieldwork for her thesis in Peru. Since the company's beginning, the business has been run from the family's farm in Tonganoxie, Kansas.

Annie, who had virtually no background in clothing design, began by working with beautiful and unusual sweaters of local artisans. A sense of style enabled her to adapt the sweaters to North American tastes. Now, the Peruvian Connection does its own designing, but the same artisans knit for the company on the same antique looms.

Annie insists on using the finest. She keeps prices low by selecting and buying raw materials directly from the producers, and maintains control over quality by checking each product before it is exported from Peru. Annie now augments Alpaca wool products with products made of pima cotton.

The Peruvian Connection uses mail order as its primary distribution system, along with three stores in the United States and one in England. Its luxury fiber clothing, blankets, rugs, and hangings are available only from the company. Customers range from enthusiasts of "cheap chic" to collectors of colonial (from Pizarro's conquest to the Republican era, 1825) native crosses. Contemporary clothing is complemented by wearable art from Peru's rich past. Authenticity and complete satisfaction are guaranteed.

FIGURE 15-4 Comparative Item Presentations from American and German Versions of the Same Peruvian Connection Catalog

In the process of building her retail mail-order business, Annie learned early on the value of a customer. After a first sale, her promotional strategy is to send periodic mailings to customers. Annie seeks new customers via market segmentation techniques, matching the profile of her present customers and calculating a "present value" of new acquisitions to justify their cost. About 260,000 customers purchase from the Peruvian Connection in the United States; another 70,000 customers are in the United Kingdom; and 38,000 are in Germany. These customers generate sales revenues in the range of $40 million, and about half of this amount is from repeat orderers.

Annie herself produces the catalogs, sales copy and photo shoots included. About six million catalogs are mailed domestically; another four million are mailed internationally.

The Peruvian Connection's global direct marketing began in the late 1980s, first to the United Kingdom, where a retail store was also opened. Even though product selection and page positioning are the same in both the United States and United Kingdom versions of the catalog, descriptive copy, and pricing differ. The U.K. catalog version contains Anglican spellings, local sizes, and pricing is in pounds sterling. Pricing must incorporate value-added tax (VAT) and often must anticipate currency fluctuation. The German catalog version, with pricing in deutsche marks, has standard copy translated into German so as to reflect cultural differences. Even though copy is basically the same, review by a native consultant is very important. Figure 15-4 shows similar catalog presentations from the American and German versions of the same catalog.

A real challenge is finding prospects to whom to mail. Annie recognized this early on as she engaged local direct marketing experts and consultants for guidance in list refinement. (It is interesting to note that demographic profiles of her customers are similar in all countries.)

However, the Peruvian Connection must accommodate various cultural differences. It considers cultural differences in payment preferences when fulfilling orders. For example, German customers do not share the U.S. propensity to use credit cards, preferring open-account billing. Foreign funds need to be managed. In addition, the Peruvian Connection considers cultural differences regarding local distribution as well as local use of the telephone and the Internet.

Source: The globalization experience presented here, with their permission, was conceived and developed by Annie and Biddy Hurlbut. Although the Peruvian Connection's mail-order catalog sales were initially confined to the United States, the company was already international in that its product originated in Peru and other South American countries. ■

Case Discussion Questions

1. What economic, social, and cultural differences does the Peruvian Connection need to consider as it applies the tools and techniques of direct marketing to diverse international markets?
2. What are the main factors that led to the international success of the Peruvian Connection?
3. If you were hired by the Peruvian Connection to expand its international direct marketing efforts, what additional information would you need in order to provide suggestions for market expansion? What are some of the avenues you might investigate and recommend for international market expansion?

Notes

1. Lawrence J. Gitman and Carl McDaniel, *The Future of Business* (Mason, Ohio: South-Western, 2002), 67.
2. Jupiter Media Matrix, Inc., "International: Global Digital Divide Narrowest for Mobile Market," *Marketing News*, July 8, 2002, 19.
3. "The DMA's International Postal Usage Survey," *The Statistical Fact Book 2003*, 25th ed. (New York: The Direct Marketing Association, Inc., 2003), 219.
4. Ibid., 220.
5. Ibid.

6. "Top 10 Global Ad Markets," *Advertising Age Global*, April 2002, 18–23.

7. Beth Negus Viveiros, "As The World Turns," *Inside the DMA*, 2002, D19.

8. Kelly J. Andrews, "The World Wide Web Lives Up to Its Name," *Target Marketing*, 22, no. 48 (June, 1999): 48.

9. Richard N. Miller, *Multinational Direct Marketing: The Methods & the Markets* (New York: McGraw-Hill, Inc., 1995), 7–8.

10. Ibid., 2.

11. Ibid.

12. Ibid.

13. Rainer Hengst, "Plotting Your Global Strategy," *Direct Marketing* 63, no. 4 (August 2000): 52–57.

14. Michael R. Czinkota and Ilkka A. Ronkainen, *International Marketing*, 7th ed. (Mason, Ohio: South-Western, 2004), 539.

15. Ibid., 545.

16. Adapted from John J. Wild, Kenneth L. Wild, and Jerry C. Y. Han, *International Business*, 2nd ed. (Upper Saddle River, NJ: Prentice Hall, 2003); adapted from William J. MacDonald, "Five Steps to International Success," *Direct Marketing* 61, no. 7 (November 1998): 32–35; Rainer Hengst, "Plotting Your Global Strategy," *Direct Marketing* 63, no. 4 (August 2000): 52–54; and Richard N. Miller, "Where in the World. . . How to Determine the Best Market for Your Product or Service," *Target Marketing* 24, no. 3 (March 2001): 57.

17. Richard N. Miller, *Multinational Direct Marketing: The Methods & the Markets* (New York: McGraw-Hill, Inc., 1995), 6–7.

18. Lawrence J. Gitman and Carl McDaniel, *The Future of Business* (Mason, Ohio: South-Western, 2002), 81.

19. Michael R. Czinkota and Ilkka A. Ronkainen, *International Marketing*, 7th ed. (Mason, Ohio: South-Western, 2004), 318.

20. William J. McDonald, *Direct Marketing: An Integrated Approach*, (New York: Irwin/McGraw-Hill, 1999), 349.

21. Tom Murry, "Reeling Them In," *The DMA Insider* (Spring 2003): 18.

22. H. Katzenstein and W. S. Sachs, *Direct Marketing*, 2nd ed. (New York: Macmillan Publishing Company, 1986), 417.

23. Lawrence J. Gitman and Carl McDaniel, *The Future of Business* (Mason, Ohio: South-Western, 2002), 83.

24. Texas Instruments Web site, <http://www.ti.com> September, 2003.

25. Terry Brennan, "Day-Timers Makes Foray Into U.D. With First 100,000-Piece Mail Test," *DM News*, November 15, 1989, 14.

26. Michael R. Czinkota and Ilkka A. Ronkainen, *International Marketing*, 7th ed. (Mason, Ohio: South-Western, 2004), 318.

27. William J. MacDonald, "Five Steps To International Success," *Direct Marketing* 61, no. 7 (1998): 35.

28. Michael R. Czinkota and Ilkka A. Ronkainen, *International Marketing*, 7th ed. (Mason, Ohio: South-Western, 2004), 318.

29. Beth Negus Viveiros, "As The World Turns," *Inside the DMA*, 2002, D19.

30. Lawrence Chaido and Lisa A. Yorgey, "The Back-End of Global Delivery: How to Transport Your Products Around the World," *Target Marketing* 21, no. 9 (September 1998): 64–66.

31. William J. MacDonald, "Five Steps To International Success," *Direct Marketing* 61, no. 7 (1998): 35–36.

32. Paper Direct Web sites, <http://www.paperdirect.com> and <http://www.paperdirect.com.uk> September, 2003.

33. "The DMA's International Postal Usage Survey," *The Statistical Fact Book 2003*, 25th ed. (New York: The Direct Marketing Association, Inc., 2003), 220.

34. Amy Traverso, "A Global Perspective," *The DMA Insider* (Fall 2002): 6.

35. William, J. MacDonald, "Five Steps to International Success," *Direct Marketing* 61, no. 7 (November 1998): 34.

36. Stephen, J. Eustace, "The World Is Your Cyber Market," *Target Marketing* 24, no. 4, (April 2001): 54.

37. Ibid.

38. Priya Ghai, "Southward Bound," *Target Marketing 24*, no. 5 (May 2001): 64.

39. Stan Rapp "Something New Under the Advertising Sun," *The DMA Insider* (Fall 2002), 10–14.

40. Michael R. Czinkota and Ilkka A. Ronkainen, *International Marketing*, 7th ed. (Mason, Ohio: South-Western, 2004), 257.

41. Ibid., 552.

42. Rose Lewis, "Before You Advertise on the Net—Check the International Marketing Laws," *Bank Marketing* (May 1996), 40–42.

43. Lisa A. Yorgey, "Navigating Taxes and Duties," *Target Marketing* 22, no. 10 (October 1999): 76.

44. Lisa A. Yorgey, "Marketing up North: Treat Canada as Another Country, Not Another State," *Target Marketing* 22, no. 4 (April 1999): 52.

45. Cornelio A. Bos and John Gustavson, "NAFTA: The Valve That Regulates Our Borders," *Target Marketing* 20, no. 7 (July 1997): 54.

46. Rainer Hengst, "Plotting Your Global Strategy," *Direct Marketing* 63, no. 4 (August 2000): 54.

47. "European Mail Order Trade Association (EMOTA)," from "2002 FEDMA's Survey on Direct and Interactive Marketing Activities in Europe," *The Statistical Fact Book 2003*, 25th ed. (New York: The Direct Marketing Association, Inc., 2003), 223.

48. Rainer Hengst, "Plotting Your Global Strategy," *Direct Marketing* 63, no. 4 (August 2000): 54.

49. Ibid.

50. Erika Rasmusson, "The Perils of International Direct Mail," *Sales & Marketing Management* 152, no. 4 (April 2000): 107.

51. Lisa A. Yorgey, "Direct Marketing in the Benelux," *Target Marketing* 22, no. 7 (July 1999): 40.

52. Laura Loro, "Zeroing in on Latin America: Infrastructure Varies by Nation, But Marketers Say Opportunity Huge," *Business Marketing* 83, no. 1 (January 1998): 19.

53. Amy Traverso, "A Global Perspective," *The DMA Insider* (Fall 2002): 8.

54. North American Publishing Company, "Southward Bound," *Target Marketing*, 24, no. 5 (May 2001): 64.

55. Cornelio A. Bos and John Gustavson, "NAFTA: The Valve That Regulates Our Borders," *Target Marketing* 20, no. 7 (July 1997): 54.

56. William J. McDonald, "American Direct Marketers in Europe and Asia: Prospect Motivations and Creative Strategy," *Direct Marketing* 61, no. 4 (August 1998): 38–42.

57. Rainer Hengst, "Plotting Your Global Strategy," *Direct Marketing* 63, no. 4 (August 2000): 52–57.

58. Ibid., 55.

59. Ibid., 55.

60. William J. McDonald, "The Ban in China: How Direct Marketing Is Affected," *Direct Marketing* 61, no. 2 (June 1998): 17.

61. William J. McDonald, "International Direct Marketing in a Rapidly Changing World," *Direct Marketing* 61, no. 11 (March 1999): 44.

62. "The DMA Report: Economic Impact—30 Countries Worldwide, 2002," *The Statistical Fact Book 2003*, 25th ed. (New York: The Direct Marketing Association, Inc., 2003), 225.

63. Ibid., 224.

64. "The 9th Survey on Direct Marketing Usage, the Japan Direct Marketing Association, 2002," *The Statistical Fact Book 2003*, 25th ed. (New York: The Direct Marketing Association, Inc., 2003), 221.

Glossary

a posteriori   after the fact.

a priori   before the fact.

accessory equipment   equipment used to aid and implement production.

accumulation   bringing together of goods from a number of sources to a larger homogenous supply.

ad clicks   the number of times a user "clicks" on an on-line ad, often measured as a function of time.

affinity   as a marketing term, relationships.

agent middlemen   do not take title to the goods but they do actively assist in transfer of title.

allocation   breaking down a homogenous supply into smaller units.

alternative hypothesis   the hypothesis that is determined when a null hypothesis is proven wrong.

annoyance   in marketing terms, it is the way people feel when they receive too much unsolicited marketing communications.

attrition   the assumed (historic) drop off in active customers from one time period to the next.

banner advertising   the digital analog to print ads, targeting a broad audience with the goal of creating awareness about the product or service being promoted.

bingo card   an insert or page of a magazine that is created by the publishers to provide a numeric listing of advertisers (also called an "information card").

bit   the smallest unit of information that a computer understands; one electronic pulse.

branding   refers to the use of a name, term, symbol, or design (or a combination of these) to identify a company's goods and services and to distinguish them from their competitors.

break even   the point at which the gross profit on a unit sale equates to the cost of making that unit sale.

broadcast media   television and radio which can be used as methods for direct response advertising.

browser   the software that enables you to view the pages on the Web.

business clusters   reveal the impact of variables on the buying behavior of businesses located in these areas.

business-to-business (B2B) direct marketing   the process of providing goods and services to industrial market intermediaries, as opposed to ultimate consumers.

call abandonment   the number of callers in telemarketing that hang up before being serviced by a telephone sales representative.

call center   a dedicated team supported by various telephone technological resources to provide responses to customer inquiries.

call center outsourcing   refers to the process of having all call center activities handled by an outside organization or a teleservice outsourcer.

catalog   a multipage direct-mail booklet that displays photographs and/or descriptive details of products/ services along with prices and order details.

cause-related marketing   a commercial activity by which businesses and charities or causes form a partnership with each other to market an image, product, or service for mutual benefit.

central limit theorem   assures us that (in a number of random samples taken from a population) the sample means (response rates) tend to be normally distributed.

channels of distribution   the linkages between producers and users.

chi-square (χ^2) test   a statistical technique for determining whether an observed difference between the test and the control in an experiment is (or is not) significant.

chief privacy officer (CPO)   a corporate officer whose responsibility it is to protect the sensitive information the corporation collects, from credit card accounts to health records.

circular   a printed piece that augments the letter to provide additional information (often called a "folder" or "brochure").

classic format   a direct-mail package consisting of an outer envelope, letter, circular, order form, and a reply envelope.

clickstream   the database created by the date-stamped and time-stamped, coded/interpreted, button-pushing events enacted by users of interactive media.

click-through rates   the number of times a user "clicks" on an on-line ad, often measured as a function of time.

code of ethics   a code that generally serves as a guideline for making ethical decisions.

cold calls   a telemarketing term that indicates there is no existing relationship with, or recognition of, the direct marketer by the customer or potential customer.

compiled lists   lists that have been generated by a third party or market research firm of individuals who do not have a response history.

confidence level   the number of standard deviations from the mean in a normal distribution.

continuity selling   offers that are continued on a regular (weekly, monthly, quarterly, annually) basis (also called "club offers").

contract manufacturing   the process by which a company contracts a local manufacturer to produce goods for the company.

control group   a group of subjects on which the experiment is not conducted.

cookie   an electronic tag on the consumer's computer that enables the Web site to follow consumers as they shop and recognize them on return visits.

cooperative mailings   provide participants, usually noncompeting direct response advertisers, with opportunities to reduce mailing cost in reaching common prospects.

cost per response (CPR)   the total promotion budget divided by the total number of orders and/or inquiries received.

cost per viewer (CPV)   the total promotion budget divided by the total number of people in the viewing audience.

coupon   an offer by a manufacturer or retailer that includes an incentive for purchase of a product or service in the form of a specified price reduction.

cross-selling   an important characteristic of direct marketing where new and related products (or even unrelated products) are offered to existing customers.

customer database   a list of customer names to which additional information has been added in a systematic fashion.

customer lifetime value (CLTV)   the discounted stream of revenue a customer will generate over the lifetime of his or her relationship or patronage with a company.

customer relationship management (CRM)   a business strategy to select and manage customers to optimize value.

customer satisfaction   the extent to which a firm fulfills a consumer's needs, desires, and expectations.

data mining   the process of using statistical and mathematical techniques to extract customer information from the customer database in order to draw inferences about each individual customer's needs and predict future behavior.

database   a collection of data arranged for ease and speed of search and retrieval.

database enhancement   adding and overlaying information to records to better describe and understand the customer.

degrees of freedom   the number of observations that are allowed to vary.

demographics   identifiable and measurable statistics that describe the consumer population.

dependent variable   a variable upon whose outcome or effect the research is interested.

derived demand   industrial demand that ultimately depends on consumer demand.

direct investment   the process whereby a company acquires an existing company or forms a completely new company.

direct marketing   an interactive system of marketing that uses one or more advertising media to effect a measurable customer response or transaction at any location and stores information about that event in a database.

dry testing   experimental research used to test a new product not yet available in the marketplace.

dual distribution   the marketer using several (two or more) competing channels of distribution to reach the same target customer.

duties   a tax charged by a government, especially on imports.

e-branding   refers to carrying out branding strategies electronically.

e-fulfillment   the integration of people, processes, and technology to ensure customer satisfaction before, during, and after the on-line buying experience.

e-mail electronic communication that travels all over the world via the Internet, but is not a part of the World Wide Web.

electronic commerce (e-commerce) the completion of buying and selling transactions on-line.

embedded ads ads that are designed to allow the viewer to receive additional information without having to link to other Web sites.

ethical conforming to the accepted professional standards of conduct.

ethics a branch of philosophy, a system of human behavior concerned with morality: the rightness and wrongness of individual actions or deeds.

experiment is designed to measure the effect of change (often called a "test" by direct marketers).

exporting when a company sells its products from its home base without any personnel overseas.

fabricated materials materials that have already undergone some processing, but require additional processing.

focus group interview a survey research tool where unstructured small groups (representative of appropriate market segments, under skilled leadership) converse in a relaxed environment about the subject of the research.

frequency the number of ad insertions purchased in a specific communication vehicle within a specified time period.

fulfillment the act of carrying out a customer's expectations by sending the product to the customer or delivering the service agreed upon.

fundraising organized activity or an instance of soliciting money or pledges, as for charitable organizations or political campaigns.

general descriptive information a category of information containing demographic or classification information.

geographics the physical characteristics of a certain area.

Global Positioning System (GPS) a segmentation tool that associates latitude and longitude coordinates with street addresses.

gross rating points a mathematical value computed by multiplying reach by frequency that measures the number of people exposed to an ad.

hits any on-line requests for data from a Web page or file.

hotline names the most recent names acquired by specific list owners, but there is no uniformity as to what chronological period "recent" describes.

house lists lists of an organization's own customers (active as well as inactive).

hypertext the links that enable you to move from one Web site to another. Most are recognizable by their *underline*.

hypertext markup language (HTML) a simple coding system used to format documents for viewing by Web clients.

hypothesis testing an assertion about the value of the parameter of a variable (the researcher decides) on the basis of observed facts such as the relative response to a test of variation in advertising.

inbound calls a category of telemarketing where customers are calling to place an order or to request more information or for customer service.

identified users the demographic profile of either visitors or users of a site during a specified period of time.

independent variable a controllable factor in an experiment.

industrial goods products that are generally used as raw materials or in the fabrication of other goods.

infomediaries companies that act as third parties by gathering personal information from a user and providing it to other sites with the user's approval.

infomercial a relatively long commercial in the format of a television program, to inform viewers of a featured product.

infrastructure is normally a leading indicator of economic development of a country and includes the essential services that support business activities.

input-output analysis derived from Census Bureau data, traces the distribution of goods from their origins to their destinations

insert a popular form of print advertisement in a magazine or newspaper.

installations consists of major equipment with long lives such as buildings.

integrated order fulfillment a term based on the idea that the process of building and delivering products should not begin until after an order has been taken.

intellectual property products of the mind or ideas.

interactive marketing two-way marketing communication with the customer or prospect.

Internet a worldwide network of computers connected to one another to enable rapid transmission of data from one point to another reaching every country in the world.

involvement devices   devices used in direct response advertising to spur action by involving the reader; examples would be tokens, stamps, punch-outs, puzzles, etc..

joint venture   two or more investors join forces to conduct a business by sharing ownership and control.

key code   a unique identifier placed on the response device or order form prior to mailing a promotional piece in order to measure results.

law of large numbers   assures us that (as sample size increases) the distribution of sample means concentrates closer to the true mean of the total population.

layout   the positioning of copy and illustrations to gain attention and direct the reader through the message in an intended sequence.

letter   the principal element of the direct-mail package that provides the primary means for communication and personalization.

licensing   similar to franchising, local businesses become authorized to manufacture or sell specific brand products for another company.

lifetime value of a customer (LTV)   the discounted stream of revenue a customer will generate over the lifetime of his or her relationship or patronage with a company (also called "customer lifetime value").

limit of error   describes the number of percentage points by which the researcher is allowed to comfortably miscalculate the actual response rate.

list brokers   those who serve as intermediaries who bring list users and list owners together.

list compilers   organizations that develop lists and data about them, often serving as their own list managers and brokers.

list managers   managers who represent the interest of list owners and have responsibility to be in contact with list brokers and list users.

list owners   those who describe and acquire prospects (as market segments) who show potential of becoming customers of the list user.

lists   a group of names, addresses, and information used by direct marketers as market segments to which promotion efforts are directed.

logistics   the management of the details of an operation.

management contracting   the process whereby a contract is signed with local foreign people or the foreign government to manage the business in the country market.

market segmentation   a marketing strategy devised to attract and meet the needs of a specific submarket.

market segments   placing people (customers or potential customers) into homogeneous groups based on certain attributes such as age, income, stage in the family life cycle, etc.

marketing concept   a philosophy and attitude which says that all planning, policies, and operations should put the needs and wants of the customer above the desire to sell a particular product or service.

marketing research   gathers, classifies, and analyzes information about the marketing process.

match code   abbreviated information about a customer record which is constructed so that each individual record can be matched, pairwise, with each other record.

mail order   a transaction within a channel, characterized by the absence of a "retail store" or a "salesperson"; direct channel from producer to user.

mean   arithmetic average; a measure of central tendency in a normal distribution.

median   an average, the midpoint of a set of values; a measure of central tendency in a normal distribution.

merchant middlemen   companies that buy goods from the previous owner, the seller, then they become sellers.

merge-purge   a computerized process used to identify and delete duplicate names/addresses within various lists.

middlemen   independent business concerns that stand between the producer and the consumer in a distribution channel.

mode   an average, the value that occurs most frequently; a measure of central tendency in a normal distribution.

morals   the judgment of the goodness or badness of human action and character.

motivations   needs that compel a person to take action or behave in a certain way.

multibuyer   an individual whose name/address that appears on two or more response lists simultaneously.

multichannel distribution   refers to a marketer using several competing channels of distribution to reach the same target customers.

multichannel marketing   the process that allows customers to select the media or channels they prefer when shopping for products and services.

negative option   the shipment of a product is sent automatically unless the customer specifically requests that it not be.

nixie   mail that has been returned by the United States Postal Service because it is undeliverable as addressed.

normal distribution completely determined by its two parameters: mean and standard deviation ("bell-shaped curve").

North American Industry Classification System (NAICS) an industrial classification system using a six-digit code that focuses on production activities.

null hypothesis the statistical hypothesis that there is no difference between the means of the groups being compared.

offer the terms under which a specific product or service is promoted to the customer.

on-line panels on-line discussions marketers conduct with people who have agreed to talk about a selected topic over a period of time.

operating supplies materials used in producing goods and services, such as ball-point pens or lubricating oil for machines.

outbound calls a category of telemarketing where firms place calls to prospects and/or customers.

outsourcing a telemarketing term, refers to the process of having all call center activities handled by an outside organization or a service bureau.

ownership information the category of information that contains data about the various products the consumer owns.

package inserts printed offers of products and services that arrive when the recipient has just made a purchase.

packing slip a form or document that identifies the products to be included with the order.

pages a measure of the number of Web pages downloaded from a specific site at a particular time.

PAR a calculation of the value of a continuity customer over time.

PAR ratio the ratio of cost of customer acquisition to PAR value.

penetration strategy a strategy used where the price of a product or service is set at a very low level to enable almost any consumer who wants to buy the product to afford to do so.

permission marketing the process of obtaining the consent of a customer before a company sends out a marketing communication to that customer via the Internet.

picking list a list identifying each item on an order list and serves as a routing guide to move the picker efficiently through a warehouse.

pixel a tiny dot of light on a computer screen (stands for "picture element").

positioning a marketing strategy that enables marketers to understand how each consumer perceives a company's product or service based on important attributes (also known as "product positioning").

positive option the process whereby the customer must specifically request shipment of a product for each offer in a series.

predictive dialers advanced hardware systems that use machines to dial and connect a telemarketing call only when the computer detects a live human voice on the other end of the line.

preprinted inserts newspaper advertisements that are usually printed ahead of the newspaper production and are provided to the newspaper to be distributed with the newspaper.

present value of a customer a measure of how much could or should be spent to acquire a customer at the yield rate assumed when discounting.

price elasticity the relative change in demand for a product given the change in the price of the product.

price penetration a strategy used if the direct marketer wants to maximize sales volume.

price skimming a strategy used when the objective of the price is to generate the largest possible return on investment (ROI) where the price must be set at the highest possible level in order to "skim-the-cream" off the top of the market and only target a select number of consumers who can afford to buy the product/service.

primary data data collected specifically for the current research problem or need.

privacy the ability of an individual to control the access others have to personal information.

privacy fundamentalists represents about twenty percent of the population and consists of people who believe that they own their name, as well as all the information about themselves, and that no one else may use it without their permission.

privacy pragmatists represents about sixty percent of the population and consists of people who look at the contact, offer, and the methods of data collection and apply a cost/benefit analysis to make a determination about a marketer's use of information.

privacy unconcerned represents about twenty percent of the population and consists of those who literally do not care about the issue of privacy at all.

product differentiation a strategy that uses innovative design, packaging, and positioning to make a clear distinction between products and services serving a market segment.

product positioning a marketing strategy that enables marketers to understand how each consumer perceives a company's product or service based on important attributes (also called "positioning").

product purchase information   a category of information that contains a variety of purchase activity data, including magazine subscription information, credit record information, and lifestyle information.

product/service policy   a formal statement that acts as a management guide as to what products will be made or sold, and what attributes these will have.

promotion   communicating information between the seller and the buyer to change attitudes and/or behavior.

psychographics   the study of lifestyles, habits, attitudes, beliefs, and value systems of individuals.

pull strategy   the process whereby consumers seek out and demand information and/or products and services from the producer (also called "pull policy").

push strategy   where information and marketing activities follow the normal path of distribution of a product—from the producer to the consumer (also called "push policy").

qualitative   relating to, or concerning explanations or reasons.

qualitative research   research that deals with behavior.

quantitative   of or relating to number or quantity.

quantitative research   research that deals with numbers.

rack jobber   a middleman that provides and maintains displays and inventories of products.

random sample   a sample in which every element of a population has an equal chance of being selected and differences occur by chance only.

randomization   of or relating to an event in which all outcomes are equally likely.

raw materials   unprocessed goods that are destined to become part of another product, subject to further processing.

reach   the number of people exposed to vehicles carrying the ad.

reference groups   the people a consumer turns to for reinforcement.

reference individuals   the people a consumer turns to for advice.

response device   the part of the direct-mail package that provides the means for action.

response lists   lists of those who have responded to a direct marketer's offer.

right to confidentiality   a consumer's right to specify to a given company that information that they freely provide should not be shared.

right to be informed   includes the consumer's right to receive any and all pertinent or requested information.

right to privacy   the ability of an individual to control the access others have to personal information.

right to selection   a consumer's right to choose or make decisions about his or her buying behavior.

run-of-paper advertisements (ROP)   small advertisements that appear in the regular section of the newspaper where positioning of the ad is at the will of the newspaper.

salting   the process whereby a direct marketer places decoys, which are either incorrect spellings or fictitious names, on a customer list to track and identify any misuse (also called "seeding").

sample   subsets of the total population for which data are available.

sample size   the number of observations in a sample, determined by first looking at two major considerations: (1) the cost of reaching the sample and (2) the amount of information we need to make an efficient decision.

sampling   a method of choosing observations from which we can predict estimations.

sampling errors   errors that occur in market research due to nonrepresentative sample selection or a lack of randomness of the sample.

search engine   an index of key words that enables Web browsers to find what they are looking for.

secondary data   data collected originally for another purpose but may have relevance to the current research needs.

seeding   the process whereby a direct marketer places decoys, which are either incorrect spellings or fictitious names, on a customer list to track and identify any misuse (also called "salting").

self-mailer   any direct-mail piece mailed without an envelope.

sensitive/confidential information   the category of information that contains facts about an individual that are considered to be the most private.

service bureaus   provide data processing, data mining, outsourcing, on-line analytical processing (OLAP), etc. to support the interchange of lists and database information.

short messaging service (SMS)   a technological breakthrough in telemarketing that provides alerts from direct marketers by delivering a text message to customers with cellular phones.

solo mailer   direct-mail pieces that promote a single product or limited group of related products.

source data   the information contained in a customer database.

spam   unsolicited e-mail messages.

standard deviation   the variance from the mean.

Standard Industrial Classification (SIC) System   a four-digit coding system of industrial segments developed by the federal government.

storyboard   a series of illustrations that show the visual portion of a television commercial.

stuffers   printed offers of products and services that are inserted in the envelope with invoice or statement.

Sunday supplements   mass circulation sections that are edited nationally but appear locally in the Sunday editions of many newspapers.

survey   a research method in which data is gathered and hypotheses are tested using questionnaires.

syndication mailings   mailings that offer a product to an established customer list.

T1   a giant pipeline or conduit through which a user may send multiple voice, data, or video signals.

take-one racks   an alternative method of print distribution where the printed material is placed on a display rack.

target market   a specific segment of people to which an organization specifically focuses its marketing efforts.

telemarketing   a medium that uses sophisticated telecommunications and information systems combined with personal selling and servicing skills to help companies keep in close contact with present and potential customers, increase sales, and enhance business productivity.

telephone script   a call guide used by telemarketers to assist a telephone operator in communicating effectively with the prospect or customer.

testing   an experiment designed to measure the effect of change.

TIGER   a system that associates latitude and longitude coordinates with street addresses (*T*opologically *I*ntegrated *G*eographic *E*ncoding *R*eferencing).

till-forbid (TF)   an offer that pre-arranges continuous shipments on a specified basis and are renewed automatically until the customer instructs otherwise.

Type I error   results when the decision maker rejects the null hypothesis (even though it is true).

Type II error   occurs when the decision maker accepts the null hypothesis (when it is not true).

up-selling   the promotion of more expensive products or services over the product or service originally discussed or purchased.

URL   universal resource locator, otherwise known as your Internet address.

users   a measurement of the number of different people or "unique visitors" who visit a particular site during a given period of time.

violation   in marketing terms, is the way people feel when they believe too much information about their personal lives is being exchanged between marketers without their knowledge and/or consent.

viral marketing   a form of electronic word of mouth where e-mail messages are forwarded from one consumer to other consumers.

virtual enterprise   a company that is primarily a marketing and customer service entity, with actual product development and distribution handled by a broad network of subcontractors.

visits   count the total number of times a user accessed a particular site during a given period of time.

wholesalers   middlemen who buy from producers and sell to resellers, ultimate users, or industrial firms.

Wide Area Telephone Service (WATS)   a type of telephone service that can handle a large volume of long-distance calls for a set fee.

World Wide Web (WWW, Web)   the portion of the Internet that has color, sound, graphics, animation, video, interactivity, and ways to move from one page to another.

Index

Credits

CHAPTER 1

2	Used with Permission of Crispies Co., Inc., d.b.a. Peace Frogs
3	Used with Permission of Crispies Co., Inc., d.b.a. Peace Frogs
15	Used with Permission of the Peruvian Connection.
16	Used with Permission of the Peruvian Connection.
24	Used with Permission of Harris Teeter.
27	Used with Permission of TreadMoves.
29	Used with Permission of TreadMoves.
30	Used with Permission of TreadMoves.

CHAPTER 2

45	Used with permission of the Direct Marketing Association.
56	Used with Permission of Lillian Vernon Corporation.
57	Used with Permission of Lillian Vernon Corporation.

CHAPTER 3

62	Used with Permission of McDonald Garden Center.
84	Used with Permission of Smithfield Packing Company.

CHAPTER 4

88	Used with Permission of Harry and David.
91	Used with Permission of Harry and David.
92	Used with Permission of Busch Gardens Williamsburg.
93	Used with Permission of Lillian Vernon Corporation.
98	Used with Permission of Lillian Vernon Corporation.

CHAPTER 5

122	Used with permission of Donna Baier Stein.
123	Used with permission of P.S. Graphics.

CHAPTER 6

138	Used with permission of P.S. Graphics.
139	Used with Permission of McDonald Garden Center.
141	Used with Permission of McDonald Garden Center.
148	Used with Permission of McDonald Garden Center.
149	Used with Permission of McDonald Garden Center.
154	Used with permission of Newport News, Inc.
155	Used with permission of Newport News, Inc.

CHAPTER 7

163	Used with Permission of McDonald Garden Center.
172	Used with permission of Geico Direct and the Martin Agency.

CHAPTER 8

199	Used with Permission of 1-800-FLOWERS.
201	Used with Permission of 1-800-FLOWERS.

CHAPTER 9

206	Used with permission of the Direct Marketing Association.
212	Used with Permission of Lillian Vernon Corporation.
216	Used with Permission of Siebel Systems.
220	Used with permission of the Direct Marketing Association.
221	Used with permission of the Direct Marketing Association.
222	Used with permission of the Direct Marketing Association.
227	Used with Permission of Dell Computer Corporation.

CHAPTER 10

233	Used with Permission of the Lillian Vernon Corporation.
234	Used with Permission of the Lillian Vernon Corporation.
235	Used with Permission of the Lillian Vernon Corporation.
236	Used with Permission of the Lillian Vernon Corporation.
237	Used with Permission of the Lillian Vernon Corporation.
245	Used with Permission of the Lillian Vernon Corporation.
246	Used with Permission of the Lillian Vernon Corporation.
247	Used with Permission of the Lillian Vernon Corporation.
258	Used with Permission of the Lillian Vernon Corporation.
259	Used with Permission of the Lillian Vernon Corporation.
260	Used with Permission of the Lillian Vernon Corporation.

CHAPTER 11

268	Used with permission of the Direct Marketing Association.
273	Used with permission of the Direct Marketing Association.
280	Used with permission of the Direct Marketing Association.
286	Used with Permission of Omaha Steaks International.

CHAPTER 12

290	Used with permission of the Direct Marketing Association.
298	Used with permission of the Direct Marketing Association.
302	Used with Permission of J.C. Penney Company, Inc.
303	Used with permission of the Direct Marketing Association (top and bottom).

CHAPTER 14

350	Used with permission of the Direct Marketing Association.
351	Used with permission of The Peninsula Rescue Mission.
356–357	Used with permission of The Peninsula Rescue Mission.
363	Used with permission of the National Congressional Committee.
368	Used with permission of The National Trust for Historic Preservation.
369	Used with permission of The National Trust for Historic Preservation.

CHAPTER 15

373	Used with permission of the Direct Marketing Association.
391	Used with Permission of the Peruvian Connection.